Thomas Jefferson

Accuracy vs. Revisionism

An Exposé

Dr. Catherine Millard

Copyright © 2020

Christian Heritage Ministries®
P.O. Box 797
Springfield, Virginia 22150
www.christianheritagemins.org
www.christianheritagetours.org

ISBN: 978-0-578-75694-3
LOC Control Number: 2020917123

© Copyright 2020 by Catherine Millard.
All rights of translation, reproduction and
adaptation reserved for all countries.

No part of this publication may be reproduced or transmitted
in any form or by any means, electronic, or mechanical, including
photocopy, recording or any other information storage or retrieval
system, without prior written permission from the author and the publisher.

Published by: Christian Heritage Ministries®
Printed in the United States of America
Photography: © Catherine Millard

Front cover:
Bronze statue of Thomas Jefferson by Rudolph Evans, the
Declaration of Independence in his left hand.
The Thomas Jefferson Memorial, Washington, D.C.

CONTENTS

Introduction

Chapter I

The College of William and Mary – Jefferson studies Law – The House of Burgesses, Effort for the Emancipation of Slaves – Reflections on his Youth to his grandson – The Roll of Fame, William and Mary College. 1

Chapter II

Rev. James Maury, Jefferson's Formative Years – Thomas Jefferson, Vestryman – Rev. James Maury's Sermons – "Hypocrisy is a very Dangerous Vice" – Thomas Jefferson to John Adams, January 11, 1817 – Jefferson to Mrs. Harrison Smith, August 6, 1816 – True Christianity vs. the Corruptions of the Priesthood. 5

Chapter III

Jefferson's Act for Establishing Religious Freedom – "The Establishment of the Anglican Church entirely put Down," 1779 – "A Vindication of the Public Life and Conduct of Thomas Jefferson, 1800" – Jefferson's Notes on the State of Virginia, Reflections on Slavery – The Virtues of Yeomanry– Act for Establishing Religious Freedom passed by the Assembly, 1786. 16

Chapter IV

Jefferson's "Notes on Religion" – The Fundamentals of Christianity – Christian Heretics – Locke's System of Christianity – The Epistles – "A Heretic is an Impugner of Fundamentals" – Protestant Christianity, Reliance on Scripture Alone – Another Plea for Episcopal Government in Religion in England – The Presbyterian Spirit – The Civil Magistrate denied Jurisdiction over the Church – The Commonwealth, "a Society of Men constituted for Protecting their Civil Interests" – "A Church is a Voluntary Society of Men" – "Truth will do well Enough if left to shift for Herself". 23

Chapter V

The French "Enlightenment" or "Reign of Terror" – Voltaire – Robespierre – Rousseau – The Jacobin Club (Jacobins) – John Locke's "Letter concerning Toleration" – Locke's Political Theories – Sir Isaac Newton – Sir Francis Bacon – Defamation of Character, Jefferson's View. 30

Chapter VI

Jefferson's Bill for Proportioning Crimes and Punishments, 1778 – His Personal Family Bible, Testimony of Edmund Bacon, Overseer – Thomas Jefferson's Library, Rare Book Collection, Library of Congress – Jefferson, Churchman at St. Anne's Parish – Subscription to support a Clergyman in Charlottesville – Concern for his Pastor's Support – Jefferson proclaims a Day of Fasting, Humiliation and Prayer – His Notice of a Fast Day, St. Anne's Parish – Jefferson's Letter to the Danbury Baptists – President Thomas Jefferson, Churchman in Washington – Secretary of State in Georgetown –

Jefferson, Churchman in Georgetown – His Contribution to erect St. John's Episcopal Church, Georgetown – Francis Scott Key, Vestryman – Jefferson, Churchman in Charlottesville – Churchman in Philadelphia – Churchman in Williamsburg – Georgetown-on-the-Potomac... 36

Chapter VII

Thomas Jefferson's Resolutions Concerning Peace with England – His Respect for sound Christian Books – A Summary View of the Rights of British America, from "The Best and Wisest of its Members" – "The Abolition of Domestic Slavery is the great object of Desire in those Colonies" – "The God who gave us Life gave us Liberty" – "We the People" penned by Thomas Jefferson – His Second Draft of "Declaration on Taking up Arms"............. 63

Chapter VIII

Thomas Paine and "Common Sense" – The Influence of "Common Sense" in British America – Congress appoints Thomas Jefferson to draft Declaration – The Declaration of Independence, July 4th, 1776 – "Mr. Jefferson and the 'Wolf,' " U.S. News and World Report – Jefferson's 28th Clause, the anti-Slavery Clause in the Declaration of Independence...................................... 73

Chapter IX

"Mr. Jefferson's Servants" by Edmund Bacon, his Overseer – Genealogy of Mr. Jefferson's Servants at Monticello – Isaac's Recollections of Mr. Jefferson at Monticello – "Mr. Jefferson's Personal Appearance and Habits" – Jefferson's Care for the Poor – Mr. Jefferson's Mule, "Dolphin" – His Meticulous Business Transactions – Thomas Jefferson, the Lawyer – His Anti-slavery Bill – Jefferson's Bill to stop Slave Importation passes Congress, 1778.................... 82

Chapter X

James Callender and Sally Hemings – James Callender's Demise – Calumny in Public Life, Jefferson's View – A 1998 Revival of Callender's Slander – Accuracy in Media's "In Defense of Jefferson" – Peter and Samuel Carr & Sally and Betsy Hemings – Ellen Randolph Coolidge's October 24, 1858 Letter – Dabney Carr, Father of Jefferson's Nephews – Jefferson's Description of Dabney Carr – Dabney Carr's untimely Death – Ellen Randolph Coolidge's Letter Misquoted – "It's Odd," The Thomas Jefferson Society's Rebuttal – Historic Revisionism: "Just a Mistake"?................... 92

Chapter XI

Madison Hemings' March 13, 1873 Interview, Accuracy vs. Fallacy: "Such is the Story that comes Down to Me" – Jefferson the Agriculturalist – Thomas Jefferson's Prayer Book Record of the Birth of his Twelve Grandchildren — Another "Just a Mistake" Revisionism by Gordon-Reed – Jefferson's Prayer Book Record of his Marriage, and the Birth of their six Children – Martha Wayles Jefferson's Death at Age 33 – Panel of twelve Scholars refutes Madison Hemings' Claims.. 101

Chapter XII

What is American History? – Thomas Jefferson, Minister Plenipotentiary to France – Polly Jefferson's Letter to her Father – Abigail Adams: Jefferson, "One of the Choice Ones of the Earth" – Minister to France – Bereaved of His Daughter, Lucy – Thomas Jefferson's Love letter to his Daughter, Polly – Polly Jefferson Refuses to go to Paris – Jefferson's Instructions on Polly's Voyage to France – His Anxiety, "I drop my Pen at the Thought" – He Repeats His Prayer for Polly – His concern for Polly's Happiness – A Father's Love for his Daughter, Martha – Thomas Jefferson to Martha Jefferson, March 28, 1787 – Martha Jefferson to her Father, April 9, 1787 – A beautiful Father-daughter Relationship – Jefferson, the Naturalist – Anxiety in Virginia over Polly's Departure – Polly Jefferson leaves for France – Her Arrival in London – Polly Arrives in Paris, A Reunion of "Great Joy" – A Year later, July 12th, 1788. 116

Chapter XIII

Jefferson's departure from France, September 26, 1789 – His Arrival at Monticello, December 23, 1789 – "Mr. Jefferson's Servants, ebullitions of Joy at his Return" – Slavery in British America – Rev. Dr. Samuel Davies, Founder of the 1740's Great Awakening in Virginia – Rev. Davies' Educational Efforts taught Slaves and White Indentured Servants to read the Bible – The Dangerous "African Trade for Slaves". 132

Chapter XIV

Monticello, "The Thomas Jefferson Foundation, Inc." – Monticello's Exhibit: "The Life of Sally Hemings, drawn from the Words of her son Madison Hemings" – "Such is the story that comes down to Me" – Accuracy vs. Fallacy 144

Chapter XV

Monticello's July 2, 2018 Press Release – A "UNESCO World Heritage Site" and "Site of Conscience" – Monticello, a "United Nations World Heritage Site" – Monticello's "A Site of Conscience" – Monticello Trustees' "Site of Conscience" based on False History – "International Coalition of Sites of Conscience" – The Significance of Monticello Trustees' "Site of Conscience" – Training Ground for Indoctrination against "racist" and "white supremacist" Thomas Jefferson, based upon Fake History – Monticello's author-Trustee "Historians" – Monticello, The Thomas Jefferson Foundation's published Mission – Monticello's Endowments, The National Endowment for the Humanities. 155

Chapter XVI

What is Museum Instruction? David M. Rubenstein, Thomas Jefferson Foundation Donor – Rubenstein's book, "The American Story: Conversations with Master Historians" – Rubenstein's Interview with Jon Meacham, Chairman of Monticello's Thomas Jefferson Foundation, Inc. on his book, "Thomas Jefferson: The Art of Power" – Meacham: "It is One of the many Hypocrisies of Jefferson's Life" – Rubenstein's next Question to Jon Meacham – Accuracy vs. Revisionism in American History – Meacham's book, "Thomas Jefferson: The Art of Power, 'A Treaty in Paris'" – The book, "In the Hands of the People" edited by Jon Meacham – The British Institution of Slavery: "America's Original Sin"? – Jefferson's Louisiana Purchase and the Lewis and Clark Expedition a "narrow" view? – The Bible's view on Original Sin – Jefferson's 1778 Bill ending the Importation of Slaves – His anti-Slavery, 28th Clause in the Declaration of Independence – Jefferson's Northwest Ordinance, Slavery Banned – The Northwest Ordinance, American Indians Protected – The Jeffersonian Principle against Sodomy – Annette Gordon-Reed and the Thomas Jefferson Memorial – Jefferson's Notes on the State of Virginia denouncing Slavery, inscribed in the Jefferson Memorial – David McCullough's book, "The American Spirit, Who we Are and What we Stand For" – Jefferson's Autobiography, Slavery in America from 1650-1778 – Accuracy vs. Revisionism – David McCullough's book, "John Adams" – Abigail Adams: "He (Jefferson) is one of the Choice Ones of the Earth" 160

Chapter XVII

The Council on Foreign Relations and Karl Marx – Origin and Goals – Members of the Council on Foreign Relations.. 185

Chapter XVIII

Monticello designated a UNESCO "World Heritage Site" in 1987 – The United States and Israel quit UNESCO in 2019 – UNESCO'S "World Heritage Sites" – UNESCO'S "List of World Heritage in Danger" – The World Heritage Emblem, "Interdependence" – UNESCO'S Scheme to pervert Public Education – Attack upon Patriotism and its Parental Encouragement – Teachers Urged to Suppress American History – A Passage from Karl Marx's Communist Manifesto – 20th Century attacks, Jefferson the Atheist? – Thomas Jefferson, the anti-Evolutionist – Was he anti-Semitic? 189

Chapter XIX

Charles Thomson's "Synopsis of the Four Evangelists" – Jefferson's "wee-little book" – "The Philosophy of Jesus of Nazareth, an Abridgment of the New Testament for the Use of the Indians…" Jefferson to Charles Thomson, "I am a Real Christian" – Jefferson's "wee-little book," the work of 2-3 nights at Washington – Jefferson's "wee-little book" and the Smithsonian Institution – The History of Jefferson's "wee-little book" – 1904, Jefferson's "wee-little book" becomes "Thomas Jefferson's Bible" – 2011, Jefferson's "wee-little book" becomes "The Jefferson Bible, by Thomas Jefferson" – Smithsonian's "The History and Conservation of the Jefferson Bible" narrative continues – Three Charters of Freedom of the American Republic – Jefferson's Writing Desk – Inauguration of Smithsonian Books' 2011 "The Jefferson Bible," a Deliberate Fake. 196

Chapter XX

A Step Further, The Museum of the Bible – "Impact of the Bible in America" exhibit: "The Jefferson Bible," 2011 Smithsonian Edition – Thomas Jefferson and Revisionism – Smithsonian Books' 2011 "The Jefferson Bible," a 21st Century Fake Title and Cover – The Museum of the Bible's "Thanksgiving in America" – Thomas Jefferson's December 9th, 1779 "Day of Publick and Solemn Thanksgiving and Prayer to Almighty God" Proclamation – "The Missing Complement of 'Jefferson's Bible' " or his "Literary Commonplace

Book"? – "The Literary Bible of Thomas Jefferson" – Inauguration of the Museum of the Bible - "The Shroud of Turin," Roman Catholic Relic – Counterfeit Papyri Fragments and Clay Objects – Ancient Gilgamesh Tablet forfeited – "All Dead Sea Scroll Fragments in the Museum of the Bible are Forgeries" – A one-of-a-kind, original "wee-little book"of known Provenance in the University of Virginia vault – The Jesuits, a Threat to this "wee-little book" – The English, 1791 and 1799 New Testament Bibles bought by Thomas Jefferson – Jefferson's reverence for the Bible..........213

Chapter XXI

The Museum of the Bible and Historic Revisionism, George Washington, John Adams and Benjamin Franklin – George Washington: "Impact of the Bible in America" exhibit – Washington's "Prayer for the Nation" – His "Sunday Evening Prayer" – George Washington's Addresses to the Churches – John Adams: "Impact of the Bible in America" exhibit – John Adams' May 9, 1798 "Day of Humiliation, Fasting and Prayer" Proclamation – John Adams' April 25, 1799 "Day of Humiliation, Fasting and Prayer" Proclamation – John Adams' 1780 Massachusetts Constitution – Benjamin Franklin: "Impact of the Bible in America" exhibit – Historic Revisionism: Benjamin Franklin – Accuracy: Franklin's Design Proposal for First U.S. Seal accepted by Congress – Biblical Symbolism of the First United States Seal – Benjamin Franklin and George Whitefield. 229

Chapter XXII

The Thomas Jefferson Memorial 245

Conclusion 250

Footnotes...251

Appendix I.   Aleksandr Solzhenitsyn (1918-2008)................................259

Appendix II. Thomas Jefferson's Last Will and Testament 261

Appendix III. The History of the United States of America –
              Mount Rushmore Historic Plaque 264

Appendix IV. Communist "Blueprint for World Conquest" 266

Appendix V. Investigation of Un-American Propaganda Activities in the United States. Hearings before a Special Committee on Un-American Activities, House of Representatives, Seventy-Sixth Congress, First Session on H. Res. 282 – September 28, 29, 30 and October 5, 6, 7, 9, 11 and 14, 1939 at Washington, D.C. – "Confessions of Stalin's Agent – This is my Story" by Kenneth Goff, alias John Keats..268

Appendix VI. The Marxists' Modus Operandi 317

Appendix VII. The American Civil Liberties Union 319

INTRODUCTION

From the pen of Aleksandr Solzhenitsyn* come the following words of wisdom:

> Modern society is hypnotized by socialism. It is prevented by socialism from seeing the mortal danger it is in. One of the greatest dangers of all is that you have lost all sense of danger. You cannot even see where it is coming from as it moves swiftly towards you. Socialism of any type leads to a total destruction of the human spirit…to destroy a people you must first sever their roots.

and

> The strength or weakness of a society depends more on the level of its spiritual life than on its level of industrialization. Neither a market economy nor even general abundance constitutes the crowning achievement of human life. If a nation's spiritual energies have been exhausted, it will not be saved from collapse by the most perfect government structure or by any industrial development. A tree with a rotten core cannot stand.

and

> The simple truth of a courageous individual is not to take part in the lie. One word of truth outweighs the world. You can resolve to live your life with integrity. Let your credo be this: let the lie come into the world, let it even triumph. But not through me.

The United States has undergone in the past fifty years, a severance of her historic roots. This is why I write the book, *Thomas Jefferson – Accuracy vs. Revisionism – An Exposé*, restoring the nation's true republican creed, established by this great founding father.

His virtues, valour, biblical standards and integrity far surpass the avalanche of revisionism aimed at destroying his reputation – in order to discredit the pivotal documents upon which this nation's liberties rest – the *Declaration of Independence* (1776), *An Act for Establishing Religious Freedom* (1786), *A Summary View of the Rights of British America* (1774), his anti-Slavery Bill (1778), and many others, authored by this illustrious founder of the American Republic.

— Catherine Millard

---

*Aleksandr Solzhenitsyn (1918-2008), authored *The Gulag Archipelago*. His exposé of Marxist infiltration, and its atheistic opposition to the liberties of the United States – largely unheeded – have now permeated the "Republic under God." (*see* Appendix I).

DEDICATION

...I shall need, too, the favour of that Being in whose hands we are, who led our forefathers, as Israel of old, from their native land, and planted them in a country flowing with all the necessaries and comforts of life; who has covered our infancy with His Providence, and our riper years with His wisdom and power; and to whose goodness I ask you to join with me in supplications that He will so enlighten the minds of your servants, guide their councils, and prosper their measures, that whatsoever they do, shall result in your good, and shall secure to you the peace, friendship, and approbation of all nations.

Thomas Jefferson
Second Inaugural Address
March 4, 1805.

Thomas Jefferson – a portrait of the founding father from life by Charles Willson Peale.

Chapter I

The College of William and Mary – Jefferson studies Law – The House of Burgesses, effort for the Emancipation of Slaves – Reflections on his Youth to his grandson – The Roll of Fame, William and Mary College.

The College of William and Mary

Thomas Jefferson entered the *College of William and Mary* on March 25th, 1760, at the age of sixteen, having been tutored by Reverend James Maury, "a correct classical scholar"[1] and pastor of *Walker's Parish*, in Albemarle County, Virginia. The young scholar was already proficient in the classics and able to read Greek and Latin authors in the original, a practice he continued throughout his life.

The Christopher Wren Building, circa 1693, oldest academic building in America, is where he lodged and boarded, attending communal meals in the Great Hall; and morning and evening prayers with singing of Psalms in the Chapel. His studies comprised natural philosophy (physics, metaphysics and mathematics) and moral philosophy (rhetoric, logic, ethics and belles lettres).[2] A dedicated and diligent student, he displayed an avid curiosity in all fields of knowledge, and frequently studied fifteen hours a day. His close friend, John Page, relates that Jefferson "could tear himself away from his dearest friends, to fly to his studies."

"It was my great fortune, and what probably fixed the destinies of my life that Dr. William Small of Scotland was then professor of Mathematics..." writes Jefferson.[3] As professor of moral philosophy, Dr. Small introduced him to the writings of John Locke, Francis Bacon and Isaac Newton.

The Christopher Wren building of the College of William and Mary, (circa 1693). Oldest academic building in continuous use in America. Williamsburg, Virginia.

First page of the original Charter for the College of William and Mary, Williamsburg, Virginia. Given by King William and Queen Mary of England "to the end that the Church in Virginia may be furnished with a Seminary of Ministers of the Gospel and that the Youth may be piously educated in Good Letters and Manners and that the Christian Faith may be propagated amongst the Western Indians, to the glory of Almighty God…" University Archives, Swem Library, College of William and Mary, Williamsburg, Virginia.

The founding fathers' Chapel, Sir Christopher Wren building, William and Mary College, Williamsburg, Virginia. Thomas Jefferson commenced and closed his studies each day with Psalms and Prayer in this Chapel.

Jefferson studies Law

After completing his two-year course of study at the College, Jefferson went on to read law for the next five years under George Wythe, a distinguished jurist, who became the first professor of law at William and Mary in 1779. "Mr. Wythe", writes Jefferson, "continued to be my faithful and beloved mentor in youth, and my most affectionate friend through life. In 1767, he led me into the practice of the law at the bar of the General Court, at which I continued until the Revolution shut up the courts of justice." [4]

The House of Burgesses – Effort for the Emancipation of Slaves

In 1769, Jefferson was elected to the legislature, in which he served until it was closed by the Revolution. Of note is that one of his first priorities was an "effort in that body for the permission of the emancipation of slaves, which was rejected; and indeed, during the regal government, nothing liberal could expect success." [5]

Under the Act of 2nd George II, no slave was to be set "free upon any pretence whatsoever, except for some meritorious services, to be adjudged and allowed by the Governor and Council." Acts of the Assembly, 1769. (No trace of this effort is recorded in the *Journal of the House of Burgesses*).

Reflections on his Youth to his Grandson

Many years later, the "Sage of Monticello", reflecting upon his youthful years, gives the following valuable advice to his eldest grandson, Thomas Jefferson Randolph:

> When I recollect that at fourteen years of age the whole care and direction of myself was thrown on myself entirely, without a relative or friend qualified to advise or guide me, and recollect the various sorts of bad company with which I associated from time to time, I am astonished that I did not turn off with some of them, and become as worthless to society as they were. I had the good fortune to become acquainted very early with some characters of very high standing, and to feel the incessant wish that I could ever become what they were. Under temptations and difficulties, I would ask myself – What would Dr. Small, Mr. Wythe, Peyton Randolph, do in this situation? What course in it will insure me their approbation? I am certain that this mode of deciding on my conduct tended more to correctness than any reasoning powers I possessed. Knowing the even and dignified lives they pursued, I could never doubt for a moment which of two courses would be in character for them; whereas, seeking the same object through a process of moral reasoning, and with the jaundiced eye of youth, I should often have erred. From the circumstances of my position, I was often thrown into the society of horse-racers, card-players, fox-hunters, scientific and professional men, and of dignified men; and many a time have I asked myself, in the enthusiastic moment of the death of a fox, the victory of a favorite horse, the issue of a question eloquently argued at the bar, or in the great council of the nation, well, which of these kinds of reputation should I prefer – that of a horse-jockey, a fox-hunter, an orator, or the honest advocate of my country's rights? Be assured, my dear Jefferson, that these little returns into ourselves, this self-catechizing habit, is not trifling nor useless, but leads to the prudent selection and steady pursuit of what is right.[6]

Roll of Fame – William and Mary College

The College of William and Mary's *Roll of Fame* honors Thomas Jefferson no less than nine times as,

> President of the United States, Signer of the *Declaration of Independence*, Governor of Virginia, Member of the Committee of Correspondence, Member of the Continental Congress, Member of the Cabinet, Minister to France, Founder of the University of Virginia and Candidate for the Presidency of the United States. And the list of his accomplishments for this nation continues…

However, the values, morals and high principles of the founder of America's political creed originated in his formative years, when these virtues were engrafted upon his young mind and heart through the teaching and example of his noble mentors.

Chapter II

Rev. James Maury, Jefferson's Formative Years – Thomas Jefferson, Vestryman – Rev. James Maury's Sermons – "Hypocrisy is a very Dangerous Vice" – Thomas Jefferson to John Adams, January 11, 1817 – Jefferson to Mrs. Harrison Smith, August 6, 1816 – True Christianity vs. the Corruptions of the Priesthood.

Rev. James Maury – Jefferson's Formative Years

In order to evaluate a person's philosophy and ideas, it is necessary to revert to the greatest formative influences which fashioned his mind, and consequently his creed and actions in life. Reverend James Maury's classical scholarship and spiritual guidance prepared Thomas Jefferson for enrollment in the prestigious *College of William and Mary*, which in turn, equipped him for his illustrious career.

Historic marker designating the site of Rev. James Maury's classical Christian Academy. Rev. Maury tutored Jefferson, preparing him for the College of William and Mary.

"Walker's Parish," circa 1745. The Rev. James Maury, Jefferson's tutor and pastor, preached at this church. Thomas Jefferson served as vestryman from 1767-1770.

Thomas Jefferson – Vestryman

This erudite scholar and Minister of the Gospel, James Maury, is buried beneath the pulpit of *Walker's Parish Church*, of which his pupil, Thomas Jefferson was a member and vestryman from 1767-1770. A new vestryman was obliged to take a number of oaths, the first of which was loyalty to King George II. Of second importance was his renunciation of the Pope's authority "within this realm," – as well as the doctrine which permitted citizens to dispose of a king by death or dethronement, should the said king have been excommunicated by the Pope. Thirdly, he had to swear allegiance to the Hanovarian family's right to the throne, as opposed to the papist Stuart family of King James II. His last oath was,

I do declare that I do believe that there is not any Transubstantiation* in the sacrament of the Lord's Supper, or in the elements of bread and wine at or after the consecration thereof by any person whatsoever.[1]

Tomb of Rev. James Maury, first pastor of Walker's Parish. "A tribute to his piety, learning and worth," he is buried beneath the pulpit of the original wood-frame church.

It follows that Thomas Jefferson, George Washington, George Mason, George Wythe, Peyton Randolph, Edmund Pendleton, and other founders of the American Republic – all of whom were vestrymen of their respective churches, renounced by solemn oath allegiance to the Pope, the Roman Catholic Church and its dogmas, which do not originate from the authoritative Holy Scriptures.

James Maury's epitaph reads:

Sacred
to the memory of the Reverend James Maury,
first pastor of Walker's Parish.
Born April 8th, 1717. Died June 9th, 1769.
As a tribute to his piety, learning and worth.

Historic plaque marking the site of Walker's Parish Church. "Here was the Doorway of the Colonial Church."

---

*Transubstantiation is the dogma held by the Roman Catholic Church that the words of Christ, "This is my body…This is my Blood of the New Covenant…" are literal; that there is a metamorphous of transubstantiation in fact, although not in appearance during the ritual Mass.

A handsome bronze plaque nearby gives the origins of this historic church as follows:

> Walker's Parish
> Here was the Doorway of the Colonial Church
> given by the Walkers and served by the Maurys
> for their Kinsfolk and Friends
> The Builders of Old Albemarle.

Rev. James Maury's Sermons

Posterity is grateful to be heir to Reverend Maury's hand-written, extant sermons, which spiritually nurtured Thomas Jefferson early in life – giving insight into this founder's philosophy. The following sermon addresses secret prayer:

The First Sermon on this Text. Matthew VI. 6.
'But thou, when thou prayest, enter into thy closet; and, when thou hast shut the door, pray to thy Father, which is in secret; and thy Father, which seeth in secret, shall reward thee openly':

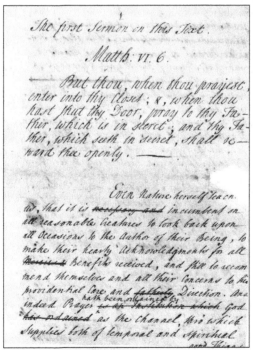

First page of Rev. James Maury's sermon from Matthew's Gospel, chapter VI, verse 6, on Secret Prayer. Courtesy of Colonial Williamsburg Library.

Even nature herself teaches, that it is incumbent on all reasonable Creatures to look back upon all occasions to the Author of their being, to make their hearty acknowledgements for all benefits received, and still to recommend themselves and all their concerns to His providential care and direction. And indeed Prayer hath been ordained by God as the channel, thro' which supplies both of temporal and spiritual, and good things regularly are conveyed. It is also a singular means of preserving in our hearts a continual sense of His Majesty and Goodness, and consequently an awful veneration for His holy Name. Our temporal necessities come constantly upon us; and every day we are assailed by temptations, which tend to draw our hearts from God and fix them on earthly and perishable objects: and therefore our petitions for daily supplies and assistances ought daily to be offered to the Father of Mercies and the God of all comforts. Public and family devotions seem here to be taken for granted by our Lord.

Now before I can conveniently enter upon a particular consideration of these Words, it will be proper to show with what intent they were spoken, and to give some little explanation of the terms.

The preceding verses plainly show us with what intent our Saviour delivered their precept. For at the beginning of the chapter, out of which the text is taken, He cautions His hearers against that ostentatious way of doing their good works, which was so common among the Pharisees; advises them to perform these duties with a pure intention to serve God and promote His glory; and not in order to catch at the empty applause of men, with a view of establishing themselves an interest in the world. Next, He proceeds to branch out this advice into more particular admonitions on these three great duties, Almsgiving, Prayer and Fasting, which the Pharisees were very prone to corrupt by pride and ostentation, which are apt to draw the esteem of the world on those who practice them, and in reality deserve the greatest regard.

"**Take heed**, that ye do not your alms before men, to be seen of them. But when thou dost thine alms let not thy left hand know what thy right hand doeth." After He had told His audience that they ought to perform their good works in as private a manner as possible, and with a singular view of promoting the happiness of their brother, the salvation of their souls, and the glory of their Creator; He proceeds in the same manner to correct the hypocrisy of their devotions. "When thou prayest, thou shall not be as the hypocrites are; for they love to pray, standing in the Synagogues and in the corners of the streets, that they may be seen of men: verily, I say unto you, they have their reward." After this caution against their vainglorious and hypocritical show of devotion, He directs them, in the text, to the practice of sincerity and secrecy in all their acts of adoration.

But thou, in contradiction to this pharisaical ostentation, when thou prayest, enter into thy closet; and, when thou hast shut thy door, pray to thy Father which is in secret. But we must here observe, that this recommendation of secret Prayer is not intended to discourage our public devotions in the Church, or domestic worship in families. But the object of this reproof is the ostentation, imprudence and insincerity of such, as used to break out into sudden sallies of devotion at the most improper times and places, only in order to obtain the applause of men.

Now as to the terms, they need not much explanation. However, it may not be improper to observe, that the original word (Greek word) which we have rendered <u>closet</u>, as properly signifies a granary or magazine, a wardrobe, or any other secure and private place, as a chamber or closet. This observation, indeed, may seem frivolous; but there are two reasons which prompted me to make it.

First, because our Lord would have our private devotions so very secret, and free from the least suspicion of vainglory, that even the place where we are might not divulge what we are doing. Now if we dedicate any one place to this particular purpose of secret devotion, every time we retire thither, we shall discover what we are about. Nay, it might be looked upon by some censorious persons as a scheme calculated to show men our great devotion and the frequency of our Prayers, or at least to let them know that much of our time is spent in that business. This is directly opposite to our Saviour's design that we should perform this duty of private Prayer in so secret a manner, as to be visible to none but God.

The other reason, which induces me to take notice of this particular, is to obviate an excuse some poor people may allege for their neglect of this duty. They may say none but persons of fortune can afford to have so many apartments in their houses, as to have a closet consecrated to this purpose; and therefore the performance of this duty cannot be required of us. But, suppose their circumstances will not allow this convenience, if they have any place near their habitations, which will screen them from the eyes of men, where none can see but Him who seeth in secret, I imagine they have everything requisite to enable them to enter into their closet, in the proper and unconstrained sense of the words, and in the very sense our Saviour intended when He uttered them.

Having thus represented to you the design with which those words were spoken; we may sum up the meaning of them thus; as if our Saviour had said "Instead of this pharisaical vainglory and hypocritical ostentation in your Prayers, of which I have been speaking, do you, who are called by my Name, perform your secret devotions with as little noise as possible, as remote from company and as disengaged from business as ye can. For which end retire to some private place, and let your devotions be imperceptible to any, but your heavenly Father, who seeth in secret. And you may depend that He, who is present in every place, shall give a public reward to those secret and cordial effusions of devotion, probably in this world, but most certainly at the solemn Day of Judgment, in the glorious Assembly of Men and Angels." From the words thus explained flow these following Heads of Discourse:

I. Private Devotion is recommended in preference to those unseasonable Prayers, which the Pharisees uttered in crowds of spectators and places of great resort.
II. The properest preparation for secret Prayer is described to be a disengagement from the cares of this world, and a retirement from company into some private place, where we can be visible to none but the all-seeing God. and,
III. Lastly, a public reward is promised to this secret and sincere kind of Devotion.

As these are points of great importance in private life; and as the conscientious practice of the precept of the text wonderfully promotes virtue in this world, and consequently influences our happiness in the next; I propose, God willing, to consider each of them fully, and to make the first the subject of this day's meditations.

First. Private Devotion is recommended in preference to those unseasonable Prayers, which the Pharisees uttered in crowds of spectators, and places of great resort: as we may gather from these words; "But thou, when thou prayest, enter into thy closet; and, when thou hast shut thy door, pray to thy Father which is in secret." And indeed it is very agreeable to reason, that secret Prayers are far preferable before those ostentatious sallies of devotion, at the most unseasonable times and in the most improper places. For,

1. **This private way** of praying in our closets is not so apt to create disturbances, as such enthusiastical and Pharisaical effusions are. In order to be sensible of the force of this argument, let us reflect a little upon the tumults and distractions, the discords and confusions, that a new-fangled set of Enthusiastics not long since created, not only in our mother country, but in many places much nearer home, by their pretended inspirations, by breaking out into Prayers among numerous crowds of people, and by extemporaneous harangues to an unruly and senseless mob. And wherever private Christians are permitted thus to encroach on the province of those, who act in public capacities, the same inversion of order, the same disturbances, the same assembly and confusion will constantly ensue. It is not therefore surprising, that our Saviour, whose every action was governed by the greatest wisdom, should prohibit private Christians from venting their extemporary effusions at undetermined seasons, and in unconsecrated and indecent places; since it is a practice always attended by so many inconveniences. Therefore, it is a practice contrary to our Saviour's doctrine, and destructive of that apostolical precept – "Let all things be done decently and in order."

2. **Another reason** whereon this preference is founded is, that secrecy in our private Devotions is a very powerful antidote against hypocrisy, and prevents us from making any disingenuous views the end of our addresses to our Father in Heaven. When we do an action in the place void of spectators, no one can charitably suppose, that any sinister intention was the end of that action. Our Saviour frequently guards His disciples against this vice of hypocrisy; as it is of such a subtle and insinuating nature, and as they had the bad example of the scribes and Pharisees daily before their eyes; which might have some tendency to corrupt them. For they turned religion into a sort of force or comedy. They, indeed, made great pretensions to sanctity; they wore large borders on their garments called phylacteries whereon were written several precepts of the Law; they were very frequent in praying in places of great resort; they were fond of standing at the corners of the street and breaking out into sudden ejaculations; and always prayed with uplifted hands, elevated eyes, and other signs of uncommon devotion; but notwithstanding they had no true religion.

The ultimate end of these extraordinary Prayers, the only aim of these **ostentational devotions**, was to establish them a reputation of sanctity; that under the cloak of holiness, they might have an opportunity to devour widows' houses. Now it is an inward purity of heart, an integrity of intention, a cordial affection to God and His holy Laws, which constitute the true Christian. The Life and Soul of all duty is, to propose no other view in discharging it, than the honour of our Maker, and the salvation of our souls. To promote this, and to exclude hypocrisy from entering into our Payers, nothing can be more proper than retirement from the eyes of men. The further we can retire from company, and the more ardently we can pour out our souls to God in acts of devotion; so much the nearer approaches we make to the Divinity, and so much the more acceptable are our addresses.

If we can once bring ourselves to a love and readiness in this duty of secret Prayer; and at the same time keep our hearts from swelling with vainglory; and abstain from proposing any worldly interest as our end: it is a comfortable assurance to our souls, that we are sincere and hearty in all these duties. For, if we do not propose to gain anything from men by these devotions; then we may expect the completion of all our requests as far as is expedient for us, and conclude that our hearts and treasure are both in Heaven.

3. **Lastly**, secret Prayer greatly lends to the destruction of pride and to promote our growth in humility. Indeed, the corruption of our nature is so great, that it is not impossible but an honest man, in the most retired place, may sometimes be a little proud of his devotions and begin to think of himself somewhat more highly than he ought. But, if it be difficult to suppress this vice when none are present to applaud us; how much greater is the danger to which we are exposed, how much greater the difficulties we must struggle withal, when surrounded by the multitudes of spectators, who launch out extravagantly in our praises; and when, besides the depravity of our own hearts to contend withal, we must stem a torrent of acclamations from an applauding multitude?

The man that can stop his ears to these enchanters, and refuse to hear these deluding charmers, must be thoroughly invested in the Christian Faith, have notions very abstracted from matter, and be under a very powerful conviction of his own infirmities and the perfections of the Supreme Being. From all this it appears that **hypocrisy is a very dangerous vice**, difficult to be resisted, and not easily detected. For such as are guilty of it have generally the greatest repulsion for Religion. Such as have the largest share of piety and devotion, commonly keep it private, make the least show and noise about it, and enjoy it between God and themselves. But notwithstanding the subtilty of hypocrisy, we may often discover it both in ourselves and in others.

We may discover it in ourselves by examining what is our real aim in the performance of all religious duties. Let us ask our consciences, what end we promote to ourselves, whether it be to gain the favour of our heavenly Father, or to procure some worldly advantage? And the answer to this question will infallibly discover our sincerity to us, or else convince us we are **hypocrites and false pretenders**.

And, as to the detection of this vice in others altho' it be God's peculiar prerogative to know the heart of man and understand his thoughts; yet, from some symptoms, which our Saviour has mentioned, we may form a tolerable conjecture who are infected with this odious and abominable disease. When a man affects to make more show of devotion in public, than he takes care to practice in private; when he breaks out into ejaculations among crowds of people where he is exposed to the view of all men, at the same time that he neglects to pray in his closet, where he is visible to none but God's all-seeing Eye; we may with good reason conclude, he labours under the disease of hypocrisy. Again, whoever studies a singularity in the unseasonable exercise of Prayer, in order to be commended as a man of extraordinary devotion and uncommon piety; whoever is fond of innovations in worship and new-invented ceremonies in Religion; whoever breaks out into enthusiastic Prayers, discourses in streets, or places where men assemble either on account of lawful business or innocent recreation; finally, whoever affects a constrained gesture, a distortion of features, and such other pretences to a more than common degree of devotion, we may, without any great breach of charity, rank under the denomination of hypocrites.

Having thus pointed out a method to discover this vice in ourselves and others; let us be persuaded to abhor and detest it. For nothing better deserves our abhorrence and detestation than this; whether we reflect on the scandal of being under the imputation of hypocrisy here; or consider, that it will involve us in eternal misery thereafter.

Nothing is more inconsistent with the Spirit of Christianity, than hypocrisy. This is a proposition, which needs not many arguments to prove it. For the Spirit of our holy Religion is a Spirit of truth and honesty, of sincerity and integrity: but the hypocrite proceeds by the crooked rule of falsity and dissimulation. **The true Christian is adorned with a Spirit of meekness and humility**; the false pretender grounds his actions on pride and vanity. The former in all religious duties is directed by the honest rule of Christian simplicity and undesigning sincerity: the latter never discharges a duty, but with some sinister views and disingenuous prospects. The one in all his actions sees God before his eyes, and makes it his ultimate end to please Him: the other leaves his Maker quite out of his thoughts and does all to be seen of men and to gain their applause. In short, the former performs his duty conscientiously here in expectation of an unseen happiness, of an invincible crown and of a spiritual reward hereafter: but whatever duty the other discharges, he does it to obtain some earthly recompence or temporal advantage.

Thus, appears the beauty of a sincere holiness, and the deformity of a hypocritical sanctity; the vanity of this, and the solidity of that; the rectitude of one, and disingenuity of the other; and the steadiness of the first and the instability of that last. Let us, therefore, study to acquire the very soul and substance, the power of Godliness; and not rest contented with only the superficial form of it. When we offer up our petitions to our Father in Heaven; let our hearts keep company with our words. When our Prayers are sent up to Heaven; let our minds thither also ascend. And after we have implored the Divine assistance; let our utmost endeavours be excepted to acquire those virtues we have mentioned in our Prayers. And when our words and thoughts unite; when we honour the Lord not only with our lips but in our hearts; and when our Prayers and endeavours go hand in hand: then and not 'till then, we may have a comfortable assurance, that our Prayers are sincere, and a well-founded confidence, that we shall not be sent empty away. Then may we depend, that our labour shall not be in vain in the Lord; that our endeavours will be crowned with the desired success; that we shall be comforted with a plentiful effusion of Grace in this life; and rewarded with an eternal weight of glory in the next; thro' the merits and mediation of Jesus Christ our Lord. Amen.

Last page of Rev. James Maury's sermon from Matthew's Gospel, chapter VI, verse 6 on Secret Prayer. Courtesy of Colonial Williamsburg Library.

"Hypocrisy is a very Dangerous Vice"

In this sermon, Rev. Maury emphasizes the fact that "hypocrisy is a very dangerous vice, difficult to be resisted, and not easily detected." "For such as are guilty of it," he asserts, "have generally the greatest repulsion for Religion. Such as have the largest share of piety and devotion, commonly keep it private, make the least show and noise about it, and enjoy it between God and themselves…" He adds that, "We may discover it in ourselves by examining what is our real aim in the performance of all religious duties." In conclusion, he exhorts his parishioners to examine their true motives: "Let us ask our consciences, what end we promote to ourselves, whether it be to gain the favour of our Heavenly Father or to procure some worldly advantage? And the answer to this question will infallibly discover our sincerity to us, or else convince us we are hypocrites and false pretenders..."

Such profound wisdom, echoing Christ's denunciation of the scribes and Pharisees as hypocrites and white-washed tombs, who love the chief seats at banquets, preferring the applause of men to the approval of God;* reflects Thomas Jefferson's refusal during his illustrious career, to make public his own Religion. Following is an example:

Thomas Jefferson to John Adams – January 11, 1817

> One of our fan-coloring biographers, who paints small men as very great, inquired of me lately, with real affection too, whether he might consider as authentic, the change of my Religion much spoken of in some circles. Now this supposed that they know what had been my Religion before, taking for it the word of their priests, whom I certainly never made the confidants of my creed. My answer was, say nothing of my Religion. Its evidence before the world is to be sought in my life; if that has been honest and dutiful to society, the Religion that has regulated it cannot be a bad one.

and again,

Jefferson to Mrs. Harrison Smith – August 6, 1816

> ...I often call to mind the occasions of knowing your worth, which the societies of Washington furnished; and none more than those derived from your much valued visit to Monticello. I recognize the same motives of goodness in the solicitude you express on the rumour supposed to proceed from a letter of mine to Charles Thomson on the subject of the Christian Religion. It is true that, on writing to the translator of the Bible and Testament, that subject was mentioned; but equally so that no adherence to any particular mode of Christianity was there expressed; nor any change of opinions suggested. A change from what? The priests indeed have heretofore thought proper to ascribe to me religious, or rather anti-religious sentiments of their own fabric, but such as soothed their resentments against the Act of Virginia for Establishing Religious Freedom. They wished him to be thought Atheist, Deist, or Devil, who could advocate freedom from their religious dictations. But I have ever thought Religion a concern purely between our God and our consciences, for which we are accountable to Him, and not to the priests...For it is in our lives, and not from our words, that our Religion must be read. By the same test the world must judge me...I have left the world in silence, to judge of causes from their effects: and I am consoled in this course, my dear friend, when I perceive the candor with which I am judged by your justice and discernment; and that notwithstanding the slanders of the saints, my fellow-citizens have found me worthy of trusts...

---

*Luke 20: 46,47; Matthew 23: 13-17.

True Christianity vs. the Corruptions of the Priesthood

Actions, however, speak louder than words, as proven by Jefferson's exemplary life and conduct. In a letter to Elbridge Gerry, he again extols mere Christianity, in contrast to the corruptions of the Anglican priesthood, which he disestablished with his *Act for Establishing Religious Freedom* in 1786:

> ...The mild and simple principles of the Christian philosophy* would produce too much calm, too much regularity of good, to extract from its disciples a support for a numerous priesthood, were they not to sophisticate it, ramify it, split it into hairs, and twist its texts till they cover the Divine morality of its Author with mysteries, and require the priesthood to explain them.

Jefferson's view of true Christianity is again seen in a letter to his friend Charles Thomson, dated January 9, 1816, in which he states that he is,

> a real Christian, that is to say, a disciple of the doctrines of Jesus, very different from the Platonists,** who call me infidel, and themselves Christians and preachers of the Gospel, while they draw all their characteristic dogmas from what its Author never said or saw...

From the above correspondence, we understand that Thomas Jefferson despised the hypocrisy of "priestcraft," reviling their misinterpretations of Scripture and fabricated dogmas.

It is for this reason that he disestablished the Church of England, enabling the "dissident" Protestants churches*** to worship in their own mode; free from the jurisdiction of the Civil Magistrate.

Both Jefferson and James Madison often referred to various Protestant denominations as Christian Religions, sects or societies.

---

*Way of Life.

Platonists: Followers of **Plato (427-347 B.C.), who was a Greek philosopher, a student of Socrates, and teacher of **Aristotle**, who further developed many of the principles of Platonism in terms of preaching, sciences. The Aristotelian Platonistic thought of the 13th century attempted to incorporate the body of Greek doctrine into Christian theology. Works in this direction have become the official attitude of the Roman Catholic Church.[2]

***Presbyterians, Baptists, Methodists, Congregationalists, Huguenots, etc.

Chapter III

Jefferson's Act for Establishing Religious Freedom – "The Establishment of the Anglican Church entirely put Down," 1779 – "A Vindication of the Public Life and Conduct of Thomas Jefferson, 1800" – Jefferson's Notes on the State of Virginia, Reflections on Slavery – The Virtues of Yeomanry– Act for Establishing Religious Freedom passed by the Assembly, 1786.

Jefferson's Act for Establishing Religious Freedom

The origins, history and circumstances in the American Colonies which prompted this bill, is explained in Jefferson's *Autobiography*. He commences with the first settlers in Virginia:

> **The first settlers of this colony were Englishmen, loyal subjects to their king and church**, and the grant to Sir Walter Raleigh contained an express Proviso that their laws "should not be against the true Christian faith, now professed in the Church of England." As soon as the state of the colony admitted, it was divided into parishes, in each of which was established a minister of the Anglican church, endowed with a fixed salary, in tobacco, a glebe house and land with the other necessary appendages. To meet these expenses all the inhabitants of the parishes were assessed, whether they were or not, members of the established church. Towards Quakers who came here they were most cruelly intolerant, driving them from the colony by the severest penalties. In process of time however, other sectarisms were introduced, chiefly of the Presbyterian family; and the established clergy, secure for life in their glebes and salaries, adding to these generally the emoluments of a classical school, found employment enough, in their farms and schoolrooms for the rest of the week, and devoted Sunday only to the edification of their flock, by service, and a sermon at their parish church.
>
> Their other pastoral functions were little attended to. Against this inactivity the zeal and industry of sectarian preachers had an open and undisputed field; and by the time of the revolution, a majority of the inhabitants had become dissenters from the established church, but were still obliged to pay contributions to support the Pastors of the minority. This unrighteous compulsion to maintain teachers of what they deemed religious errors was grievously felt during the regal government, and without a hope of relief. But the first republican legislature which met in '76 was crowded with petitions to abolish this spiritual tyranny. These brought on the severest contests in which I have ever been engaged. Our great opponents were Mr. Pendleton & Robert Carter Nicholas, honest men, but zealous churchmen. The petitions were referred to the Committee of the Whole House on the state of the country; and after desperate contests in that committee, almost daily from the 11th October to the 5th December, we prevailed so far only as to repeal the laws which rendered criminal the maintenance of any religious opinions, the forbearance of repairing to church, or the exercise of any mode of worship; and further, to exempt dissenters from contributions to the support of the established church; and to suspend, only until the next session levies on the members of that church for the salaries of their own incumbents. For although the majority of our citizens were dissenters, as has been observed, a majority of the legislature were churchmen. Among these however were some reasonable and liberal men, who enabled us, on some points, to obtain feeble majorities.

"The Establishment of the Anglican Church entirely put Down" – 1779

Jefferson's explanation continues,

> **But our opponents** carried in the general resolutions of the committee of November 19 a declaration that religious assemblies ought to be regulated, and that provision ought to be made for continuing the succession of the clergy, and superintending their conduct. And in the bill now passed (entitled: "An Act for exempting the different societies of dissenters from contributing to the support and maintenance of the church as by law established, and its ministers, and for other purposes therein mentioned." Passed by the House of Delegates, December 5th. Concurred in by the Senate December 9th. Re-enacted January 1, 1778)* was inserted an express reservation of the question Whether a general assessment should not be established by law, on every one, to the support of the pastor of his choice; or whether all should be left to voluntary contributions; and on this question, debated at every session from '76 to '79 (some of our dissenting allies, having now secured their particular object, going over to the advocates of a general assessment) we could only obtain a suspension from session to session until '79, when the question against a general assessment was finally carried, and the establishment of the Anglican church entirely put down.[1]

There is no doubt that Jefferson's *Act for Establishing Religious Freedom* caused great animosity, followed by vehement denunciations of this courageous founding father's Religion, as portrayed by the following vindication of his public life and conduct, penned in 1800:

A Vindication of the Public Life and Conduct of Thomas Jefferson, 1800

A July, 1800 publication entitled, *Address to the People of the United States, with an Epitomé and Vindication of the Public Life and Character of Thomas Jefferson*, sheds further light on the subject:

> **"To the People of the United States**
>
> Fellow Citizens,
>
> …Republican citizens of America, will you believe it, and shall the groundless calumny yet find currency in our land, that Jefferson is an anti-federalist and enemy to the Constitution of the United States? Reflect, and ask yourselves whether, if in the prophetic spirit that dictated his remarks on the Constitution, as before quoted, the convention of four States had refused to accede to it, until amendments were obtained, you would probably now have cause to regret the existence in your country of an alien and sedition law, of the lately adopted doctrine of constructive treason, and above all, of the ruinous and disgraceful Treaty of Great Britain?
>
> Equally repulsive is the malign suggestion that Mr. Jefferson is an enemy to Religion. The public records of his native State present to the world in the Statute Book of their laws, the celebrated act "for establishing Religious freedom" – drawn by the pen, and offered to the assembly of Virginia, by

---

*Editor's note in parenthesis.

the hand of their enlightened and illustrious fellow-citizen: Read, ye fanatics, bigots, and religious hypocrites, of whatsoever clime or country ye be – and you, base calumniators, whose efforts to traduce are the involuntary tribute of envy to a character more pure and perfect than your own; read, learn and practice the RELIGION OF JEFFERSON, as displayed in the sublime truths and inspired language of his ever memorable "Act for establishing Religious Freedom," thus –

WELL AWARE that Almighty God hath created the mind free; that all attempts to influence it by temporal punishments or burdens, or by civil incapacitations tend only to beget habits of hypocrisy and meanness, and are a departure from the plan of the holy Author of our Religion, who being Lord both of body and mind, yet chose not to propagate it by coercions on either, as was in His Almighty power to do; that the impious presumption of legislators and rulers, civil as well as ecclesiastical, who, being themselves but fallible and uninspired men have assumed dominion over the faith of others, setting up their own opinions and modes of thinking as the only true and infallible, and as such endeavouring to impose them on others, hath established and maintained false religions over the greatest part of the world, and through all time:

That to compel a man to furnish contributions of money for the propagation of opinions which he disbelieves, is sinful and tyrannical; that even the forcing him to support this or that teacher of his own religious persuasion is depriving him of the comfortable liberty of giving his contributions to the particular Pastor whose morals he would make his pattern, and whose powers he feels most persuasive to righteousness, and is withdrawing from the ministry those temporal rewards, which proceeding from an approbation of their personal conduct, are an additional incitement to earnest and unremitting labors for the instruction of mankind; that our civil rights have no dependence on our religious opinions, more than our opinions in physics or geometry; that therefore the proscribing any citizen as unworthy the public confidence, by laying upon him an incapacity of being called to offices of trust and emolument, unless he profess or renounce this or that religious opinion, is depriving him injuriously of those privileges and advantages to which in common with his fellow citizens he had a natural right;

that it tends also to corrupt the principles of that very Religion it is meant to encourage, by bribing, with a monopoly of worldly honors and emoluments, those who will externally profess and conform to it: that though indeed these are criminal who do not withstand such temptation, yet neither are those innocent who lay the bait in their way; that to suffer the civil magistrate to intrude his powers into the field of opinion and to restrain the profession or propagation of principles on supposition of their ill tendency, is a dangerous fallacy, which at once destroys all religious liberty, because he being of course judge of that tendency, will make his opinions the rule of judgment, and approve or condemn the sentiments of others only as they shall square with or differ from his own; that it is time enough for the rightful purposes of civil government, for its officers to interfere when principles break out into overt acts against peace and good order; and finally, that truth is great and will prevail if left to herself, that she is the proper and sufficient antagonist to error, and has nothing to fear from the conflict, unless by human interposition disarmed of her natural weapons, free argument and debate, errors ceasing to be dangerous when it is permitted freely to contradict them.

Be it therefore enacted by the General Assembly – That no man shall be compelled to frequent or support any religious worship, place, or ministry whatsoever, nor shall be enforced, restrained, molested or burthened in his body or goods, nor shall otherwise suffer on account of his religious opinions or belief; but that all men shall be free to profess, and by argument to maintain, their opinions in matters of religion and that the same shall in no wise diminish, enlarge or affect their civil capacities.

And though we well know that this assembly elected by the people for the ordinary purposes of legislation only, have no power to restrain the acts of succeeding assemblies, constituted with powers equal to our own and that therefore to declare this act irrevocable, would be of no effect in law, yet we are free to declare, that the rights hereby asserted are of the natural rights of mankind, and that if any act shall be hereafter passed to repeal the present, or to narrow its operation, such act will be an infringement of natural right.

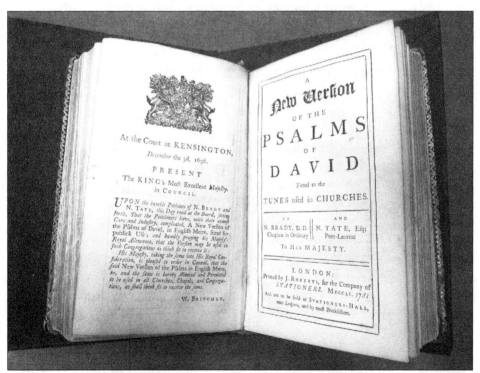

Thomas Jefferson's Prayer Book, opened to the Psalms of David.
University of Virginia Archives, Charlottesville, Virginia.

Jefferson's Notes on the State of Virginia – Reflections on Slavery

"A Vindication of the Public Life and Conduct of Thomas Jefferson" continues – this time on the subject of Slavery:

Further, if the opponents of Mr. Jefferson require additional proof of the ardent piety and religious fervour of his mind, let them read in his ***Notes on Virginia***, page 237, his reflections on the subject of slavery, expressive of his wishes for a gradual emancipation, which are concluded by the following pious apostrophe,

'Can the liberties of a nation be thought secure when we have removed their only firm basis, a conviction in the minds of the people that these liberties are the gift of God? That they are not to be violated but with His wrath? Indeed I tremble for my country when I reflect that God is just; that His justice cannot sleep forever: that considering numbers, nature and natural means only, a revolution of the wheel of fortune, an exchange of situation is among possible events: that it may become probable by supernatural interference! The Almighty has no attribute which can take side with us in such a contest. – But it is impossible to be temperate and to pursue this subject through the various considerations of policy, of morals, of history, natural and civil. We must be contented to hope they will force their way into everyone's mind. I think a change already perceptible since the origin of the present (American)* revolution. The spirit of the master is abating, that of the slave rising from the dust; his condition mollifying, the way I hope preparing, under the auspices of Heaven, for total emancipation, and that this is disposed, in the order of events, to be with the consent of the masters, rather than by their extirpation.'

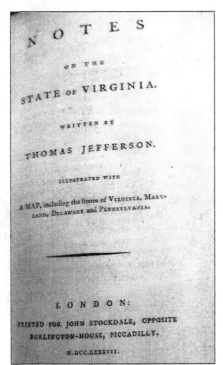

Title page of Thomas Jefferson's original *Notes on the State of Virginia*. Printed in London, 1787. University of Virginia Archives, Charlottesville, Virginia.

Thomas Jefferson's *Notes on the State of Virginia*, printed in London, 1787. (Written by Jefferson in 1781.) University of Virginia Archives, Charlottesville, Virginia.

*Author's text in parenthesis.

Notes on the State of Virginia – The Virtues of Yeomanry

Lastly, Jefferson's character is praised for the value he places on the cultivators of the earth:

> Again, in the same *Notes on Virginia*, page 240, evincing his anxiety to cultivate a spirit of genuine virtue in the public mind, as the sure preservative of Republican liberty, he expresses a no less exalted sentiment of the cultivators of the soil, the yeomanry of our country, than a just confidence in the order of Providence to perpetuate, through their labour, the sacred flame of moral and religious virtue:
>
> 'Those,' says Jefferson, 'who labour in the earth are the chosen people of God, if ever He had a chosen people, whose breasts He has made His peculiar deposit for substantial and genuine virtue. It is the focus in which He keeps alive that sacred fire, which otherwise might escape from the face of the earth. – Corruption of morals in the mass of cultivators is a phenomenon of which no age nor nation has furnished an example. It is the mark set on those, who not looking up to Heaven, to their own soil and industry, as does the husbandman, for their subsistence, depend for it on the casualties and caprice of customers. Dependence begets subservience and venality, suffocates the germ of virtue, and prepares fit tools for the designs of ambition...It is the manners and spirit of the people which preserve a republic in vigour. A degeneracy in these is a canker which soon eats to the heart of its laws and constitution.'
>
> signed: 'Americanus'
Pennsylvania, July, 1800." [2]

One of a series of mural paintings depicting Thomas Jefferson's accomplishments and writings. Main Reading Room, *The John Adams Building*, Library of Congress, Washington, District of Columbia.

Act for Establishing Religious Freedom passed by the Assembly in 1786

The *Act for Establishing Religious Freedom* was Jefferson's particular joy, and ranked in his mind with the *Declaration of Independence*. It was originally introduced to the Assembly on June 13, 1779, and was promptly the subject of memorials, both pro and con, to that body.

The Assembly eventually passed the bill into law in 1786. Jefferson, then in Paris, promptly had an edition printed with the title, *An Act for Establishing Religious Freedom, passed by the Assembly of Virginia in the beginning of the year 1786.*

In the same year it was again printed in Paris as, *Acte de la République de Virginie, qui établit la liberté de Religion.* It was again printed as, *Republican Notes on Religion: and An Act Establishing Religious Freedom, passed in the Assembly of Virginia, in the Year 1786. By Thomas Jefferson, Esquire, President of the United States. Danbury. Printed by Thomas Row, 1803. 8vo pp. 11.*

Chapter IV

Jefferson's "Notes on Religion" – The Fundamentals of Christianity – Christian Heretics – Locke's System of Christianity – The Epistles – "A Heretic is an Impugner of Fundamentals" – Protestant Christianity, Reliance on Scripture Alone – Another Plea for Episcopal Government in Religion in England – The Presbyterian Spirit – The Civil Magistrate denied Jurisdiction over the Church – The Commonwealth, "a Society of Men constituted for Protecting their Civil Interests" – "A Church is a Voluntary Society of Men" – "Truth will do well Enough if left to shift for Herself".

Jefferson's "Notes on Religion"

Many are familiar with Jefferson's *Act for Establishing Religious Freedom*, but few are aware of his meticulous manuscript, ***Notes on Religion***,[1] endorsed by himself as "Early in the Revolution." They were materials and notes for his speeches in the House of Delegates on the petitions for the disestablishment of the Anglican Church. A close study of these "Notes on Religion" prove that Thomas Jefferson understood and differentiated "Christian Heretics" from the fundamentals of Christianity. He writes,

> **The fundamentals of Christianity** as found in the Gospels are, 1. Faith, 2. Repentance. That faith is everywhere explained to be a belief that Jesus was the Messiah who had been promised. Repentance was to be proved sincerely by good works. The advantages accruing to mankind from our Saviour's mission are these: 1. The knowledge of one God only. 2. A clear knowledge of their duty, or system of morality, delivered on such authority as to give it sanction. 3. The outward forms of religious worship wanted to be purged of that farcical pomp and nonsense with which they were loaded. 4. An inducement to a pious life, by revealing clearly a future existence in bliss, & that it was to be the reward of the virtuous.

Christian Heretics

Jefferson prefaced his ***Notes on Religion*** with an elaborate explanation of the false doctrine of "Christian Heretics," concluding with "John Locke's System of Christianity", as follows,

> "**Sabellians**. Christian heretics. That there is but one person in the Godhead. That the 'Word' and Holy Spirit are only virtues, emanations or functions of the deity.
>
> **Sorcinians**. Christian heretics. That the Father is the one only God. That the Word is no more than an expression of the godhead and had not existed from all eternity; that Jesus Christ was God no otherwise than by his superiority above all creatures who were put in subjection to him by the Father. That he was not a mediator, but sent to be a pattern of conduct to men. That the punishments of hell are not eternal.

Arminians. They think with the Romish church (against the Calvinists) that there is a universal grace given to all men, and that man is always *free* and at liberty to receive or reject grace. That God creates men free, that his justice would not permit him to punish men for crimes they are predestinated to commit. They admit the presence of God, but distinguish between foreknowing and predestinating.

Arians. Christian heretics. They avow there was a time when the Son was not, that he was created in time mutable in nature, and like the angels liable to sin; they deny the three persons in the Trinity to be of the same essence.

Apollinarians. Christian heretics. They affirm there was but one nature in Christ, that his body as well as soul was impassive and immortal, and that his birth, death, and resurrection was only in appearance.

Macedonians. Christian heretics. They teach that the Holy Ghost was a mere creature, but superior in excellence to the angels.

Locke's system of Christianity is this: Adam was created happy and immortal; but his happiness was to have been *Earthly* and *Earthly* immortality. By *sin* he lost this – so that he became subject to total death (like that of brutes) to the crosses and unhappiness of this life. At the intercession however of the Son of God, this sentence was in part remitted. A life conformable to the law was to restore them again to immortality. And moreover to them who *believed* their *faith* was to be counted for righteousness. Not that faith without works was to save them; St. James. chapter 2, says expressly the contrary; and all make the fundamental pillars of Christianity to be faith and *repentance*. So that a reformation of life (included under *repentance*) was essential, and defects in this would be made up by their *faith*; i.e. their faith should be counted for righteousness. As to that part of mankind who never had the Gospel preached to them, they are, 1. **Jews**. 2. **Pagans**, or **Gentiles**. The Jews had the law of works revealed to them. By this therefore they were to be saved: and a lively faith in God's promises to send the Messiah would supply small defects. 2. The Gentiles. St. Paul says – Romans 2: 13 'the Gentiles have the law written in their hearts,' i.e. the law of nature: to which adding a *faith* in God and His attributes that on their repentance He would pardon them, they also would be justified. This then explains the text 'there is no other *Name* under heaven by which a man may be saved', i.e. the defects in good works shall not be supplied by a faith in Mahomet, or any other except Christ.

The Epistles were written to persons *already Christians*. A person might be a Christian then before they were written. Consequently the fundamentals of Christianity were to be found in the preaching of our Saviour, which is related in the Gospels. These fundamentals are to be found in the epistles dropped here and there, and promiscuously* mixed with other truths. But these other truths are not to be made fundamentals. They serve for edification indeed and explaining to us matters in worship and morality, but being written occasionally it will readily be seen that their explanations are adapted to the notions and customs of people they were written to. But yet every sentence in them (tho' the writers were inspired) must not be taken

---

*synonym: mingled

up and made a fundamental, without assent to which a man is not to be admitted a member of the Christian church here, or to His kingdom hereafter. **The Apostles Creed** was by them taken to contain all things necessary to salvation, and consequently to a communion...

A Heretic is an Impugner of Fundamentals. What are fundamentals? The Protestants will say those doctrines which are clearly and precisely delivered in the Holy Scriptures...
Episcopy. Greek_____. Latin: Episcopus. Italian: Vescovo. French: Evesque. Saxon: Byscop. Bishop (overseer). The Epistles of Paul to Timothy and Titus are relied on (together with Tradition) for the Apostolic institution of bishops.

Protestant Christianity – Reliance on Scripture Alone

As to tradition, if we are Protestants, we reject all tradition and rely on the Scripture alone, for that is the essence and common principle of all the Protestant churches. As to Scripture, I Timothy 3: 2. 'A bishop must be blameless, etc. (Greek word) verse 8; 'likewise must the deacons be grave, etc. (Greek word) ministers.' Chapter 5, verse 6, he calls Timothy a 'minister (Greek word)'; Chapter 4, verse 14. 'neglect not the gift that is in thee, which was given thee by prophecy with the laying on the hands of the presbytery, (Greek word)'; Chapter 5. 'rebuke not an elder; (Greek word).' 5:17; – 'let the elders that rule well, etc. (Greek word).' 5: 19; 'against an elder (Greek word) receive not an accusation.' 5: 22. 'lay hands suddenly on no man, (Greek words).' 6: 11. He calls Timothy man of God (Greek words), 2 Timothy 1: 6. 'stir up the gift of God, which is in thee, by the putting on of *my* hands (Greek words)' but ante chapter 4 verse 14, he said it was by the hands of the presbytery. This imposition of hands then was some ceremony or custom frequently repeated, and certainly is a good proof that Timothy was ordained by the elders (and consequently that they might ordain) as that it was by Paul. I. 11. Paul calls himself 'a preacher,' 'an apostle,' 'a teacher. (Greek words).' Here he designates himself by several synonyms as he had before done Timothy. Does this prove that every synonym authorizes a different order of ecclesiastics. 4: 5. 'do the work of an Evangelist, make full proof of thy ministry (Greek words).' Timothy then is called 'Greek words.' 4:11. He tells Timothy to bring Mark with him, for 'he is profitable to me for the ministry.' (Greek word). Epistle to Titus, 1.1, he calls himself 'a servant of God' (Greek word) 1: 5 'for this cause left I thee in Crete that thou shouldst set in order the things that are wanting, and ordain (Greek word) *elders* in every city, as I had appointed thee.' If any be blameless, the husband of one wife, having faithful children, not accused of riot or unruly, for a *bishop* must be blameless as the steward of God, etc. Here then it appears that as the elders appointed the bishops, so the bishops appointed the elders, i.e., they are synonyms. Again when telling Titus to appoint *elders* in every city he tells him what kind of men they must be, for said he a bishop must be etc., so that in the same sentence he calls elders bishops. 3: 10 'a man that is a *heretic* after the first and second admonition, reject, (Greek word).' James 5: 14. 'is any sick among you? Let him call for the elders (Greek word) of the church, and let them pray over him, anointing him with oil in the name of the Lord.'

Another plea for Episcopal government in Religion in England is its similarity to the political government by a king. No bishop, no king. This then with us is a plea for government by a presbytery which resembles republican government. The clergy have ever seen this. The bishops were always mere tools of the Crown.

The Presbyterian spirit is known to be so congenial with friendly liberty, that the patriots after the restoration finding that the humour of people was running too strongly to exalt the prerogative of the Crown, promoted the dissenting interest as a check and balance, and thus was produced the **Toleration Act**.

St. Peter gave the title of *clergy* to all God's people till Pope Higinus and the succeeding prelates took it from them and appropriated it to priests only. I Milt. 230...

A modern bishop to be moulded into a primitive one must be elected by the people, undiocest, unrevenued, unlorded. I Milt. 255. From the dissensions among sects themselves arises necessarily a right of choosing a necessity of deliberating to which we will conform, but if we choose for ourselves, we must allow others to choose also, and to reciprocally. This establishes religious liberty.

Why require those things in order to ecclesiastical communion which Christ does not require in order to life eternal? How can that be the church of Christ which excludes such persons from its communion as he will one day receive into the Kingdom of Heaven.

The arms of a religious society or church are exhortations, admonitions and advice, and ultimately expulsion or excommunication. This last is the utmost limit of power.

How far does the duty of toleration extend?

1. No church is bound by the duty of toleration to retain within her bosom obstinate offenders against her laws.
2. We have no right to prejudice another in his *civil* enjoyments because he is of another church. If any man err from the right way, it is his own misfortune, no injury to thee; nor therefore art thou to punish him in the things of this life because thou supposeth he will be miserable in that which is to come – on the contrary according to the spirit of the Gospel, charity, bounty, liberality is due to him.

The Civil Magistrate denied Jurisdiction over the Church

Each church being free, no one can have jurisdiction over another one, not even when the Civil Magistrate joins it. It neither acquires the right of the sword by the Magistrate's coming to it, nor does it lose the rights of instruction or excommunication by his going from it. It cannot by the accession of any new member acquire jurisdiction over those who do not accede. He brings only himself, having no power to bring others. Suppose for instance two churches, one of Arminians, another of Calvinists in Constantinople, has either any right over the other? Will it be said the orthodox one has. Every church is to itself orthodox; to *others* erroneous or heretical.

No man complains of his neighbor for ill management of his affairs, for an error in sowing his land, or marrying his daughter, for consuming his substance in taverns, pulling down building & in all these he has his liberty: but if he do not frequent the church, or there conform to ceremonies, there is an immediate uproar.

The care of every man's soul belongs to himself. But what if he neglect the care of it? Well what if he neglect the care of his health or estate, which more nearly relate to the state. Will the Magistrate make a law that he shall not be poor or sick? Laws provide against injury from others; but not from ourselves. **God himself will not save men against their wills**.

If I be marching on with my utmost vigour in that way which according to the sacred geography leads to Jerusalem straight, why am I beaten and ill used by others because my hair is not of the right cut; because I have not been dressed right, because I eat flesh on the road, because I avoid certain by-ways which seem to lead into briars, because among several paths I take that which seems shortest and cleanest, because I avoid travelers less grave and keep company with others who are more sour and austere, or because I follow a guide crowned with a mitre and clothed in white; yet these are the frivolous things which keep Christianity at war.

If the Magistrate command me to bring my commodity to a public store house, I bring it because he can indemnify me if he erred and I thereby lose it; but what indemnification can he give one for the Kingdom of Heaven?

I cannot give up my guidance to the Magistrates, because he knows no more of the way to Heaven than I do, and is less concerned to direct me right than I am to go right. If the Jews had followed their Kings, among so many, what number would have led them to idolatry? Consider the vicissitudes among the Emperors, Arians, Athana, etc., or among our princes.

Why persecute for difference in religious opinion?

1. For love to the person.
2. Because of tendency of these opinions.

1. When I see them persecute their nearest connection and acquaintance for gross vices, I shall believe it may proceed from love. Till they do this, I appeal of their own consciences if they will examine, when you do not find some other principle.

2. Because of tendency. Why not then level persecution at the crimes you fear will be introduced? Burn or hang the adulterer, cheat, etc. Or exclude them from offices. Strange should be so zealous against things which tend to produce immorality, and yet so indulgent to the immorality when produced. These moral vices all men acknowledge to be diametrically against Christianity and obstructive of salvation of souls, but the fantastical points for which we generally persecute are often very questionable; as we may be assured by the very different conclusions of people. Our Saviour chose not to propagate His Religion by temporal punishments or civil incapacitation, if He had, it was in His Almighty power. But He chose to extend it by its influence on reason, thereby showing to others how they should proceed.

The Commonwealth is 'a Society of Men constituted for Protecting their Civil Interests.'

Civil interests are 'life, health, indolency of body, liberty and property.' That the Magistrate's jurisdiction extends only to civil rights appears from these considerations:

1. The Magistrate has no power but what the people gave. The people have not given him the care of souls because you cannot, you cannot, because no man has *right* to abandon the care of his salvation to another.

No man has *power* to let another prescribe his faith. Faith is not faith without believing. No man can conform his faith to the dictates of another. The life and essence of religion consists in the internal persuasion or belief of the mind. External forms of worship, when against our belief are hypocrisy and impiety. Romans 14: 23. 'he that doubteth is damned if he eat, because he eateth not of faith: for whatsoever is not of faith, is sin?'

2. If it be said the Magistrate may make use of arguments and so draw the heterodox to truth, I answer, every man has a commission to admonish, exhort, convince another of error.

A Church is a Voluntary Society of Men

A church is 'a *voluntary* society of men, joining themselves together of their own accord, in order to the public worshipping of God in such a manner as they judge acceptable to Him and effectual to the salvation of their souls.' It is *voluntary* because no man is *by nature* bound to any church. The hope of salvation is the cause of his entering into it. If he find anything wrong in it, he should be as free to go out as he was to come in.

What is the power of that church. As it is a society, it must have some laws for its regulation. Time and place of meeting. Admitting and excluding members, etc. Must be regulated, but as it was a spontaneous joining of members, it follows that its laws extend to its own members only, not to those of any other voluntary society, for then by the same rule some other voluntary society might usurp power over them.

Christ has said 'wheresoever two or three are gathered together in His name, He will be in the midst of them.' This is His definition of a society. He does not make it essential that a bishop or presbyter govern them. Without them it suffices for the salvation of souls.

Compulsion in religion is distinguished peculiarly from compulsion in every other thing. I may grow rich by art I am compelled to follow. I may recover health by medicines I am compelled to take against my own judgment, but I cannot be saved by a worship I disbelieve and abhor.

Whatsoever is lawful in the Commonwealth, or permitted to the subject in the ordinary way, cannot be forbidden to him for religious uses: and whatsoever is prejudicial to the Commonwealth in their ordinary uses and therefore prohibited by the laws, ought not to be permitted to churches in their sacred rites. For instance, it is unlawful in the ordinary course of things or in a private house to murder a child. It should not be permitted any sect then to sacrifice children: it is ordinarily lawful (or temporarily lawful) to kill calves or lambs. They may therefore be religiously sacrificed, but if the good of the State required a temporary suspension of killing lambs, as during a siege, sacrifices of them may then be rightfully suspended also. This is the true extent of toleration.

Truth will do well enough if left to shift for herself. She seldom has received much aid from the power of great men to whom she is rarely known and seldom welcome. She has no need of force to procure entrance into the minds of men. Error indeed has often prevailed by the assistance of power or force. Truth is the proper and sufficient antagonist to error. If anything pass in a religious meeting seditiously and contrary to the public peace, let it be punished in the same manner and no otherwise than as if it had happened in a fair or market. These meetings ought not to be sanctuaries for faction and flagitiousness."[2]

The above-cited *Notes on Religion* disclose Jefferson's Scriptural reasoning underlying his *Act for Establishing Religious Freedom*, considered by him to be, after the *Declaration of Independence*, his greatest accomplishment – granting freedom of worship to dissident Protestant denominations, outside the jurisdiction of the Civil Magistrate.

Chapter V

The French "Enlightenment" or "Reign of Terror" – Voltaire – Robespierre – Rousseau – The Jacobin Club (Jacobins) – John Locke's "Letter concerning Toleration" – Locke's Political Theories – Sir Isaac Newton – Sir Francis Bacon – Defamation of Character, Jefferson's View.

The French "Enlightenment" or "Reign of Terror"

From "John Locke's System of Christianity," in Jefferson's *Notes on Religion*, we understand that Locke, whose writings Jefferson studied, was a true believer in Jesus Christ the Messiah, and His gospel. This refutes the widely-propagated revisionist teaching that Thomas Jefferson's democratic creed proceeded from "Enlightenment" ideas – equating them with those of the "Reign of Terror, Enlightenment" movement. The French "Enlightenment" has its origins in the writings of Voltaire, Rousseau, Robespierre, Diderot, and their followers, all of whom were atheists.

Following are the French "Enlightenment" leaders' true identity:

Voltaire (1694-1778), whose real name was Francois Marie Arouet, was educated by the Jesuits at the *College de Louis-le-Grand*. In early youth he became associated with *La Societé du Temple*, a group of free-thinkers (Freemasons). His satirical writings earned him eleven months' imprisonment in the Bastille (1717). He was again incarcerated in 1725. At the age of sixty, unwelcome in France, he moved his residence close to Geneva, but found himself at odds with the Swiss Protestants. Voltaire's *Dictionnaire Philosophique* (1764) was an intellectual battery aimed at Religion. As a deist, Volaire based God in part, on the necessity for rationalizing conscious existence. He advocated the role of chance in human affairs, discrediting Christianity and the belief in Providence, which he termed "non-existent." Returning to Paris in 1778, he died shortly thereafter. In 1791, the French Revolutionists of the "Reign of Terror" deposited his remains in the Pantheon.[1]

Robespierre, Maximilien Marie Isidore de (1768-1794), French Revolutionist, was born in Arras, and educated there, and at the *College de Louis-le-Grand* by the Jesuits. An ardent proponent of the political theories of Rousseau, he stood with the extreme Left in the Constituent Assembly. Unable to make any headway against the Bourgeoisie in France, he transferred his activities to the Jacobin Club. He urged the execution of Louis XVI as a matter of public policy. In 1793, he was elected to the General *Committee of Public Safety*, where he played an important role as the propagandist and apologist of the Committee during the "Reign of Terror." In 1794, he procured a passage of a law abridging the procedure of the Tribunal, thus opening the way for the excesses of the Great Terror.[2]

Rousseau (1712-1778), a French philosopher and political theorist, was born in Geneva, Switzerland. His work, *Emile* (1762), which he considered to be the "best and most important of all his writings," is a treatise on the nature of education and the nature of man. When the book was condemned by the French Parliament, the author fled. *Emile* was banned in Paris and Geneva, and publicly burned in 1762, due to a segment entitled, *Profession of Faith of the Savoyard Vicar*. During the "Reign of Terror" this treatise became the basis for the future new system of education in France. Rousseau is regarded as the author, above all others, who inspired the French Revolution, or "Great Terror." [3]

The **"Enlightenment"** is a term which refers to a philosophic movement of the 18th century that questioned religious and secular authority, and attempted to make reason the foundation of society, and of man's philosophy. In France, it led to the editing of the *Encyclopédie* by **Diderot**, to which atheists like Voltaire and Rousseau contributed. It is based on the assumption that man is capable of understanding the world without any recourse to God or His supernatural assistance.[4]

The Jacobin Club (Jacobins), founded by **Robespierre**, was the most influential political club of the French Revolution, which identified itself with extreme egalitarianism and violence, leading to the *Revolutionary Government* from 1793-1794 in France. Called "the Jacobins" because its meetings were held in a Monastery of the Dominicans known in Paris as "Jacobins." By July, 1790, there were about 1,200 members in Paris, and 153 affiliate clubs throughout France. The purpose of the Jacobins was to protect the progress of the French Revolution against possible reaction from opponents. With the establishment of the Revolutionary dictatorship, beginning mid-1793, the local Jacobin Clubs became instruments of the "Reign of Terror." In 1793, there were about 5,000 - 8,000 clubs throughout France, with a membership of 500,000. The Clubs monitored people of suspect opinions, leading to the de-Christianizing movement and the organization of Revolutionary gatherings. **The fall of Robespierre** (July 27, 1794), resulted in the closure of the Club, which had become a symbol of terror and dictatorship.[5]

John Locke's "Letter Concerning Toleration"

In stark contrast to the European atheistic "Enlightenment," **John Locke** (1632-1704) authored *A Letter Concerning Toleration* (1689), which became a foundation in the quest for **Religious Freedom of Protestants**. In 1699, the Virginia House of Burgesses confirmed the Act of Toleration. The same year, John Locke wrote to **Reverend Dr. James Blair**, missionary from Scotland to Virginia (1685), who founded the College of William and Mary in 1693. Locke thanked this man of God for "all the great compliments you make to me on this occasion:

> Sir,
>
> ...Grateful reflections on what had been done, with an overgreat opinion, expressed of that service which you imagine you had from my hand in the doeing of it. I shall not undertake to answer all the great compliments you make me on this occasion. I take them, as I ought, to be the language of your civility. But this gives me leave to say that if I have been any way

instrumental in procuring any good to the country you are in, I am as much pleased with it as you can be. The flourishing of the plantations under their due and just regulations being that which I doe and shall always aim at – whilst I have the honour to sit at the board I now doe. I hope the College grows and flourishes under your care...

I am, sir,
Your most humble servant,
John Locke

Locke's Political Theories

The 2nd Treatise on Government (1690), Locke's most important political work, was written as a reply to Sir Robert Filmer, a proponent of the Divine Right of Kings, who endeavoured to trace the right of monarchical government to Adam. Locke's reply became much more than a refutation. Having denied Filmer's conception of the source of civil authority, Locke proposed an alternative by describing the condition of men without government, or in the "state of nature." In order to protect "life, liberty and property," men exchange the "state of nature" for the "state of society," agreeing, for practical reasons, to accept the judgment of a Magistrate in matters of conduct. Locke then points to the fallacy of a doctrine which holds that a ruler may himself arbitrarily abridge these natural rights of life, liberty and property: absolutism is an unacceptable form of government because it is in opposition to the very principles upon which all government is founded. Thus the monarch who disregards the basic tenet of popular consent, and injures, for his own selfish ends, those whom he had agreed to protect, has in fact instituted a State of War, and the alleged revolutionist merely defends himself against unauthorized attack. The importance of Locke's political doctrines extends far beyond 17th century England. His writings exercised great influence upon the founders of the American Republic; particularly **Thomas Jefferson**, who de-throned monarchial rule in the British American Colonies with his immortal *Declaration of Independence*.[6]

Equally contradictory to the European atheistic "Enlightenment" ideas, are the writings and philosophy of **Isaac Newton**, in concert with the works of **John Locke** and **Francis Bacon**, which Jefferson studied at the College of William and Mary:

Sir Isaac Newton (1642-1727) was a genius in the realm of science. His discoveries of the *System of the Universe*; the *Law of Gravity; Mathematical Principles of Natural Philosophy; a New Calculus*; the *Parabolic Curve; Optics – A Treatise of Light*; and the *Reflecting Telescope*, among many others, revolutionized the world. His genius extended to an understanding of the force exercised by the sun and the moon, causing *Tides*. Elected to the *Royal Society of London* and *l'Academie des Sciences de Paris*, his brilliant analytical discoveries were made before the age of twenty-three. In a letter written to Rev. Dr. Bentley in 1692, Newton states that,

If I have done the public any service in this way, it is due to nothing but industry and patient thought.[7]

Portrait of Sir Isaac Newton by Enoch Seeman, c. 1726.

Newton's amazing discoveries led him to conclude that there was "a very First Cause;" "A Supernatural Power;" "A Creator;" "A Being Incorporeal, Living, Intelligent, Omnipresent" who created the Universe, men and women; as well as animals in their species, maintaining his creation by "Divine Power." "Whence is it," he asks, "that nature does nothing in vain, and whence arises all that order and beauty, which we see in the world? Was the eye contrived without skill in Optics, and the ear without knowledge of sounds?...and whence is the instinct in animals?" "The diurnal rotations of the planets could not be derived from gravity, but required a Divine Arm to impress them," he asserts. His *Observations on the Apocalypse of St. John* the Evangelist in relation to Daniel's prophecies of the Messiah, and the End Times are insightful and profound. A scholar of the Bible, the last ten years of Newton's life were spent studying the Scriptures. His *Theological Notebook* discloses an adherence to, and acknowledgment of God the Father, God the Son and God the Holy Spirit. A true scientist, Isaac Newton proved that science and the Bible are totally compatible.[8]

Sir Francis Bacon (1561-1626) was educated at Trinity College, Cambridge. Bacon's handsome bronze statue adorns the Library of Congress' Main Reading Room, to the right of the pillar "Philosophy," bearing a quotation from his writings:

The Enquiry, Knowledge and Belief of Truth is the Sovereign Good of Human Nature.

His work, *Novum Organum*, was actually published as part of a much larger work, *Instauratio Magna*, "the Great Instauration." The word "instauration" was intended to show that the state of human knowledge was to simultaneously press forward while also returning to that enjoyed by man before the Fall. The engraved title page for *Instauratio Magna*, published in 1620, bears a prominent Latin inscription at the bottom taken from the Old Testament, translated to mean,

Many shall run to and fro and knowledge shall be increased. Daniel 12: 4.

Francis Bacon's inscription above the pillar for – "Philosophy," Main Reading Room, Library of Congress Thomas Jefferson Building, Washington, D.C.

Statue of Sir Francis Bacon representing "Philosophy," Main Reading Room, Library of Congress, Thomas Jefferson Building, Washington, D.C.

It follows that the atheistic "Enlightenment" philosophy in Europe was at antipodes with that of Locke, Newton and Bacon, whom Thomas Jefferson called "the three greatest men the world has produced."

Defamation of Character – Jefferson's View

On the subject of defamation of public character, Thomas Jefferson wrote to his friend John Jay, on January 25, 1786, stating that "it is a part of the price we pay for liberty." It reads,

> It really is to be lamented that after a public servant has passed a life in important and faithful services, after having given the most plenary satisfaction in every station, it should yet be in the power of every individual to disturb his quiet, by arraigning him in a Gazette and by obliging him to act as if he needed a defence, an obligation imposed on him by unthinking minds which never give themselves the trouble of seeking a reflection unless it be presented to them. However, it is a part of the price we pay for liberty, which cannot be guarded but by the freedom of the press, nor that be limited without danger of losing it. To the loss of time, of labour, of money, then, must be added that of quiet, to which those must offer themselves who are capable of serving the public and all this is better than European bondage.

Although a constant target of calumny in public life, this founding father saw the loss of time, labour, resources and quiet, as necessary evils to be borne by those capable of serving their fellow citizens in a free society – and preferable to European bondage.

Chapter VI

Jefferson's Bill for Proportioning Crimes and Punishments, 1778 – His Personal Family Bible, Testimony of Edmund Bacon, Overseer – Thomas Jefferson's Library, Rare Book Collection, Library of Congress – Jefferson, Churchman at St. Anne's Parish – Subscription to support a Clergyman in Charlottesville – Concern for his Pastor's Support – Jefferson proclaims a Day of Fasting, Humiliation and Prayer – His Notice of a Fast Day, St. Anne's Parish – Jefferson's Letter to the Danbury Baptists – President Thomas Jefferson, Churchman in Washington – Secretary of State in Georgetown – Jefferson, Churchman in Georgetown – His Contribution to erect St. John's Episcopal Church, Georgetown – Francis Scott Key, Vestryman – Jefferson, Churchman in Charlottesville – Churchman in Philadelphia – Churchman in Williamsburg – Georgetown-on-the-Potomac.

Jefferson's Bill for Proportioning Crimes and Punishments, 1778

In keeping with his Christian philosophy of life and an adherence to the Ten Commandments, Jefferson authored a "Bill for Proportioning Crimes and Punishments," consisting of XXXII sections. It is hereunder excerpted:

> **Section I.** Whereas it frequently happens that wicked and dissolute men, resigning themselves to the dominion of inordinate passions, commit violations on the lives, liberties, and property of others, and the secure enjoyment of these having principally induced men to enter into society, government would be defective in its principal purpose, were it not to restrain such criminal acts by inflicting due punishments on those who perpetuate them; but it appears at the same time equally deducible from the purposes of society, that a member thereof, committing an inferior injury, does not wholly forfeit the protection of his fellow citizens, but after suffering a punishment in proportion to his offence, is entitled to their protection from all greater pain, so that it becomes a duty in the Legislature to arrange in a proper scale the crimes which it may be necessary for them to repress, and to adjust thereto a corresponding gradation of punishments.
>
> And whereas the reformation of offenders, though an object worthy the attention of the laws, is not effected at all by capital punishments which exterminate instead of reforming, and should be the last melancholy resource against those whose existence is become inconsistent with the safety of their fellow citizens: which also weaken the State by cutting off so many, who, if reformed, might be restored sound members to society, who, even under a course of correction, might be rendered useful in various labours for the public, and would be, living, and long-continued spectacles to deter others from committing the like offences.
>
> And forasmuch as the experience of all ages and countries hath shown, that cruel and sanguinary laws defeat their own purpose, by engaging the benevolence of mankind to withhold prosecutions, to smother testimony, or to listen to it with bias; and by producing in many instances a total dispensation and impunity under the names of pardon and privilege of clergy: when, if the punishment were only proportioned to the injury, men would feel it their inclination, as well as their duty, to see the laws observed; and

the power of dispensation, so dangerous and mischievous, which produces crimes by holding up a hope of impunity, might totally be abolished, so that men while contemplating to perpetrate a crime would see their punishment ensuing as necessarily as effects follow their causes; for rendering crimes and punishments, therefore, more proportionate to each other.

Section II. Be it enacted by the General Assembly, that no crime shall be henceforth punished by the deprivation of life or limb, except those hereinafter ordained to be so punished.

Section V. Whoever commiteth murder by poisoning, shall suffer death by poison.

Section VI. Whosoever commiteth murder by way of duel, shall suffer death by hanging; and if he were the challenger, his body, after death, shall be gibbeted. He who removeth it from the gibbet shall be guilty of a misdemeanor, and the officer shall see that it be replaced.

Section X. Whosoever shall be guilty of manslaughter, shall, for the first offence, be condemned to hard labour for seven years in the public works; shall forfeit one half of his lands and goods to the next of kin to the person slain; the other half to be sequestered during such term, in the hands, and to the use, of the commonwealth, allowing a reasonable part of the profits for the support of his family. The second offence shall be deemed murder.

Section XII. In other cases of homicide the law will not add to the miseries of the party, by punishments or forfeitures.

Section XIV. Whosoever shall be guilty of rape, (*polygamy*), or sodomy with man or woman, shall be punished; if a man, by castration, if a woman, by boring through the cartilage of her nose a hole of one half inch in diameter at the least.

Section XVI. Whosoever shall counterfeit any coin current by law within this commonwealth, or any paper bills issued in the nature of money, or of certificates of loan, on the credit of this commonwealth, or of all or any of the United States of America, or any Inspectors' notes for tobacco, or shall pass any such counterfeited coin, paper bills, or notes, knowing them to be counterfeit; or, for the sake of lucre, shall diminish each, or any such coin, shall be condemned to hard labour six years in the public works, and shall forfeit all his lands and goods to the commonwealth.

Section XX. Whosoever committeth a robbery, shall be condemned to hard labour four years in the public works, and shall make double reparation to the persons injured.

Section XXIV. Grand larceny shall be where the goods stolen are of the value of five dollars; and whosoever shall be guilty thereof, shall be forthwith put in the pillory for one half hour, shall be condemned to hard labour two years in the public works, and shall make reparation to the person injured.

Section XXIX. All attempts to delude the people, or to abuse their understanding by exercise of the pretended arts of witchcraft, conjuration, enchantment, or sorcery, or by pretended prophecies, shall be punished by ducking and whipping, at the discretion of a jury, not exceeding fifteen stripes.

Section XXXII. Pardon and privilege of clergy, shall henceforth be abolished, that none may be induced to injure through hope of impunity. But if the verdict be against the defendant, and the court, before whom the offence is heard and determined, shall doubt that it may be untrue for default of testimony, or other cause, they may direct a new trial to be had.*

As God's Scriptural admonitions in the Ten Commandments and His law establish the basis for Anglo-American crimes and punishments – including sins of immorality – the illustrious author of the **Declaration of Independence** would doubtless be censored and ostracized by 21st century media for his denunciation of immorality, sodomy, witchcraft, sin and tyranny; as well as for his allotted punishments of these criminal offenses. Should they do so, they would be elevating themselves above the documents of America's liberty, under which they live.

The founders of the American Republic, moreover, referred to their unique new nation as, "A Republic under God," and "God's American Israel" – in keeping with the Scripture penned by **Patrick Henry** on the back of his 1765 Stamp Act Resolves:

> Righteousness exalteth a nation, but sin is a reproach to any people.
> Proverbs 14:34**

Patrick Henry's original 1765 Stamp Act Resolves (Signature page). University of Virginia Archives, Charlottesville, Virginia.

* The text of the Act is printed from the *Report of the Revisors*. Jefferson's hand-written manuscript was enclosed in the letter to his friend and mentor, George Wythe on November 1, 1778.
** Entire text of Scripture verse.

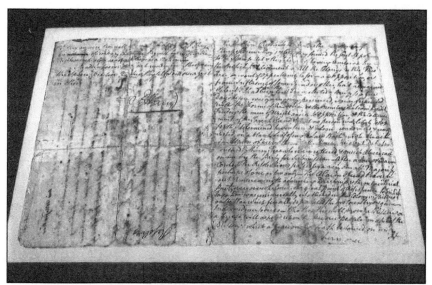

Patrick Henry's 1765 original Stamp Act Resolves. (Back page). University of Virginia Archives, Charlottesville, Virginia.

Jefferson's Personal Family Bible – Testimony of Edmund Bacon, Overseer

Another attack on the character of Thomas Jefferson has been the revisionists' unrelenting accusations that Thomas Jefferson was averse to the Bible, being anti-Christian. An eye-witness account over a period of twenty years is far more credible than the unscrupulous calumnies published by the enemies of Jefferson's *Act for Establishing Religious Freedom*. Captain Edmund Bacon, overseer at Monticello for twenty years, recounts in detail his esteemed master's love of the Bible in ***The Private Life of Thomas Jefferson***, an 1862 publication:

> Mr. Jefferson had a very large library. When the British burnt Washington, the library the belonged to Congress was destroyed, and Mr. Jefferson sold them his. He directed me to have it packed in boxes and sent to Washington. John Hemings, one of his servants, made the boxes, and Burwell and I packed them up mostly. Dinsmore helped us some, and the girls, Ellen, Virginia and Cornelia, (Jefferson's granddaughters) would come in sometimes and sort them out and help us a good deal. There was an immense quantity of them. There were sixteen wagonloads. I engaged the teams. Each wagon was to carry three thousand pounds for a load, and to have four dollars a day for delivering them in Washington. If they carried more than three thousand pounds, they were to have extra pay. There were all kinds of books – books in a great many languages that I knew nothing about. There were a great many religious books among them – more than I have ever seen anywhere else. All the time Mr. Jefferson was President I had the keys to his library, and I could go in and look over the books, and take out any one that I wished, and read and return it. I have written a good many letters from that library to Mr. Jefferson in Washington.

Thomas Jefferson's personal Bible, King James Authorized translation from the original Tongues, circa 1752. Rare Book Collection, University of Virginia, Charlottesville, Virginia.

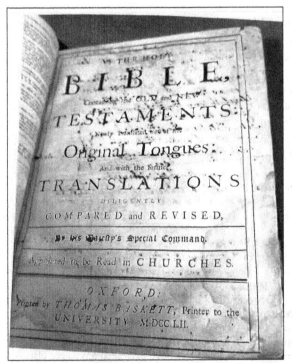

Title Page of Thomas Jefferson's personal Bible, "The Holy Bible containing the Old and New Testaments newly translated out of the original Tongues. Oxford: 1752." Rare Book Collection, University of Virginia, Charlottesville, Virginia.

Mr. Jefferson had a sofa or lounge upon which he could sit or recline, and a small table on rollers, upon which he could write or lay his books. Sometimes he would draw this table up before the sofa and sit and read or write; and other times he would recline on his sofa, with his table rolled up the sofa, astride it. **He had a large Bible**, which nearly always lay at the head of his sofa. Many and many a time I have gone into his room and found him reading that Bible. You remember I told you about riding all night from Richmond, after selling that flour, and going into his room very early in the morning, and paying over to him the new United States Bank money. *That* was one of the times I found him with the big Bible open before him on his little table, and he busy reading it. And I have seen him reading it in that way many a time. Some people, you know, say he was an atheist. Now if he was an atheist, what did he want with all those religious books, and **why did he spend so much of his time reading his Bible**?

When Chancellor **George Wythe** died, he willed to Mr. Jefferson his library. It was very large and nearly filled up the room of the one he sold to Congress. Mr. Jefferson studied law with Chancellor Wythe. They thought a great deal of each other.[1]

It is interesting to note that this large family Bible (King James Version, circa 1752) so often read by Jefferson (as well as his Prayer Book), were not included in the 1815 sale of his collection to Congress. They were retained at Monticello for his continuous use, and are now housed in a vault at the *University of Virginia*, which he founded in 1819.

Thomas Jefferson's Prayer Book. Rare Book Collection, University of Virginia, Charlottesville, Virginia.

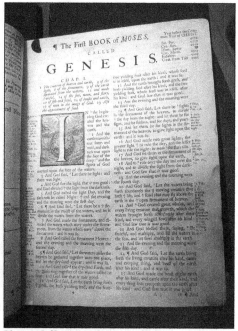

Thomas Jefferson's personal family Bible, (King James 1611 Authorized), opened to Genesis, the First Book of the Bible. Rare Book Collection, University of Virginia, Charlottesville, Virginia.

Thomas Jefferson's Library – Rare Book Collection, Library of Congress

Jefferson's Library of Congress Collection is meticulously catalogued by himself. There are no less than a hundred and ninety entries under the category: **Religion**, of which numerous are Bibles in multiple languages; including doctrinally-sound concordances, the works of John Wesley, and other notable Christian writings. A perusal of this collection which he titled, **Religion**, discloses his own Religion – Protestant Christianity – and none other. On the title page of this catalogue, Jefferson's famous words are quoted:

> …I am for freedom of Religion, and against all maneuvers to bring about a legal ascendancy of one sect over another…

Following are some of these entries for the reader to assess:

His well-worn, beautifully leather-bound, four-volume Bible holds preeminence in this collection. Its Jefferson Collection Rare Book card catalogue entry (BS.195. T55) describes his Bible as:

> Bible. English. 1808.
> Thomson
>
> The Holy Bible containing the Old and New Covenant, commonly called the Old and New Testament translated from the Greek by Charles Thomson, late Secretary to the Congress of the Unitec States. Philadelphia. Printed by J. Aitken, 1808. The Bible on which Dr. Daniel Boorstin book the oath of office as the 12th Librarian of Congress, November 12, 1975.

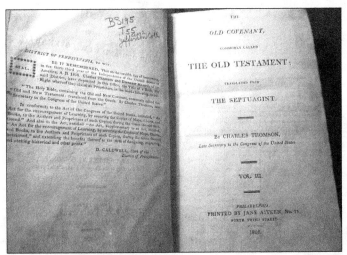

The Holy Bible containing the Old and New Covenant, commonly called the Old and New Testament, translated from the Septuagint (Greek), Vol III, by Charles Thomson, Late Secretary to the Congress of the United States. Jefferson Library, Rare Book Collection, Library of Congress.

Other entries in the collection include:

- Old and New Testament and Apocrypha 1798.

- Greek New Testament 1583.

- Greek and Latin New Testament 1578.

- Latin New Testament 1735.

- Bible – New Testament Greek 1800.

- Hammond's New Testament – a Paraphrase and Annotation upon all the Books of the New Testament, briefly explaining all the difficult places therein.

- The New Testament of our Lord and Saviour Jesus Christ, translated out of the original Greek, 1802.

- The History of Jesus by Thompson and Price, 1805.

- The History of our Blessed Lord and Saviour Jesus Christ: with the Lives of the Holy Apostles, and their successors for three hundred years after the crucifixion.

- Newman's Concordance to the Bible, 1650.

- Cruden's Concordance, 1738.

- Clarke's Concordance to the Holy Bible, 1696.

- Brown's Dictionary of the Holy Bible.

- *Truth of the Christian Religion* by Hugo Grotius in six books, Written in Latin by Grotius, and now translated into English, with an addition of a seventh book against the present Roman Church, 1694. (Hugo Grotius was the father of International Law).

- *Evidences of Christianity*, a view of the evidences of Christianity in three parts. Part I: Of the direct Historical Evidence of Christianity, and wherein it is distinguished from the evidence alleged for other miracles. Part II: Of the Auxiliary Evidence of Christianity. Part III: A brief Consideration of some popular objections, 1795.

- *Barclay's Minute Philosopher*, in seven dialogues, containing an apology for the Christian Religion, against those who are called Freethinkers, 1732.

- The works of Reverend John Witherspoon, D.D., LL.D., late President of the College, at Princeton, New Jersey. To which is prefixed an account of the author's life, in a sermon occasioned by his death, by the Reverend Dr. John Rodgers of New York, in three volumes. (Dr. Witherspoon was the only preacher-signer of the *Declaration of Independence*). It was

>   Witherspoon, in 1781, noting the differences in the English language as spoken in America, who coined the word "Americanism."
>
> – *Primitive Christianity Revived*, by William Whiston, Volume I: Epistles of Ignatius; Volume II: The Apostolical Constitutions in Greek and English; Volume III: An Essay on those Apostolical Constitutions; Volume IV: An account of the Primitive faith, concerning the Trinity and Incarnation.
>
> – A *Scriptural Account of the Millenium*: being a Selection from the Prophecies concerning Christ's Second Coming, and personal glorious reign on earth a thousand years. To which are added a number of arguments to shew that this event has not yet taken place. Also, some observations, calculated to stimulate man to an enquiry into the matter make the necessary preparation for that all important event. By Benjamin Gorton, 1802.
>
> – *Tracts in Religion*: The Blessings of America. A sermon preached in the Middle Dutch Church, on the 4th July, 1791, being the Anniversary of the Independence of America. By William Linn.
>
> – *Principles of Civil Union and Happiness considered and Recommended*. A sermon by Elizur Goodrich.
>
> – *The Inquirer*: Being An examination of the Question lately agitated, respecting the legitimate Powers of Government, whether they extend to the Care of Religion, and warrant making and enforcing Laws for the Purpose of establishing, supporting or encouraging the Christian Religion. 1801.
>
> – *Prideaux' Connections*. 2 vol. fol. The Old and New Testament connected in the History of the Jews and neighboring Nations, from the Declension of the Kingdoms of Israel and Judah to the Time of Christ, by Humphrey Prideaux, 1719.[2]

The above list of books on the subject of Religion in Jefferson's library represents but a small fraction of his collection on Christianity. It is reminiscent of a well-equipped and balanced library of Bibles and Christian works of the highest caliber. It also shows Thomas Jefferson's extensive personal collection of Old and New Testaments, intact. These hold preeminence in his library of books entitled, "Religion." This precludes "deism," "atheism" and alien false religions which are non-existent in this founding father's extensive collection. Biblical sermons, such as "The Blessings on America' also show the inseparable link between Christianity and the nation's government. It would seem questionable whether one would collect such an extensive library on Bibles and Bible-related materials if the Word of God was not an integral part of one's life.

Jefferson – Churchman at St. Anne's Parish

Another oft-repeated criticism against Jefferson is that he was "far from being a churchman." Yet, in the published historic records of St. Anne's Parish – Christ

Church (circa 1745), we read:

"Our most famous Colonial parishioner was Thomas Jefferson."

St. Anne's Episcopal Parish, established in 1745. "Christ Church, Glendower," where Jefferson served as vestryman.

He was also a member of the vestry, writing the following testimonial for his pastor, **Reverend Charles Clay**:

15 August, 1779

Parish of Saint Anne, Albemarle.

The Reverend Charles Clay has been many years Rector of this parish, and has been particularly known to me. During the whole course of that time his deportment has been exemplary as became a Divine, and his attention to parochial duties unexceptionable. In the earliest stage of the present contest with Great Britain, while the clergy of the Established Church in general took the adverse side, or kept aloof from the cause of their country, he took a decisive and active part with his countrymen, and has continued to prove his whiggism, unequivocal, and his attachment to the American cause to be sincere and zealous. As he has some thought of leaving us, I feel myself obliged, in compliance with the common duty of bearing witness to the truth when called on, to give this testimonial of his merit, that it may not be altogether unknown to those with whom he may propose to take up his residence.

Given under my hand, this 15th day of August, 1779.
TH: Jefferson.

At the height of the American Revolution, prior to this testimonial, and after the General Assembly in Virginia had acted upon Jefferson's Freedom of Religious Worship Act – Jefferson initiated a "Subscription to support a Clergyman" (Rev. Charles Clay) in Charlottesville, dated February, 1777:

Subscription to Support a Clergyman in Charlottesville

February, 1777.

WHEREAS, by a late Act of General Assembly, freedom of Religious opinion and worship is restored to all, and it is left to the members of each religious society to employ such teachers as they think fit for their own spiritual comfort and instruction, and to maintain the same by their free and voluntary contributions: We, the subscribers, professing the most universal affection for other religious sectaries who happen to differ from us in points of conscience, yet desirous of encouraging and supporting the Calvinistical Reformed church, and of deriving to ourselves, through the ministry of its teachers, the benefits of Gospel knowledge and religious improvement; and at the same time of supporting those, who, having been at considerable expence in qualifying themselves by regular education for explaining the Holy Scriptures, have dedicated their time and labour to the service of the said church; and moreover, approving highly the political conduct of the Reverend Charles Clay, who, early rejecting the tyrant and tyranny of Britain, proved his Religion genuine by its harmony with the liberties of mankind, and, conforming his public prayers to the spirit and the injured rights of his country, ever addressed the God of battles for victory to our arms, while others impiously prayed that our enemies might vanquish and overcome us: do hereby oblige ourselves, our heirs, executors, and administrators to pay to the said Charles Clay of Albemarle, his executors or administrators, the several sums affixed to our respective names on the 25th day of December next, and also to make the like annual payment on the 25th day of December in every year following until we shall withdraw the same, or until the legislature shall make other provision for the support of the said Clergy. In consideration whereof, we expect that the said Charles Clay shall perform Divine service and preach a sermon in the town of Charlottesville on every 4th Saturday till the end of the next session of General Assembly and after that on every 4th Sunday, or oftener, if a regular rotation with the other churches which shall have put themselves under his cure will admit a more frequent attendance.

And we further mutually agree with each other that we will meet at Charlottesville on the 1st of March in the present year and on_____in every year following, so long as we continue our subscriptions and there make choice by ballot of three Wardens to collect our said subscriptions to take care of such books and vestments as shall be provided for the use of our church to call meetings of our Congregation when necessary, and to transmit such other business relating to our said Congregation as we shall hereafter confide to them.

February, 1777.

TH: Jefferson, six pounds.
Phillip Mazzei, sixteen shillings & eight pence.
Randolph Jefferson, two pounds, ten shillings.
Nicholas Lewis, three pounds, ten shillings.
Samuel Taliaferro, twenty shillings.
Hastings Marks, twenty shillings.
Peter Marks, twenty-five shillings.
Richard Gaines, ten shillings.
Lewis Cradock, ten shillings.
Edward Butler, ten shillings.
Benjamin Calvert, ten shillings.
Richard Moore, ten shillings.
John (…), ten shillings.
A.S. Bryan, twenty shillings.
Thomas Garth, fifteen shillings.
James Minor, twenty shillings.
William Tandy, twenty shillings.
Jonathan Jouet, one pound, ten shillings.
Thomas Key, two pounds.
Richard Anderson, two pounds.

Concern for his Pastor's Support

The above testifies to Thomas Jefferson's concern for his Pastor's support and care – a contribution of six pounds per annum being the most generous of all subsequent subscriptions listed. It also explains his motivation in authoring the 1777 *Freedom of Religion Act*: to allow "the members of each Religious Society to employ such teachers as they think fit for their own spiritual comfort and instruction, and to maintain the same by their free and voluntary contributions."

Jefferson proclaims a Day of Fasting, Humiliation and Prayer

Moreover, in 1774, at the outbreak of the Revolution, when the American colonists were being taxed without representation, and as a result of their opposition to a tax on the importation of tea, Great Britain announced closure of the Port of Boston. It was thus that Thomas Jefferson and Patrick Henry drafted a Proclamation on the 24th of May, 1774, designating June 1st, 1774 to be "set apart as a Day of Fasting, Humiliation and Prayer, devoutly to implore the Divine Interposition for averting the heavy calamity:"

TUESDAY, the 24th of MAY, 14 GEO. III. 1774.

THIS House being deeply impressed with apprehension of the great dangers to be derived to *British America,* from the hostile invasion of the City of *Boston,* in our sister Colony of *Massachusetts Bay,* whose commerce and harbour are on the 1st Day of *June* next to be stopped by an armed force, deem it highly necessary that the said first Day of June be set apart by the members of this House as a Day of Fasting, Humiliation and Prayer, devoutly to implore the Divine Interposition for averting the heavy calamity, which threatens destruction to our civil rights, and the evils of civil war; to give us one heart and one mind firmly to oppose, by all just and proper means, every injury to *American* rights, and that the minds of his Majesty and his parliament may be inspired from above with wisdom, moderation and justice, to remove from the loyal people of *America* all cause of danger from a continued pursuit of measures pregnant with their ruin.

Ordered, therefore, that the members of this House do attend in their places at the hour of ten in the forenoon, on the said 1st Day of *June* next, in order to proceed with the Speaker and the Mace to the Church in this city for the purposes aforesaid; and that the Reverend Mr. *Price* be appointed to read Prayers, and the Reverend Mr. *Gwatkin* to preach a sermon suitable to the occasion.

Ordered, that this Order be forthwith printed and published

By the HOUSE of BURGESSES.
GEORGE WYTHE, C. H. B.

Notice of a Fast Day – St. Anne's Parish

To his own Parish of St. Anne, Jefferson and his co-delegate, John Walker of the "late" House of Burgesses dissolved by the British, penned these lines recommending that the parishioners "set apart some convenient day of fasting, humiliation and prayer, devoutly to implore the Divine Interposition in behalf of an injured and oppressed people:"

June, 1774

To the Inhabitants of the Parish of Saint Anne

The members of the late House of Burgesses having taken into their consideration the dangers impending over British America from the hostile invasion of a sister colony, thought proper that it should be recommended to the several parishes in this colony that they set apart some convenient day for fasting, humiliation and prayer, devoutly to implore the Divine Interposition in behalf of an injured and oppressed people; and that the minds of his Majesty, his ministers, and parliament, might be inspired with wisdom from above, to avert from us the dangers which threaten our civil rights, and all the evils of civil war. We do therefore recommend to the inhabitants of the Parish of Saint Anne that Saturday, the 23rd instant be by them set apart for the purpose aforesaid, on which day will be prayers and a sermon suited to the occasion by the Reverend Mr. Clay at the new Church on Hardware River, which place is thought the most centrical to the parishioners in general.

JOHN WALKER*
THOMAS JEFFERSON

Jefferson's Letter to the Danbury Baptists

Many years later, Jefferson's letter to a Committee of the *Danbury Baptist Association*, in the State of Connecticut, was penned in reply to their Public Address applauding his stance for Religious freedom. It is excerpted below in order to clarify the true meaning and significance, in context, of the First Amendment's Freedom of Religion Clause. Here we see that Jefferson agrees with these fundamental, biblical Christians, assuring them that the government will no longer encroach upon their mode of worship; and that the disestablished Anglican Church will no longer have jurisdiction over them:

> ...Believing with you that Religion is a matter which lies solely between man and his God, that he owes account to none other for his faith or his worship, that the legitimate powers of government reach actions only, and not opinions, I contemplate with sovereign reverence that act of the whole American people which declared that their legislature should "make no law respecting an **establishment of Religion**, or prohibiting the free exercise thereof," thus building a wall of separation between Church and State. Adhering to this expression of the supreme will of the nation in behalf of the rights of conscience, I shall see with sincere satisfaction the progress of those sentiments which tend to restore to man all his natural rights, convinced he has no natural right in opposition to his social duties...

TH: Jefferson
Jan. 1, 1802 [3]

President Thomas Jefferson – Churchman in Washington

At the time that Jefferson was president, the only place for worship in the newly-established city was a tobacco house that had been converted into a plain and humble chapel. The services were attended by about fifty people. During his first winter in office, Jefferson regularly attended these services. Later, he began a custom of Sunday preaching in the Hall of Representatives, at which he was a most regular attendant during his entire administration. The scarlet-uniformed Marine Band led the congregation in hymns and psalms. An historical account entitled, *The First Forty Years of Washington Society,* furnishes eye-witness evidence of "Thomas Jefferson, the Churchman," as follows:

---

*Jefferson's fellow-member from Albemarle County, in the House of Burgesses.

"Christ Church," first Episcopal Church in Washington Parish (c.1794) – a converted warehouse, corner of New Jersey Avenue and D Street, S.E., Washington City. Archives of Christ Church, Capitol Hill.

...At this time (1800), the only place for public worship in our new city was a small, very small, frame building at the bottom of Capitol Hill. It had been a tobacco-house belonging to Daniel Carrrol of Duddington Manor, and was purchased by a few Episcopalians for a mere trifle and fitted up as a church in the plainest and rudest manner. During the first winter, Mr. Jefferson regularly attended service on the Sabbath-day in the humble church. The congregation seldom exceeded fifty or sixty, but generally consisted of about a score of hearers. He could have no motive for this regular attendance, but that of respect for public worship, choice of place or preacher he had not, as this was the only church in the new city. The custom of preaching in the Hall of Representatives had not yet been attempted, though after it was established by Mr. Jefferson, he was a most regular attendant during his whole administration. The seat he chose the first Sabbath, and the adjoining one, which his private Secretary occupied, was ever afterwards by the courtesy of the congregation, left for him and his Secretary...Not only the chaplains, but the most distinguished clergymen who visited the city, preached in the Capitol. I remember hearing Mr. E. Everet, afterwards a member of Congress, deliver an eloquent discourse to a most thronged and admiring audience...As Congress is composed of Christians of every persuasion, each denomination in its turn has supplied Chaplains to the two Houses of Congress, who preach alternately in the Hall of Representatives...Clergymen who, during the Session of Congress visited the city, were invited by the chaplains to preach...[4]

The log tobacco barn, where Thomas Jefferson worshipped, was *Christ Episcopal Church's* first house of worship and prayer. It was located at New Jersey Avenue and D Street, S.E., across from the Navy Yard. Jefferson contributed $50.00 annually to the church, for several years. He could often by seen, Prayer Book in hand, walking to the church, a few blocks south of the new Capitol building.

It was the first Episcopal Church in Washington Parish, created by the Maryland Vestry Act of 1794, "An Act to form a new Parish by the name of Washington Parish, to include the City of Washington and Georgetown on the Potomac."[5]

Secretary of State in Georgetown

During George Washington's presidency, Secretary of State Thomas Jefferson resided in Georgetown,* then Maryland, three miles from the site chosen for the City of Washington. The first person to preach the Gospel in Georgetown was **Reverend Dr. Stephen Bloomer Balch**, in 1780.

At that time, a log building serving as a place of worship for German Lutherans, was the only church in town. However, there was no pastor, nor a visible congregation when Rev. Balch preached there, and being invited to return, he accepted the call. In March, 1780, he established the first Presbyterian Church at M and 30th Streets in Georgetown. It was called the *Bridge Street Presbyterian Church*, later becoming the *Georgetown Presbyterian Church*.

From 1780 until his death in 1833, Dr. Balch, who had studied at the College of New Jersey (Princeton) under the nurturing hand of Rev. Dr. John Witherspoon, the college's greatest educator, faithfully ministered to the congregants of Georgetown and the Georgetown community, becoming the Principal of the *Columbian Academy*, an esteemed and well-known school. **George Washington** sent his two wards, the sons of his deceased brother, Samuel, to be educated by Rev. Balch, requesting that both boys, George Steptoe, and Lawrence Augustine Washington, board with him.[6]

George Washington's letter to Rev. Dr. Balch recounts this for posterity:

Portrait of Rev. Dr. Stephen Bloomer Balch from an engraving by John Sartian.

The Bridge Street Presbyterian Church, which stood at the corner of 30th and M Streets, N.W., Georgetown, until 1873, when it was torn down and materials used in a new church on P Street, near 31st.

Tablet in honor of Stephen Bloomer Balch, D.D., presented by philanthropist, William Wilson Corcoron. Renwick Chapel, Oak Hill Cemetery, Georgetown, District of Columbia.

*As recorded in *A Portrait of Old Georgetown*, 1933, p.47, by Grace Dunlop Ecker.

Mount Vernon
30th October, 1784

To the Rev. Dr. Balch

Sir,

If you will now, or at any other time, furnish me with an account of the expenses which have been incurred for schooling, boarding and clothing of my nephews, I will transmit you the money. Such of the latter as are proper for them, I hope will be obtained on the best terms, as the cost of them shall be regularly paid. I think it would be very proper to have them taught the French language and such parts of the mathematics as will bring them acquainted with practical surveying, which is useful to every man who has landed property. As they are fatherless and motherless children, I commit them to your benevolent care and protection.

I am, Sir,
Yours,
G. Washington

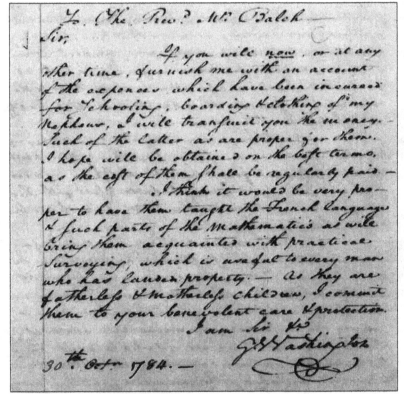

George Washington's October 30, 1784 letter to Rev. Dr. Balch, committing his two ophaned nephews to his friend's "benevolent care and protection." Courtesy of the Manuscript Division, Library of Congress, Washington, D.C.

Jefferson – Churchman in Georgetown

George Washington worshipped at the Bridge Street Presbyterian Church on occasion, probably while visiting Martha Custis Peter, Martha Washington's granddaughter, who lived with her husband Thomas Peter and family at Tudor Place in Georgetown.[7] It is recorded that **Thomas Jefferson**, as well as Albert Gallatin, Secretary of the Treasury, also worshipped at Dr. Balch's church occasionally.[8] As Secretary of State, Jefferson subscribed $75.00 in 1793 for the church's enlargement, contributing another $70.00, and a harmonium a few years later, to enhance worship services.[9] An Act of Incorporation of this famous church was passed by Congress, and signed by President Thomas Jefferson on March 28, 1806. Andrew Jackson, 7th U.S. President, held a pew at the Georgetown Presbyterian Church while Senator from Tennessee..[10]

Framed copy of Act of Incorporation of the Presbyterian Congregation in Georgetown, signed by President Thomas Jefferson on March 28, 1806. Georgetown Presbyterian Church, Georgetown, District of Columbia.

The Reverend Walter Addison, an Episcopal Minister, hearing that there were some Episcopal families in Georgetown, paid it a visit, was invited by Dr. Blach to hold an Episcopal Service in his church, and encouraged by him to organize an Episcopal congregation. Rev. Addison continued to visit Georgetown and to hold services occasionally during the years 1794 and 1795. In the summer of 1796, the first effort was made to organize a congregation and build a church. A list of 112 subscribers, dated August 1796, shows contributions were to be applied "to building the walls and covering in a Protestant Episcopal Church in Georgetown." The next extant record is a meeting of the citizens of Georgetown, in January, 1803, to take measures for renewing the effort to build an Episcopal Church. The Minutes of this meeting commences as follows: "At a meeting of a number of the inhabitants of Georgetown, at Mr. Semmes' Tavern, on Friday evening, 28th January, pursuant to a notice in the *Washington Federalist*, for the purpose of adopting regulations for building a Protestant Episcopal Church…" There are recorded the names of one hundred and fifty-four subscribers, whose subscriptions amount to twenty-five hundred dollars. Among the subscribers is **Thomas Jefferson**, who contributed fifty dollars. The name of Rev. Dr. Stephen Bloomer Balch also appears on the subscription list. Of note, is that Jefferson's contribution ranks among the most generous of the hundred and fifty-four subscribers.[11]

A page of the Alphabetical List of Subscribers to erect St. John's Church, Georgetown, circa 1803. Thomas Jefferson's name, with his subscription of fifty dollars is dated July 22, 1803.

St. John's Episcopal Church in Georgetown was inaugurated in 1804, and consecrated to God's service in 1809 by Bishop Thomas Claggert, who also consecrated the new gothic edifice of *Christ Episcopal Church – Navy Yard* on Capitol Hill the same day. Following Thomas Jefferson's example of regular Sunday worship services, James Madison and John Quincy Adams both worshipped at Christ Church, on Capitol Hill.

St. John's Episcopal Church, circa 1804, Georgetown, District of Columbia. President Thomas Jefferson contributed to the building of this church.

Jefferson's Contribution to erect St. John's Episcopal Church, Georgetown

St. John's Episcopal Church in Georgetown displays a prominent plaque affixed to a rock adorning its front entranceway:

St. John's Episcopal Church, Georgetown Parish

This first Episcopal congregation in Georgetown was founded in 1796 by the Reverend Walter Dulaney Addison. Other founders and benefactors include Thomas Hyde, Thomas Corcoran, Benjamin Stoddert and Francis Scott Key. **President Thomas Jefferson** contributed to the building fund. This Federal-style building, based on a design by William Thornton, architect of the Capitol, was opened in 1804 and consecrated in 1809. The foundations, walls and bell tower are original. Founded as a Christian community for the worship of God, the dissemination of the Gospel, and the furnishing of spiritual and material help to those in need, St. John's remains dedicated to these purposes. "In the beginning was the Word, and the Word was with God, and the Word was God." John 1: 1.

Historic marker in front of St. John's Episcopal Church, Georgetown, circa 1804. Founded in 1796 by Rev. Walter Dulaney Addison. Designed by William Thornton, Architect of the Capitol.

Francis Scott Key - Vestryman

Early in 1804, the trustees of *St. John's Church*, Georgetown, advertised their want of a Rector. In March, they were visited by the Reverend John Sayrs of Port Tobacco Parish, who served as the first pastor of the church. **Francis Scott Key*** was a founding member and vestryman, becoming Rev. Sayrs' devoted parishioner and intimate friend.

At his untimely death in 1809, Key penned a moving epitaph to this great man of God, "who lived and died a humble minister of his benignant purposes to man." The epitaph was engraved upon Rev. Sayrs' marble sarcophagus, which lay beneath St. John's sanctuary until the church's renovation years later, when it was discovered.[12]

It is now displayed on a wall within the church for all to read:

---

*Francis Scott Key, author of *The Star-spangled Banner,* was also a founder of the first Bible Society in the District of Columbia.

A painting of the young Francis Scott Key. From, *Portrait of Old Georgetown*, 1933.

John J. Sayrs
First Rector
Who served as Faithful Minister of Christ
Died January 6, A.D. 1809.

Here once stood forth a Man, who from the world,
Though bright its aspect to his youthful eye,
Turn'd with affection ardent to his God,
And lived and died an humble minister
Of his benignant purposes to Man.
Here lies he now – yet grieve not thou for him,
READER! He trusted in that love where none
Have ever vainly trusted. Rather let
His marble speak to thee, and should'st thou feel
The rising of a new and solemn thought,
Wak'd by this sacred place and sad memorial,
O listen to its impulse! 'tis Divine –
And it shall guide thee to a life of joy,
A death of hope and endless bliss hereafter.

From the foregoing evidence, it cannot be doubted the Thomas Jefferson was not only an active churchman in his own parish churches, but that he also began the first Sabbath-day worship services in the U.S. Hall of Representatives; that he generously subscribed to his own pastor's* material needs, in addition to supporting newly-formed congregations such as *Christ Church – Navy Yard,* the *Bridge Street Presbyterian Church* and *St. John's Episcopal Church* in Georgetown, District of Columbia.

What is striking is that, as heir to the Scriptural sermons and guidance of his tutor and pastor, **Rev. James Maury,** Thomas Jefferson continued this foundational legacy throughout his life:

Jefferson – Churchman in Charlottesville

Captain Edmund Bacon, his Monticello overseer, further testifies to this fact,

> …Mr. Jefferson never debarred himself from hearing any preacher that came along. There was a Mr. Hiter, a Baptist preacher, that used to preach occasionally at the Charlottesville Courthouse. He had no regular church, but was a kind of missionary – Rode all over the country and preached. He wasn't much of a preacher, was uneducated, but he was a good man. Everybody had confidence in him, and they went to hear him on that account. Mr. Jefferson nearly always went to hear him when he came around. I remember his being there one day in particular. His servant came with him and brought a seat – a kind of campstool upon which he sat. After the sermon there was a proposition to pass around the hat and raise money to buy the preacher a horse. Mr. Jefferson did not wait for the hat. I saw him unbutton his overalls, and get his hand into his pocket, and take out a handful of silver, I don't know how much. He then walked across the courthouse to Mr. Hiter and gave it into his hand. He bowed very politely to Mr. Jefferson and seemed very much pleased…[13]

Churchman in Philadelphia

In the Handbook of Christ Church (1695-1945), "Commemorating the 250th Anniversary Year of CHRIST CHURCH in Philadelphia," under the subtitle "Famous People who attended Christ Church – Those who signed the Declaration of Independence" – **Thomas Jefferson** stands out among ten founders of the American Republic.

Under the sub-title: SHRINE OF AMERICAN PATRIOTS, we see Jefferson's name again listed among members of the Continental Congress who worshipped at "the nation's Church," CHRIST CHURCH, Philadelphia, called "birthplace of liberty:"

---

*Reverend Charles Clay of St. Anne's Parish, Albemarle.

Christ Episcopal Church, (circa 1727) Church Street, Philadelphia, Pennsylvania.

On June 25, 1775, members of the Continental Congress met in Christ Church to hear Dr. William Smith preach on, *The Present Situation in American Affairs*. This sermon, according to the Rt. Rev. William Stevens Perry, Bishop of Iowa, 1897, 'shaped popular sentiment in the direction of resistance to arbitrary and alien rule.'

On July 7, 1775, members of Congress heard the Rev. Jacob Duché* preach on *The Duty of Standing Fast in our Spiritual and Temporal Liberties*.

Again, on July 20, 1775, Dr. Duché preached on, *The American Vine*. These sermons were printed and circulated throughout England and Europe where they caused much controversy. Those known to have been present on these occasions included such American patriots as: **Thomas Jefferson**, Benjamin Franklin, John Adams, John Jay, Patrick Henry, Peyton Randolph, Richard Henry Lee, John Hancock, Samuel Adams, Roger Sherman, Philip Livingston, George Clinton and Philip Schuyler.

Worthy of note is that a resolution, observed to the present day, was adopted on October 5, 1785 by the General Convention at Christ Church when deputies from seven States, "on motion resolved: That the Fourth of July shall be observed by this church forever as a *Day of Thanksgiving to Almighty God* for the inestimable blessings of religious and civil liberty vouchsafed to the United States of America."

*Appointed first Chaplain of the First Continental Congress, 1774.

Churchman in Williamsburg

Thomas Jefferson's Pew no. 17, facing the altar rail, front row to the left of the aisle. Bruton Parish Episcopal Church, Williamsburg, Virginia, where Thomas Jefferson worshipped while in Williamsburg.

Thomas Jefferson's marked pew adorns Bruton Parish Church, circa 1715, in Williamsburg, the capital of Virginia from 1699-1780. His pew, no. 17, is situated directly opposite the communion rail on the left side of the aisle. Facing Jefferson's pew across the aisle to the right, is General George Washington's pew. It was at this famous church, established in 1674, that Jefferson and Washington, together with the members of the House of Burgesses, convened to hear a sermon, pray and worship God on June 1, 1774 – observing the Day of Fasting, Humiliation and Prayer, drafted by **Thomas Jefferson** and Patrick Henry. Of this notable day, George Washington wrote in his diary,

"…went to church and fasted all day."

Bruton Parish Episcopal Church, circa 1715, Williamsburg, Virginia, the founding fathers' church during the American Revolution. James Blair, D.D. was the first Rector. Painting by Thomas Charles Millington, 1836.

The foregoing evidence clearly refutes the accusation that Thomas Jefferson was "far from being a churchman." The church attendance of 21st century Christians in America may well fall short of Jefferson's practice of regular church attendance, as proven by written historic records.

Moreover, when Samuel Greenhow informed him that in Virginia there were families without Bibles, requesting a contribution for the Bible Society which he represented, Jefferson responded in a letter dated January 21, 1814, expressing surprise at such a dilemma, and enclosed his gift of $50.00.[14]

Georgetown-on-the-Potomac

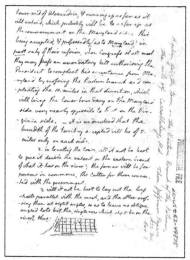

Last page of "A Plan for the town on the Eastern Branch of the Potomac, the site of Carrollsburg, Maryland, by Secretary of State, Thomas Jefferson. Site of the new capital city – Washington, D.C.

"Georgetown-on-the-Potomac" is the parent of Washington City. An Act was passed by Congress on July 16, 1790, to establish the permanent capital city of the United States, and on the 30th day of March, 1791, President Washington, then in Georgetown, issued his proclamation concerning the permanent seat of government of the United States as being located in the District of Columbia. This proclamation closes as follows:

> In testimony whereof, I have caused the seal of the United States to be affixed to these presents, and sign the same with my hand. Done in Georgetown, aforesaid, the 30th day of March, in the year of our Lord, 1791, and the Independence of the United States the fifteenth.
>
> By the President: GEORGE WASHINGTON.
> Thomas Jefferson.

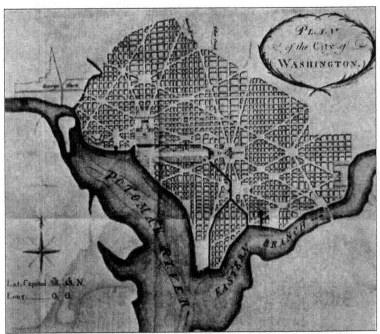

Plan of the City of Washington, June, 1791 by Pierre Charles L'Enfant.

Thomas Jefferson, third President of the United States; author of the *Declaration of Independence* and the *Statute of Virginia for Religious Freedom*. Marble bas-relief portrait over the Gallery door, to the left of the Speaker's Chair, House of Representatives, U.S. Capitol, Washington, D.C.

Chapter VII

Thomas Jefferson's Resolutions Concerning Peace with England – His Respect for sound Christian Books – A Summary View of the Rights of British America, from "The Best and Wisest of its Members" – "The Abolition of Domestic Slavery is the great object of Desire in those Colonies" – "The God who gave us Life gave us Liberty" – "We the People" penned by Thomas Jefferson – His Second Draft of "Declaration on Taking up Arms".

Thomas Jefferson's Resolutions Concerning Peace with England

Among Jefferson's manuscripts are *Resolutions Concerning Peace with England*, demonstrating a manly stand for Colonial America's attainment of Peace with Great Britain, only "in a manner consistent with our National Faith and Federal Union:"

June 7, 1778

RESOLUTIONS CONCERNING PEACE WITH ENGLAND

Resolved unanimously that a proposition from the Enemy to all or any of these United States for Peace or truce separate from their Allies is insidious and inadmissible.

Resolved unanimously that a proposition from the Enemy for treating with any Assembly or Body of men in America other than the Congress of these United States is insidious and inadmissible.

Resolved unanimously that this Assembly will not listen to any Proposition nor suffer any Negotiation inconsistent with their National Faith and Federal Union.

Resolved unanimously that this Assembly will exert the utmost Power of the State to carry on the War with vigour and effect until Peace shall be obtained in a manner consistent with our National Faith and Federal Union.*

It follows that the hallmark of the American Revolution was "National Faith and Federal Union" devoid of treachery, bribery, corruption and tyrannical dictatorship, as practiced during France's Revolutionary "Reign of Terror" – where internal civil conflict caused the decapitation of multitudes of her nobles and leaders, including King Louis XVI and his wife.

Jefferson's Respect for sound Christian Books

At the height of the Revolution, in a letter written to **Reverend Samuel Henley** from Williamsburg, Jefferson's shows his respect and appreciation for sound Christian books, as well as his concern for their preservation:

---

*The work of Thomas Jefferson, these Resolutions, however, do not appear in the *Journal of the House of Delegates*.

Williamsburg, June 9, 1778

Reverend Sir:

Mr. Madison I believe, informed you by letter written some time ago that one of your boxes of books left in his care burst open in removing it from the college to the President's House for greater security. This accident discovered them to be in a state of ruin. They had contracted a dampness and stuck together in large blocks, insomuch that they could not sometimes be separated without tearing the cover. I happened to be in town and was of opinion with Mr. Madison that it was necessary to overhaul them and give them air. Indeed we both thought – I think it would be for your interest to have them sold, as books are now in considerable demand here, and, packed as they are in boxes, they must sustain injury. There are many of them which I would be glad to take myself at their sterling cost and would remit you the money by the way of France. That cost might be fixed either by note from yourself, informing me what they cost you, or by the estimate of anybody here in whom you trust. Upon a presumption that you could not but approve of the proposal to have them disposed of and the money remitted, for the reasons before given and others which you may apprehend but would be improper for me to explain, I have taken the liberty of laying apart many of them for myself, leaving with Mr. Madison a catalogue of them, and ready to return them to him if you shall direct it. I shall be glad of your answer as soon as possible, and will gladly serve you in the care of any interest you may have left here. The reasons are obvious which restrain this letter to matters of business. As soon as the obstacles to friendly correspondence are removed I shall be glad at all times to hear from you. I am Reverend Sir,

Your friend and servant,
TH: Jefferson

A Summary View of the Rights of British America from "The Best and Wisest of their Members"

Thomas Jefferson's contributions to the cause of freedom from tyrannical rule are many, the greatest of which is the American *Declaration of Independence*. This pivotal document, announcing to the world that the thirteen British American Colonies were no longer under monarchial rule, was preceded by,

**A Summary View of the Rights of British America,
set forth in some Resolutions intended for the
Inspection of the present delegates of the People
of Virginia now in Convention.
By a NATIVE and MEMBER of the HOUSE
of BURGESSES
Printed by Clementina Rind 1774.**

The Preface of the Editors reveals that its author was absent due to an accidental illness when it was presented, and that, without his knowledge, the Delegates deemed its communication to the public appropriate, naming Thomas Jefferson "the best and wisest of their members."

The Preface of the Editors.

The following piece was intended to convey to the late meeting of DELEGATES the sentiments of one of their body, whose personal attendance was prevented by an accidental illness. In it the sources of our present unhappy differences are traced with such faithful accuracy, and the opinions entertained by every free American expressed with such a manly firmness, that it must be pleasing to the present, and may be useful to future ages. It will evince to the world the moderation of our late convention, who have only touched with tenderness many of the claims insisted on in this pamphlet, though every heart acknowledged their justice. Without the knowledge of the author, we have ventured to communicate his sentiments to the public, who have certainly a right to know what the best and wisest of their members have thought on a subject in which they are so deeply interested.

Following is an excerpt from Jefferson's *A Summary View of the Rights of British America*:

"**Resolved**, that it be an instruction to the said deputies, when assembled in general congress with the deputies from the other states of British America, to propose to the said congress that an humble and dutiful address be presented to his Majesty, begging leave to lay before him, as Chief Magistrate of the British empire, the united complaints of his Majesty's subjects in America; complaints which are excited by many unwarrantable encroachments and usurpations, attempted to be made by the Legislature of one part of the empire, upon those rights which God and the laws have given equally and independently to all. To represent to his Majesty that these his states have often individually made humble application to his imperial throne to obtain, through its intervention, some redress of their injured rights, to none of which was ever even an answer condescended; humbly to hope that this their joint address, penned in the language of truth, and divested of those expressions of servility which would persuade his Majesty that we were asking favours, and not rights, shall obtain from his Majesty a more respectful acceptance. And this his Majesty will think we have reason to expect when he reflects that he is no more than the chief officer of the people, appointed by the laws, and circumscribed with definite powers, to assist in working the great machine of government, erected for their use, and consequently subject to their superintendence. And in order that these our rights, as well as the invasions of them, may be laid more fully before his Majesty, to take a view of them from the origin and first settlement of these countries...

By the **act for the suppression of riots and tumults in the town of Boston**, passed also in the last session of parliament, a murder committed there is, if the governor pleases, to be tried in a court of King's Bench, in the island of Great Britain, by a jury of Middlesex. The witnesses, too, on receipt of such a sum as the governor shall think it reasonable for them to expend, are to enter into recognizance to appear at the trial. This is, in other words, taxing them to the moment of their recognizance, and that amount may be whatever a governor pleases; for who does his Majesty think can be prevailed on to cross the Atlantic for the sole purpose of bearing evidence to a fact? His expenses are to be borne, indeed, as they shall be estimated by a governor; but who are to feed the wife and children whom he leaves behind and who have had no other subsistence but his daily labour?

Those epidemical disorders too, so terrible in a foreign climate, is the cure of them to be estimated among the articles of expense, and their danger to be warded off by the almighty power of parliament? And the wretched criminal, if he happen to have offended on the American side, stripped of his privilege of trial by peers of his vicinage, removed from the place where alone full evidence could be obtained, without money, without council, without friends, without exculpatory proof, is tried before judges predetermined to condemn. The cowards who would suffer a countryman to be torn from the bowels of their society, in order to be thus offered a sacrifice to parliamentary tyranny, would merit that everlasting infamy now fixed on the authors of the act! A clause for a similar purpose had been introduced into an act passed in the twelfth year of his Majesty's reign, entitled, "An Act for the better securing and preserving his Majesty's dockyards, magazines, ships, ammunition and stores," against which, as meriting the same censures, the several colonies have already protested.

That these are acts of power, assumed by a body of men, foreign to our constitutions, and unacknowledged by our laws, against which we do, on behalf of the inhabitants of British America, enter this our solemn and determined protest; and we do earnestly entreat his Majesty, as yet the only mediatory power between the several states of the British empire, to recommend to his parliament of Great Britain the total revocation of these acts, which, however nugatory they be may yet prove the cause of further discontents and jealousies among us.

That we next proceed to consider the conduct of his Majesty, as holding the executive powers of the laws of these states, and mark out his deviations from the line of duty. By the constitution of Great Britain, as well of the several American states, his Majesty professes the power of refusing to pass into a law any bill which has already passed the other two branches of legislature. His Majesty, however, and his ancestors, conscious of the impropriety of opposing their single opinion to the united wisdom of two houses of parliament, while their proceedings were unbiased by interested principles, for several ages past have modestly declined the exercise of this power in that part of his empire called Great Britain.

But by change of circumstances, other principles than those of justice simply obtained an influence on their determinations; the addition of new states to the British empire has produced an addition of new, and sometimes opposite interests. It is now, therefore, the great office of his Majesty, to resume exercise of his negative power, and to prevent the passage of laws by any one legislature of the empire, which might bear injuriously on the rights and interests of another. Yet this will not excuse the wanton exercise of this power which we have seen his Majesty practice on the laws of the American legislatures. For the most trifling reasons, and sometimes for no conceivable reason at all, his Majesty has rejected laws of the most salutary tendency.

The abolition of domestic slavery is the great object of desire in

those colonies, where it was unhappily introduced in their infant state.* But previous to the enfranchisement of the slaves we have, it is necessary to exclude all further importations from Africa; yet our repeated attempts to effect this by prohibitions, and by imposing duties which might amount to a prohibition, have been hitherto defeated by his Majesty's negative: Thus preferring the immediate advantages of a few African corfairs** to the lasting interests of the American states, and to the rights of human nature deeply wounded by this infamous practice. Nay, the single interposition of an interested individual against a law was scarcely ever known to fail of success, though in the opposite scale were placed the interests of a whole country. That this is so shameful an abuse of a power trusted with his Majesty for other purposes, as if not reformed, would call for some legal restrictions.

With equal inattention to the necessities of his people here has his Majesty permitted our laws to lie neglected in England for years, neither confirming them by his assent, nor annulling them by his negative; so that such of them as have no suspending clause we hold on the most precarious of all tenures, his Majesty's will and such of them as suspend themselves till his Majesty's assent be obtained, we have feared, might be called into existence at some future and distant period, when the time and change of circumstances shall have rendered them destructive to his people here. And to render this aggrievance still more oppressive, his Majesty by his instructions has laid his governors under such restrictions that they can pass no law of any moment unless it have such suspending clause; so that, however immediate may be the call for legislative interposition, the law cannot be executed till it has twice crossed the Atlantic, by which time the evil may have spent its whole force...

But your Majesty, or your governors, have carried this power beyond every limit known, or provided for, by the laws: **After dissolving one House of Representatives**, they have refused to call another, so that for a great length of time, the legislature provided by the laws has been out of existence. From the nature of things, every society must at all times possess within itself the sovereign powers of legislation. The feelings of human nature revolt against the supposition of a state so situated as that it may not in any emergency provide against dangers which perhaps threatened immediate ruin. While those bodies are in existence to whom the people have delegated the powers of legislation, they alone possess and may exercise those powers; but when they are dissolved by the lopping off one or more of their branches, the power reverts to the people, who may exercise it to unlimited extent, either assembling together in person, sending deputies, or in any other way they may think proper. We forbear to trace consequences further; the dangers are conspicuous with which this practice is replete...

That these are our grievances which we have thus laid before his Majesty, with that freedom of language and sentiment which becomes a free people claiming their rights, as derived from the laws of nature, and not as the gift of their Chief Magistrate: Let those flatter who fear, it is not an American art. To give praise which is not due might be well from the venal, but would ill beseem those who are asserting the rights of human nature. They know, and will therefore say, that kings are the servants, not the proprietors of the people. Open your breast, sire, to liberal and expanded

---

* In 1619 in Virginia by Great Britain
** Slaves

thought. Let not the name of George the third be a blot in the page of history. You are surrounded by English counsellors, but remember that they are parties. You have no minister for American affairs, because you have none taken up from among us, nor amenable to the laws on which they are to give you advice. It behooves you, therefore, to think and to act for yourself and your people. The great principles of right and wrong are legible to every reader; to pursue them requires not the aid of many counsellors. The whole art of government consists in the art of being honest...

Jefferson concludes his *"Summary View of the Rights of British America"* to the King of England and her colonies, with this profound truth:

"The God who gave us Life gave us Liberty"

The God who gave us life gave us liberty at the same time; the hand of force may destroy, but cannot disjoin them. This, sire, is our last, our determined resolution: and that you will be pleased to interpose with that efficacy which your earnest endeavors may ensure to procure redress of these our great grievances to quiet the minds of your subjects in British America, against any apprehensions of future encroachment, to establish fraternal love and harmony through the whole empire, and that these may continue to the latest ages of time, is the fervent prayer of all British America.[1]

Of this copy Jefferson wrote to **Meriwether Jones**, on October 19, 1804:

I received last night your favor the 15th. I have but a single copy of the pamphlet you ask for and that is bound up in a volume of pamphlets of the same year and making one of a long suite of volumes of the same nature. I mention this to impress you with the value I set on the volume as part of the history of the times, and to justify a request of attention in the use and return of it. It happens that Mr. Duval sets out this afternoon for Richmond and furnishes an opportunity of conveying it to you. It should be noted in the republication that the title, the motto and the preface were of the editors, and, with the piece itself, were printed without my knowledge. I had drawn the paper at home, set out for the Convention, was taken ill on the road and sent on the paper to Peyton Randolph, moderator of the Convention. It was laid by him on the table of the convention for the perusal of the members, and by them justly deemed ahead of the sentiments of the times: but some of them deemed it useful to publish it and they affixed the title, epigraph and preface. I was informed by Parson Hurt who was in England when it arrived there that it ran through several editions there.

"We the People" – Penned by Thomas Jefferson

Hence, from the majestic pen of Thomas Jefferson came the first principles of the rights and liberties of *"We the People:"*

1. A free people claiming their rights as derived from the laws of nature, and not as the gift of their Chief Magistrate.

2. That kings are the servants, not the proprietors of the people.

3. That the abolition of domestic slavery is the great object of desire in the British American Colonies, where it was unhappily introduced in their infant state by Great Britain.

4. That repeated attempts to abolish slavery by prohibitions, have been defeated by His Majesty's negative power.

5. That God who gave us life, gave us liberty at the same time; that the hand of force may destroy, but cannot disjoin them, and,

6. That the fervent prayer of all British America is to establish fraternal love and harmony throughout the whole empire, through the restoral of her rights, and the redress of her great grievances.

Jefferson's Second Draft of "Declaration on Taking up Arms"

The appointment of the Continental troops was the first major step taken by the United Colonies towards war. On June 26, 1775, Congress requested that Thomas Jefferson draw up a draft of *Declaration on Taking up Arms*. Jefferson's second draft, presented to the Committee on July 6, 1775, is hereunder reprinted:

A Declaration by the representatives of the United colonies of America now sitting in General Congress, setting forth the causes and necessity of their taking up arms.

The large strides of late taken by the *legislature of Great Britain* towards establishing over these colonies their absolute rule, and the hardiness of the present attempt to effect by force of arms what by law or right they could never effect, *render* it necessary for us also to change the ground of opposition, and to close with their last appeal from reason to arms. And it behooves those, who *are called to this great decision*, to be assured that their cause is approved before supreme reason; so is it of great avail that its justice be made known to the world, whose affections will ever take part with those encountering oppression.

Our forefathers, inhabitants of the island of Great Britain, left their native land to seek on these shores a residence for civil & religious freedom. At the expence of their blood, to the ruin of their fortunes, with the relinquishment of everything quiet & comfortable in life, they effected settlements in the inhospitable wilds of America; and there established civil societies with various forms of constitution. To continue their connection with the friends whom they had left, they arranged themselves by charters of compact under the same common king, who thus completed their powers of full and perfect legislation and became the link of union between the several parts of the empire. Some occasional assumptions of power by the parliament of Great Britain, however unacknowledged by the constitution of our governments, were finally acquiesced in thro' warmth of affection. Proceeding thus in the fullness of mutual harmony and confidence, both parts of the empire increased in population & wealth with a rapidity unknown in the history of man.

The political institutions of America, its various soils and climates opened a certain resource to the unfortunate & to the enterprising of every country, and ensured to them the acquisition & free possession of property. Great Britain too acquired a lustre and a weight among the powers of the earth which her internal resources could never have given her. To a communication of the wealth and power of every part of the empire we may surely ascribe in some measure the illustrious character she sustained through her last European war, & its successful event. At the close of that war it pleased our sovereign to make a change in his counsels. The new ministry finding all the foes of Britain subdued took up the unfortunate idea of subduing her friends also. By them & her parliament then for the first time assumed a power of unbounded legislation over the colonies of America; and in the course of ten years have given such decisive specimens of the spirit of this new legislation, as leaves no room to doubt the consequence of acquiescence under it.

By several acts of parliament passed within that time they have undertaken to give and grant our money without our consent: a right of which we have ever had the exclusive exercise: they have interdicted all commerce to one of our principal towns, thereby annihilating this property in the hands of the holders; they have cut off the commercial intercourse of whole colonies with foreign countries; they have extended the jurisdiction of courts of admiralty beyond their ancient limits; they have deprived us of the inestimable privilege of trial by jury of the vicinage, in cases affecting both life & property; they have declared that American Subjects charged with certain offenses shall be transported beyond sea to be tried before the very persons against whose pretended sovereignty the offense is supposed to be committed; they have attempted fundamentally to alter the form of government in one of these colonies, a form secured by charters on the part of the crown and confirmed by acts of its own legislature; they have erected in a neighboring province acquired by the joint arms of Great Britain & America, a tyranny dangerous to the very existence of all these colonies. But why should we enumerate their injuries in the detail?

By one act they have suspended the powers of one American legislature, & by another have declared they may legislate for us themselves in all cases whatsoever. These two acts alone form a basis broad enough whereon to erect a despotism of unlimited extent. And what is to secure us against this dreaded evil? The persons assuming these powers are not chosen by us, are not subject to our control or influence, are exempted by their situation from the operation of these laws, and lighten their own burthens in proportion as they increase ours. These temptations might put to trial the severest characters of ancient virtue: with what new armour then shall a British parliament encounter the rude assault? towards these deadly injuries from the tender plant of liberty which we have brought over, & with so much affection fostered on these our own shores, we have pursued every temperate, every respectful measure. We have supplicated our king at various times, in terms almost disgraceful to freedom; we have reasoned, we have remonstrated with parliament in the most mild & decent language; we have even proceeded to break off our commercial intercourse with our fellow subjects, as the last peaceful admonition that our attachment to no nation on earth should supplant our attachment to liberty.

And here we had well hoped was the ultimate step of the controversy. But subsequent events have shown how vain was even this last remain of confidence in the moderation of the British ministry. During the course of the last year their troops in a hostile manner invested the town of Boston in the province of Massachusetts bay, and from that time have held the same beleaguered by sea & land. On the 19th day of April in the present year they made an unprovoked assault on the inhabitants of the said province at the town of Lexington, murdered eight of them on the spot and wounded many others. From thence they proceeded in all the array of war to the town of Concord, where they set upon another party of the inhabitants of the same province, killing many of them also, burning houses, & laying waste property, until repressed by the people suddenly assembled to oppose this cruel aggression. Hostilities thus commenced on the part of the ministerial army have been since by them pursued without regard to faith or to fame.

The inhabitants of the town of Boston in order to procure their enlargement having entered into treaty with General Gage their Governor it was stipulated that the said inhabitants, having first deposited their arms with their own magistrates, should have liberty to depart from out of the said town taking with them their other effects. Their arms they accordingly delivered in, and claimed the stipulated license of departing with their effects. But in open violation of plighted faith & honour, in defiance of the sacred obligations of treaty which even savage nations observe, their arms deposited with their own magistrates to be preserved as their property, were immediately seized by a body of armed men under orders from the said General, the greater part of the inhabitants were detained in the town, and the few permitted to depart were compelled to leave their most valuable effects behind. We leave the world to its own reflections on this atrocious perfidy. That we might no longer doubt the ultimate aim of these ministerial maneuvers, General Gage, by proclamation bearing date the 12th day of June, after reciting the grossest falsehoods and calumnies against the good people of these colonies, proceeds to declare them all, either by name or description, to be rebels & traitors, to supersede the exercise of the common law of the said province, and to proclaim and order instead thereof the use and exercise of the law martial.

This bloody edict issued, he has proceeded to commit further ravages & murders in the same province, burning the town of Charlestown, attacking & killing great numbers of the people residing or assembled therein; and is now going on in an avowed course of murder & devastation, taking every occasion to destroy the lives & properties of the inhabitants. To oppose his arms we also have taken up arms. We should be wanting to ourselves, we should be perfidious to posterity, we should be unworthy that free ancestry from which we derive our descent, should we submit with folded arms to military butchery & depredation, to gratify the lordly ambition, or sate the avarice of a British ministry.

We do then most solemnly, before God and the world declare that, regardless of every consequence, at the risk of every distress, the arms we have been compelled to assume we will use with the perseverance, exerting to their utmost energies all those powers which our Creator hath given us, to preserve that liberty which he committed to us in sacred deposit & to protect from every hostile hand our lives & our properties. But that this our declaration may not disquiet the minds of our good fellow subjects in any parts of the empire, we do further assure them that we mean not in any wise to affect that union with them in which we have so long & so happily lived and which we wish so much to see again restored. That necessity must be hard indeed which may force upon us that desperate measure, or induce us to avail ourselves of any aid which their enemies might proffer. We did not embody a soldiery to commit aggression on them; **we did not raise armies for glory or for conquest; we did not invade their island carrying death or slavery to its inhabitants**.

In defense of our persons and properties under actual violation, we took up arms. When that violence shall be removed, when hostilities shall cease on the part of the aggressors, hostilities shall cease on our part also. For the achievement of this happy event, we call for & confide in the good offices of our fellow subjects beyond the Atlantic. Of their friendly dispositions we do not cease to hope; aware, as they must be, that they have nothing more to expect from the same common enemy, than the humble favour of being last devoured. And we devoutly implore assistance of Almighty God to conduct us happily thro' this great conflict, to dispose his majesty, his ministers, & parliament to reconciliation with us on reasonable terms, & to deliver us from the evils of a civil war. [2]

On a meeting of the Committee, John Dickinson, one of the Committee members, objected that it was too harsh, and wanted softening, etc. Whereupon the Committee desired him to retouch it, which he did in the form which they reported, and which was adopted by Congress on July 6th, 1775.

Chapter VIII

Thomas Paine and "Common Sense" – The Influence of "Common Sense" in British America – Congress appoints Thomas Jefferson to draft Declaration – The Declaration of Independence, July 4th, 1776 – "Mr. Jefferson and the 'Wolf,' " U.S. News and World Report – Jefferson's 28th Clause, the anti-Slavery Clause in the Declaration of Independence.

Thomas Paine and "Common Sense"

Thomas Paine, was an Englishman by birth, a Quaker by education, aged about forty years, and an inhabitant of America a little over a year. He was by nature and education fitted for the task he assumed; an ardent lover of liberty, trained in the school of equal rights instituted by George Fox and his followers, bold and intrepid in thought, simple, clear and fearless in his expressions, scathing in his sarcasms, and terrible in his denunciations, he was emphatically the man for the times. A compeer of Franklin, Rittenhouse, Clymer, Samuel Adams, Benjamin Rush and men of that class, his influence among the patriots was as great, as his genius and power of argument were subduing and convincing to the royalists. His first work was to prepare an essay on the existing relations between the Colonies and the mother country; and when it was completed, he submitted it to the gentlemen above mentioned, and asked them what title he should give it. Rush replied, call it, **"Common Sense."**

In order that the reader may form a correct idea of the character of the pamphlet, following are a few extracts from it, as a part of the history of the nation two hundred and forty-four years ago:

"Common Sense"

> The design and end of government is freedom and security. In the early ages of the world, mankind were equals in the order of creation: the heathen introduced government by kings, which the will of the Almighty, as declared by Gideon and the prophet Samuel, expressly *disapproved*. To the evil of monarchy we have added that of hereditary succession; and as the first is a lessening of ourselves, so the second might put posterity under the government of a rogue or a fool. Nature disapproves it, otherwise she would not so frequently turn it into ridicule.
>
> **England**, since the conquest, hath known some few good monarchs, but groaned beneath a much larger number of bad ones. The most plausible plea, which has ever been offered in favor of hereditary succession is, that it preserves a nation from civil wars; whereas the whole history of England disowns the fact.
>
> **Thirty Kings**, and two minors have reigned in that distracted kingdom since the conquest, in which time there have been no less than eight civil wars and nineteen rebellions. In short, monarchy and succession have laid not this kingdom only, but the world in blood and ashes. The nearer any government approaches to a Republic, the less business there is for a king; in England a king hath little more to do than to make war and give away places.

Volumes have been written on the struggle between England and America, but the period of debate is closed. Arms must decide the contest; the appeal was the choice of the king, and the continent hath accepted the challenge.

The sun never shone on a cause of greater worth. 'Tis not the affair of a city, a country, a province, or a kingdom, but of a continent, of at least one-eighth part of the habitable globe. 'Tis not the concern of a day, a year, or an age; posterity are virtually involved in it even to the end of time.

But Great Britain has protected us, say some. She did not protect us from our enemies on our account, but from her enemies on her own account. America would have flourished as much, and probably more, had no European power had anything to do with governing her. France and Spain never were, nor perhaps ever will be, our enemies as Americans, but as subjects of Great Britain.

Britain is the parent country, say some; then the more shame upon her conduct. Nothing can settle our affairs so expeditiously as an open and *determined declaration for independence*. It is unreasonable to suppose that France or Spain will give us assistance, if we mean only to use that assistance for the purpose of repairing the breach. While we profess ourselves the subjects of Britain, we must in the eyes of foreign nations be considered as rebels.

A Manifesto published and dispatched to foreign courts, setting forth the miseries we have endured, and declaring that we had been driven to the necessity of breaking off all connection with her, at the same time assuring all such courts of our desire of entering into trade with them, would produce more good effects to this continent, than if a ship were freighted with petitions to Britain.

Every quiet method for peace hath been ineffectual; our prayers have been rejected with disdain; reconciliation is now a fallacious dream. Bring the doctrine of reconciliation to the touch-stone of nature; can you hereafter, love, honor, and faithfully serve the power that hath carried fire and sword in your land? Ye that tell us of harmony, can ye restore to us the time that is past? The blood of the slain, the weeping voice of nature cries, 'tis time to part. The last chord is now broken; the people of England are presenting addresses against us.

A Government of our own is our natural right. Ye that love mankind, that dare oppose not only tyranny, but the tyrant, stand forth! Every spot of the old world is overrun with oppression; Freedom hath been hunted round the globe; Europe regards her like a stranger; and England hath given her warning to depart; O! RECEIVE THE FUGITIVE and prepare an asylum for mankind.[1]

The Influence of "Common Sense" in British America

Thomas Paine was editor of the *Pennsylvania Magazine*. He was author of various other political papers which exerted a powerful influence in forwarding the cause of independence. In *The Crisis*, first appeared the phrase, "These are times that try men's souls!"

"**Common Sense**" appeared on the 8th of January, 1776. On the same day, the royal proclamation was received in Congress, and the day previous, the news of the disaster at Norfolk arrived. It was read in Congress, read in the army, in private houses, workshops, from pulpits, stores, taverns, read everywhere, and with an effect to render the king's manifesto nugatory, and to fire the people with indignation, and arouse the spirt of retaliation for the outrages inflicted upon the town of Norfolk.

Upon the king's speech being read in Congress, **Samuel Adams** arose and exclaimed, "The Tyrant! His speech breathes the most malevolent spirit, and determines my opinion of its author as a man of a wicked heart. I have heard that he is his own minister. Why, then should we cast the odium of distressing mankind upon his minions? Guilt must lie at his door: Divine vengeance will fall on his head."

The staunch patriot, indignant at the imputation of being a rebel, calling to his support **George Wythe** of Virginia, the two commenced at once instituting strong efforts in the direction of a confederation of the thirteen Colonies, and independence from British rule.

On June 7th, 1776, a delegate from Virginia, **Richard Henry Lee**, introduced the following resolution to the Continental Congress, that, "these United Colonies are, and of right ought to be, free and independent States." John Adams, delegate from Massachusetts wrote a glowing report thereon:

> Yesterday, the greatest question was decided which ever was debated in America; and a greater perhaps never was, nor will be, decided among men. A resolution was passed without one dissenting colony, that those United Colonies are, and of right ought to be, free and independent States.

Congress appoints Thomas Jefferson to draft Declaration

Thomas Jefferson, as chairman of the Committee* appointed by Congress to draw up this statement, penned the first draft. The events which preceded its adoption by Congress were related by Jefferson in a letter to James Madison on August 30th, 1823 from Monticello:

> …Pickering's observations…'that it contained no new ideas, that it is a common-place compilation, its sentiments hackneyed in Congress for two years before, and its essence contained in Otis' pamphlet,' may all be true. Of that I am not to be the judge. Richard Henry Lee charged it as copied from Locke's treatise on government. Otis' pamphlet I never saw, and whether I had gathered my ideas from reading or reflection, I do not know. I know only that I turned to neither book nor pamphlet while writing it. I did not consider

---

*Thomas Jefferson, John Adams, Benjamin Franklin, Robert Livingston and Roger Sherman.

it as any part of my charge to invent new ideas altogether, and to offer no sentiments which had never been expressed before…During the debate I was sitting by Dr. Franklin, and he observed that I was writhing a little under the acrimonious criticisms on some of the parts; and it was on that occasion, that by way of comfort, he told me the story of John Thompson, the hatter, and his new sign…In opposition, however, to Mr. Pickering, I pray God that these principles may be eternal, and close the prayer with my affectionate wishes for yourself of long life, health and happiness.

The *Declaration of Independence* was drafted at the private lodgings of Mr. Jefferson, in the house of Jacob Graff (circa 1775), still standing at the corner of 7th and Market streets in Philadelphia. Jefferson writes, "I rented the second floor, consisting of a parlor and bedroom ready furnished. In that parlor I wrote habitually, and in it wrote this paper particularly."

It was not until the 2nd of July, 1776 that the Declaration itself was adopted; nor till the 4th that it was decided, and it was signed by every member present, except Mr. Dickinson.

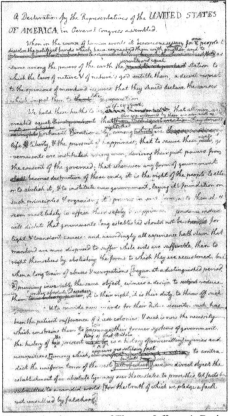

First hand-written page of Thomas Jefferson's Declaration of Independence presented to the Continental Congress, June, 1776.

The Declaration of Independence
Adopted by Congress, July 2, 1776
Signed by Congress, July 4, 1776

In Congress, July 4, 1776. The Unanimous Declaration of the thirteen United States of America. WHEN IN THE COURSE OF HUMAN EVENTS it becomes necessary for one people to dissolve the political bands which have connected them with another, and to assume among the powers of the earth, the separate and equal station to which the Laws of nature and nature's God entitle them, a decent respect to the opinions of mankind requires that they should declare the causes which impel them to the separation.

We hold these truths to be self-evident, that all men are created equal, that they are endowed by their Creator with certain unalienable rights, that among these are life, liberty, and the pursuit of happiness. That to secure these rights, governments are instituted among men, deriving their just powers from the consent of the governed. That whenever any form of government becomes destructive of these ends, it is the right of the people to alter or to abolish it, and to institute new government, laying its foundation on such principles and organizing its powers in such form, as to them shall seem most likely to effect their safety and happiness. Prudence, indeed, will dictate that governments long established should not be changed for light and transient causes; and accordingly all experience hath shown, that mankind are more disposed to suffer, while evils are sufferable, than to right themselves by abolishing the forms to which they are accustomed. But when a long train of abuses and usurpations, pursuing invariably the same object, evinces a design to reduce them under absolute despotism, it is their right, it is their duty, to throw off such government, and to provide new guards for their future security. Such has been the patient sufferance of these Colonies, and such is now the necessity which constrains them to alter their former systems of government. The history of the present King of Great Britain is a history of repeated injuries and usurpations, all having, in direct object, the establishment of an absolute tyranny over these States. To prove this, let facts be submitted to a candid world.

He has refused his assent to laws, the most wholesome and necessary for the public good.

He has forbidden his Governors to pass laws of immediate and pressing importance, unless suspended in their operation till his assent should be obtained; and when so suspended, he has utterly neglected to attend to them.

He has refused to pass other laws for the accommodation of large districts of people, unless those people would relinquish the right of representation in the legislature, a right inestimable to them and formidable to tyrants only.

He has called together legislative bodies at places unusual, uncomfortable, and distant from the depository of their public records, for the sole purpose of fatiguing them into compliance with his measures.

He has dissolved representative houses repeatedly, for opposing with manly firmness his invasions on the rights of the people.

He has refused for a long time, after such dissolutions, to cause others to be elected; whereby the legislative powers, incapable of annihilation, have returned to the people at large for their exercise; the State remaining in the meantime exposed to all the dangers of invasion from without and convulsions within.

He has endeavoured to prevent the population of these states; for that purpose obstructing the laws of naturalization of foreigners; refusing to pass others to encourage their migration hither, and raising the conditions of new appropriations of lands.

He has obstructed the administration of justice, by refusing his assent to laws for establishing judiciary powers.

He has made judges dependent on his will alone, for the tenure of their offices, and the amount and payment of their salaries.

He has erected a multitude of new offices, and sent hither swarms of officers to harass our people, and eat out their substance.

He has kept among us, in times of peace, standing armies without the consent of our legislatures.

He has affected to render the military independent of, and superior to, the civil power.

He has combined with others to subject us to a jurisdiction foreign to our constitution, and unacknowledged by our laws; giving his assent to their acts of pretended legislation:

For quartering large bodies of armed troops among us:

For protecting them, by a mock trial, from punishment for any murders which they should commit on the inhabitants of these States:

For cutting off our trade with all parts of the world:

For imposing taxes on us without our consent:

For depriving us, in many cases, of the benefits of trial by jury:

For transporting us beyond seas to be tried for pretended offences:

For abolishing the free system of English laws in a neighbouring Province, establishing therein an arbitrary government, and enlarging its boundaries so as to render it at once an example and fit instrument for introducing the same absolute rule into these Colonies:

For taking away our Charters, abolishing our most valuable laws, and altering fundamentally the forms of our governments:

For suspending our own legislatures, and declaring themselves invested with power to legislate for us in all cases whatsoever.

He has abdicated government here, by declaring us out of his protection and waging war against us.

He has plundered our seas, ravaged our coasts, burnt our towns, and destroyed the lives of our people.

He is, at this time, transporting large armies of foreign mercenaries to complete the works of death, desolation and tyranny, already begun, with circumstances of cruelty and perfidy scarcely paralleled in the most barbarous ages, and totally unworthy the head of a civilized nation.

He has constrained our fellow citizens taken captive on the high seas to bear arms against their country, to become the executioners of their friends and brethren, or to fall themselves by their hands.

He has excited domestic insurrections amongst us, and has endeavoured to bring on the inhabitants of our frontiers, the merciless Indian savages, whose known rule of warfare is an undistinguished destruction of all ages, sexes, and conditions.

In every stage of these oppressions we have petitioned for redress in the most humble terms: our repeated petitions have been answered only by repeated injury. A prince whose character is thus marked by every act which may define a tyrant is unfit to be the ruler of a free people.

Nor have we been wanting in attention to our British brethren. We have warned them from time to time of attempts by their legislature to extend an unwarrantable jurisdiction over us. We have reminded them of the circumstances of our emigration and settlement here. We have appealed to their native justice and magnanimity, and we have conjured them by the ties of our common kindred to disavow these usurpations, which would inevitably interrupt our connections and correspondence. They too have been deaf to the voice of justice and consanguinity. We must, therefore, acquiesce in the necessity, which denounces our separation, and hold them, as we hold the rest of mankind, enemies in war, in peace, friends.

We, therefore, the Representatives of the United States of America, in General Congress assembled, appealing to the Supreme Judge of the world for the rectitude of our intentions, do, in the name, and by authority of the good people of these Colonies, solemnly publish and declare, That these United Colonies are, and of right ought to be, Free and Independent States; that they are absolved from all allegiance to the British Crown, and that all political connection between them and the State of Great Britain, is and ought to be totally dissolved; and that as Free and Independent States, they have full power to levy war, conclude peace, contract alliances, establish commerce, and to do all other acts and things which Independent States may of right do. And for the support of this declaration, with a firm reliance on the protection of Divine Providence, we mutually pledge to each other our lives, our fortunes, and our sacred honor. [2]

"Mr. Jefferson and the 'Wolf' " – U.S. News and World Report

Ever ready to attack and discredit Thomas Jefferson and his immortal document, the *Declaration of Independence*, U.S. News and World Report, in its February 1, 1993 article entitled, "Mr. Jefferson and the 'Wolf,' " quotes the following lines of his Declaration: "We hold these truths to be self-evident, that all men are created equal, that they are endowed by their Creator with certain unalienable rights, that among these are life, liberty, and the pursuit of happiness," adding, "Thomas Jefferson did not write 'all *white* men are created equal.' He wrote, 'all men.' Was its author a colossal hypocrite?"

The fatal error made by *U.S. News and World Report* in their attack on the integrity and truthfulness of the Declaration's author, is their deliberate omission of Jefferson's 28th clause in his final draft presented to Congress. It was struck out prior to its adoption by the thirteen United Colonies, the two southernmost states, Georgia and South Carolina refusing to sign it as written, due to its anti-Slavery clause – but reprinted in its entirety in Jefferson's *Autobiography*, prefaced with, "... I will state the form of the Declaration as originally reported..."

Jefferson's 28th Clause – The anti-Slavery Clause

He (the King of England)* has waged cruel war against human nature itself, violating its most sacred rights of life and liberty in the persons of a distant people, who never offended him, captivating and carrying them into slavery in another hemisphere, or to incur miserable death in their transportation thither. This piratical warfare, the opprobium of <u>infidel</u> powers, is the warfare of the CHRISTIAN King of Great Britain. Determined to keep open a market where MEN should be bought and sold, he has prostituted his negative for suppressing every legislative attempt to prohibit or to restrain this execrable commerce: and that this assemblage of horrors might want no fact of distinguished die, he is now exciting those very people to rise in arms among us, and to purchase that liberty of which he has deprived them, by murdering the people on whom he also obtruded them; thus paying off former crimes committed against the LIBERTIES of one people, with crimes which he urges them to commit against the LIVES of another. ³

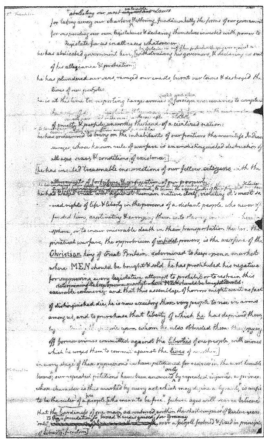

A page of Thomas Jefferson's hand-written Declaration of Independence containing his 28th Clause – the anti-Slavery Clause, as presented to the Continental Congress, June, 1776.

*Authors's text in parenthesis.

Is *U.S. News and World Report* "a colossal hypocrite" in misleading its readership into believing that the famed author of the *Declaration of Independence* lacked integrity and honesty in penning his immortal statement, "We hold these truths to be self-evident, that all men are created equal..."? Jefferson rightly accuses King George III of "prostituting his negative (power) for suppressing every legislative attempt to prohibit or to restrain this execrable commence" for lucrative gain.

The anti-Slavery Clause, with its denunciation of the King of England's refusal to abolish slavery in British America – thwarting the founders' repeated attempts to do so – certainly proves Jefferson's belief that "all men are created equal," his 1774 *A Summary View of the Rights of British America,* and his 1785 *Notes on the State of Virginia* agreeing thereto.

Chapter IX

"Mr. Jefferson's Servants" by Edmund Bacon, his Overseer – Genealogy of Mr. Jefferson's Servants at Monticello – Isaac's Recollections of Mr. Jefferson at Monticello – "Mr. Jefferson's Personal Appearance and Habits" – Jefferson's Care for the Poor – Mr. Jefferson's Mule, "Dolphin" – His Meticulous Business Transactions – Thomas Jefferson, the Lawyer – His Anti-slavery Bill – Jefferson's Bill to stop Slave Importation passes Congress, 1778.

"Mr. Jefferson's Servants" by Edmund Bacon, his Overseer

The Private Life of Thomas Jefferson, published in 1862, gives an eye-witness account of "Mr. Jefferson's Servants" by Captain Edmund Bacon, overseer of Monticello for twenty years:

> Mr. Jefferson was always very kind and indulgent to his servants. He would not allow them to be at all overworked...His orders to me were constant: that if there was any servant that could not be got along without the chastising that was customary, to dispose of him. He could not bear to have a servant whipped, no odds how much he deserved it. I remember one case in particular. Mr. Jefferson gave written instructions that I should always sell the nails that were made in his nailery. We made from sixpenny to twentypenny nails and always kept a supply of each kind on hand. I went one day to supply an order, and the eightpenny nails were all gone, and there was a full supply of all the other sizes. Of course they had been stolen. I soon became satisfied that Jim Hubbard, one of the servants that worked in the nailery, had stolen them and charged him with it. He denied it powerfully. I talked with Grady, the overseer of the nailery about it, and finally I said, "Let us drop it. He has hidden them somewhere, and if we say no more about it, we shall find them." I examined his house and every place I could think of, but for some time I could find nothing of the nails. One day after a rain, as I was following a path through the woods, I saw muddy tracks on the leaves leading off from the path. I followed them until I came to a treetop, where I found the nails buried in a large box. There were several hundred pounds of them. From circumstances I knew that Jim had stolen them. Mr. Jefferson was at home at the time, and when I went up to Monticello I told him of it. He was very much surprised and felt very badly about it. Jim had always been a favorite servant. He told me to be at my house next morning when he took his ride, and he would see Jim there. When he came, I sent for Jim, and I never saw any person, white or black, feel as badly as he did when he saw his master. He was mortified and distressed beyond measure. He had been brought up in the shop, and we all had confidence in him. Now his character was gone. The tears streamed down his face, and he begged pardon over and over again. I felt very badly myself.
>
> Mr. Jefferson turned to me, and said, "Ah, sir, we can't punish him. He has suffered enough already." He then talked to him, gave him a heap of good advice, and sent him to the shop. Grady had waited, expecting to be sent for to whip him, and he was astonished to see him come back and go to work after such a crime. When he came to dinner – he boarded with me then – he told me that when Jim came back to the shop, he said, "Well, I'se

been a-seeking religion a long time, but I never heard anything before that sounded so, or made me feel so, as I did when master said, 'Go, and don't do so any more;' and now I'se determined to seek religion till I find it;" and sure enough, he afterwards came to me for a permit to go and be baptized. I gave him one and never knew of his doing anything of the sort again. He was always a good servant afterwards.

Mr. Jefferson had a large number of favorite servants that were treated just as well as could be. Burwell (1783-1827+)* was the main, principal servant on the place. He did not go to Washington. Mr. Jefferson had the most perfect confidence in him. He told me not to be at all particular with him – to let him do pretty much as he pleased, and to let him have pocket money occasionally, as he wanted it.

Once or twice every week while Mr. Jefferson was President, I opened every room in the house and had it thoroughly aired. When I was so busy that I could not attend to this myself, I would send the keys to Burwell, and he would air the house, and was, if possible, more particular than I was. He stayed at Monticello and took charge of the meat house, garden, etc., and kept the premises in order. Mr. Jefferson gave him his freedom in his will, and it was right that he should do it....

They (the servants)* have often told my wife that when Mrs. Jefferson died they stood around the bed. Mr. Jefferson sat by her, and she gave him directions about a good many things that she wanted done. When she came to the children, she wept and could not speak for some time. Finally she held up her hand, and spreading out her four fingers, she told him she could not die happy if she thought her four children were ever to have a stepmother brought in over them. Holding her other hand in his, Mr. Jefferson promised her solemnly that he would never marry again. And he never did...

Sally Hemings (1773-1835)* went to France with Maria Jefferson (1778-1804)** when she was a little girl. Mr. Jefferson was Minister to France, and he wanted to put her in school there. They crossed the ocean alone. I have often heard her tell about it. When they got to London, they stayed with Mr. Adams, who was Minister there, until Mr. Jefferson came or sent for them. I have read a beautiful letter that Mrs. Adams wrote to her sister, Mrs. Cranch, about her. Here it is:

"I have had with me for a fortnight a little daughter of Mr. Jefferson's, who arrived here with a young Negro girl, her servant, from Virginia. Mr. Jefferson wrote me some months ago that he expected them, and desired me to receive them. I did so, and was amply repaid for my trouble. A finer child of her age I never saw. So mature and understanding, so womanly a behavior, and so much sensibility, united, are rarely to be met with. I grew so fond of her, and she was so attached to me, that, when Mr. Jefferson sent for her, they were obliged to force the little creature away. She is but eight years old. She would sit, sometimes, and describe to me the parting with her

---

 * Author's text in parenthesis.
** Mary, or Polly Jefferson. At the Convent of Panthemont, on the outskirts of Paris where she boarded with her sister, Martha (1772-1836), and her servant, she was called Mademoiselle *Polie*, which changed to *Marie*, pronounced *Maria* in Virginia.

aunt*, who brought her up, the obligations she was under to her, and the love she had for her little cousins, till the tears would stream down her cheeks; and how I had been her friend, and she loved me. Her papa would break her heart by making her go again. She clung round me so that I could not help shedding a tear at parting with her. She was a favorite of every one in the house. I regret that such fine spirits must be spent in the walls of a convent. She is a beautiful girl, too."

...John Hemings (1775-1830)** was a carpenter. He was a first-rate workman — a very extra workman. He could make anything that was wanted in woodwork. He learned his trade of Dinsmore. He made most of the woodwork of Mr. Jefferson's fine carriage. Joe Fosset made the iron-work. He was a very fine workman; could do anything it was necessary to do with steel or iron. He learned his trade of Stewart. Mr. Jefferson kept Stewart several years longer than he would otherwise have done in order that his own servants might learn his trade thoroughly. Stewart was a very superior workman, but he would drink. And Burwell was a fine painter. He painted the carriage and always kept the house painted. He painted a good deal at the University...

No servants ever had a kinder master than Mr. Jefferson. He did not like slavery. I have heard him talk a great deal about it. He thought it a bad system. I have heard him prophesy that we should have just such trouble with it as we are having now..." [1]

Genealogy of Mr. Jefferson's Servants at Monticello

I. **Betty Hemings*** (1735-1807) and her twelve children:**
Mary (1753-92+) Pastry Cook.
Martin (1755/6-1807) trusted house servant.
Bett or Betty Brown (1759-1827+) Seamstress.
Nance (1761-1827+).
Robert or Bob (1762-1819) Barber.
James (1765-96) Monticello Cook.
Thenia (1767-95+)
Critta (1769-1827+)
Peter (1770-1827+)
Sally (1773-1835) Servant of Mary Jefferson.
John (1775-1830+) Carpenter.
Lucy (1777-86)

II. **Mary's four children:**
Daniel (1772-83+)
Molly (1777-1790+)
Joe or Joe Fosset (1780-1827+) Blacksmith.
Betsy (1783-1857)

*Thomas Jefferson's sister-in-law, Mrs. Elizabeth Eppes.
**Author's text in parenthesis.
***Betty Hemings' twelve children presumably had four fathers. Her name, Hemings came to her from her father, an English sea Captain; her mother was a full-blooded African slave of John Wayles, Thomas Jefferson's father-in-law. Source: Library of Congress, History and Genealogy Division.

III. **Bett's eight children:**
Billy (1777-78)
Wormley (1781-1851+) Gardener.
Burwell (1783-1827+) faithful servant.
Brown (1785-1806) Nail maker.
Melinda (1787-97+)
Edwin (1793-1816+)
Robert (1799-1817?)
Mary (1801-1827+)
IV. **Nance's child:**
Billy (1780-179?)
V. **Critta's child:**
Jamey, called Jamey (Jim) Hubbard (1787-1812+)
VI. **Sally's five children:**
Harriet (1795-97)
Beverley (1778-1822+)
Harriet (1802-1822+) Spinner and Weaver.
Madison (1805-73+) Carpenter, trained by his uncle John.
Eston (1808-54?)

ISAAC and his Immediate Family*

I. **Great George (1730-1799) and his wife, Ursula (1737-1800)**
Great George and Ursula's four children:
Little George (1759-1799)
Bagwell (1768-1826+)
Archy (1773-74)
Isaac (1775-1849?) and his wife, Iris (1775-97+)
II. **Isaac and Iris' two children:**
Squire (1793-97+)
Joyce (1796-97+) a boy.

Isaac's Recollections of Mr. Jefferson at Monticello

The simplicity of Isaac's Memoir of his forty-three years (1781-1824) at Monticello is its hallmark of truth. Charles W. Cambell's handwritten manuscript of Isaac's recollections, was recorded by him in Petersburg, Virginia in 1849, where he found Isaac living in quiet retirement after his many years of faithful service to Jefferson. Both Edmund Bacon's and Isaac's narratives are unique, in that each knew his subject from eye-witness testimony. They are so much in agreement that their authenticity provides historical accuracy. Following are some lines from Isaac's recollections of Mr. Jefferson:

*Source: Library of Congress, History and Genealogy Division.

Old Master (Jefferson)* had six sisters: Polly married a Bolling; Patsy (Martha) married old Dabney Carr in the low grounds, one married William Skipwith; Nancy married old Hastings Marks. Old Master's brother, Mass Randall (Randolph Jefferson)* was a mighty simple man: used to come out among black people, play the fiddle and dance half the night; hadn't much more sense than Isaac...Mr. Jefferson bowed to everybody he meet; talked wid his arms folded. Gave the boys in the nail factory a pound of meat a week, a dozen herrings, a quart of molasses, and peck of meal. Give them that wukked the best a suit of red or blue; encouraged them mightily. Isaac calls him a mighty good master. [2]

To Isaac's Recollections must be added Edmund Bacon's description of his virtues:

"Mr. Jefferson's Personal Appearance and Habits"

Captain Edmund Bacon recounts, in detail, "the Sage of Monticello's" personal appearance and habits, lived out for twenty years before his scrutiny, at close-range:

Mr. Jefferson was six feet, two and a half inches high, well-proportioned, and straight as a gun barrel...His skin was very clear and pure – just as he was in principle...His countenance was always mild and pleasant. You never saw it ruffled. No odds what happened, it always maintained the same expression. When I was sometimes very much fretted and disturbed, his countenance was perfectly unmoved. I remember one case in particular. We had about eleven thousand bushels of wheat in the mill, and coopers and everything else employed. There was a big freshet – the first after the dam was finished. It was raining powerfully. I got up early in the morning and went up to the dam. While I stood there, it began to break, and I stood and saw the freshet sweep it all away. I never felt worse. I did not know what we should do. I went up to see Mr. Jefferson. He had just come from breakfast.

"Well, sir," said he, "have you heard from the river?" I said, "Yes, sir; I have just come from there with very bad news. The milldam is all swept away." "Well, sir," said he, just as calm and quiet as though nothing had happened, "we can make a new dam this summer, but we will get Lewis' ferryboat, with our own, and get the hands from all the quarters, and boat in rock enough in place of the dam to answer for the present and next summer. I will send to Baltimore and get ship bolts, and we will make a dam that the feshet can't wash away." He then went on and explained to me in detail just how he would have the dam built. We repaired the dam as he suggested, and the next summer we made a new dam that I reckon must be there yet.

Mr. Jefferson was always an early riser – arose at daybreak or before. The sun never found him in bed. I used sometimes to think, when I went up there *very* early in the morning, that I would find him in bed; but there he would be before me, walking on the terrace...

He did not use tobacco in any form. He never used a profane word or anything like it. He never played cards. I never saw a card in the house at

---

*Author's text in parenthesis.

Monticello, and I had particular orders from him to suppress card-playing among the Negroes, who, you know, are generally very fond of it. I never saw any dancing in his house, and if there had been any there during the twenty years I was with him I should certainly have known it. He was never a great eater, but what he did eat he wanted to be very choice. He never ate much hog meat. He often told me, as I was giving out meat for the servants, that what I gave one of them for a week would be more than he would use in six months...He was very fond of vegetables and fruit and raised every variety of them.

He was very ingenious. He invented a plough that was considered a great improvement on any that had ever been used. He got a great many premiums and medals for it. He planned his own carriage, buildings, garden, fences, and a good many other things. He was nearly always busy upon some plan or model..." [3]

Jefferson's care for the Poor

Mr. Jefferson was very liberal and kind to the poor. When he would come from Washington, the poor people all about the country would find it out immediately and would come in crowds to Monticello to beg him. He would give them notes to me directing me what to give them. I knew them all a great deal better than he did. Many of them I knew were not worthy – were just lazy, good-for-nothing people, and I would not give them anything. When I saw Mr. Jefferson, I told him who they were and that he ought not to encourage them in their laziness. He told me that when they came to him and told him their pitiful tales, he could not refuse them, and he did not know what to do. I told him to send them to me. He did so, but they never would come. They knew what to expect.

In, I think, the year 1816, there was a very severe frost, and the corn was almost destroyed. It was so badly injured that it would hardly make bread, and it was thought that the stock was injured by eating it. There was a neighborhood at the base of the Blue Ridge where the frost did not injure the corn. They had a good crop, and the people were obliged to give them just what they were disposed to ask for it. I went up there and bought thirty barrels for Mr. Jefferson of a Mr. Massey – gave him ten dollars a barrel for it. That spring the poor trifling people came in crowds for corn. I sent the wagon after what I had bought, and by the time it would get back, Mr. Jefferson had given out so many of his little orders that it would pretty much take the load. I could hardly get it hauled as fast as he would give it away. I went to Mr. Jefferson and told him it never would do; we could not give ten dollars a barrel for corn, and haul it thirty miles, and give it away after that fashion. He said, "What can I do? These people tell me that have no corn, and it will not do to let them suffer." I told him again, I could tell him what to do. Just send them all to me. I knew them all a great deal better than he did and would give to all that were really deserving.

There was an old woman named____ who used to trouble us a great deal. She had three daughters that were bad girls – large, strapping, lazy things – and the old woman would beg for them. One day she went to Mr. Jefferson in a mean old dress, and told him some pitiful story, and he gave her a note to me directing me to give her two bushels of meal. I did so. The same day she went to Mrs. Randolph* and got three sides of bacon – middling meat. There was more than she could carry and she had two of her daughters' illegitimate children to help her carry it home. When she got to the river, the old Negro who attended the ferry was so mad to see her carrying off the meat that he would not ferry her over. So she laid the meat on the edge of the boat, and they ferried themselves across. When the boat struck the bank it jarred the meat off, and it went to the bottom of the river, and she had a great deal of trouble to get it.[4]

Mr. Jefferson's Mule – "Dolphin"

Afterwards she went to Mr. Jefferson and told him the meal I gave her was not good – would not make bread – and he sent her to me again. I told her the meal in the mill was all alike, and she could only get better by going to the Blue Ridge for corn. She said she had no horse, it was too far to walk, and she could not go. I told her I would furnish her a mule. Mr. Jefferson had an old mule that must have been thirty or forty years old, called Dolphin. He was too old to work and we did not like to kill him. His hair grew very long, and he was a sight to look at. He was too old to jump much, but he would tear down the fence with his nose and go over the plantation pretty much as he pleased. I was very anxious to get rid of the mule and of the old woman too, and I thought that maybe if I loaned her the mule she would not come back. So I told her she could have the old mule and go get her corn. She came and stayed overnight, so as to get an early start. My wife gave her a coffee sack, and I gave her an order on Massey, and she started off on old Dolphin. When she got up there the people knew nothing about her, and she could do so much better begging, that sure enough, she never came back at all. Mr. Jefferson used to enjoy telling people how I got rid of the old woman and Dolphin…

Some six weeks or two months after the old woman had gone, I saw something moving about in the wheat field, and, sure enough, there was Dolphin home again. After this there were a couple of Kentucky drovers named Scott and Dudley, from whom we used to buy a good many mules for the plantation, came along with a drove. I told them about the trouble we had with Dolphin. They said they would take him away so that he would trouble us no more, and I gave him to them. They sheared off his long hair and trimmed him up so that he looked quite well. They found one in the drove that matched him very well, and went on a few miles, and sold the pair to Hon. Hugh Nelson. He was a Congressman…It wasn't long before Dolphin was back, and I told Mr. Jefferson. He laughed and said, "You treat him so much better than anybody else will, that he will come back and see you." When Mr. Nelson's overseer came over for him I asked him how old he supposed he was. He said he could not tell. I then told him his history. He took him off, and we never saw any more of Dolphin.[5]

Jefferson's meticulous Business Transactions

…Mr. Jefferson was very particular in the transaction of all his business.

*Martha Jefferson Randolph, Jefferson's daughter.

> He kept an account of everything. Nothing was too small for him to keep an account of. He knew exactly how much of everything was raised at each plantation, and what became of it; how much was sold, and how much fed out...⁶

From the foregoing eye-witness account, the virtues of patience, discipline, self-control, industriousness, temperance, moderation, inventiveness, repulsion for vice and vain pursuits; care for the poor and needy (regardless of his own personal loss); selflessness; kindness, and mercy are all exemplified in the life of Thomas Jefferson. Are these virtues not a reflection of his immersion in the Bible, which Captain Bacon asserts he witnessed his master "reading many and many a time" on a continuing basis?

Thomas Jefferson – the Lawyer

As a lawyer, Thomas Jefferson argued that slavery was "a violation of the law of nature;" that under those laws, "all men are created free, everyone comes into the world with a right to his own person, which includes the liberty of moving and using it at his own will." This shows that he was clearly not in sympathy with a slave-holding community, living under an established Anglican church and ruled by a royal Governor, as attested to in his writings.

Jefferson's Anti-Slavery Bill

From his *Autobiography*, we read Jefferson's initiation of a bill in Congress to free the Slaves:

> The bill on the subject of slaves was a mere digest of the existing laws respecting them, without any intimation of a plan for a future and general emancipation. It was thought better that this should be kept back, and attempted only by way of amendment, however the bill should be brought on. The principles of the amendment however were agreed on, that is to say, the freedom of all born after a certain day, and deportation at a proper age. But it was found that the public mind would not yet bear the proposition, nor will it bear it even at this day. Yet the day is not distant when it must bear and adopt it, or worse will follow. Nothing is more certainly written in the book of fate than that these people are to be free, nor is it less certain that the two races, equally free, cannot live in the same government. Nature, habits, opinion, have drawn indelible lines of distinction between them. It is still in our power to direct the process of emancipation and deportation peaceably and in such slow degree as that the evil will wear off insensibly and their place be pari passu* filled up with free white laborers. If on the contrary, it is left to force itself on, human nature must shudder at the prospect held up... Commerce between master and slave is despotism.⁷

Jefferson's statement that "it was found that the public mind would not yet bear the proposition," that is, of abolishing slavery in the British American colonies – is evidence that the middle-class slave-holding populace in British America could

---
*slowly but surely

not tolerate relinquishing the institution of slavery, begun in 1619 by the Crown of England.

However, the 20th and 21st century media in this nation have indoctrinated millions into believing that only the plantation-owning founders of the American Republic are to be blamed and held accountable for this evil – contrary to historic fact.

In opposition to the widespread media coverage that Thomas Jefferson was a "slave-driver" who visited this great moral evil upon the nation, it follows that he was diametrically opposed to it. Like other representatives in Congress, however, he was unhappily subject to the Crown of England who enforced the evil in his empire for lucrative gain.

Jefferson's Bill to stop Slave Importation passes Congress– 1778

It was only in 1778, after the signing of the *Declaration of Independence*, that Jefferson's bill to prevent the importation of slaves was passed by Congress: His *Autobiography* furnishes the details:

"Monticello", beautiful home of Thomas Jefferson and his family in Charlottesville, Virginia. Designed by Jefferson who was a self-taught architect, The name, translated from Italian means, "Little Hill."

The first establishment in Virginia which became permanent was made in 1607. I have found no mention of Negroes in the colony until about 1650. The first brought here as slaves were by a Dutch ship; after which the English commenced the trade and continued it until the revolutionary war. That suspended, ipso facto, their further importation for the present, and the business of the war pressing constantly on the legislature, this subject was not acted on finally until the year '78 when I brought in a bill to prevent their further importation. This passed without opposition, and stopped the increase of the evil by importation, leaving to future efforts its final eradication.[8]

Chapter X

James Callender and Sally Hemings – James Callender's Demise – Calumny in Public Life, Jefferson's View – A 1998 Revival of Callender's Slander – Accuracy in Media's "In Defense of Jefferson" – Peter and Samuel Carr & Sally and Betsy Hemings – Ellen Randolph Coolidge's October 24, 1858 Letter – Dabney Carr, Father of Jefferson's Nephews – Jefferson's Description of Dabney Carr – Dabney Carr's untimely Death – Ellen Randolph Coolidge's Letter Misquoted – "It's Odd," The Thomas Jefferson Society's Rebuttal – Historic Revisionism: "Just a Mistake"?

James Callender and Sally Hemings

Among the calumnies heaped upon the author of America's *Declaration of Independence*, to defame and destroy the highly principled character of Thomas Jefferson, is the following:

The rewriting of Jefferson's impeccable moral character began in 1802, when a dishonest, enraged Scotsman by the name of James T. Callender publicized an allegation against Thomas Jefferson, that Sally Hemings was his concubine. A Scot who fled from England in the 1790's in order to escape sedition charges, Callender was a pamphleteer who had vented his journalistic rage upon the British government, distancing himself from London. He was employed by the *Philadelphia Gazette*, an affiliate of the Republican Party, the nation's first opposition party founded by Thomas Jefferson, where he displayed his splendid journalistic ability.

In 1797, Vice-President Thomas Jefferson made a visit to his printing office in Philadelphia. Unaware of Callender's total lack of scruples, Jefferson continued subscribing to his writings, even sending him $50.00 when he was out of work. In 1799, James Callender was employed by the Republican Richmond *Examiner*, of which Jefferson's friend, Meriwether Jones, was editor. The Scot continued his invective against the Federalists in unabated fury. Callender was found guilty under the Sedition Act of 1798, and charged for libel against President John Adams. He was sentenced to a $200 fine and nine months' imprisonment in the Richmond jail. However, he continued writing from his jail cell in Richmond.

After being inaugurated as third U.S. President on March 4, 1801, President Jefferson granted pardon to those convicted under the Sedition law – promising Callender a reimbursement of his fine. As government bureaucratic delays ensued, Jefferson generously paid part of the remission from his personal funds. The belligerent Scotsman, however, angered by the government's delay in repayment, and ungrateful for Jefferson's partial remission, promptly sought the position of Richmond Postmaster with an annual salary of $1,500, in recompense for his alleged services to the Republican Party. Callender's communications with James Madison, then Secretary of State, and his attempted contacts with President Jefferson, proved unsuccessful.

James Callender then resorted to damaging President Jefferson's reputation by calumny.* Breathing threats against the President, he acquired a position in Richmond on the Federalist *Recorder,* vilifying Jefferson with unfounded, false accusations concerning Sally Hemings, which were immediately seized by the Federalist press and republished throughout the nation to advance their cause. However, the pamphleteer never proved these spurious accusations, nor were there any journalists who visited Monticello to authenticate Callender's fictitious charges. No libel laws existing in those days, Callender precipitated his scheme of defaming Jefferson's character in order to destroy him.

It is reported that James T. Callender was constantly at odds with his fellowmen. The Federalist Richmond *Recorder's* readership nonetheless increased considerably after his calumnious attacks on Jefferson. A man who was often inebriated, his body was retrieved in the James River in three feet of water, in July, 1803.

Front page sample of *The Recorder,* Vol. II, No. 62, in which James Callender initiated his calumnious attack on Thomas Jefferson in 1802. Callender's fraudulent allegation was in retaliation to President Jefferson's refusal to appoint him Postmaster of Richmond. Courtesy of the Virginia State Library and Archives.

James Callender's demise

After his demise, the Richmond *Examiner* published the following:

> Callender had threatened to put an end to his existence, by drowning himself, for several weeks previous to his actual death…It may be inferred that he got excessively drunk for the express purpose of putting an easy end to his life.

---

*calumny: trickery; slander; from *calvi*, to deceive. 1. slander; a false accusation of a crime or offense, knowingly or maliciously made to hurt someone's reputation. 2. slander. Synonyms: traducement, aspersion, defamation, detraction, libel, backbiting, opprobrium. *Webster's Dictionary.*

A reputed historian wrote that, "almost every scandalous story about Jefferson which is still whispered or believed" has its origin in the calumny of Callender. Many others are of the same view. The notorious name of James T. Callender is therefore the source of this slanderous rewriting of U.S. history.

Calumny in Public Life – Jefferson's View

In a letter to Samuel Smith dated August 22, 1798, Jefferson writes his view on calumny in public life:

> At a very early period of my life, I determined never to put a sentence into any newspaper. I have religiously adhered to the resolution through my life, and have great reason to be contented with it. Were I to undertake to answer all the calumnies of the newspapers, it would be more than all my own time, and that of twenty aides could effect. I have thought it better to trust to the justice of my countrymen, that they would judge me by what they see of my conduct on the stage where they have placed me, and what they knew of me before the epoch since which a particular party has supposed it might answer some views of theirs to vilify me in the public eye. Some, I know, will not reflect how apocryphal is the testimony of enemies so palpably betraying the views with which they give it. But this is an injury to which duty requires everyone to submit whom the public think proper to call into its councils. I thank you, my dear sir, for the interest you have taken for me on this occasion. Though I have made up my mind not to suffer calumny to disturb my tranquility, yet I retain all my sensibilities for the approbation of the good and just.

A 1998 Revival of Callender's Slander

The monstrous calumny to defame Jefferson, thereby discrediting his philosophy of self-government, and his reputation as the principal founder of American political thought, was vehemently revived in 1998. *Nature Magazine*, a British publication, reported this fallacy as truth in November, 1998. Revisionists throughout America immediately championed their cause through national newspapers, television and media. *Accuracy in Media*, however, a well-known and respected organization, published a rebuttal entitled: "In Defense of Jefferson." It is hereunder reprinted:

Accuracy in Media's – "In Defense of Jefferson"

> Nature Magazine omitted facts when it claimed in its November issue that scientific evidence proved that President Thomas Jefferson fathered a child by his slave Sally Hemings. Reed Irvine, chairman of *Accuracy in Media*, reports that the January issue of Nature will admit that the magazine did not tell the whole story. The scientific journal will print a letter from one of the study's authors that says that genetic evidence shows that Jefferson was only one of many Jefferson men (25 of whom lived in the Monticello area) who could have fathered Sally's son, Eston. (The most likely candidate, according to historian Herbert Barger, is Jefferson's younger brother Randolph, a widower who often visited Monticello and was known to dance

and play the fiddle with the slaves.) It remains to be seen whether the media and the numerous liberal historians who trumpeted the claims of Jefferson's paternity will follow Nature's lead in acknowledging reasonable doubt.

Both *Nature Magazine* (British) and *Science Magazine** (American) published articles in their January, 1999 editions, quoting foremost DNA experts worldwide who validated the lack of evidence, pointing to Randolph Jefferson as the most likely candidate. DNA had been taken from Field Jefferson, Thomas Jefferson's uncle. However, the American 20th century media deliberately ignored these scientific facts, intensifying their slanderous attack on Thomas Jefferson.

Peter and Samuel Carr & Sally and Betsy Hemings

Evidence incriminates the two nephews of Thomas Jefferson, Peter and Samuel Carr, his sister Martha's sons, whose father, Dabney Carr, was a beloved college friend. Carr's three sons and three daughters became wards of Jefferson at the untimely death of their thirty-year-old father.

There is proof that Sally's, and her niece, Betsy Hemings' children were sired by Peter and Samuel Carr, from the communication between Thomas Jefferson Randolph, Jefferson's eldest grandson, and Jefferson's biographer, Henry S. Randall. A letter dated June 1, 1868 from Henry Randall to James Parton, another biographer of "the Sage of Monticello," describes their conversation as follows:

> Walking about mouldering Monticello one day with Colonel Thomas Jefferson Randolph…he showed me a smoke blackened and sooty room in one of the collonades and informed me it was Sally Hemings' room. He asked me if I knew how the story of Mr. Jefferson's connection with her originated. I told him I did not…Colonel Randolph informed me that Sally Hemings was the mistress of Peter Carr and her niece Betsy the mistress of Samuel – and from these connections sprang the progeny which resembled Mr. Jefferson…
>
> The Colonel said their connection with the Carrs was perfectly notorious at Monticello and scarcely disguised by the latter – never disavowed by them. Samuel's proceedings were particularly open…Colonel Randolph said that a visitor at Monticello dropped a newspaper from his pocket or accidentally left it. After he was gone, he (Colonel Randolph) opened the paper and found some very insulting remarks about Mr. Jefferson's "mulato children"…Peter and Samuel Carr were lying not far off under a shade tree. He took the paper and put it in Peter's hands, pointing to the article. Peter read it, tears coursing down his cheeks, and then handed it to Samuel. Samuel also shed tears. Peter exclaimed, "Ar'nt you and I a couple of____pretty fellows to bring this disgrace on poor old uncle who has always fed us! We ought to be____ by____!..."

---

*Science magazine is an academic journal of the American Association for the Advancement of Science, and one of the world's top academic journals.

Do you ask why I did not state, at least hint the above facts in my life of Jefferson? I wanted to do so, but Colonel Randolph, in this solitary case alone, prohibited me from using at my discretion the information he furnished me with. When I rather pressed him on the point, he said, pointing to the family graveyard, "You are not bound to prove a negation. If I should allow you to take Peter Carr's corpse into Court and plead guilty over it to shelter Mr. Jefferson, I should not dare again to walk by his grave: he would rise and spurn me." I am exceedingly glad Colonel Randolph did overrule me in this particular. I should have made a *shameful* mistake. If I had *unnecessarily* defended him (and it was purely unnecessary to offer any defense) at the expense of a dear nephew – and a noble man– hating a single folly. – ...

Ellen Randolph Coolidge's October 24, 1858 Letter

Further to the above evidence, on October 24, 1858, Ellen Randolph Coolidge, Jefferson's granddaughter, wrote to her husband, Joseph Coolidge, Jr., stating,

"no female domestic ever entered his (Jefferson's)* chambers except at hours when he was known not to be there, and none could have entered without being exposed to the public gaze." She added that, "dusky Sally" was "pretty notoriously the mistress of a married man, a near relative of Mr. Jefferson's, and there can be small question that her children were his...I will tell you in confidence what Jefferson (Thomas Jefferson Randolph) told me under the like condition. Mr. Southall and himself being young men together, heard Peter Carr say, with a laugh, that 'the old gentleman had to bear the blame for his and Sam's (Col. Carr) misdeeds.' There is a general impression that the four children of Sally Hemings were *all* the children of Col. Carr, the most notorious good-natured Turk that ever was master of a black seraglio** kept at other men's expense. His deeds were as well known as his name."

Dabney Carr – Father of Jefferson's Nephews

Dabney Carr, Jefferson's closest college friend, became his brother-in-law by intermarrying with his sister, Martha. As boys, they had studied together under a favorite oak tree at Monticello. A promise was made between them, that whoever died first, would be buried by the other at the foot of this tree. The untimely death of his beloved friend occurred when Jefferson was away from home. Upon his return, he discovered that Dabney had been buried at Shadwell. Jefferson promptly had his body disinterred and buried beneath their oak tree, which originated the graveyard at Monticello.

Jefferson's description of Dabney Carr

I well remember the pleasure expressed in the countenance and conversation of the members generally on this début of Mr. Carr, and the hopes they

---

* Author's text in parenthesis.
** seraglio: the palace of a Turkish sultan or noble; a harem; a place where a Moslem keeps his wives or concubines. *Webster's Dictionary of the English Language, Unabridged..*

conceived as well from the talents, as from the patriotism it manifested…His character was of high order. A spotless integrity, sound judgment, handsome imagination, enriched by education and reading, quick and clear in his conceptions, of correct and ready elocution, impressing every hearer with the sincerity of the heart from which it flowed. His firmness was inflexible in whatever he thought was right; but when no moral principle stood in the way, never had man more of the milk of human kindness, of indulgence, of softness, of pleasantry of conversation and conduct. The number of his friends and the warmth of their affection, were proofs of his worth, and of their estimate of it.[1]

And again, in 1770, Jefferson writes to his friend, John Page,

He (Dabney Carr)* speaks, thinks and dreams of nothing but his young son. This friend of ours, Page, in a very small house, with a table, half a dozen chairs, and one or two servants, is the happiest man in the universe. Every incident in life he so takes as to render it a source of pleasure. With as much benevolence as the heart of man will hold, but with an utter neglect of the costly apparatus of life, he exhibits to the world a new phenomenon in life – the Samian sage in the tub of the cynic.

Dabney Carr's untimely Death

Jefferson's beloved friend, Dabney Carr, died on the 16th of May, 1773 at the age of thirty. The following moving inscription was discovered among Jefferson's papers after his death:

Inscription on my Friend Dabney Carr's Tomb

Lamented shade, whom every gift of heaven
Profusely blest; a temper winning mild;
Nor pity softer, nor was truth more bright.
Constant in doing well, he neither sought
Nor shunned applause. No bashful merit sighed
near him neglected: sympathizing he
wiped off the tear from Sorrow's clouded eye
with kindly hand, and taught her heart to smile.
                    Mallet's *Excursion*.

Send for a plate of copper to be nailed on the tree at the foot of his grave, with this inscription:

Still shall thy grave with rising flowers be dressed
And the green turf lie lightly on thy breast;
There shall the morn her earliest tears bestow,
There the first roses of the year shall blow,
While angels with their silver wings o'ershade,
The ground now sacred by thy reliques made.

*Author's text in parenthesis.

On the upper part of the stone inscribe as follows:

> Here lie the remains of
> DABNEY CARR
> Son of John and Jane Carr, of Louisa County,
> Who was born_____, 1744.
> Intermarried with Martha Jefferson, daughter of
> Peter and Jane Jefferson, 1765;
> And died at Charlottesville, May 16, 1773
> Leaving six small children.
> To his Virtue, Good Sense, Learning, and Friendship,
> this stone is dedicated by Thomas Jefferson,
> who, of all men living, loved him most.[2]

At his death, Dabney Carr's six children, Peter, Samuel and Dabney, and their three sisters, became wards of Thomas Jefferson. They were welcomed into his family, his sister Martha depending upon her brother for their protection and affection.

Ellen Randolph Coolidge's Letter Misquoted

It is interesting to note that, in spite of Ellen Randolph Coolidge's October 24, 1858 well known, published letter, there would be a 20th century author who deliberately misquoted it to prove a false premise. This disinformation was brought to her attention by the President of the *Thomas Jefferson Heritage Society* for correction. Her response was, "Your charge that I intentionally altered the text of Ellen Randolph Coolidge's letter to her husband, Joseph, is flat wrong. Any mistake that appears in my work is just that – a mistake."

The following rebuttal was published in the Fall, 2012, No. 12 edition of *Jefferson Notes*, a publication of the *Thomas Jefferson Heritage Society*:

"IT'S ODD" – The Thomas Jefferson Society's Rebuttal

> In her 1997 book, *Thomas Jefferson and Sally Hemings: An American Controversy*, Annette Gordon-Reed included as appendix E a typescript of an October 24, 1858 letter from Ellen Randolph Coolidge (one of Thomas Jefferson's granddaughters) to her husband.
>
> **ODD** that the typescript would have an altered sentence. The sentence by Ellen Coolidge referring to Jefferson's bedchambers read that "no female domestic ever entered his chambers except at hours when he was known not to be there and none could have entered without being exposed to the public gaze." Gordon-Reed's version dropped "there and none could have entered without being exposed to," and added the word "in." So, the sentence by Gordon-Reed then read that "no female domestic ever entered his chambers except at hours when he was known not to be in the public gaze."
>
> **ODD** such a "mistake" could be made which comprised both the dropping of a ten word phrase and the addition of a new word. Coolidge's intent is clear,

which is that someone could not enter Jefferson's bed chambers without being observed. Gordon-Reed's altered version reversed the meaning Coolidge had intended.

ODD that Gordon-Reed would feel the need to prepare a typescript, when one was available in the files of Monticello. A correct typescript of the letter had also appeared in the May 18, 1974 *New York Times* as part of an article by Dumas Malone.

ODD that when this serious discrepancy was called to her attention by John Works, then President of the *Thomas Jefferson Heritage Society*, she responded that "your charge that I intentionally altered the text of Ellen Randolph Coolidge's letter to her husband, Joseph, is flat wrong. Any mistake that appears in my work is just that – a mistake." Gordon-Reed did not explain how the "mistake" occurred.

ODD that when the in-house Research Committee at Monticello issued their January 2000 Report, it included a photocopy of the hand written letter from Ellen Coolidge, but also included as a typescript Appendix E from the Gordon-Reed book, rather than the correct typescript Monticello had in its own files.

ODD that Gordon-Reed would address this issue in her subsequent book, *The Hemingses of Monticello* (page 698, n. 51), but not discuss the critical aspect of the discrepancy, i.e., could a domestic have entered Jefferson's chambers without observation by the Jefferson family, the other slaves, or the many visitors to Monticello. In this book, she simply concludes that everyone knew about Hemings. So, Coolidge's letter must have been just a…mistake.

Historic Revisionism – "Just a Mistake"?

Annette Gordon-Reed's reversal of the meaning intended by Ellen Wayles Randolph Coolidge's letter to her husband reflects academic dishonesty, particularly in light of her published Biography asserting that she is "the author of *Thomas Jefferson and Sally Hemings – An American Controversy* (1997), which examines the scholarly writing on the relationships between Thomas Jefferson and Sally Hemings."

Webster's Dictionary describes "scholarship" as "the systematized knowledge of a learned man (or woman), exhibiting accuracy, critical ability and thoroughness; erudition." The removal of ten words from a scholarly writing of America's history – thus reversing its meaning – exhibits a lack of accuracy, critical ability, thoroughness and erudition in her work. Gordon-Reed's Biography also describes her as having "published *The Hemingses of Monticello: An American Family* (2008) which won the Pulitzer Prize in history". The reader may wonder, under what historic scholarship criteria is this prize awarded? As Professor of History in the Faculty of Arts and Sciences at Harvard University, the highest calibre of accuracy and integrity is expected of Gordon-Reed by her students and readers alike. Her refusal to correct a deliberate omission of ten words from Thomas Jefferson's granddaughter's letter is a clear indication of her intent to perpetuate a fallacy.

Furthermore, Gordon-Reed, together with David McCullough,* (also awarded the Pulitzer Prize in American History) are on the Board of Trustees of Monticello, *The Thomas Jefferson Foundation, Inc*; as well as Pulitzer Prize-winner, Jon Meacham, its chairman, and author of *Thomas Jefferson: The Art of Power* (Random House, 2012) – endorsed by Annette Gordon-Reed. The front book jacket overview of Meacham's book states, "Here, too, is the personal Jefferson, a man of appetite, sensuality, passion" – quite in keeping with Gordon-Reed's portrayal of "the Sage of Monticello" via Madison Hemings' 1873 fallacious interview, "Such is the story that comes down to me."

---

*Honorary Trustee of *The Thomas Jefferson Foundation, Inc*. Member of Yale's secret society, "Skull and Bones" also called "The Brotherhood of Death."

Chapter XI

Madison Hemings' March 13, 1873 Interview, Accuracy vs. Fallacy: "Such is the Story that comes Down to Me" – Jefferson the Agriculturalist – Thomas Jefferson's Prayer Book Record of the Birth of his Twelve Grandchildren — Another "Just a Mistake" Revisionism by Gordon-Reed – Jefferson's Prayer Book Record of his Marriage, and the Birth of their six Children – Martha Wayles Jefferson's Death at Age 33 – Panel of twelve Scholars refutes Madison Hemings' Claims.

Madison Hemings' March 13, 1873 Interview

On March 13, 1873, the *Waverly (Ohio) Pike County Republican* weekly newspaper published an interview with Madison Hemings, aged 68. In it, he made the following fallacious statements:

Accuracy vs. Fallacy

Fallacy no. 1. "Such is the story that comes down to me.... Their stay (my mother's and Maria's)* was about eighteen months. But during that time, my mother became Mr. Jefferson's concubine, and when he was called back home, she was *enciente* by him."

Accuracy: There are numerous fallacies in this interview account. Mary Jefferson (eight years) and her servant, Sally Hemings (fourteen years) arrived in Paris on July 15, 1787, at which time Mary and her maid joined Martha (Patsy) Jefferson, at the Convent of Panthemont on the outskirts of Paris. Jefferson resided in central Paris with Colonel Humphreys, the Secretary of the American legation, and his private secretary, William Short, at the corner of la Grande Route des Champs Elysées et la Rue Neuve de Berry at a house belonging to le Compte de l'Avongeac.[1] Thomas Jefferson departed from Paris with his two daughters and American staff on September 26th, 1789 – twenty-six+ months after their arrival in Paris – *not* eighteen months. Should the reader believe Madison Hemings' story, his mother, then aged fifteen, would have departed Paris for America at the end of December, 1788 – alone and pregnant, but would not have cleared the French Customs authorities, as she belonged to the newly-established United States of America legation to France.

Fallacy no. 2. "But during that time (mid-July, 1787 – December, 1788)** my mother became Mr. Jefferson's concubine, and when he was called back home, she was *enciente* by him."

Accuracy: Thomas Jefferson was not "called back home" but was granted a temporary, six-month, leave-of-absence by Congress to visit his family in Virginia and take care of his personal matters at Monticello.*** Should we believe Madison

---
* In Paris.
** Author's text in parenthesis.
*** Thomas Jefferson to Randolph Jefferson, January 11, 1789: "I have asked of Congress a leave of absence for six months, and if I obtain it in time, I shall expect to sail from hence in April, and to return in the Fall..."

Hemings' account, in December 1788, his mother, who resided at the Convent of Panthemont with Jefferson's daughters, was "enceinte" (pregnant) at age fifteen, unbeknownst to the principal, professors, masters and staff of the Convent, the French authorities, or the American legation to France. Furthermore, the French word "enceinte" could not have been known by Madison, as he is quoted in this interview as stating, "I learned to read by inducing the white children to teach me the letters and something more; what else I know of books, I have picked up here and there, till now I can read and write." A person who admits to having attained an educational level of mere reading and writing the English language would be incapable of expressing himself in the French language; nor could he articulate in the polished, collegiate English of this interview.

Fallacy no. 3. "He (Thomas Jefferson)* desired to bring my mother back to Virginia with him, but she demurred. She was just beginning to understand the French language well, and in France she was free, while if she returned to Virginia, she would be re-enslaved."

Accuracy: A fifteen-year-old minor, the servant of Mary Jefferson, lodging with Thomas Jefferson's two daughters on the outskirts of Paris – Sally Hemings could neither read nor write the English and French languages. Nor was she "free" in France, slavery being first abolished by *la Republique Française* in 1794, six years after Madison Hemings' allegation that his mother left France. In 1802, Napoleon revoked the 1794 decree, restoring slavery and the slave trade in France and its colonies. In 1815, the French Republic abolished the slave trade, but the decree did not come into effect until 1826. France finally re-abolished slavery in 1848 with a general and unconditional emancipation. Are Americans therefore to believe that Sally Hemings' negotiating leverage with Thomas Jefferson consisted of exchanging slavery in France for slavery in Virginia?

Fallacy no. 4. "So she refused to return with him. To induce her to do so, he (Jefferson)* promised her extraordinary privileges, and made a solemn pledge that her children should be freed at the age of twenty-one years…We were free from the dread of having to be slaves all our lives long, and were measurably happy."

Accuracy: As established by historic fact, Sally Hemings was not "free" in France, slavery being enforced until 1794. She could not therefore have used this bargaining leverage, according to Madison Hemings, to "refuse to return to Virginia" – neither France nor Virginia having abolished slavery. Secondly, what children is Madison referring to in 1788, in France? At age fifteen, his mother had no children, her genealogy** proving that her first child, Harriet, was born in 1795 (d. 1797), after which she had four more children. Is the reader to believe that Madison's fifteen-year-old mother, in "negotiating" with the illustrious, virtuous and revered Thomas

---

* Author's text in parenthesis.
** Source: Library of Congress, History and Genealogy Division.

Jefferson, had a prophetic "dream" that she already had five children, striking a bargain with him to set them all free at age twenty-one – for the sake of exchanging enslavement in France for enslavement in Virginia?

A March 13, 1873 edition of the *Waverly (Ohio) Pike County Republican* weekly newspaper, in which appeared the fraudulent claims of Madison Hemings, aged 68, slandering President Thomas Jefferson. Courtesy of the Virginia State Library and Archives.

At the time of this 1873 interview, Madison Hemings, aged 68, was well acquainted with Thomas Jefferson's Last Will and Testament, signed and dated March 17, 1826, which made no distinction between the emancipation of his grandmother, Betty Hemings' children and grandchildren, adding – "I humbly and earnestly request of the Legislature of Virginia a confirmation of the bequest of freedom to these servants...." Moreover, Madison's statement, "...(he)* made her

*Author's text in parenthesis.

a solemn pledge that her children would be freed at the age of twenty-one years... We were free from the dread of having to be slaves all our lives long, and were measurably happy," does not match up with the facts – Beverley having run away in 1822 at the age of twenty-four, three years after his 21st birthday; while Harriet also ran away in 1822, at age twenty, and was then freed by Jefferson; who freed Betty Hemings' son, Robert (1762-1819) in 1794, her son, James (1765-96+) in 1796* and her daughter Bett's son, Burwell (1783-1827+) in his will, prior to Madison and Eston Hemings, as follows:

> I give to my good, affectionate, and faithful servant, Burwell, (Betty Hemings' daughter, Bett's son, born 1783)** his freedom, and the sum of three hundred dollars, to buy necessaries to commence his trade of painter and glazier, or to use otherwise, as he pleases.
>
> I give also to my good servants, John Hemings (Betty Hemings' son, born 1775),** and Joe Fosset (Betty Hemings' daughter, Mary's son, born 1780)**, their freedom, at the end of one year after my death; and to each of them respectively, all the tools of their respective shops or callings; and it is my will that a comfortable log-house be built for each of the three servants so emancipated on some part of my lands convenient to them with respect to the residence of their wives, and to Charlottesville, and the University, where they will be mostly employed, and reasonably convenient also to the interests of the proprietor of the lands, of which houses I give the use of one, with the curtilage of an acre to each, during his life, or personal occupation thereof.
>
> I give also to John Hemings the service of his two apprentices, Madison and Eston Hemings, until their respective ages of twenty-one years, at which period, respectively, I give them their freedom; and I humbly and earnestly request of the Legislature of Virginia a confirmation of the bequest of freedom to these servants, with permission to remain in this State, where their families and connections are, as an additional instance of the favor of which I have received so many other manifestations in the course of my life, and for which I now give them my last, solemn, and dutiful thanks...
>
> March 17, 1826.
TH: Jefferson

Fallacy no. 5. "In consequence of his promise, on which she implicitly relied, she returned with him to Virginia. Soon after their arrival, she gave birth to a child, of whom Thomas Jefferson was the father. It lived but a short time. She gave birth to four others, and Jefferson was the father of them all. Their names were Beverly,*** Harriet, Madison (myself), and Eston – three sons and one daughter.

Accuracy: The above statement by Madison Hemings implies that fifteen-year-old Sally Hemings was pregnant crossing the Atlantic from France to America in December, 1788, eighteen months after their arrival in France, without being apprehended by the French authorities – which is impossible. And where was "it"

---

* Source: Library of Congress, History and Genealogy Division.
** Author's text in parenthesis.
*** Spelled, Beverley.

born? This allegation is disproved by Sally Hemings' genealogy, which records her first child, Harriet's birth as 1795, (died two years later in 1797.) Secondly, Madison's mother had *five* children, (Harriet, 1795-97); Beverley (1798-1822+); Harriet (1802-22+); Madison (1805-73+) and Eston (1808-54?) –not *four* children, as alleged by Madison Hemings.

Fallacy no. 6. 'We all became free agreeably to the treaty entered into by our parents before we were born,"

Accuracy: No written "treaty" exists. Thomas Jefferson's Last Will and Testament is dated and signed March 17, 1826, approximately three and a half months prior to his death on July 4, 1826, at which time Madison Hemings was twenty-one and a half years old, surpassing the twenty-one-year-old date of being granted the "extraordinary privileges" of emancipation he affirmed were promised in this "treaty." Moreover, Beverley ran away in 1822 at age twenty-four, and Harriet also ran away in 1822 at age twenty, then freed by Jefferson – while in 1826, eighteen-year-old Eston had another three years' apprenticeship with John Hemings prior to manumission, according to Jefferson's will.

In this interview, Madison makes another fatal error. He states:

Fallacy no. 7. "Unlike Washington, he (Jefferson)* had but little taste or care for agricultural pursuits."

Accuracy: Jefferson wrote, "No occupation is so delightful to me as the culture of the earth, and no culture comparable to that of the garden…But though an old man, I am but a young gardener." [2]

Jefferson meticulously catalogued his collection of 6,700[+] volumes sold to the Library of Congress in 1815. Now housed in its Rare Book Collection, he classified each subject. They include numerous books on *Agriculture, Anatomy, Zoology, Botany, Animals, Vegetables* and *Minerals*.

Jefferson, the Agriculturalist

The site of Monticello, on land Jefferson inherited from his father at the age of fourteen, was the center of a 5,000-acre plantation that was largely self-sufficient, and included four adjacent farms. Jefferson began planting wheat as his main cash crop in 1794. Other crops such as corn, potatoes, and small grains were cultivated with a variety of experimental techniques, including crop rotation and contour plowing. Cattle, hogs and sheep were also raised to support the plantation.

At Monticello Jefferson centered his house on an oval manmade "level" below which he laid out a series of four circuitous roads called "roundabouts," as well as gardens and orchards. The grounds became a kind of living laboratory for the study of useful and ornamental plants from around the world. His Garden Book chronicles a lifetime of gardening activities.

*Author's text in parenthesis.

By 1807, anticipating his retirement from public life, Jefferson prepared a scheme for his **flower gardens**. This plan included twenty oval-shaped flower beds at the four corners of the house, and a graveled "roundabout" walk with a flower border on the west or garden side of the house. The oval beds were planted with a variety of flowers such as the "Columbian Lilly," brought back by the Lewis and Clark expedition, the native cardinal flower, and recent European imports such as the tulip, sweet William, and Maltese cross. One flower bed was planted with *Jeffersonia diphyll*a, a spring-blooming flower named in Jefferson's honor.

For many other varieties that he wished to grow, Jefferson planned "a winding walk surrounding the lawn before the house with a narrow border of flowers on each side." The flower border was divided into eighty-seven ten-foot compartments, in which, he noted, "I am fond of placing handsome plants or fragrant, those of mere curiosity I do not aim at."

Numerous trees planted about Monticello included shade and flowering trees in "clumps" at the four corners of the house. Jefferson occasionally took visitors on tours of his "pet trees," especially the recently introduced species like the copper beech, mimosa, and gingko. At least five trees planted in his lifetime have survived – two tulip poplars (a species he described as the "Juno" of the tree world), a sugar maple, the lone survivor of his attempt at a sugar orchard, a European larch, and a red cedar.

When Jefferson mentioned his "garden," he was referring to his **vegetable, or kitchen, garden** on the sunny southern slope of the mountain. Over 250 varieties of vegetables and herbs were grown here, including sesame, which he cultivated for its oil; sea kale, a winter vegetable tasting like asparagus; tomatoes, a relatively unknown fruit; and nearly twenty varieties of English pea, believed to be his favorite vegetable.

In its final form the garden resembled a terraced shelf eighty feet wide and a thousand feet long, cut into the hillside and supported by a stone wall. At the base of the steep slope below Mulberry Row was the northwest border, where early season vegetables took advantage of the late winter sun.

The main part of the terraces contained twenty-seven growing beds, or squares, which were divided into areas for "roots" (including beets and onions), "leaves" (lettuce and spinach), and "fruits" (beans and peppers).

At the midpoint of the stone wall, Jefferson constructed a pavilion. Below the wall was a seven-acre orchard with a nursery, vineyards, and other fruit and vegetable terraces. The entire garden and orchard area was surrounded by a ten-foot-high "paling" fence with boards "so near as not to let even a young hare in." [3]

The foregoing detailed account of Jefferson's agricultural pursuits proves irrefutably in his own words, that "no occupation is so delightful to me as the culture of the earth…" This is just another incontestable proof that Hemings' interview is a forgery.

Fallacy no. 8. Madison Hemings states: "His (Jefferson's)* daughter Martha married Thomas Mann Randolph, by whom she had thirteen children. Two died in infancy. The names of the living were Ann, Thomas Jefferson, Ellen, Cornelia, Virginia, Mary, James, Benj. Franklin, Lewis Madison, Septemia and Geo. Wythe."

Thomas Jefferson's Prayer Book Record of the Birth of his Twelve Grandchildren

Accuracy: Martha Jefferson Randolph had *twelve* children, *one* of whom died in infancy, not "thirteen children. Two died in infancy" – as meticulously recorded by her father, Thomas Jefferson within his Prayer Book, and preserved for safe-keeping in the Rare Book vault of the University of Virginia. Hand-written by Jefferson, they are:

1. Anne Cary Randolph was born 1791 Jan. 23
2. Thomas Jefferson Randolph was born 1792 Sept. 12
3. Ellen Wayles Randolph was born 1794 Aug. 30 Died 1795 July 26
4. Ellen Wayles Randolph was born 1796 Oct. 13
5. Cornelia Randolph was born 1799 July 26
6. Virginia Randolph 1801 Aug. 22
7. Mary Jefferson Randolph was born 1803 Nov. 2
8. James Randolph 1806 Jan. 17
9. Benjamin Randolph was born 1808 July 16
10. Lewis Randolph was born 1810 Jan. 31
11. Septimia Randolph was born 1814 Jan 3
12. George Wythe Randolph was born 1818 Mar. 10

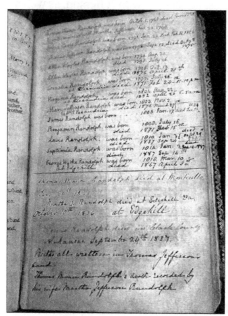

Thomas Jefferson's Prayer Book record of his daughter Martha's marriage to Thomas Mann Randolph, Jr., the birth of their twelve children, and death of their third child in infancy. Rare Book Collection, University of Virginia, Charlottesville, Virginia.

*Author's text in parenthesis.

Madison Hemings further incriminates himself by stating that the name of Thomas Jefferson's fourth grandson was "Lewis Madison," whereas his name was Meriwether Lewis Randolph – *not* Lewis Madison Randolph. Martha Jefferson Randolph named her five sons after her beloved and esteemed father, and his closest friends in public life as follows,

I. Thomas Jefferson Randolph
II. James Madison Randolph
III. Benjamin Franklin Randolph
IV. Meriwether Lewis Randolph
V. George Wythe Randolph

Hemings further misspells two additional names of Jefferson's grandchildren, "Ann" – correctly spelled "Anne" and "Septemia" in lieu of "Septimia Randolph" meaning "seventh."

Another "Just a Mistake" Revisionism by Annette Gordon-Reed

In her book, *Thomas Jefferson and Sally Hemings – An American Controversy*, (1997) Annette Gordon-Reed, under her chart "the Hemingses and Wayleses," connects Madison Hemings' fallacious genealogical links between his grandmother, Betty Hemings, and John Wayles, father-in-law to Jefferson; as well as reinforcing Madison's false statement that Martha Jefferson Randolph had "thirteen children. Two died in infancy." This she did by deceptively removing Martha Jefferson Randolph's second daughter, recorded in Jefferson's Prayer Book as, "Ellen Wayles Randolph was born 1794 Aug. 30 Died 1795 July 26," prior to her third daughter's birth, bearing the same name, "Ellen Wayles Randolph was born 1796 Oct. 13," – thereby eliminating Madison's glaring historical error of attributing thirteen children to Martha Jefferson Randolph, in lieu of twelve, one having died at the age of eleven months. To further bolster this cover-up removal of Jefferson's second granddaughter, Gordon-Reed reiterates Madison Hemings' misspelling of Jefferson's seventh granddaughter as "Septemia," but recorded by Jefferson as "Septimia Randolph," her name stemming from the Latin word "Septimus" meaning seventh. Additionally, in her chart of "The Jeffersons and Randolphs" genealogy, Gordon-Reed records the birth of Jefferson's second grandson, James Madison Randolph as "b. Jan. 18, 1806," whereas Jefferson's Prayer Book record of his grandson's birth is "1806 Jan. 17."

In her 1997 book's genealogical chart of Sally Hemings, Gordon-Reed attributes six children to Madison's mother, adding, – "Unnamed daughter (1799)" – which contradicts Madison Hemings' statement that soon after his mother's return from France, "she gave birth to a child...It lived but a short time. She gave birth to four others...." The latter, in turn, contradicts the accurate genealogy of Sally Hemings' recorded as having borne *five* children, beginning in 1795: Harriet (1795-97); Beverley (1798-1822+): Harriet (1802-22+); Madison (1805-73+) and Eston (1808-54?). These serious misstatements fact are again, "scholarship" à la mode de – "just a mistake," but serving to calumniate Thomas Jefferson.

Fallacy no. 9. Madison Hemings continues, "As to myself, I was named Madison by the wife of James Madison, who was afterwards President of the United States. Mrs. Madison happened to be at Monticello at the time of my birth, and begged the privilege of naming me, promising my mother a fine present for the honor. She consented, and Mrs. Madison dubbed me by the name I now acknowledge, but like many promises of white folks to the slaves she never gave my mother anything."

Accuracy: Not content with renaming Jefferson's fourth grandson, "Lewis Madison" in lieu of his correct name, "Meriwether Lewis Randolph," Madison Hemings is here elevating himself above Jefferson's second grandson, whose name was "James Madison Randolph," thus attributing to himself the honor bestowed upon James Madison (President Thomas Jefferson's Secretary of State, and "father of the U.S. Constitution") by Martha Jefferson Randolph, in giving her second son the namesake "James Madison Randolph." Additionally, the stately and distinguished Dolley Madison would not have "begged the privilege" of ascribing to the illegitimate son of Peter Carr, her illustrious husband's name.

James Madison, portrait of the founding father from life by Gilbert Stuart.

Here again, we evidence a recurring theme in Madison's Hemings' "Such is the story that comes down to me," – exalting himself and his family above two U.S. Presidents, among the most illustrious founding fathers of America, by asserting that his mother had "bargaining power" to manipulate Thomas Jefferson and the wife of James Madison into fawning at her feet as underlings. Of course, according to the "story" fabricated by Madison Hemings' interview, "it was a privilege and an honor" for the distinguished Mrs. James Madison, hostess at the White House during Jefferson's presidency, to beg the mother of Peter Carr's out-of-wedlock child to give him her husband's name. Hemings also degrades and disparages Mrs. Madison by accusing her of lying to his mother: "like many promises of white folks to the slaves, she never gave my mother anything."

The foregoing "interview" resembles a modernized – but inferior – version of *Don Quixote*, dubbed by the French, "la folie des grandeurs," meaning, "the embecility (pride) of great aspirations."

Also meticulously recorded by Jefferson in his Prayer Book is the date of his marriage to Martha Wayles, the birth of their six children, the death of four, and his wife's untimely death after the birth of their sixth child:

Know all men by these presents that we Thomas Jefferson and Francis Eppes are held and firmly bound to our sovereign lord the king his heirs and successors in the sum of fifty pounds current money of Virginia, to the paiment of which well and truly to be made we bind ourselves jointly and severally, our joint and several heirs executors and administrators in witness whereof we have hereto set our hands and seals this twenty third day of December in the year of our lord one thousand seven hundred and seventy one The condition of the above obligation is such that if there be no lawful cause to obstruct a marriage intended to be had and solemnized between the abovebound Thomas Jefferson and Martha Skelton of the county of Charles city, widow, for which a license is desired, then this obligation is to be null and void; otherwise to remain in full force.

Marriage banns for Thomas Jefferson and Martha Wayles Skelton. They were married on January 1st, 1772.

Thomas Jefferson's Prayer Book record of his marriage, and the birth of their Six Children

Thomas Jefferson was born April 2, 1743 Old Stile
Martha Wayles was born Oct. 19, 1748, Old Stile
They intermarried, Jan. 1, 1772.

1. Martha Jefferson was born Sept. 27, 1772.
2. Jane Randolph Jefferson born April 3, 1774 at 11 o'clock A.M. She died September, 1774.
3. A son born May 28, 1777 H. 10 p.m. Died June 18, 1777. H. 10 M. 20.
4. Mary Jefferson born August 1, 1778. Died April 17, 1804, between 8 and 9 a.m.
5. A daughter born in Richmond. Feb. 5, 1780 at 10:45 p.m. She weighed 10 ½ lbs. She died April 15, 1781 at 10 o'clock A.M.
6. Lucy Elizabeth Jefferson born May 8, 1782 at 1 o'clock A.M. Died 1784.

Martha (Wayles) Jefferson died Sept. 6, 1782 at 11:45 a.m. aged Y. 33 M. 10 D. 8

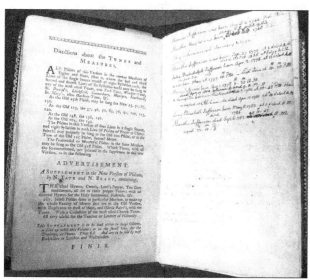

Last page of Thomas Jefferson's Prayer Book recording his hand-written account of his marriage to Martha Wayles (1772) – the birth of their six children, and deaths. University of Virginia Archives, Charlottesville, Virginia.

Silhouette of Jefferson's wife, Martha Wayles Jefferson, the only known extant image. Courtesy of the Virginia State Library and Archives.

Hemings' "interview" continues,

Fallacy no. 10. "On the death of John Wales*, my grandmother, his concubine, and her children by him fell to Martha, Thomas Jefferson's wife, and consequently became the property of Thomas Jefferson, who in the course of time became famous, and was appointed Minister to France during our revolutionary troubles, or soon after independence was gained. About the time of the appointment and before he was ready to leave the country his wife died, and as soon after her interment as he could attend to and arrange his domestic affairs in accordance with the changed circumstances of his family in consequence of this misfortune

*Spelled, Wayles.

(I think not more than three weeks thereafter) he left for France, taking his eldest daughter with him. He had sons born to him, but they died in early infancy, so he then had but two children, Martha and Maria. The latter was left home, but afterwards was ordered to follow him to France. She was three years or so younger than Martha. My mother accompanied her as a body servant. When Mr. Jefferson went to France, Martha was just budding into womanhood."

Accuracy: Firstly, there is no evidence whatsoever – written, or eye-witness, that Betty Hemings was John Wayles' concubine – apart from Madison Hemings' tall story. His statement, "About the time of the appointment, and before he was ready to leave the country his wife died" is historically false, as Martha Wayles Jefferson, according to her husband's meticulously-recorded Prayer Book entry, died on September 6, 1882 at 11:45 a.m., aged 33 years, 10 months and 8 days.

Contrary to Hemings' statement that Jefferson's appointment as Minister to France was prior to his wife's death, are Jefferson's own words on Congress' appointment **two months** subsequent to his beloved wife's death. From his *Autobiography* we read,

> I had, two months before that, lost the cherished companion of my life, in whose affections, unabated on both sides, I had lived the last ten years in unchequered happiness. With the public interests, the state of my mind concurred in recommending the change of scene proposed; and I accepted the appointment.[4]

His departure for France took place more than a year and a half later, leaving from Boston on July 5, 1784 on *The Ceres* with his eleven-year-old eldest daughter, Martha, and his private secretary William Short.

Fallacy No. 11: Another blatant fallacy is Madison's statement that "He (Jefferson)* had sons born to him, but they died in early infancy…"

Accuracy: Thomas Jefferson records in his Prayer Book his six children's births, there being only *one* son recorded – his third child: "A son born May 28, 1777 at 10 p.m. Died June 18, 1777 at 10:20." Madison Hemings' fallacious story continues: "…so he then had but two children, Martha and Maria." Jefferson's Prayer Book record proves, to the contrary that, after his wife's death, he had *three* children left, not two: "Martha Jefferson was born Sept. 27, 1772." "Mary Jefferson born August 1, 1778." "Lucy Elizabeth Jefferson born May 8, 1782 at 1 o'clock A.M." The devastating news of his daughter, Lucy Elizabeth's death was announced to Jefferson in Paris in a letter from his sister-in-law, Mrs. Francis Eppes, dated October 13, 1784.

*Author's text in parenthesis.

Martha Wayles Jefferson's Death at Age 33

Jefferson's daughter, Martha, recounts this tragic event in her manuscript,

> During my mother's life he (Jefferson)* bestowed much time and attention on our education – our cousins, the Carrs, and myself – and after her death, during the first month of desolation which followed, I was his constant companion while we remained at Monticello…As a nurse no female ever had more tenderness nor anxiety. He nursed my poor mother in turn with aunt Carr and her own sister – sitting up with her and administering her medicines and drink to the last. For four months that she lingered he was never out of calling; when not at her bedside, he was writing in a small room which opened immediately at the head of her bed. A moment before the closing scene, he was led from the room in a state of insensibility by his sister, Mrs. Carr, who, with great difficulty, got him into the library, where he fainted, and remained so long insensible that they feared he never would revive. The scene that followed I did not witness, but the violence of his emotion, when, almost by stealth, I entered his room by night, to this day I dare not describe to myself. He kept his room three weeks, and I was never a moment from his side. He walked almost incessantly night and day, only lying down occasionally, when nature was completely exhausted, on a pallet that had been brought in during his long fainting-fit. My aunts remained constantly with him for some weeks – I do not remember how many. When at last he left his room, he rode out, and from that time he was incessantly on horseback, rambling about the mountain, in the least frequented roads, and just as often through the woods. In those melancholy rambles I was his constant companion – a solitary witness to many a burst of grief, the remembrance of which has consecrated particular scenes of that lost home beyond the power of time to obliterate.[5]

The following epitaph was written by Jefferson for his wife's tomb:

> To the Memory of
> MARTHA JEFFERSON,
> Daughter of John Wayles;
> Born October 19th, 1748, O.S..;
> Intermarried with
> THOMAS JEFFERSON
> January 1st, 1772;
> Torn from him by Death
> September 6th, 1782;
> This Monument of his Love is inscribed.
>
> ———
>
> If in the melancholy shades below,
> The flames of friends and lovers cease to glow,
> Yet mine shall sacred last; mine undecayed
> Burn on through death and animate my shade.** [6]

---

* Author's text in parenthesis.
** These four lines were written in Greek in the original epitaph.

Madison's deceptive narrative is unending:

Fallacy no. 12. "The latter (Mary)* was left home, but afterwards was ordered to follow him to France. She was three years or so younger than Martha."

Accuracy: According to Jefferson's Prayer Book entry of his six children's births, Mary was born on August 1, 1778 – hence she was *six* years younger than her elder sister, Martha, born on September 27, 1772 – *not* three years, as asserted by Hemings.

Fallacy no. 13. "When Mr. Jefferson went to France, Martha was just budding into womanhood."

Accuracy. At their departure for France on July 5th, 1784, Martha Jefferson was a little girl of eleven years. An eleven-year-old daughter is in no wise "just budding into womanhood."

Fallacy no. 14. Madison Hemings' interview continues to amaze readers as to its bold misstatements of historic fact – "Such is the story that comes down to me. Elizabeth Hemings (his grandmother)* grew to womanhood in the family of John Wales**....was taken by the widower Wales as his concubine, by whom she had six children – three sons and three daughters, viz. Robert, James, Peter, Critty, Sally and Thena. These children went by the name of Hemings."

Accuracy: There is no evidence whatsoever to this fraudulent claim by Madison Hemings, defaming Thomas Jefferson's wife's family. Furthermore, Hemings misspells two of his aunts' names, namely "Critty" for "Critta" and "Thena" for "Thenia," Additionally, his claim that "These children went by the name of Hemings," excludes John Hemings, born in 1775 after the birth of the "three sons and three daughters (who)* went by the name of Hemings," as asserted by Madison. "The story that comes down to me" is Hemings' thesis throughout his published, March 13, 1873 interview with a journalist of the *Waverly (Ohio) Pike County Republican* weekly newspaper – "just a story."

Fallacy no. 15. Madison states; "She (Betty Hemings, his grandmother)* had seven children by white men and seven by colored men – fourteen in all."

Accuracy: To the contrary, Betty Hemings' genealogy proves that she had twelve children, who had presumably four fathers – *not* fourteen. Madison Hemings attributed two additional non-existent births to his own grandmother. Betty Hemings (1735-1807) bore her first child, Mary, in 1753 at age eighteen, and her last child, Lucy, in

---

* Author's text in parenthesis.
** Spelled, Wayles.

1777, at the age of forty-two. Following are the recorded births of Betty Hemings' twelve children: Mary (1753-92+), Martin (1755/6-1807), Bett "Betty Brown" (1759-1827+), Nance (1761-1827+), Robert (1762-1819), James (1765-96), Thenia (1767-95+), Critta (1769-1827+), Peter (1770-1827+), Sally (1773-1835), John (1775-1830+) and Lucy (1777-86.)*

Madison Hemings' interview ends thus, "My post office address is, Pee Pee, Pike County, Ohio."

This interview, proven to contain at least fifteen historically fraudulent claims, must be rejected as fallacious inventions by one or more persons, aimed at defaming both Thomas Jefferson's, and his wife, Martha Wayles Jefferson's, reputation and character. In fact, a Court of Law would disqualify it as a deliberate forgery.

Panel of Twelve Scholars refutes Madison Hemings' Claims

In August, 2011, a panel of twelve scholars, formed at the behest of the *Thomas Jefferson Heritage Society*, and chaired by Robert F. Turner, former professor at the University of Virginia, concluded that,

- Claims that the relationship between Hemings and Jefferson started in Paris are unlikely, because she was living with his daughters at their boarding school across the city at the time.

- The "Jefferson family" DNA used in the 1998 test came from descendants of his uncle, which the scholars said means any one or two dozen Jefferson men living in Virginia at the time Eston was conceived could have been the father.

- The 1802 rumors centered on Thomas Woodson, who was said to have been one of Sally Hemings' children. But tests of three Woodson descendants failed to show a link to Jefferson family DNA.

- Also, no documentation supports claims he was Hemings' child.

- Oral tradition from Eston Hemings' family initially said he was not the son of the President, but rather of an "uncle" which the scholars think is a reference to Randolph Jefferson, the President's brother, who would have been referred to as "uncle" by Jefferson's daughters.

    (The foregoing excerpted front-page article appeared in the August 31, 2011 edition of the *Washington Times*.)

---

*Source: Library of Congress, History and Genealogy Division.

Chapter XII

What is American History? – Thomas Jefferson, Minister Plenipotentiary to France – Polly Jefferson's Letter to her Father – Abigail Adams: Jefferson, "One of the Choice Ones of the Earth" – Minister to France – Bereaved of His Daughter, Lucy – Thomas Jefferson's Love letter to his Daughter, Polly – Polly Jefferson Refuses to go to Paris – Jefferson's Instructions on Polly's Voyage to France – His Anxiety, "I drop my Pen at the Thought" – He Repeats His Prayer for Polly – His concern for Polly's Happiness – A Father's Love for his Daughter, Martha – Thomas Jefferson to Martha Jefferson, March 28, 1787 – Martha Jefferson to her Father, April 9, 1787 – A beautiful Father-daughter Relationship – Jefferson, the Naturalist – Anxiety in Virginia over Polly's Departure – Polly Jefferson leaves for France – Her Arrival in London – Polly Arrives in Paris, A Reunion of "Great Joy" – A Year later, July 12th, 1788.

What is American History?

American history is not a narrative or a "story that comes down to me," but concrete, verified, factual, written records, such as Thomas Jefferson's *Farm Book*, in which he meticulously recorded the births of all his servants born at Monticello.

A page from Thomas Jefferson's *Farm Book* entry.

Thomas Jefferson – Minister Plenipotentiary to France

An examination of Jefferson's voyage and stay in France, from factual, original writings of American history ensues.

Thomas Jefferson's wife, Martha Wayles Jefferson – honored by Jefferson as "the cherished companion of my life," died on September 6, 1782. Two months later, he accepted Congress' appointment as Minister Plenipotentiary, together with Benjamin Franklin and John Adams, in negotiating with foreign nations. Awaiting definite orders from Congress in Philadelphia, he placed Martha Jefferson, his eleven-year-old daughter, in a boarding school in that city prior to their July 5, 1784 departure. Mary Jefferson (b. 1778) and Lucy Elizabeth Jefferson (b. 1782), being too young to sustain the journey, were left in the nurturing care of his sister-in-law and her husband, Mr. and Mrs. Francis Eppes. While in Philadelphia, he received the following letter from his six-year-old daughter, Mary:*

Polly Jefferson's Letter to her Father

Eppington, April 11, 1784

My dear Papa,

I want to know what day you are going to come and see me, and if you will bring sister Patsy (Martha)** and my baby with you. I was mighty glad of my sashes, and gave Cousin Bolling one.

I can almost read.

Your affectionate daughter,
Polly Jefferson.[1]

Upon their arrival in Paris, he placed his beloved daughter, Martha, at the Convent of Panthemont on the outskirts of Paris, where she boarded – Jefferson's lodging being in central Paris. Here is his daughter Martha's own account of their voyage and arrival in Paris:

> He (Jefferson)** sailed from Boston in a ship of Colonel Tracy's (*The Ceres*, Captain St. Barbe), the passengers – only six in number – of whom Colonel Tracy himself was one, were to a certain degree select, being chosen from many applying...We landed in Portsmouth, where he was detained a week by the illness of his little travelling companion, suffering from the effects of the voyage. On his first arrival in Paris he occupied rooms in the Hôtel d'Orleans, Rue des Petits Augustins, until a house could be got ready for him. His first house was in the Cul-de-sac Têtebout, near the Boulevards. At the end of the year he removed to a house belonging to M. le Compte de l'Avongeac, at the corner of the Grande Route des Champs Elysées and the Rue Neuve de Berry, where he continued as long as he remained in Paris. Colonel Humphreys, the Secretary of the legation, and Mr. Short, his private

---

* Also called *Polly* or *Maria*.
** Author's text in parenthesis.

secretary, both lived with him. The house was a very elegant one even for Paris, with an extensive garden, court and outbuildings, in the handsomest style...He kept me with him till I was sent to a convent in Paris, where his visits to me were daily for the first month or two, till in fact I recovered my spirits.²

Abigail Adams: Jefferson – "One of the Choice ones of the Earth"

Mrs. Abigail Adams, in a letter to her sister from Paris, writes of her acquaintance with Thomas Jefferson,

We see as much company in a formal way as our revenues will admit and Mr. Jefferson, with one or two Americans, visits us in the social, friendly way. I shall really regret to leave Mr. Jefferson; he is one of the choice ones of the earth. On Thursday, I dine with him at his house. On Sunday he is to dine here. On Monday, we all dine with the Marquis (de Lafayette.)*

She further elaborates to her niece, describing Jefferson's life in Paris,

Well, my dear niece, I have returned from Mr. Jefferson's. When I got there, I found a pretty large company. It consisted of the Marquis and Madame de Lafayette; the Count and Countess de____; a French Count who had been a general in America, but whose name I forget; Commodore Jones; Mr. Jarvis, an American gentleman lately arrived (the same who married Amelia B____)...a Mr. Bowdoin, an American also; I ask the Chevalier de la Luzerne's pardon – I had liked to have forgotten him; Mr. Williams, of course, as he always dines with Mr. Jefferson; and Mr. Short...I think I have mentioned Mr. Short before in some of my letters; he is about the stature of Mr. Tudor; a better figure, but much like him in looks and manners; consequently a favorite of mine...

Minister to France

As Minister to France, and friend to the Marquis de Lafayette, Jefferson's house was a chosen resort for the many distinguished French Officers who had participated in America's Revolutionary War. A philosopher, and author of the celebrated *Notes on the State of Virginia*, his company was sought after by those reputed to be the greatest savants and intellects, gathering in France's cultural capital. When Dr. Franklin returned to America, honored and venerated by the French for his virtues, wit, wisdom and diplomacy, the Premier, le Compte de Vergennes, said to Jefferson, "You replace Dr. Franklin." To which "the Sage of Monticello" responded, "I succeed him, no one could replace him." Jefferson wrote the following of his predecessor in France,

> At these (court gatherings)* he (Benjamin Franklin)* sometimes met with the old Duchess de Bourbon, who being a chess-player of about his force, they very generally played together. Happening once to put her king

*Author's text in parentheses.

into prise, the Doctor took it. "Ah," says she, "we do not take kings so." "We do in America," said Franklin...The Emperor Joseph II, then in Paris incognito under the title of Count Falkenstein, was overlooking the game in silence, while the company was engaged in animated conversation on the American question. "How happens it, Monsieur le Compte," said the Duchess, "that while we all feel so much interest in the cause of the Americans, you say nothing for them"? "I am a king by trade," he said.

Another of Jefferson's writings on the venerable Dr. Franklin merits inclusion here:

> The Dr. told me at Paris the following anecdote of the Abbé Raynal. He had a party to dine with him one day at Passy, of whom one half were Americans, the other half French, and among the last was the Abbé. During the dinner, he (the Abbé) got on his favorite theory of the degeneracy of animals and even of man in America, and urged it with his usual eloquence. The Dr. (Franklin)* at length noticing the accidental stature and position of guests at table said, "Come, Monsieur l'Abbé, let us try this question by the fact before us. We are here, one half Americans and one half French, and it happens that the Americans have placed themselves on one side of the table, and our French friends are on the other. Let both parties rise, and we will see on which side nature has degenerated." It happened that his American guests were Carmichael, Harmer, Humphreys and others of the finest stature and form; while those of the other side were remarkably diminutive, and the Abbé himself, particularly a mere shrimp. He parried the appeal, however, by a complimentary admission of exceptions, among which the Dr. himself was a conspicuous one.[3]

The friendship that was formed between Thomas Jefferson and John Adams in France weathered all political differences in later years, a voluminous correspondence reflecting their mutual respect and esteem, until the day on which they both died – July 4th, 1826 – the jubilee of the signing of the *Declaration of Independence*.

Bereaved of His Daughter, Lucy

Shortly after his arrival in Paris, Jefferson received a letter from his sister-in-law, with the devastating news of his daughter, Lucy Elizabeth's death. It reads,

Eppington, October 13, 1784.

Dear Sir,

It is impossible to paint the anguish of my heart on this melancholy occasion. A most unfortunate whooping-cough has deprived you and us of two sweet Lucys within a week. Ours was the first that fell a sacrifice. She was thrown into violent convulsions, lingered out a week, and then died. Your dear angel was confined a week to her bed, her sufferings were great, though nothing like a fit; she retained her senses perfectly, called me a few minutes before she died and asked distinctly for water. Dear Polly (Mary)* has had

*Author's text in parentheses.

it most violently, though always kept about, and is now quite recovered... Life is scarcely supportable under such severe afflictions. Be so good as to remember me most affectionately to my dear Patsy (Martha),* and beg she will excuse my not writing till the gloomy scene is a little forgotten. I sincerely hope you are both partaking of everything that can in the smallest degree entertain and make you happy. Our warmest affections attend you both.

Your sincere friend,
E. Eppes

It was hence that Jefferson was most anxious to have his daughter Mary (Polly) conveyed to him in France, as we shall see from the following correspondence –

Thomas Jefferson's Love letter to his Daughter, Polly

Paris, September 20th, 1785

My dear Polly,

I have not received a letter from you since I came to France. If you knew how much I loved you and what pleasure the receipt of your letters gave me at Philadelphia, you would have written to me, or at least have told your Aunt what to write, and her goodness would have induced her to take the trouble of writing it. I wish so much to see you, that I have desired your Uncle and Aunt to send you to me. I know, my dear Polly, how sorry you will be, and ought to be, to leave them and your cousins, but your sister and myself cannot live without you, and after a while, we will carry you back to Virginia. In the meantime you shall be taught here to play on the harpsichord, to draw, to dance, to read and talk French, and such other things as will make you more worthy of the love of your friends; but above all things, by our care and love of you, we will teach you to love us more than you will do if you stay so far from us. I have had no opportunity since Colonel de Maire went, to send you anything; but when you come here you shall have as many dolls and play things as you want for yourself, or to send to your cousins whenever you shall have opportunities. I hope you are a very good girl, that you love your Uncle and Aunt very much, and are very thankful to them for all their goodness to you; that you never suffer yourself to be angry with anybody, and that you give your play things to them who want them, that you do whatever anybody desires of you that is right, that you never tell stories, never beg for anything, mind your books and your work when your Aunt tells you, never play but when she permits you, nor go where she forbids you; remember, too, as a constant charge, not to go out without your bonnet, because it will make you very ugly, and then we shall not love you so much. If you always practice these lessons we shall continue to love you as we do now, and it is impossible to love you any more. We shall hope to have you with us next summer, to find you a very good girl, and to assure you of the truth of our affection for you. Adieu, my dear child,

Yours affectionately
TH: Jefferson

*Author's text in parenthesis.

Polly (Mary) Jefferson was the image of her mother, in beauty, graciousness, well-bred manners and loveliness. The father longed to enfold his beloved daughter in his arms, and have his two only daughters near him in Paris, at the Convent of Panthemont.

Polly Jefferson Refuses to go to Paris

However, seven-year-old Polly was not so easily persuaded by her father's negotiations and promises to her, as her letters show,

> Dear Papa,
>
> I long to see you, and hope that you and sister Patsy are well; give my love to her and tell her that I long to see her, and hope that you and she will come very soon to see us. I hope that you will send me a doll. I am very sorry that you have sent for me. I don't want to go to France. I had rather stay with Aunt Eppes. Aunt Carr, Aunt Nancy and cousin Polly Carr are here.
>
> Your most happy and dutiful daughter,
>
> Polly Jefferson [4]

and again,

> Dear Papa,
>
> I should be very happy to see you, but I cannot go to France, and hope that you and sister Patsy are well.
>
> Your affectionate daughter, adieu,
> Polly Jefferson [5]

and still again,

> Dear Papa,
>
> I want to see you and sister Patsy, but you must come to Uncle Eppes' house.
>
> Polly Jefferson [6]

Jefferson's Instructions on Polly's voyage to France

Thomas Jefferson's pleas and assurances to Polly, however, were accompanied by numerous letters to his sister-in-law, Mrs. Eppes, and her husband, instructing them on how to convey his daughter safely to him in Paris.

On August 30th, 1785, he writes to Mr. Eppes, recommending Polly's conveyance across the Atlantic, in the custody of "some good lady passing from America to

France, or even England, would be most eligible…a careful Negro woman, such as Isabel, for instance, if she has had the small-pox, would suffice…"

He adds that "my anxieties on this subject could induce me to endless details…" and that, "my dear Poll hangs on my mind night and day:"

August 30th 1785

Dear Sir,

I must now repeat my wish to have Polly sent to me next summer. This, however, must depend on the circumstance of a good vessel sailing from Virginia in the months of April, May, June or July. I would not have her set out sooner or later on account of the equinoxes. The vessel should have performed one voyage at least, but not be more than four or five years old. We do not attend to this circumstance till we have been to sea, but there the consequence of it is felt. I think it would be found that all the vessels which are lost are either on the first voyage or after they are five years old; at least there are a few exceptions to this. With respect to the person to whose care she should be trusted, I must leave it to yourself and Mrs. Eppes altogether. Some good lady passing from America to France, or even England, would be most eligible, but a careful gentleman who would be so kind as to superintend her would do. In this case some woman who has had the small-pox must attend her. A careful Negro woman, such as Isabel, for instance, if she has had the small-pox, would suffice under the patronage of a gentleman. The woman need not come farther than Havre, l'Orient, Nantes, or whatever port she should land at, because I could go there for the child myself, and the person could return to Virginia directly. My anxieties on this subject could induce me to endless details, but your discretion and that of Mrs. Eppes saves me the necessity. I will only add that I would rather live a year longer without her than have her trusted to any but a good ship and summer passage. Patsy is well. She speaks French as easily as English; while Humphreys, Short and myself are scarcely better at it than when we landed…

I look with impatience to the moment when I may rejoin you. There is nothing to tempt me to stay here. Present me with the most cordial affection to Mrs. Eppes, the children, and the family at Hors-du-monde. I commit to Mrs. Eppes my kisses for dear Poll, who hangs on my mind night and day.

TH: Jefferson

Jefferson's Anxiety – "I drop my Pen at the Thought"

Three weeks later, Jefferson writes to his sister-in-law, urging his daughter Mary's departure to France, expressing his anxiety at the thought "that such a child, so dear to me, is to cross the ocean, is to be exposed to all the sufferings and risks…I drop my pen at the thought – but she must come…"

Paris, September 22, 1785

Dear Madam,

The Fitzhughs having stayed here longer than they expected, I have (since writing my letter of August 30, to Mr. Eppes) received one from Dr. Currrie of August 5, by which I have the happiness to learn you are all well, and my Poll also. Every information of this kind is like gaining another step, and seems to say, we "have got so far safe." Would to God the great step was taken and taken safely. I mean that which is to place her on this side of the Atlantic. No event of your life has put it into your power to conceive how I feel when I reflect that such a child, and so dear to me, is to cross the ocean, is to be exposed to all the sufferings and risks, great and small, to which a situation on board a ship exposes everyone. I drop my pen at the thought – but she must come. My affections would leave me balanced between the desire to have her with me, and the fear of exposing her; but my reason tells me the dangers are not great, and the advantages to her will be considerable.

I send by Mr. Fitzhugh some garden and flower seed and bulbs; the latter, I know, will fall in your department. I wish the opportunity had admitted the sending more, as well as some things for the children; but Mr. Fitzhugh being to pass a long road both here and in America, I could not ask it of him. Pray write to me, and write me long letters. Currie has sent me one worth a great deal for the details of small news it contains. I mention this as an example for you. You always know facts enough which would be interesting to me to fill sheets of paper. I pray you then to give yourself up to that kind of inspiration, and to scribble on as long as you recollect anything unmentioned, without regarding whether your lines are straight or your letters even. Remember me affectionately to Mr. Skipwith and the little ones of both houses; kiss dear Polly for me, and encourage her for the journey.

Accept assurances of unchangeable affection from, dear Madam,

Your sincere friend and servant,
TH: Jefferson

Jefferson Repeats his Prayer for Polly

On January 7th, 1786, he writes again to his sister-in-law, "to repeat a prayer I urged, that you would confide my daughter only to a French or English vessel having a Mediterranean pass,"

I wrote you last on the 11th December, by way of London, that conveyance being uncertain, I write the present, chiefly to repeat a prayer I urged in that, that you would confide my daughter only to a French or English vessel having a Mediterranean pass. This attention, though of little consequence in matters of merchandise, is of weight in the mind of a parent which sees even possibilities of capture beyond the reach of any estimate. If a peace be concluded with the Algerians in the meantime, you shall be among the first to hear it from myself. I pray you to believe it from nobody else, as far as respects the conveyance of my daughter to me.

He reiterates his gratitude to Mrs. Eppes and the anxiety of being separated from his daughter, Polly, in another letter written a few weeks later to her husband:

> I know that Mrs. Eppes' goodness will make her feel a separation from an infant who has experienced so much of her tenderness. My unlimited confidence in her has been the greatest solace possible under my own separation from Polly. Mrs. Eppes' good sense will suggest to her many considerations which render it of importance to the future happiness of the child that she should neither forget nor be forgotten by her sister and myself.

His Concern for Polly's Happiness

On December 14th, 1786, Jefferson again writes to his wife's sister that, "though I am distressed when I think of this voyage, yet I know it is necessary for her happiness:"

> Paris, December 14th, 1786
>
> Dear Madam,
>
> I perceive indeed, that our friends are kinder than we have sometimes supposed them, and that their letters do not come to hand. I am happy that yours of July 30th has not shared the common fate. I received it about a week ago, together with one from Mr. Eppes announcing to me that my dear Polly will come to me the ensuing summer. Though I am distressed when I think of this voyage, yet I know it is necessary for her happiness. She is better with you, my dear Madam, than she could be anywhere else in the world, except with those whom nature has allied still more closely to her. It would be unfortunate through life, both to her and us, were those affections to be loosened which ought to bind us together, and which should be the principal source of our future happiness. Yet this would be too probably the effect of absence at her age. This is the only circumstance which has induced me to press her joining us...
>
> Yours affectionately,
> TH: Jefferson

A Father's Love for his Daughter, Martha

While awaiting Polly's arrival, Jefferson's letters of loving advise, guidance and instruction flowed from his heart to his beloved daughter, Martha. Following is one dated March 6, 1786:

> To Martha Jefferson:
>
> I need not tell you what pleasure it gives me to see you improve in every useful thing and agreeable. The more you learn the more I love you; and I rest the happiness of my life on seeing you beloved by all the world, which you will be sure to be, if to a good heart you join those accomplishments so peculiarly pleasing in your sex. Adieu, my dear child; lose no moment

in improving your head, nor any opportunity of exercising your heart in benevolence.

TH: Jefferson

In another letter, this time from Aix-en-Provence, dated March 28th, 1787, Jefferson advises his daughter that "nothing could contribute more to my interest in your future happiness, (moral rectitude always excepted), than your contracting a habit of industry and activity." Jefferson's superintendence of his daughter's curriculum and education resulted in her being honored in adulthood as, "the noblest woman in Virginia:"

Thomas Jefferson to Martha Jefferson, March 28, 1787

Aix-en-Provence, March 28th, 1787

I was happy, my dear Patsy, to receive, on my arrival here, your letter, informing me of your good health and occupation. I have not written to you sooner because I have been almost constantly on the road. My journey hitherto has been a very pleasing one. It was undertaken with the hope that the mineral waters of this place might restore strength to my wrist…It is your future happiness which interests me, and nothing can contribute more to it (moral rectitude always excepted) than the contracting a habit of industry and activity. Of all the cankers of human happiness, none corrodes with so silent, yet so baneful an influence as indolence. Body and mind both unemployed, our being becomes a burden, and every object about us loathsome, even the dearest. Idleness begets ennui,* ennui the hypochondriac, and that a diseased body. No laborious person was ever yet hysterical. Exercise and application produce order in our affairs, health of body and cheerfulness of mind, and these make us precious to our friends. It is while we are young that the habit of industry is formed. If not then, it never is afterwards. The fortune of our lives, therefore, depends on employing well the short period of youth. If at any moment, my dear, you catch yourself in idleness, start from it as you would from the precipice of a gulf. You are not, however, to consider yourself as unemployed while taking exercise. That is necessary for your health, and health is the first of all object. For this reason, if you leave your dancing master for the summer, you must increase your other exercise.

I do not like your saying that you are unable to read the ancient print of your *Livy* but with the aid of your master. We are always equal to what we undertake with resolution. A little degree of this will enable you to decipher your *Livy*. If you always lean on your master, you will never be able to proceed without him. It is a part of the American character to consider nothing as desperate; to surmount every difficulty by resolution and contrivance. In Europe there are shops for every want; its inhabitants, therefore, have no idea that their wants can be supplied otherwise. Remote from all other aid, we are obliged to invent and execute; to find means within ourselves, and not to lean on others. Consider, therefore, your conquering your *Livy* as an exercise in the habit of surmounting difficulties; a habit which will be necessary to you in the

*boredom

country where you are to live, and without which you will be thought a very helpless person, and less esteemed.

Music, drawing, books, invention, and exercise, will be so many resources to you against ennui. But there are others which, to this object, add that of utility. These are the needle and domestic economy. The latter you cannot learn here, but the former you may. In the country life in America there are many moments when a woman can have recourse to nothing but her needle for employment. In a dull company, and in dull weather, for instance, it is ill-manners to leave them; no card-playing there among genteel people – that is abandoned to blackguards.* The needle is then a valuable resource.

You ask me to write you long letters. I will do it, my dear, on condition you will read them from time to time, and practice what they inculcate. Their precepts will be dictated by experience, by a perfect knowledge of the situation in which you will be placed, and by the fondest love for you. This it is which makes me wish to see you more qualified than common. My expectations from you are high, yet not higher than you may attain. Industry and resolution are all that are wanting. Nobody in this world can make me so happy, or so miserable, as you. Retirement from public life will ere long become necessary for me. To your sister and yourself, I look to render the evening of my life serene and contented. Its morning has been clouded by loss after loss, till I have nothing left but you. I do not doubt your affections or dispositions. But great exertions are necessary, and you have little time left to make them. Be industrious, then, my dear child. Think nothing insurmountable by resolution and application, and you will be all that I wish you to be.

You ask if it is my desire that you should dine at the Abbess's table? It is. Propose it as such to Madame de Frauleinheim, with my respectful compliments, and thanks for her care of you. Continue to love me with all the warmth with which you are beloved by, my dear Patsy,

Yours affectionately,
TH: Jefferson

Martha's affectionate and obedient response to her father included the news of her sister's departure for France the following month:

Martha Jefferson to her Father – April 9, 1787

Convent of Panthemont.
April 9th, 1787

My dear Papa,

I am very glad that the beginning of your voyage has been so pleasing, and I hope that the rest will not be less so, as it is a great consolation for me, being deprived of the pleasure of seeing you, to know at least that you are happy. I hope your resolution of returning in the end of April is always the same. I do not doubt but what Mr. Short has written you word that my

---

*blackguard: n. one who uses scurrilous language; a scoundrel; a villain. *Webster's Dictionary.*

sister sets off with Fulwar Skipworth in the month of May, and she will be here in July. Then, indeed, shall I be the happiest of mortals; united to what I have the dearest in the world, nothing more will be requisite to render my happiness complete. I am not so industrious as you or I would wish, but I hope that in taking pains, I very soon shall be. I have already begun to study more. I have not heard any news of my harpsichord; it will be really very disagreeable if it is not here before your arrival. I am learning a very pretty thing now, but it is very hard. I have drawn several little flowers, all alone, that the master even has not seen; indeed he advised me to draw as much alone as possible, for that is of more use than all I could do with him. I shall take up my *Livy* as you desire it. I shall begin it again, as I have lost the thread of the history. As for the hysterics, you may be quiet on that head, as I am not lazy enough to fear them. Mrs. Barett has wanted me out, but Mr. Short told her that you had forgotten to tell Madame l'Abbess to let me go out with her.

There was a gentleman a few days ago that killed himself because he thought that his wife did not love him. They had been married ten years. I believe that if every husband in Paris was to do as much, there would be nothing but widows left. I shall speak to Madame Thaubeneu about dining at the Abbess's table.

As for needlework, the only kind that I could learn here would be embroidery, indeed netting also; but I could not do much of those in America, because of the impossibility of having proper silks; however, they will not be totally useless. You say your expectations of me are high, yet not higher than I can attain. Then be assured, my dear Papa, that you shall be satisfied in that, as well as in any other thing that is in my power; for what I hold most precious is your satisfaction, indeed I should be miserable without it. You wrote me a long letter, as I asked you; however, it would have been much more so without so wide a margin.

Adieu, my dear Papa. Be assured of the tenderest affection of your loving daughter,

Martha Jefferson

Pray answer me very soon – a long letter, without a margin. I will try to follow the advice they contain with the most scrupulous exactitude.

A beautiful Father-daughter Relationship

The correspondence between Jefferson and his daughter, Martha, reflects a beautiful father-daughter relationship, filled with mutual love, respect and attachment. In the following letter, dated May 3rd, 1787, she urges his speedy return for her sister's arrival,

Panthemont
May 3rd, 1787

My dear Papa,

I was very sorry to see, by your letter to Mr. Short, that your return would be put off. However, I hope not much, as you must be here for the arrival of my sister. I wish I was myself all that you tell me to make her; however, I will try to be as near like it as I can...

A Virginia ship coming to Spain met with a corsair of the same strength. They fought, and the battle lasted an hour and a quarter. The Americans gained and boarded the corsair, where they found chains that had been prepared for them. They took them, and made use of them for the Algerians themselves. They returned to Virginia, from whence they are to go back to Algiers to change the prisoners, to which, if the Algerians will not consent, the poor creatures will be sold as slaves. Good God! Have we not enough? **I wish with all my soul that the poor Negroes were all freed...**

Adieu, my dear Papa, and believe me to be for life your most tender and affectionate child,

Martha Jefferson

Jefferson – the Naturalist

As we have seen from the foregoing, Jefferson's letters of instruction, encouragement and fatherly love to his daughter, Martha, were numerous, such as the following one, reflecting his appreciation for nature, and imparting his feelings of "inexpressible comfort to have you both with me once more:"

May 21st, 1787

I write to you, my dear Patsy, from the Canal of Languedoc, on which I am at present sailing, as I have been for a week past, cloudless skies above, limpid waters below, and on each hand, a row of nightingales in full chorus...

As you have trees in the garden of the Convent, there might be nightingales in them, and this is the season of their song. Endeavor, my dear, to make yourself acquainted with the music of this bird, that when you return to your own country, you may be able to estimate its merit in comparison with that of the mocking-bird. The latter has the advantage of singing through a great part of the year, whereas the nightingale sings but about five or six weeks in the Spring, and a still shorter term, and with a more feeble voice in the fall.

I expect to be at Paris about the middle of next month. By that time we may begin to expect our dear Polly. It will be a circumstance of inexpressible comfort to me to have you both with me once more. The object most interesting to me for the residue of my life, will be to see you both developing daily those principles of virtue and goodness which will make you valuable to others and happy in yourselves, and acquiring those talents and that degree of science which will guard you at all times against ennui, the most dangerous poison of life. A mind always employed is always happy.

This is the true secret, and the grand recipé, for felicity. The idle are only wretched…

Be good and be industrious, and you will be what I shall most love in the world. Adieu, my dear child,

Yours affectionately,
TH: Jefferson

Anxiety in Virginia over Polly's Departure

In March, 1787, Polly's aunt writes these anxious lines to her brother-in-law, stating that every stratagem used to persuade his daughter to visit her father has failed:

I never was more anxious to hear from you than at present, in hopes of your countermanding your orders with regard to dear Polly. We have made use of every stratagem to prevail on her to consent to visit you without effect. She is more averse to it than I could have supposed. Either of my children would with pleasure take her place for the number of good things she is promised. However, Mr. Eppes has two or three different prospects of conveying her, to your satisfaction, I hope, if we do not hear from you.

Polly Jefferson leaves for France

The day before Polly's departure for France, her aunt pens these stressful words,

This will, I hope, be handed you by my dear Polly, who I most ardently wish may reach you in the health she is in at present. I shall be truly wretched till I hear of her being safely landed with you. The children will spend a day or two on board the ship with her, which I hope will reconcile her to it. For God's sake, give us the earliest intelligence of her arrival.

Jefferson's beautiful little daughter played with her cousins on board ship for a few days, acclimatizing herself with her new surroundings, and at a time when she slept, they disembarked. When Polly awoke, the ship was well at sea, on route to France – and into the arms of her devoted, anxious father.

Her Arrival in London

On July 2nd, 1787, Thomas Jefferson conveys to Francis Eppes the assuring news of his daughter Polly's arrival in London in the custody of Captain Ramsay,

Paris, July 2nd, 1787

Dear Sir,

The present is merely to inform you of the safe arrival of Polly in London, in good health. I have this moment dispatched a servant for her. Mr. Ammonit did not come, but she was in the best hands possible, those of Captain Ramsay.

Mrs. Adams (Abigail Adams)* writes me she was so much attached to him that her separation from him was a terrible operation. She has now to go through the same with Mrs. Adams. I hope that in ten days she will join those from whom she is no more to be separated. As this is to pass through post offices, I send it merely to relieve the anxieties which Mrs. Eppes and yourself are so good as to feel on your account, reserving myself to answer both your favors by the next packet.

I am, with very sincere esteem, dear Sir, your affectionate friend and servant,

TH: Jefferson.

Polly Arrives in Paris – A Reunion of "Great Joy"

On July 28th, 1787, Jefferson writes to his sister-in-law that Polly's arrival has given her sister and himself "great joy:"

Dear Madam,

Your favors of March 31st and May 7th have been duly received; the last by Polly, whose arrival has given us great joy. Her disposition to attach herself to those who are kind to her had occasioned successive distresses on parting with Captain Ramsay first, and afterwards with Mrs. Adams. She had a very fine passage, without a storm, and was perfectly taken care of by Captain Ramsay. He offered to come to Paris with her, but this was unnecessary. I sent a trusty servant to London to attend her here.

A parent may be permitted to speak of his own child when it involves an act of justice to another. The attentions which your goodness has induced you to pay her prove themselves by the fruits of them. Her reading, her writing, her manners in general, show what everlasting obligations we are all under to you. She will surely not be the least happy among us when the day shall come in which we may all be reunited. She is now established in the convent, perfectly happy…

She became a universal favorite with the young ladies and the mistresses. She writes you a long letter, giving you an account of her voyage and journey here. She neither knew us, nor should we have known her had we met with her unexpectedly. Patsy enjoys good health, and will write to you. She has grown much the last year or two and will be very tall. She retains all her anxiety to get back to her country and her friends, particularly yourself. Her dispositions give me perfect satisfaction, and her progress is well; she will need, however, your instruction to render her useful to her own country. Of domestic economy, she can learn nothing here, yet, she must learn it somewhere, as being of more solid value than anything else…

Polly was called at the Convent of Panthemont, Mademoiselle *Polie*; shortly thereafter, *Marie*, and upon their return to America, it became the Virginian pronunciation, *Maria* instead of Mary.

---

*Author's text in parenthesis.

A Year Later - July 12th, 1788

A year later, on July 12th, 1788, Jefferson writes to his sister-in-law, Mrs. Eppes, informing her that he and his two daughters "pass one day in every week together, and talk of nothing but Eppington, Hors-du-Monde and Monticello,"

Dear Madam,

Your kind favor of January 6th has come duly to hand...I would write to Mrs. Skipwith* but I could only repeat to her what I say to you, that we love you both sincerely, and pass one day in every week together, and talk of nothing but Eppington, Hors-du-Monde and Monticello, and were we to pass the whole seven, the theme would still be the same.

God bless you both, Madam, your husbands, your children, and everything near and dear to you, and be assured of the constant affection of your sincere friend and humble servant,

TH. Jefferson

---

*Jefferson's sister-in-law.

Chapter XIII

Jefferson's departure from France, September 26, 1789 – His Arrival at Monticello, December 23, 1789 – "Mr. Jefferson's Servants, ebullitions of Joy at his Return" – Slavery in British America – Rev. Dr. Samuel Davies, Founder of the 1740's Great Awakening in Virginia – Rev. Davies' Educational Efforts taught Slaves and White Indentured Servants to read the Bible – The Dangerous "African Trade for Slaves".

Jefferson's Departure from France – September 26, 1789

Thomas Jefferson, his daughters Martha and Mary, and his American legation staff departed from France on September 26th, 1789. Martha Jefferson leaves the following recorded account of their return voyage to America:

> In returning, he was detained ten days at Havre de Grace, and after crossing the Channel, ten more at Cowes, in the Isle of Wight, which were spent in visiting different parts of the island, when the weather permitted, among others, Carisbrook Castle, remarkable for the confinement of Charles the First, and also for a well of uncommon depth.
>
> We sailed on the 23rd October, 1789, in company of upwards of thirty vessels which had collected there and been detained as we were by contrary winds. Colonel Trumbull, who chartered the ship for my father in London, applied to Mr. Pitt to give orders to prevent his baggage from being searched on his arrival, informing Mr. Pitt at the same time that the application had been made without his knowledge. The orders to such an effect were accordingly issued, I presume, as he was spared the usual vexation of such a search.
>
> The voyage was quick and not unpleasant. When we arrived on the coast, there was so thick a mist as to render it impossible to see a pilot, had any of them been out. After beating about three days, the captain, a bold as well as an experienced seaman, determined to run in at a venture, without having seen the Capes. The ship came near to running upon what was conjectured to be the middle ground, when anchor was cast at 10 o'clock P.M. The wind rose, and the vessel drifted down, dragging her anchor, one or more miles. But she had got within the Capes, while a number which had been less bold were blown off the coast, some of them lost, and all kept out three or four weeks longer. We had to beat up against a strong head-wind, which carried away our topsails; and we were very near being run down by a brig coming out of port, which, having the wind in her favor, was almost upon us before we could get out of the way. We escaped, however, with only a part of our rigging.
>
> My father had been so anxious about his public accounts, that he would not trust them to go until he went with them. We arrived at Norfolk in the forenoon, and in two hours after landing, before an article of our baggage was brought ashore, the vessel took fire and seemed on the point of being reduced to a mere hull. They were in the act of scuttling her, when some abatement in the flames was discovered, and she was finally saved. So great had been the activity of her crew, and of those belonging to other ships in the harbor which came to their aid, that everything in her was saved. Our trunks, and perhaps also the papers, had been put in our staterooms, and the doors

incidentally closed by the Captain. They were so close that the flames did not penetrate; but the powder in a musket in one of them was silently consumed, and the thickness of the travelling-trunks alone saved their contents from the excessive heat. I understood at the time that the state-rooms alone, of all the internal partitions, escaped burning.[1]

His Arrival at Monticello – December 23, 1789

Norfolk had not recovered from the effects of the war, and we should have found it difficult to obtain rooms but for the politeness of the gentlemen at the hotel (Lindsay's) who were kind enough to give up their own rooms for our accommodation. There were no stages in those days. We were indebted to the kindness of our friends for horses; and visiting all on the way homeward, and spending more or less time with them all in turn, we reached Monticello on the 23rd of December.[2]

"Mr. Jefferson's Servants – ebullitions of Joy at his Return"

Martha Jefferson's historic account continues,

The Negroes discovered the approach of the carriage as soon as it reached Shadwell* and such a scene I never witnessed in my life. They collected in crowds around it, and almost drew it up the mountain by hand. The shouting, etc. had been sufficiently obstreperous before, but the moment it arrived at the top it reached the climax.

When the door of the carriage was opened, they received him (Thomas Jefferson)** in their arms and bore him to the house, crowding around and kissing his hands and feet – some blubbering and crying – others laughing. It seemed impossible to satisfy their anxiety to touch the very earth which bore him. These were the first ebullitions of joy for his return, after a long absence, which they would of course feel; but perhaps it is not out of place here to add that they were at all times very devoted in their attachment to him.[3]

Prior to his departure from Paris, Jefferson had written to his overseer apprising him of his return to Monticello. The servants, overcome with joy, requested a holiday on the day of his arrival, which was naturally granted. All his servants from various farms gathered together for his home-coming – the elderly, men, women and children, all eagerly waiting to welcome him back. Their anticipation and excitement was so great, that they descended the mountain as far as Shadwell, un-hitching the horses, and drawing the carriage with strong arms up to the front entrance of Monticello:

The appearance of the young ladies, before whom they fell back and left the way clear for them to reach the house, filled them with admiration. They had left them when scarcely more than children, and now returned – Martha, a tall and stately-looking girl of seventeen years, and little Maria, now in her eleventh year, more beautiful and, if possible, more lovable

---

* Shadwell is four miles from Monticello.
** Author's text in parenthesis.

than when, two years before, her beauty and loveliness had warmed into enthusiasm the reserved, but kind-hearted Mrs. Adams. The father and his two daughters were then at last once more domiciled within the walls of their loved Monticello. How grateful it would have been for Jefferson never again to have been called away from home to occupy a public post…[4]

The foregoing recorded account of the esteem, admiration and attachment which Jefferson's servants demonstrated for their master, reinforces both Isaac's and his overseer, Edmund Bacon's eye-witness testimonies – dispelling the 21st century media's calumny of Thomas Jefferson being a "slave driver."

Slavery in British America

Furthermore, slavery in America was initiated in 1619 by the British, whose entire world empire was infected with this evil – only to be abolished in Britain and her colonies by the decree of King William IV, a Protestant king, in 1833.

In addition, slavery in America was not confined to her founding fathers, who have been vehemently attacked and vilified due to this practice in British America, but who attempted over and over again to eradicate it by legislative declarations, addresses, and even prohibitions – thwarted consistently by the Crown of England.

Rev. Dr. Samuel Davies, Founder of the 1740's Great Awakening in Virginia

Slavery in British America was prevalent among the middle-class population, as proven and articulated by Reverend Dr. Samuel Davies' January 8, 1757 sermon to his primarily middle-class congregation, entitled: *The Duty of Christians to Propagate their Religion among Heathen, earnestly recommended to the masters of Negro Slaves in Virginia*. It is hereunder reprinted:

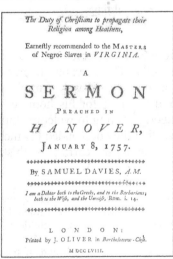

Title page of Rev. Samuel Davies' January 8, 1757 Sermon. Library of Congress, Rare Book Collection, Washington, D.C..

TROISIEME ET QUATRIÈME ANNÉE
DU REGNE DE SA MAJESTÉ
WILLIAM IV, ROI,

CHAP. LXXIII

Acte pour abolir l'esclavage dans toutes les colonies Britannniques, pour développer l'industrie des Esclaves libérés, et pour indemniser les personnes ayant droit jusqu'ici au service de ces mêmes Esclaves.

(28 Août 1833.)

Translation: Third and Fourth Year of the reign of His Majesty William IV, King. Act to abolish slavery in all the British colonies, to develop industry for the freed slaves, and to indemnify persons having the right up to the present time to the service of these slaves.

(August 28, 1833.)

King William IV's Act to abolish Slavery in all the British Colonies, August 28, 1833.

The Duty of Christians to Propagate their Religion Among Heathens Earnestly recommended to the Masters of Negro Slaves in VIRGINIA.

A
SERMON
Preached in
HANOVER,
January 8, 1757.

By SAMUEL DAVIES, *A.M.*

I am a Debtor both to the Greeks, and to the Barbarians; both to the Wise, and the Unwise. Romans 1:14.

LONDON:
Printed by J. OLIVER in Bartholomew-Close.
MDCCLVIII.

GENESIS XVIII. 19

"For I know him, that he will command his children and his household after him, and they shall keep the Way of the LORD, to do Justice and Judgment."

A creature formed for immortality, and that must be happy or miserable through an *everlasting* duration, is certainly a Being of vast importance, however mean and insignificant he may be in other respects. His immortality gives him a kind of *infinite* value. Let him be white or black, bond or free, a native or foreigner, it is of no moment in this view: he is to live *forever!* to be forever *happy,* or forever *miserable!* Happy or miserable in the *highest degree!* This places him upon a kind of equality with **Kings and Princes;** nay, with **Angels and Archangels**: for it is this that adds importance and dignity to the most exalted parts of the human, and even of the angelic nature.

In this view, the crowds of neglected Negro Slaves among us, have often appeared to me as creatures of the utmost importance. The *same* immortality is entailed upon them, as upon us. They are candidates for the *same* eternal state with us, and bound for the *same* Heaven or Hell. How awful and important a Trust, then, is *the care of a soul!* The soul even of a poor Negro Slave! To be entrusted with the care of forming and educating an *Immortal* for his everlasting state! To be instrumental in preparing him for eternal Joys, or eternal Torments! To be accountable for our management in this trust, to the supreme Judge of the Universe, with whom there is no respect of persons! To be rewarded for our faithfulness; or punished for our negligence, as having promoted the happiness or been accessory to the ruin of an immortal soul! – Pause, and think of these things, and they will certainly appear very solemn and weighty.

This solemn and important trust, I must tell you, brethren, is committed, not only to parents, with regard to their children, those dear other selves; but to *Masters*, with regard to their Servants and Slaves, of whatever country or colour they are. And as this duty is most scandalously neglected in this Christian country; and the neglect is likely to be followed with the most dangerous and ruinous consequences to thousands, both Masters and Slaves; permit me to address you upon this Head, with the utmost plainness and solemnity. You are my witnesses, that I have looked upon the poor Negroes as a part of my ministerial charge; and used various endeavours to bring them to the faith and practice of Christianity, not without promising appearances of success, in sundry instances. It affords me no small pleasure to reflect, and I mention it with gratitude to God and man, that my endeavours of this kind have, of late, met with no opposition from the Masters, of whatever denomination, in any one instance that I can recollect. And it affords me a still greater pleasure to reflect, that sundry of you not only consent that your Negroes should receive instructions from me, but also zealously concur with me, and make conscience of your own duty to them, in this respect. But alas! Are there not some among you, and are there not thousands in our country, who must be conscious of their willful negligence; nay, who, perhaps, are rather instrumental in hardening their Slaves in sin, and confirming their prejudices against our holy Religion, than in promoting their conversion to God? Were your Negroes but so many *Brutes*, you might treat them as you do your horses, fodder them, and make them work for you, without once endeavouring to make them sharers with you in the glorious privileges of Religion, the distinguishing prerogative of Human Nature. But I hope you have Divinity and Philosophy enough to know, this is not the case, Let me therefore plainly lay your duty before you, with regard to them, in order to engage you to the practice of it. For sure, you are not hardy enough to neglect the practice, in spite of conviction. Sure, you dare not sin on still, and continue your career to ruin with your eyes open.

Abraham is often proposed as a pattern to Believers in general; and I may particularly recommend his example to your imitation, in your conduct towards your domestics. Here you have his character drawn by the All-knowing God Himself: "I know him, that he will command his children, and his household after him, and they shall keep the Way of the Lord." He not only instructed, advised, persuaded, entreated; but he used his *Authority*; he COMMANDED – not only his children, but his household; which included his Servants, *Slaves*, and all his Domestics of every order. *Abraham's* family was like the generality of ours, in this, that he had hereditary *Slaves* in it, who were his property during life. We repeatedly read of his "Servants *born in his house*, and *bought with money of strangers*:" (Genesis 17:12, 13, 23, 27) both which were probably *Slaves*.

And he had so numerous a family of them, that, when he went upon an expedition to rescue *Lot* from captivity, we are told, "he armed his trained Servants, born in his own house, three hundred and eighteen." (Genesis 14:14). Where, by the by, it is remarkable, and the remark is very pertinent to the present state of our Country, that by instilling good principles into them, and by humane treatment, this numerous crowd of *Slaves* were become so faithful to their Master, that he could safely confide in them, without fear of their deserting him in the engagement, and going over to the enemy, in hopes to recover their liberty. All these, as well as *Ishmael,* and his favourite *Isaac,* he had instructed in the true Religion. He had laid his commands upon them to serve the Lord, not only during his life, but "after him," i.e. after his decease. Though he was mortal, he endeavoured to make Religion immortal in his family. He was solicitous to leave the world with the joyful hope, that his Domestics would retain and observe his pious instructions, when he should be no more their Head.

It is sufficient to recommend this example to our imitation, that it is the example of *faithful Abraham*. But it is still more strongly enforced by the express approbation of God Himself. "The Lord said, shall I hide from Abraham the thing that I do?" No, I may trust him even with my secrets: "For I know him;" I approve of him; I have full proof of him, and therefore may safely trust him; "because (*the original Hebrew may be rendered 'forasmuch as'*) he will command his children and household, and they shall keep the way of the Lord:" being once entered in the way of the Lord by his instructions, they will keep it. "Train up a child in the way in which he should go, and when he is old, he will not depart from it." (Proverbs 22:6).

It is not my present design to consider the general duty of Family-Religion and good Education, though my text is a very proper foundation for it. But I intend only to inculcate ***the particular duty of instructing Slaves in the true Religion,*** and using all proper means to enter them in the Way of the Lord. To give you directions how to perform it, before you are convinced it is your duty, would be useless and preposterous. And therefore,

My first and principal business shall be, *To convince you, that this is really your duty, and that it is a duty of the utmost importance and necessity.*

Here, I take it for granted, you are, at least, professed *Christians* yourselves; i.e. you profess to believe that the Christian Religion is divine, and to embrace it as *your* Religion. Otherwise, instead of persuading you to endeavor to Christianize your Negroes, I would first persuade you to become Christians yourselves. I would then deal with you, as with your Heathen Negroes, and labour to convince you of the Truth and Divinity of the Religion of Jesus, from whose numerous topics of argument, by which so clear and important a truth may be demonstrated. But you are fond of wearing the Christian name; you present your children to be initiated into the Christian church by baptism; you acknowledge the truth of the Scriptures, by complying with the usual ceremony of kissing the Bible in taking an oath; you attend upon the forms of worship in the Christian church, and externally conform to them. These things you do; and these things are certainly a strong profession that you are Christians. And none of you, I presume, will dare to renounce it, rather than admit the conviction that I would now force upon your minds from this consideration.

Therefore, taking this for granted, I need no other principle to convince you of the duty I am now recommending. And I shall reason from the nature and design of Christianity – from the worth and importance of the souls of your poor Slaves – from the happy influence Christianity would have upon them, even for your own interest – from the seal and generosity of others in this affair – and from your relation to them as their Masters.

1. **If you consider the *nature* and *design* of Christianity, you cannot but be convinced of this duty.**

    Christianity, in its own nature, is calculated to be **a *universal Religion*,** and is equally the concern of *all* the sons of men. It proposes *one* God, as the object of *universal* adoration to White and Black, Bond and Free: *one* Lord Jesus Christ, as a *common* Saviour for Britons, Africans, and Americans: *one* Holy Spirit, by whom alone sinners of *all* nations, colours, and characters, can be sanctified: one faith to be embraced, *one* Rule of Morality to be observed, by Masters and Servants, rich and poor*: one* Heaven and *one* Hell, as the last mansions of *all* the millions of mankind; to which they shall be adjudged according to their moral character, and, if they have heard the Gospel, according to their acceptance or non-acceptance of it; and not according to the trifling distinctions of country, colour, liberty or slavery. **Christianity is a Religion for sinners**; for sinners of *all* kindreds, and nations, and languages. They *all* need those instructions, which its heavenly light sheds upon a benighted world. They all need that pardon, which it offers; that Grace, which it communicates; and that Salvation, which it ensures. In short, *all* its doctrines intimately concern them: *all* its precepts are binding upon them: *all* its blessings are needed by them: *all* its promises and threatenings shall be accomplished upon them, according to their characters. And must it not then be the grand concern of *all?* Yes; as there is but one air for Whites and Blacks, Masters and Servants to breathe in; one earth for them to walk upon; so there is but *one common* Christian Religion for them *all*, by which they can please God, and obtain Salvation. To be a sinful creature of the race of Man, under the Gospel, is sufficient alone to render it his greatest concern, and a matter of absolute necessity, to be a Christian. And to be entrusted with the care of such a creature, is alone a sufficient foundation for the duty I am recommending; and strongly binds it upon every one of us, to whom that trust is committed.

And as Christianity is, in its own nature, the common concern of all, and calculated to be the universal Religion of mankind; so it is *designed* by its great Author to be propagated among all. No corner of our world was left out in the Commission, which the gracious Founder of our Religion gave to the teachers of it. "Go ye into *all* the world", says He, "and preach the Gospel to *every* creature"; i.e. to every creature of the human race. (Mark 16:15.) The great God "now commandeth *all* men "*everywhere* to repent." (Acts 17:30.) And when the Apostles went out to discharge their extensive Commission, the Holy Spirit concurred with them, and rendered their labours successful in Asia, Europe and Africa, without distinction. He put no difference between Jews and Gentiles, but purified the hearts of both by the same faith! (Acts 15:9.) The doors of the Church were thrown wide open, for the admission of all, that would come in upon the terms of the Gospel. The **Roman Centurion,** the **Ethiopian Eunuch, Onesimus,** a **run-away Slave,** were as welcome, as the **Jews in Jerusalem.** "All were one in Christ Jesus; in whom there is neither Greek nor Jew, Barbarian, Scythian, Bond or Free." (Colossians 3:11.) A black skin, African birth or extract, or a state of Slavery, does not disqualify a man for the blessings of the Gospel; does not exclude him from its invitations, nor cast him out of the charge of its ministers. If history may be credited, the Gospel did once flourish in Africa, and penetrated far into those inhospitable deserts, which are now the regions of Mahometism, or Heathen idolatry.

And we have all the certainty which the **sure Word of Prophecy** can afford, that it will yet visit that miserable country. Yes, brethren, "the earth shall be full of the knowledge of the Lord, as the waters cover the sea." (Isaiah 11:9.) The kingdoms of this world shall yet become the kingdoms of our Lord, and of His Christ." (Revelation 11:15.) And "from the rising of the sun unto the going down of the same, his Name shall be great among the Gentiles; and in *every* place incense shall be offered to his Name. (Malachi 1:11.) "Ethiopia," Guinea and Negro-land "shall yet stretch out their hands unto God." (Psalm 68:31.) Negroes and Slaves are included in that **"Fullness of the Gentiles,"** which, Paul tells us, "shall come in." (Romans 11:25.) And may the happy few, who in this land of their bondage, have been made partakers of "the glorious liberty of the sons of God," be the first-fruits of this blessed harvest to Christ in Africa!

And now, brethren, do you not begin to feel this argument conclude? Is Christianity adapted and intended to be the *universal* Religion of mankind?

And must it not then be the duty of Christians, to do their utmost to spread it through the world? Is it the design of Heaven, that it shall be propagated among all nations? And is it not the duty of Christians, especially of Masters, who have a command over others, to concur in this gracious design, and do all in their power to hasten that blessed period, which has been so long the eager wish and hope of Believers? The man that can be inactive and indifferent in such an affair as this, must have a temper directly contrary to that Religion which he professes; must be entirely careless about the glory of God and the Redeemer, and the happiness of his fellow-creatures, and disaffected to the gracious designs of Providence towards them. Has he imbibed the spirit of the Christian Religion, who can keep, perhaps, half a score of Heathens under his roof, and oblige them to drudge and toil for him all their lives; and yet never labours to gain them to the faith of Christ? Alas! How can he keep his conscience easy in such a course? But,

2. **The example of Christ and his Apostles obliges you to this duty.**

The example of Christ must certainly be a Law to his followers; and in vain do they pretend to that character, unless they conform themselves to it. And what did Christ do in this case? Why, he left all the glories of his native Heaven; He assumed human nature with all its common infirmities, and, in circumstances of uncommon abasement, he spent three and thirty tedious and painful years in this wretched world, and passed through an uninterrupted series of poverty, fatigue, ill-treatment and persecution; He at length died in ignominy and torture upon a Cross. And what was all this for? It was for *Africans*, as well as Britons: it was for the *Negroes,* as well as Whites: it was for poor Slaves, as well as for their Masters. Yes, for poor Negroes and Slaves, he thought it worth his while to shed the Blood of his Heart. As "God would have all men to be saved, and to come to the knowledge of the Truth," so Christ "gave himself a ransom for all;" (I Timothy 2:4, 6.) i.e. for some of *all ranks* and *all nations*. In this extent, at least, the words must be taken. This we may learn also from the songs of Heaven, which run in this strain, "Thou art worthy – for Thou was slain, and hast redeemed us unto God by thy Blood, out of *every* kindred, and tongue, and people, and nation." (Revelation 5:9.) You see, brethren, some of *every* kindred, and tongue, and people, and nation, share in the benefits of this redemption, and therefore join in the Song of Praise. Africans and Americans, as well as Europeans and Asiatics, bear their part in this celestial concert. And Oh! That the poor Negroes among us, who have so peculiar an ear for music and psalmody, may join in it, with still superior ecstasy and harmony!

I am sure, such of you as are lovers of Christ, begin already to feel the force of this argument. Did he live and die, to save poor Negroes? And shall not we use all the means in our power, to make them partakers of this Salvation? Did he pour out the Blood of his Heart for them? And shall we begrudge a little labour and pains to instruct them? **We are not called to agonize and die upon a cross for them: but Jesus was; and He did not refuse.** And shall we refuse those easier endeavours for their Salvation, which are required on our part? If we are capable of such a conduct, it is high time for us to renounce all pretensions of regard to Him, and His example.

The example of the *Apostles* also, and the primitive ministers of the Gospel, binds us to the same duty. When they received their extensive Commission, the love of Christ carried them through the world, to discharge it, among Jews and Gentiles, among Masters and Servants. Wherever they found a sinner, they preached to him "Repentance towards God, and faith towards the Lord Jesus

Christ," without regard to the cutaneous distinction of colour, or the humble state of a Servant, or a Slave. "The *poor* had the Gospel preached unto them;" and among such it was most successful. "Not many mighty, not many noble after the flesh, were called: but God chose the weak, the foolish, the base and despised things of the world – that no flesh should glory in his Presence." (I Corinthians 1:26-29.)

Paul, in particular, the Chief of the Apostles, and who was eminently the Apostle of the Gentiles, shunned no fatigues or dangers, to carry this joyful news to the remotest and most barbarous parts of the world. For this end, he became a wandering Pilgrim from country to country: he braved the dangers of sea and land, and all the terrors of persecution; and at last gloriously died in the attempt. Servants and Slaves were not beneath his care. Many parts of his writings are addressed to them; from whence we learn, that many of them had embraced the Gospel, which he had published in their ears. He thought it an object worthy of his apostolic office, to give them directions for their behavior, and to exhort them to be cheerfully contented with their mortifying condition in life. "Let every man", says he, "abide in that calling, wherein he was called."

Christianity makes no alterations in matters of property, in civil distinctions or employments. "Art thou called, being a *Servant?* Care not for it – for he that is called, being a Servant is the Lord's Free-man." (I Corinthians 7:20, 21, 22.) The servants he here speaks to, were probably not indentured servants or hirelings, but what we call *Slaves*. And in those times it was a much more common practice, than it is now among the civilized nations of Europe, to make *Slaves* of the prisoners taken in war. But even to these, Paul says, "If thou art called, being a servant, or a Slave, *care not* for it:" A Christian may be happy, even in a state of Slavery. Liberty, the sweetest and most valuable of all blessings, is not essential to his happiness: for if he is destitute of civil Liberty, he enjoys a Liberty still more noble and divine: "He is the Lord's free man." The Son hath made him free from the tyranny of sin and Satan; and therefore he is free indeed. What a striking instance is this, both of apostolic zeal for poor Slaves, and of the invaluable advantages of being a Christian, which can render the lowest and most laborious station in life so insignificant, that a man need not care for it, but continue in it with a generous indifference! –

I shall only add one instance more, and that is the case of **Onesimus,** Philemon's Servant. He had been once unprofitable to his master, and run away from him, as some of your Negroes do now. But in his ramblings, he happened to come in Paul's way, while a prisoner in Rome. The Apostle did not despise the unhappy renegade, but esteemed his conversion to Christianity a prize worth labouring for. He therefore communicated the Gospel to him; and it pleased God to open his heart to receive it, and he became a sincere convert. Upon this, the Apostle wrote a letter to his master in his favour, which is still preserved among his immortal Epistles, for the benefit of the Church in all ages. He shows all the affection and concern of a father for him, and does not disdain to call him *his son*, dear to him as his own bowels. "I beseech thee, "says he to his master, "for *my son* Onesimus, whom I have begotten in my bonds: who in time past was unprofitable, but now is profitable to thee, and me: whom I have sent again: thou therefore receive him that is *mine own bowels* – for perhaps he therefore departed for a season, that thou shouldst receive him forever; not now as a servant, but above a servant, a *brother beloved*, especially to me; but how much more to thee, both in the flesh and in the Lord? If thou count me therefore a partner, receive him *as myself*. If he hath wronged thee, or oweth thee ought, put that on mine account. I Paul have written it with my own hand, I will repay it. Yea, brother, let me have joy of thee in the Lord: refresh my bowels in the Lord, by thy compliance." (Epistle to **Philemon**.) What fatherly affection and solicitude, what ardent zeal is here, for a poor run-away Slave! How different is this from the prevailing spirit of the Christians of our age? Had the Apostles and their Fellow-labourers been as careless about propagating the Gospel among Heathens, as the generality among us are, Christianity would have soon died in that corner of the world, where it had its birth; and we and the rest of mankind would now have been as much Heathens, as the African Negroes!

But do these examples lay no obligation upon us to follow them? Did the *Apostles* discover such an ardent zeal for the Salvation even of Servants and Slaves; and shall we be quite negligent and careless about it? Did they take so much pains, pass through such severe sufferings, risk their lives, and even lose them, in the generous attempt? And shall not we take the easier measures required us for their conversion? Alas! Is the spirit of primitive Christianity entirely lost upon earth? Or is Christianity declined with age, and become an insignificant thing, unworthy of zealous propagation? Or have the souls of Slaves lost their value, so that it is no matter what becomes of them? How can you pretend to learn your Religion from the Apostles; and yet have crowds of Negroes in your houses or quarters, as ignorant Heathens, as when they left the wilds of Africa, without using any means for their conversion? Will ye not endeavor to be followers of the Apostles in this respect, as they also were of Christ? If their example has no weight, methinks the conduct of Jews, Heathens, and Mahometans may shame you. They are all zealous to gain proselytes to their Religion, though antiquated, or false. And will not you labour to proselytize your Domestics to the *divine Religion of Jesus*?...

Rev. Davies' Educational efforts taught Slaves and White Indentured Servants to Read the Bible

During his twelve-year tenure, Rev. Davies paved the way for other "dissenter" Christian churches. He also led pioneering efforts in education, specifically teaching slaves and white indentured servants to read the Bible.

The Dangerous "African Trade for Slaves"

On the eve of the American Revolution, citizens of Hanover County assembled inside the courthouse to adopt the "Hanover Resolutions." These Resolution's appeared in the *Virginia Gazette* on July 28th, 1774.

At a meeting of the Freeholders of Hanover County, at the Courthouse, on Wednesday the 20th of July, 1774, the following address was agreed upon, emphasizing their desire to abolish the dangerous "African Trade for Slaves:"

Hanover Courthouse, ca. 1735. Hanover, Virginia.

To: John Syme and Patrick Henry, Junior Esquires.

Gentlemen,

...**We are Freemen**. We have a right to be so, and to enjoy all the privileges and immunities of our fellow subjects in England; and while we retain a just sense of that freedom, and those rights and privileges necessary for its safety and security, we shall never give up the ***Right of Taxation***. Let it suffice to say, once for all, we will never be taxed but by our own Representatives. This is the great badge of freedom, British America hath been hitherto distinguished by it; and when we see the British Parliament trampling upon that right, and acting with determined resolution to destroy it, we would wish to see the united wisdom and fortitude of America collected for its defense...

The African Trade for Slaves we consider as most dangerous to Virginia and the welfare of this country. We therefore most earnestly wish to see it totally discouraged...Resolved, the above Address be transmitted to the printers, to be published in the Gazettes.

William Pollard, Clerk." [5]

Chapter XIV

Monticello, "The Thomas Jefferson Foundation, Inc." – Monticello's Exhibit: "The Life of Sally Hemings, drawn from the Words of her son Madison Hemings" – "Such is the story that comes down to Me" – Accuracy vs. Fallacy.

Monticello – "The Thomas Jefferson Foundation, Inc."

Regardless of **Madison Hemings'** counterfeit, March 13, 1873 interview published in the *Waverley (Ohio) Pike County Republican* weekly, displaying at least fifteen proven fallacious historic statements, the Monticello Trustees of *The Thomas Jefferson Foundation, Inc.* continue to vigorously promote his interview as a standard of truth; at the same time promoting their fellow-Trustee, Annette Gordon-Reed's works, replete with "just a mistake" historic inaccuracies – in their online and on-site exhibit entitled:

> "The Life of Sally Hemings – Daughter, mother, sister, aunt. Inherited as property. Seamstress. World Traveler. Enslaved woman. Concubine. Negotiator. Liberator. Mystery."

The exhibit reads as follows:

> "Sally Hemings. (1773-1835) is one of the most famous – and least known – African American women in U.S. history. For more than 200 years, her name has been linked to Thomas Jefferson as his "concubine," obscuring the facts of her life and her identity. Scroll down to learn more about this intriguing American.
>
> View the Life of Sally Hemings exhibit at Monticello online.
> OVERVIEW
> 'Such is the story that comes down to me.'

> **Madison Hemings, son of Sally Hemings and Thomas Jefferson**, Pike County (Ohio) Republican, 1873."

Following are fallacious statements made on this globally promoted Monticello Trustees' "The Life of Sally Hemings. Drawn from the words of her son Madison Hemings" production:

Fallacy no. 1. "Though enslaved, Sally Hemings helped shape her life and the lives of her children, who got an almost 50-year head start on emancipation, escaping the system that had engulfed their ancestors and millions of others. Whatever we may feel about it today, this was important to her.

– Pulitzer Prize-winning historian Annette Gordon-Reed, 2017."

The Pulitzer Prize originated with Hungarian-born journalist Joseph Pulitzer (1847-1911), who endowed Columbia University with two million dollars for the establishment of a School of Journalism and for the annual award of prizes – the Pulitzer Prizes in American journalism and letters. The prizes are awarded by the Trustees of Columbia who act upon the recommendations made by the Advisory Council of the *Pulitzer School of Journalism* at Columbia.[1]

Accuracy: How was Sally Hemings instrumental in obtaining "an almost 50-year head start on emancipation" for her children? Thomas Jefferson's Last Will and Testament made no differentiation between the emancipation of Betty Hemings' children and her grandchildren. In actuality, Betty Hemings' son, **Robert "Bob"** was freed in 1794; her son, **James** was freed in 1796, and her daughter Bett's son, **Burwell**, was freed in 1826 in Jefferson's will. Sally Hemings' sons, Madison and Eston were emancipated at the age of twenty-one, upon completing their apprenticeship to John Hemings, after Betty Hemings' sons Robert, James, and her grandson, Burwell, were freed.*

Next, the Trustees of Monticello's exhibit asserts,

Fallacy no. 2. "Unlike countless enslaved women, Sally Hemings was able to negotiate with her owner. In Paris, where she was free, the 16-year-old agreed to return to enslavement at Monticello in exchange for "extraordinary privileges" for herself and freedom for her unborn children. Over the next 32 years Hemings raised four children – Beverly, Harriet, Madison, and Eston – and prepared them for their eventual emancipation. She did not negotiate for, or ever receive, legal freedom in Virginia."

Accuracy: Sally Hemings was not free in Paris, where she lodged at the Convent of Panthemont with Martha and Mary Jefferson. As already established, slavery was abolished for the first time in France in 1794. According to Madison Hemings' 1873 interview, the duration of his mother's stay in France was "about eighteen months," that is, mid-July, 1787 – late December, 1788, which would make her fifteen years old at her departure. His mother being equally enslaved in France as in Virginia, she could not possibly have had "bargaining leverage" for her non-existent children, nor could she receive "extraordinary privileges" by exchanging slavery in France for slavery in Virginia – just prior to the French "Reign of Terror" engulfing that country.

The third historically erroneous statement, is made by Annette Gordon-Reed:

Fallacy no. 3. "It seems especially appropriate to tell one part of the story of slavery through life at a place that holds such symbolic importance for many Americans – Monticello. For it is there that we can find the absolute best, and the absolute worst, that we have been as Americans. We should not get too far into

---

*Source: Library of Congress, History and Genealogy Division.

the twenty-first century without looking back at the Hemingses and their time to remember and learn.

– The Hemingses of Monticello: An American Story, Annette Gordon-Reed, 2008."

Accuracy: As Gordon-Reed's targeted figure is "the Sage of Monticello" at his own home, her thesis is to defame and calumniate Thomas Jefferson in favor of the Hemingses, using Madison Hemings' 1873 interview, heretofore proven truncated with historically false statements, as her primary political weapon against him. Madison Hemings' interview being disqualified as a deliberate forgery, we only discover the absolute best in the author of the *Declaration of Independence*, from recorded eye-witness accounts of his servant Isaac, and his overseer for twenty years, Captain Edmund Bacon.

The fourth fallacious statement is quoted from Madison Hemings' interview:

Fallacy no.4. " 'On the death of John Wales,* my grandmother, his concubine, and her children by him fell to Martha, Thomas Jefferson's wife, and consequently became the property of Thomas Jefferson…' Madison Hemings.

Sally Hemings left no written accounts, a common consequence of enslavement. Jefferson's plantation records and reminiscences, especially those of her son Madison, are the most important sources about her life."

Accuracy: Apart from Madison Hemings' discredited 1873 interview, there is absolutely no written or eye-witness evidence to the fictitious statement that Betty Hemings was the "concubine" of John Wayles, Martha Wayles Jefferson's father – which Madison terms "such is the story that comes down to me." It is just that – "a story" of no known provenance.

The Trustees of Monticello's exhibit text continues embellishing the "story" with their fabricated genealogy of Thomas Jefferson's father-in-law, John Wayles; connecting, and asserting that: "Martha Jefferson and Sally Hemings are half-sisters."

Scholarship of this nature in academia is classified as – "flat wrong."

Fallacy no. 5. In their quest to link Martha Wayles Jefferson, Thomas Jefferson's wife, to Betty Hemings' daughter Sally, the Trustees of Monticello's exhibit asks the question: "What do they share?" The answer is already prepared for the historically vulnerable reader:

*Spelled, Wayles.

"– Same father (John Wayles)
 – Little documentation and no images of either
 – Both described as industrious
 – Both had at least six children and lost children in infancy."

Accuracy: The false linkage is further proved by the fact that Martha Wayles Jefferson had "*exactly* six children," as recorded by her husband, Thomas Jefferson, in his Prayer Book – not "at least six children;" while his servant, Sally Hemings had exactly five children, not "at least six children," according to her genealogy – all her five children acknowledged to have been sired by Jefferson's nephews, the Carr brothers. Additionally, Thomas and Martha Jefferson lost four children in infancy. His servant, Sally Hemings and Peter Carr's first child, Harriet (1795-97) died in infancy, the remaining four living to adulthood.

Fallacy no. 6. "...Madison Hemings later stated that Elizabeth Hemings and Wayles had six children together. Likewise, Sally would go on to bear at least six children to her master."

Accuracy: This assumption of "Sally Hemings bearing at least six children to her master" is founded uniquely upon the deliberately forged 1873 interview by Madison Hemings and must therefore be rejected as a disqualified counterfeit.

The Monticello Trustees' exhibit text continues,

Fallacy no. 7. "She was just beginning to understand the French language well, and in France she was free... Madison Hemings."

Accuracy: Slavery as an institution existed in the 1780's in France – only to be abolished for the first time in 1794. This statement, "in France she was free," has been historically proven to be false. In addition, understanding a language phonetically does not imply literacy in reading or writing. Sally Hemings could neither read nor write the French and English languages.

Fallacy no. 8. "They (James and Sally Hemings)* lived at Jefferson's residence, the Hôtel de Langeac. Maria (Polly) and Martha (Patsy), Jefferson's older daughter who was already in Paris, lived primarily at the Abbaye Royale de Panthemont, where they were boarding students."

Accuracy: This account by the Trustees of Monticello's exhibit is fallacious – written records proving that Thomas Jefferson resided, with Colonel Humphreys, Secretary of the American legation to France, and his private secretary, William Short, at a house belonging to M. le Compte de l'Avongeac, at the corner of des Champs Elysées et la Rue Neuve de Berry, in central Paris – not at an Hôtel. Martha Jefferson's written account states, "On his (Jefferson's)* first arrival in

*Author's text in parenthesis.

Paris he occupied rooms in the Hôtel d'Orleans, Rue des Petits Augustins, until a house could be got ready for him...At the end of the year he moved to a house belonging to M. le Compte de l'Avongeac, at the corner of the Grande Route des Champs Elysées and the Rue Neuve de Berry, where he continued as long as he remained in Paris..." Neither did his servant, Sally, "live at Jefferson's residence," she being permanently domiciled at the Convent of Panthemont on the outskirts of Paris as a maid to Jefferson's daughter, Mary (Polly). A second inaccuracy is that both Martha and Mary lived permanently – *not primarily*, at this prestigious Convent (Abbaye) de Panthemont.

Building upon the foregoing historic fallacies, the Trustees of Monticello continue their "story that comes down to me" from Madison Hemings' forged interview, asking the question, "Why did she return to Monticello?" They respond to their own question as follows:

Fallacy no. 9. "Madison Hemings recounted that his mother 'became Mr. Jefferson's concubine' in France. When Jefferson prepared to return to America, Hemings said his mother refused to come back, and only did so upon negotiating 'extraordinary privileges' for herself and freedom for her future children. He also noted that she was pregnant when she arrived in Virginia, and that the child 'lived but a short time.' No other record of that child has been found..."

Accuracy: Historic evidence refutes this statement. Sally Hemings was permanently domiciled as Mary Jefferson's maid, at the Convent of Panthemont, a long distance from Thomas Jefferson's residence, where Colonel Humphreys, Mr. Short, his private secretary, and the staff of the American legation to France lived with him. The distance between the two residences is also proven by letters of correspondence between Jefferson and his daughters at Panthemont. Further to the above, Jefferson's letter of July 12, 1788 to his sister-in-law, Mrs. Elizabeth Eppes, states that he spent one day in each week with his daughters. In addition, as Sally Hemings was equally a slave in France as in Virginia, there was no possibility of a "bargaining leverage" available as ascribed to her by Madison Hemings' "interview."

Fallacy no. 10. "1789 – Hemings arrived back in Virginia and slavery at the age of 16. According to Madison Hemings, she was pregnant with Jefferson's child."

Accuracy: This statement refutes Madison Hemings' 1873 interview that "their stay (Mary Jefferson's and his mother's in Paris)* was about eighteen months," therefore ascribing his mother's departure from France to late December, 1788 – not 1789. The accurate date of Thomas Jefferson's departure from France is recorded as September 26, 1789. According to Madison's statement, Sally Hemings was 15 years old upon her departure from France, that is, "eighteen months" subsequent to the actual arrival date of Mary Jefferson and her servant in Paris, recorded as July 15, 1787.

*Author's text in parenthesis.

Fallacy no. 11: "LIFE AT MONTICELLO. 'It was her duty, all her life which I can remember, up to the time of father's death, to take care of his chamber and wardrobe, look after us children and do such light work as sewing.' Madison Hemings."

Accuracy: Thomas Jefferson's granddaughter, Ellen Wayles Randolph Coolidge's October 24, 1858 letter to her husband Joseph, states to the contrary: "No female domestic ever entered his chambers except at hours when he was known not to be there and none could have entered without being exposed to the public gaze."

The Trustees of Monticello, therefore, by emphasizing this statement of Madison Hemings, are endorsing their fellow-Trustee, Annette Gordon-Reed's revised version of Ellen Coolidge's letter, as declared in her 1997 book, *Thomas Jefferson and Sally Hemings: An American Controversy*, where she misquotes Jefferson's granddaughter as writing: "no female domestic ever entered his chambers except at hours when he was known not to be in the public gaze." This counterfeit statement is used to falsify historic records, and thereby incriminate Thomas Jefferson.

Intensifying their falsehood, the Trustees of Monticello's exhibit continues its "just a mistake" narrative by asserting – contrary to Madison Hemings' statement that his mother departed from Paris about eighteen months after her arrival – that is, at the end of 1788, the following:

Fallacy no. 12. "Sally Hemings returned with Jefferson and his daughters to Monticello in 1789. There she performed the duties of an enslaved household servant...Sally Hemings had at least six children fathered by Thomas Jefferson. Four survived to adulthood. Decades after their negotiation, Jefferson freed all of Sally Hemings' children – Beverley and Harriet left Monticello in the early 1820's; Madison and Eston were freed in his will and left Monticello in 1826. Jefferson did not grant freedom to any other enslaved family unit."

Accuracy: Sally Hemings' genealogy proves that she had five children, Harriet (1795-97); Beverley (1798-1822+); Harriet (1802-22+); Madison (1805-73+) and Eston (1808-54?)* – not "at least six children" – all acknowledged to have been sired by Jefferson's Carr nephews. Beverley (1798-1822+) ran away in 1822 at the age of twenty-four, therefore, he was not freed by Thomas Jefferson "at age twenty-one," as asserted in Madison Hemings' historically disqualified interview. Harriet (1802-22+) ran away in 1822 at age twenty, and was then freed by Jefferson; while Madison and Eston, together with a number of Betty Hemings' other children and grandchildren, were freed under the terms of Jefferson's will, signed on March 17, 1826, as follows:

Immediate freedom was granted to Burwell (1783-1827+) son of Bett Hemings, Betty Hemings' grandson; Betty Hemings' two sons, Robert (1762-1819) and James (1765-96) having been freed in 1794 and 1796, respectively. Madison (1805-73+)

*Source: Library of Congress, History and Genealogy Division.

and Eston (1808-54?), sons of Betty Hemings' daughter, Sally, were freed under the following conditions:

> I give also to John Hemings the service of his two apprentices, Madison and Eston Hemings until their respective ages of twenty-one years, at which period, respectively, I give them their freedom, and I earnestly request of the Legislature of Virginia a confirmation of the bequest of freedom to these servants, with permission to remain in this State, where their families and connections are...

The above lines from Jefferson's Last Will and Testament refute the Trustees of Monticello's exhibit statement that "Madison and Eston were freed in his will and left Monticello in 1826." Eston was eighteen years of age in 1826 when Jefferson died, necessitating the completion of his apprenticeship to John Hemings for another three years until he reached the age of twenty-one – in 1829 – according to Jefferson's will. Moreover, their statement that "Jefferson did not grant freedom to any other family unit" is countered by his granting freedom to his servants Robert in 1794, James in 1796, Burwell in 1826; John, and Joe Fosset in his will.

Fallacy no. 13. The "Life of Sally Hemings" online exhibit goes on to display a (circa 1900) photograph of Beverly Frederick Jefferson, accusing Thomas Jefferson of being his grandfather, as follows, "Beverly Frederick Jefferson, a grandson of Sally Hemings and Thomas Jefferson, is pictured with three of his sons. No images of Sally Hemings or her children are known."

The exhibit's revisionist, undocumented version of Sally Hemings' "**seven children's**" birth dates are then confidently listed, as follows:

"1790 – Sally Heming' first child is born. According to Madison Hemings, "It lives but a short time."
1795 – A daughter, Harriet Hemings, was born. She died two years later in 1797.
1798 – A son, Beverley was born. He survived to adulthood, becoming a carpenter and fiddler.
1799 – An unnamed daughter was born and died.
1801 – Harriet was born. She was their only surviving daughter, and was a spinner in Jefferson's textile factory.
1805 – A son, Madison was born. He survived to adulthood, becoming a carpenter and joiner.
1808 – Son, Eston was born. He also survived to become a carpenter and a musician."

Accuracy: Once again, the foregoing is the Trustees of Monticello's "history according to Madison Hemings' disproven interview," rewriting Sally Hemings genealogy by adding two non-existent children's births, in order to suit their purpose of character assassination; namely, Madison Hemings' fabricated statement, "It lived but a short time," to which they have added the date 1790. And yet another non-existent, unrecorded birth date is listed – 1799. Sally Hemings' *five* children were all acknowledged to have been sired by the Carr nephews. Indeed, this is "scholarship" à la mode de their fellow-Trustee, Annette Gordon-Reed – "just a mistake."

Fallacy no. 14. The Monticello Trustees' exhibit states further: "1822 – Beverley and Harriet Hemings were allowed to leave Monticello without being legally freed."

Accuracy: Genealogical records prove that Beverley ran away in 1822 at the age of twenty-four; and that Harriet also ran away in 1822 at age twenty, and was then freed by Thomas Jefferson.

Next, we read,

Fallacy no. 15. "On Harriet Hemings: 'This girl who was born a slave...then lives a life of a free white woman, but it has to be a secret. She leaves her mother...and she can never come back.'"

Accuracy: The above statement reflects a fictional novel, filled with intrigue – but contrary to historic evidence that Harriet Hemings was freed by Thomas Jefferson.

The Trustees of Monticello's exhibit thesis, as now factually exposed, utilizes Madison Hemings' forged, discredited 1873 interview as their springboard, thus fulfilling perfectly UNESCO'S goal which is aptly stated in the *Forty-five Current Communist Goals for America*:

Goal no. 30: Discredit the American founding fathers. Present them as selfish aristocrats who had no concern for the 'common man.'[2]

However, the Thomas Jefferson Foundation Trustees' militant political quest to demolish Thomas Jefferson's reputation, thereby discrediting his writings in the eyes of America's youth, does not stop here. This exhibit's advertising skill recruits visitors to,

> "Finding Sally Hemings at Monticello – The Life of Sally Hemings Exhibit. An immersive multimedia exhibit based on the recollections of Sally Hemings' son Madison. Included in any Day Pass to Monticello. PLAN YOUR VISIT"!

To which should be added – "and be indoctrinated into fake history."

A Network of Calumny, Character Assassination and Slander

In conclusion, the Trustees of Monticello – *The Thomas Jefferson Foundation, Inc.* – together with their fellow-Trustee, Annette Gordon-Reed, have built an entire network of calumny, character assassination, slander, abuse and scandal, based upon a single, fallacious, disproven 1873 interview with Madison Hemings – truncated with the grossest historic errors, in order to deliberately corrupt and misinform millions of vulnerable American youths, unabashedly exposing them via their online and on-site Monticello exhibit, to a counterfeit, sordid drama, which never existed – but is, according to Gordon-Reed's credo – "just a mistake" – to the detriment of Thomas Jefferson's – and America's, true historic identity.

Is this libel to be tolerated and allowed to continue exploiting America's children, who are being indoctrinated by the Trustees of Monticello's exhibits, literature and online programs into believing outrageous lies about the greatest founding father of their nation, at his own home – while patriotic, history-loving (but uninformed) American citizens are urged to donate their funds towards the Thomas Jefferson Foundation's published mission of historic "preservation and education?"

The Monticello Trustees' exhibit concludes its slanderous attack on Thomas Jefferson's noble, innocent character by depending, once again, upon their fellow-Trustee, Annette Gordon-Reed's counterfeit political weapon against the impeccably moral, virtuous, and humble "Sage of Monticello:"

> "The power aspect of it is very real because obviously he could have sold her if he wanted to. She could not refuse his advances…but his wife Martha could not say no to him either…I think it would be easy for Jefferson to rationalize this relationship because males were supposed to dominate women.
> – Annette Gordon-Reed"

This deceptively-written exhibit's narrative script clinches its character defamation of the author of the *Declaration of Independence* with the following brazen condemnation, based purely upon Madison Hemings' fradulent 1873 interview:

> "This is a painful and complicated American story. Thomas Jefferson was one of our most important founding fathers, and also a life-long slave owner who held Sally Hemings and their children in bondage. Sally Hemings should be known today, not just as Jefferson's concubine, but as an enslaved woman who – at age 16 – negotiated with one of the most powerful men in the nation to improve her own condition and achieve freedom for her children."

The Thomas Jefferson Foundation, Inc. Trustees' exhibit concludes with, "Look Closer: Learn more through our Additional Resources," the first of which is, of course, *The Hemingses of Monticello: An American Family*, circa 2008, by Annette Gordon-Reed.

Should the historically vulnerable viewer follow this advise – and learn more via Gordon-Reed's advertised book, *The Hemingses of Monticello: An American Family*, circa 2008 – a sample of "l'histoire à la mode de Gordon-Reed" is her interpretation of Patsy Jefferson's May 3, 1787 letter to her father:

> "Even fifteen-year-old Patsy Jefferson got caught up in the spirit of the times. In 1787, not long before her sister arrived with Sally Hemings, she issued a literal cri de coeur when she wrote to her father, 'I wish with all my soul that the poor negroes were all freed. It grieves my heart when I think that these

our fellow creatures should be treated so terribly as they are by many of our country men.' Patsy wrote this when there was only one enslaved black person in her immediate world: her uncle. She cannot have written those words, had those thoughts, without considering how her wish, if carried out, would have affected him..." [3]

However, Patsy Jefferson's May 3, 1787 letter to her father was taken out of context by Gordon-Reed to prove an historically false premise – accusing James Hemings, Jefferson's cook in Paris, of being Patsy Jefferson's uncle. Patsy's "cri de coeur" (heart's cry) came clearly from the subject matter of her prior words, excised by Gordon-Reed. In context, Martha (Patsy) Jefferson's May 3, 1787 letter to her father reads:

> A Virginia ship coming to Spain met with a corsair of the same strength. They fought and the battle lasted an hour and a quarter. The Americans gained and boarded the corsair, where they found chains that had been prepared for them. They took them, and made use of them for the Algerians themselves. They returned to Virginia, from whence they are to go back to Algiers to change the prisoners, to which, if the Algerians will not consent, the poor creatures will be sold as slaves. Good God! Have we not enough? I wish with all my soul that the poor negroes were all freed...

Patsy Jefferson's "cri de coeur" was for the "poor (Algerian) creatures," who would be "sold as slaves" if "the Algerians would not consent" to "change the prisoners" whom a Virginia ship captured in a battle against a corsair (pirate ship) with "chains that had been prepared for them." Patsy is lamenting the possible enslavement of the Algerian (North African) captives, should their own people in Algiers refuse to change the prisoners.

For Gordon-Reed – well-acquainted with Patsy Jefferson's entire letter – to come to the conclusion that "she cannot have written those words, had those thoughts without considering how her wish, if carried out, would have affected him" (James Hemings), is once again, historic revisionism par excellence. This devious portrayal of American history is designed to defame Thomas Jefferson's and his wife, Martha Wayles Jefferson's, sterling reputation and honor.

Further to the above, chapter 16 of *The Hemingses of Monticello – An American Family* is entitled, "His Promises on which she Implicitly Relied" – a direct quotation taken from Madison Hemings' historically disproven "interview." Gordon-Reed then quotes six sentences therefrom, upon which her chapter is based, adding:

> "There is much to consider about this very simple, yet powerful, explanation of what happened between Sally Hemings and Thomas Jefferson in France..." [4]

Throughout her book, Gordon-Reed treats Madison Hemings' "such is the story that comes down to me" as a *fait accompli* upon which she implicitly relies in weaving her incredulous, slanderous "story" aimed at destroying Thomas Jefferson's and his wife, Martha Wayles Jefferson's noble character.

Nonetheless, *The Hemingses of Monticello – An American Family* won the National Book Award. Once again, a reader may query the historic scholarship criteria upon which such an award is based, as American history stands upon factual, recorded evidence. This precludes a newspaper "interview" containing at least fifteen glaring historic inaccuracies which eliminate its credibility.

In addition, under the title *The Hemings Family Tree – 2*, Gordon-Reed attributes seven children to Sally Hemings, adding – "child, 1790" and "daughter 1799-1800," [5] thus contradicting the genealogical chart in her 1997 book, *Thomas Jefferson and Sally Hemings – An American Controversy*, in which she records six children born to Sally Hemings. The latter, in turn, contradicts Sally Hemings' genealogy, which records exactly five children born to her: Harriet (1795-97), Beverley (1798-1822+), Harriet (1802-22+), Madison (1805-73+) and Eston (1808-54?)*

The Hemingses of Monticello – An American Family book's first six pages are devoted to praise from, *The New Yorker, The New Republic, New York Review of Books, San Francisco Chronicle, Seattle Times, Tennessean, Boston Globe, Booklist* starred review, *Newsweek, Richmond Times-Dispatch, Publishers Weekly,* starred review, *Kirkus Reviews, Washington Post, Slate, Chicago Tribune, New York Times, The Oregonian, Atlanta Journal Constitution, Philadelphia Inquirer, Roll Call, Library Journal, The Network Journal, Politics & Prose Holiday Newsletter 2008, Bookpage,* and a review in *William and Mary Quarterly*. On the back cover we read, "A monumental and Original Book" – *The Washington Post;* and, "One of the best books of the Year" – *Washington Post, Los Angeles Times, San Francisco Chronicle, Boston Globe, St. Louis Post-Dispatch, Chicago Tribune.*

Goal no. 20 of the *Forty-five Current Communist Goals for America* reads: "Infiltrate the press. Get control of book-review assignments, editorial writing, policy-making positions." [6]

As the Trustees of Monticello – *The Thomas Jefferson Foundation, Inc.*, and their Pulitzer Prize-winning fellow-Trustee, Annette Gordon-Reed, are peddling derogatory, revisionist history on the life, conduct and legacy of an American founding father of the highest calibre, and therefore worthy of the highest honor and gratitude from his countrymen, this exhibit demonstrating Marxist propaganda should be immediately banned from the hallowed name and memory of Thomas Jefferson and his home, Monticello; and replaced with the Trustees' published mission of historic "preservation and education," – by factually portraying the life of Thomas Jefferson, "Author of the *Declaration of American Independence*, Author of the *Statute of Virginia for Religious Freedom*, and *Father of the University of Virginia*" – Jefferson's three greatest accomplishments, as per his hand-written epitaph.

*Source: Library of Congress, History and Genealogy Division.

Chapter XV

Monticello's July 2, 2018 Press Release – A "UNESCO World Heritage Site" and "Site of Conscience" – Monticello, a "United Nations World Heritage Site" – Monticello's "A Site of Conscience" – Monticello Trustees' "Site of Conscience" based on False History – "International Coalition of Sites of Conscience" – The Significance of Monticello Trustees' "Site of Conscience" – Training Ground for Indoctrination against "racist" and "white supremacist" Thomas Jefferson, based upon Fake History – Monticello's author-Trustee "Historians" – Monticello, The Thomas Jefferson Foundation's published Mission – Monticello's Endowments, The National Endowment for the Humanities.

Monticello's July 2, 2018 Press Release

A July 2, 2018 Monticello Press Release informed its vast network of readers that,

> "*The Thomas Jefferson Foundation*, the private non-profit organization that owns and operates Monticello, announces new leadership for its board of trustees. Effective January, 2019, Jon Meacham will assume the role of chairman of the board…Meacham, who has served on the board since 2013, is a presidential historian, contributing writer to the *New York Times* Book Review, contributing editor of TIME and Pulitzer Prize-winning author of numerous books, including the best-selling *Thomas Jefferson: The Art of Power*. A member of the Council on Foreign Relations…a former executive editor at *Newsweek*, Meacham is a regular guest on Morning Joe and other broadcasts…The foundation also announces that Melody C. Barnes was elected vice chair of the board and began serving in that capacity on June 15, 2018."

A "UNESCO World Heritage Site" and "Site of Conscience"

> " 'As a **UNESCO World Heritage Site and a Site of Conscience**, Monticello offers a rich and complex history of the founding era and its reliance on slavery. Our vision is to bring history forward into national and global dialogues by engaging audiences with Jefferson's world and ideas and inviting them to experience the power and place of Monticello,' said Leslie Greene Bowman, president of the Thomas Jefferson Foundation. 'Who better than Jon and Melody to lead us in those conversations – on civic engagement, race and the legacy of slavery, religious freedom and the progress of our democracy' ?
>
> 'Melody Barnes is a Senior fellow and Compton Visiting Professor in World Politics, Miller Center, University of Virginia. She is a co-founder and principal of MB2 Solutions, LLC, a domestic strategy firm. Barnes also serves as chair of the Aspen Institute Forum for Community Solutions and Opportunity Youth Incentive Fund and vice chair of the advisory board of the Institute for Contemporary Art at VCU. From January, 2009 to January, 2012, Barnes served as an assistant to the President of the United States (Barak Obama)* and director of the White House Domestic Policy

*Author's text in parenthesis.

Council. 'Monticello is at an important juncture, having just completed a $76 million campaign that fueled a transformative period of restoration and exhibits. Jon and Melody will lead us through the next chapter, in our on-going determination to share an honest, complicated and inclusive history of Monticello – common ground for all Americans,' said Donald A. King, Jr., chairman of the board of trustees."

Monticello – a "United Nations World Heritage Site"

"The Thomas Jefferson Foundation was incorporated in 1923 to preserve Monticello, the home of Thomas Jefferson in Charlottesville, Virginia. Monticello is recognized as a National Historic Landmark, a United States World Heritage Site, and a Site of Conscience. Because it is a private, non-profit organization, the foundation's regular operating budget does not receive on-going government support to fund its two-fold mission of preservation and education."

About 440,000 people visit Monticello each year - particularly America's vulnerable youth, leaders-in-the-making, who are being indoctrinated into a false, defamatory, sordid revisionism, "through the eyes of Madison Hemings" – fulfilling perfectly UNESCO's Marxist Agenda of vilifying the victims, and victimizing the villains, thus totally discrediting the author of *The Declaration of Independence* and his virtuous political thought.

"A Site of Conscience"

The Trustees of Monticello – *The Thomas Jefferson Foundation's* published "Mission and Vision Statement" for their "Site of Conscience" reads as follows:

The International Coalition of Sites of Conscience is a worldwide network of 'Sites of Conscience' – historic sites, museums and memory initiatives – that activate the power of places of memory to engage the public with a deeper understanding of the past and inspire action to shape a just future. The Coalition supports its members in many ways, including providing direct funding for civic engagement programs, introducing members to a global network of similarly minded sites, helping them establish best practices and new partnerships; organizing leadership and program development opportunities; offering dialogue training; and conducting strategic advocacy for individual members and the sites of Conscience Movement as a whole. Learn more at: www.sitesofconscience.org.

Upon learning more at: www.sitesofconscience.org, the reader discovers the true identity of a "Site of Conscience," which is preceded by a large photograph of an unruly mob of protestors waving provocative banners subsequent to the May 25, 2020 events. Their ensuing letter is a recruitment appeal to historic, cultural and civic institutions to join their Marxist cause of anarchy against law and order:

"Monticello – International Coalition of Sites of Conscience – Celebrating 20 years of Memory to Action. The Past is Present: Sites of Conscience Solidarity.

Dear Friends,

The historic system of racism in the United States lays a path of destruction through our present, claiming lives at the hands of the police and an inequitable public health system. The International Coalition of Sites of Conscience mourns the lives lost and impacted in the newest wave of these new cycles...Everyday protestors are confronting American history in the streets, and the nation's historic and cultural institutions must stand with them. As historians, survivors, activists, artists and archivists, the Coalition knows that the inequities of the past permeate the present and will devastate the future unless we act to build a better alternative. This may feel daunting, but with the light of history and the love and compassion we seed in telling each other our stories, we can shape a future rooted in our shared humanity, in dignity and justice.

We commend all who are shining a light on white supremacy and its persistent and insidious role in the United States...

In Solidarity,
The International Coalition of Sites of Conscience."

Monticello Trustees' "Site of Conscience" based on False History

The above-cited **"International Coalition of Sites of Conscience"** letter, endorsed and promoted by the *Trustees* of Monticello, frames Thomas Jefferson as a "white supremacist" and "its persistent and insidious role in the United States" and as a "racist," by using Jefferson's beloved home, fame and signature to indoctrinate millions of unwary American citizens – particularly youth – with counterfeit history.

This is done through their Marxist literature, exhibits and media battle – which forces upon the public mind Madison Hemings' forged 1873 "interview" – the sole basis for their claim to Jefferson's "sordid, immoral, dishonest, slave-abusing, debauched and 'hypocritical' life and conduct." Their successful goal is to foam anarchy, rage and revenge against America's history and heritage, inciting riots, violent protests, government subversion and desecration – defacing valuable historic sculpture, art and architecture memorializing America's heroic legacy in nationwide memorials and landmarks; in order to eradicate from public view and memory the Judeo-Christian heritage unique to "this nation under God" – and replace it with UNESCO's Marxist (atheist) idols of their One World Order.

Monticello's author-Trustee "Historians"

Foremost among Monticello's author-*Trustee* "historians" are Pulitzer Prize-winning John Meacham, Chairman of the Board; Annette Gordon-Reed, and David McCullough, the latter *Trustee Emeritu*s being a member of Yale University's secret society "Skull and Bones," also called, "The Brotherhood of Death."

The Thomas Jefferson Foundation's major donors are David M. Rubenstein, media billionaire, self-styled "philanthropist-patriot," and chairman of the Council on Foreign Relations; and the National Endowment for the Humanities – who provide funding to undermine America's liberties through psychological weapons of defamation, vilification, misinformation, ridicule and anger-provoking revisionism of Thomas Jefferson's historically-documented noble and virtuous character. Rubenstein's Bloomberg Television, "The David Rubenstein Show," advertises Meacham and McCullough as "master historians," and "the biggest names in American history" exploring "the subjects they've come to so intimately know and understand." The former falsely accuses Thomas Jefferson by reiterating verbatim Madison Hemings' fallacious 1873 "interview" in his book, *Thomas Jefferson: The Art of Power*, while the latter, in his book, *John Adams*, labels Jefferson "…the Virginia aristocrat and slave master who lived in a style fit for a prince, as removed from his fellow citizens and their lives as it was possible to be…" The Trustees of Monticello's on-line and on-site exhibit, *The Life of Sally Hemings – through the Words of her son, Madison* is founded uniquely upon Madison Hemings' 1873 historically-disqualified interview, being reinforced by quotations from Annette Gordon-Reed's book, *The Thomas Jefferson-Sally Hemings Controversy – An American Story* – which, in turn, is squarely based upon Madison Hemings' forged interview.

Monticello's Pulitzer Prize-winning, "master historians," and self-styled "philanthropist-patriots" are on a literary crusade to discredit, defame and slander Thomas Jefferson's noble character – a stepping-stone to dismantling his republican creed of self-government – under the guise of the un-American, unpatriotic hypocrisy of 21st century fake historians.

The Monticello, Thomas Jefferson Foundation Trustees' unscrupulous calumny visited upon Thomas Jefferson is now having its toll on the liberties of Americans. I challenge every God-fearing patriotic American who loves this country to re-claim Thomas Jefferson's Monticello from the tentacles of UNESCO'S United Nations World Heritage Site control – returning this foremost National Historic Site to the American people where it belongs, as an *American Heritage Site* – teaching the Jeffersonian principles of patriotism and self-government, as opposed to anarchy, protest, civil rights activism and subversion to the God-ordained laws of peace and harmony.

Monticello – The Thomas Jefferson Foundation's published Mission

The Foundation's published statement is that, "Since its founding (1923), the Foundation has dedicated itself to a two-fold mission of preservation and education…as a private, non-profit organization, we rely on the generosity of donors like you to accomplish our dual mission of preservation and education."

Monticello's Endowments – The National Endowment for the Humanities

The Foundation's 2018 published Endowments for its two-fold mission of "preservation and education" is $74,721,720 – receiving in May, 2020, an additional $75,000 from the National Endowment for the Humanities (NEH), an independent federal agency and one of the largest funders of humanities programs in the United States, according to the Monticello Press Release of May 26, 2020.

The May 26, 2020 Press Release states,

" 'The National Endowment for the Humanities has been an invaluable and long-standing supporter of our work at Monticello' said Leslie Greene Bowman, president and C.E.O. of the *Thomas Jefferson Foundation*. 'From the restoration of Mulberry Row to archeological excavations to the galleries in the David M. Rubenstein Visitor Center, our guests directly benefit from their generosity… For more than nearly three decades, the National Endowment for the Humanities has been a generous benefactor of various historical and educational initiatives at Monticello. Projects supported by NEH grants include the 1993 *Worlds of Thomas Jefferson* exhibition; the construction of Monticello's Visitor Center; efforts to reveal the landscape of slavery through the restoration of Mulberry Row and Monticello's dependencies; the ground-breaking digitalization of archaeological research through the Digital Archaeological Archive of Comparative Slavery (DAACS); and the Capstone Public Summit on Race and the Legacy of Slavery: *Memory, Mourning, Mobilization: The Legacy of Slavery and Race in America*. Through support for these and other initiatives, the NEH has advanced Monticello's long-standing efforts to share themes of equality and freedom in meaningful ways with millions of global citizens through new exhibitions and live historical interpretation.' "

Goal no. 30 of the *Forty-five Current Communist Goals for America* reads: "Discredit the American founding fathers. Present them as selfish aristocrats who had no concern for the 'common man." [1]

Chapter XVI

What is Museum Instruction? David M. Rubenstein, Thomas Jefferson Foundation Donor – Rubenstein's book, "The American Story: Conversations with Master Historians" – Rubenstein's Interview with Jon Meacham, Chairman of Monticello's Thomas Jefferson Foundation, Inc. on his book, "Thomas Jefferson: The Art of Power" – Meacham: "It is One of the many Hypocrisies of Jefferson's Life" – Rubenstein's next Question to Jon Meacham – Accuracy vs. Revisionism in American History – Meacham's book, "Thomas Jefferson: The Art of Power, 'A Treaty in Paris'" – The book, "In the Hands of the People" edited by Jon Meacham – The British Institution of Slavery: "America's Original Sin"? – Jefferson's Louisiana Purchase and the Lewis and Clark Expedition a "narrow" view? – The Bible's view on Original Sin – Jefferson's 1778 Bill ending the Importation of Slaves – His anti-Slavery, 28th Clause in the Declaration of Independence – Jefferson's Northwest Ordinance, Slavery Banned – The Northwest Ordinance, American Indians Protected – The Jeffersonian Principle against Sodomy – Annette Gordon-Reed and the Thomas Jefferson Memorial – Jefferson's Notes on the State of Virginia denouncing Slavery, inscribed in the Jefferson Memorial – David McCullough's book, "The American Spirit, Who we Are and What we Stand For" – Jefferson's Autobiography, Slavery in America from 1650-1778 – Accuracy vs. Revisionism – David McCullough's book, "John Adams" – Abigail Adams: "He (Jefferson) is one of the Choice Ones of the Earth."

What is Museum Instruction?

What is museum instruction? It is historic education through paintings, art, architectural themes, sculpture, stained-glass windows, memorials, exhibits, visual re-enactments and "factual"* events about the nation's past. As the adage goes, an image is worth a thousand words; hence museum instruction is historic education at its highest level of retention.

David M. Rubenstein – Thomas Jefferson Foundation Donor

Monticello's Visitors' Center bears the name of David M. Rubenstein, who is chairman of the Council on Foreign Relations, the Harvard Global Advisory Council, the Smithsonian Institution and the John F. Kennedy Center for the Performing Arts, and has served as deputy domestic policy advisor to U.S. President Carter. He is a board member of the World Economic Forum and Chairman Emeritus of the Brookings Institution. He has provided $20 million to *The Thomas Jefferson Foundation, Inc.* towards their stated mission of historic "preservation and education."

Rubensteins' book, "The American Story: Conversations with Master Historians"

Also the author of *The American Story: Conversations with Master Historians*,

---

*fact: reality; truth; actuality; the state of things as they are. *Webster's Dictionary.*

foreword by Librarian of Congress, Carla Hayden, (Simon and Schuster, 2019), the book is advertised as, "In these dialogues, the biggest names in American history explore the subjects they've come to so intimately know and understand." He hosts Bloomberg Television's – "The David Rubenstein Show," interviewing authors declared by him to be "master historians" among whom are Jon Meacham and David McCullough. On September 19, 2018, the C.E.O. of Amazon, and owner of *The Washington Post*, Jeff Bezos, was interviewed by him on "The David Rubenstein Show."

Rubenstein's Interview with Jon Meacham, Chairman of Monticello's Thomas Jefferson Foundation, Inc. on his book, "Thomas Jefferson: The Art of Power"

Rubenstein's book, *The American Story: Conversations with Master Historians*, is promoted as "A sweeping journey across the American story through conversations with our greatest historians" and, "David M. Rubinstein captures the brilliance of our most celebrated historians, as well as the souls of their subjects."[1] It is dedicated to, "…the teachers of American history and civics." Mr. Rubinstein, in his interview with "master historian" John Meacham on his book, *Thomas Jefferson: The Art of Power* (Random House, 2012) directs his sixth question to this author as follows:

> "In recent years, a lot of discussion has occurred about his (Thomas Jefferson's)* relationship with a slave, Sally Hemings. He fathered six children with her, and he appears to have been an attentive father to those children, and he more or less stayed with her until he died. How do you explain a slave owner like that having a relationship with an enslaved person? Was that common or not common, and how did he hide it? When it was made public in those days, he never denied it, really, and he never affirmed it. Lastly, based on DNA evidence or anything else, do you have any doubt that the Sally Hemings-Thomas Jefferson relationship was true?"[2]

Meacham: "It is One of the many hypocrisies of Jefferson's Life"

Jon Meacham's reply, excerpted, follows:

> "To take them in reverse order, I do not have any doubt. Even in the absence of the DNA evidence, which is 99.9 percent convincing, I do not believe that a man so driven by appetite for power, for books, for food, for wine, for art, for knowledge, could at the age of forty, after his wife died, simply stop short of indulging the most sensuous appetite of all. If you disbelieve the Sally Hemings story, then you are disbelieving a perennially coherent, oral history tradition from the African American community, and you are ascribing to Jefferson a kind of discipline that is almost superhuman. I do believe that it happened. It was common…It is one of the many hypocrisies of Jefferson's life. His children by Sally Hemings were the only slaves he freed. Let me take just a second about how the Jefferson-Hemings

*Author's text in parenthesis.

relationship began. It began in Paris...Sally Hemings was his wife's half sister, so the Hemings family itself, in the odd world of slavery...was a privileged slave family, as horribly ironic as that statement is. They were to be taken very good care of and overseers were not to give them orders. If I may, they were family. And so when Sally Hemings arrives in Paris, when Jefferson is the American minister there from 1785 to 1789, the relationship begins." [3]

Rubenstein's next Question to Jon Meacham

Mr. Rubinstein's next question is, "She was fourteen?" To which Jon Meacham responds,

> "No, she was sixteen...In what I find one of the most moving and courageous moments in the whole Jefferson saga, here's this woman – this girl, as you say – Sally Hemings. She is in Paris, she has become pregnant by the man who owns her, who totally controls her fate, and he wants her to go back with him when he returns home to become the first secretary of state. If she stays in France, all she has to do is go down to the Paris City Hall and declare that she is a slave being held in France, and she will be free...In what I find to be one of the most compelling moments, she negotiates with one of the most powerful men in the world, and she bends him to her will. She says, 'I will go back with you if any children we have are freed at the age of their majority.'...But that relationship did last until the day Jefferson died forty years later...Let me quickly say something about the press...Jefferson dealt with this regarding the story of Hemings, beginning in September 1801. He had not been president for a year when the story – almost entirely accurate, with just two little mistakes – appeared in a Richmond newspaper, written by an alienated former ally of his..." [4]

The above-quoted excerpted, *Question and Answer* interview by David Rubenstein, with Jon Meacham, Pulitzer Prize-winning, "master historian," chairman of the Board of Trustees of Monticello's *The Thomas Jefferson Foundation, Inc.* and fellow-member of the Council on Foreign Relations, is accompanied by an oval profile of Thomas Jefferson, crowned with a laurel wreath halo, captioned, "A study in contradictions: the author of the *Declaration of Independence* was also a lifelong slave owner."

Accuracy vs. Revisionism in American History

For an author advertised as a "master historian" and one of "our greatest historians," Jon Meacham's historic fallacies are inexcusable.

Revisionism 1: Meacham states that "I do not have any doubt" (that the Sally Hemings-Thomas Jefferson relationship was true.) And that the DNA evidence "is 99.9 percent convincing..."

Accuracy: DNA experts published rebuttals to *Nature Magazine's* November, 1998 article incriminating Thomas Jefferson via DNA "evidence." Their articles, appearing in both *Nature* (British) and *Science* (American) magazines in January, 1999, affirmed that DNA was taken from Field Jefferson, an uncle – there being at least two dozen men in the Charlottesville area during that time period with identical DNA. DNA experts, as well as foremost, credible historian scholars have confirmed these facts – while Thomas Jefferson's nephew, Peter Carr, admitted to siring Sally Hemings' children in written historic records.

Revisionism 2: "…If you disbelieve the Sally Hemings story, then you are disbelieving a perennially coherent, oral history tradition from the African American community…"

Accuracy: As the oral tradition of Madison Hemings' March 13, 1873 interview published by *The Waverly (Ohio) Pike County Republican* weekly newspaper – and touted on the Monticello Trustee's "The Life of Sally Hemings…" online and on-site exhibit – contains at least fifteen glaring historic fallacies, it refutes Jon Meacham's assertion that "a perennially coherent, oral history tradition" is true. Madison Hemings' interview states that, "Such is the story that comes down to me" – his oral "story" being proven incoherent and historically false.

Revisionism 3: "It is one of the many hypocrisies in Jefferson's life. His children by Sally Hemings were the only slaves he freed."

Accuracy: To the contrary, Thomas Jefferson freed Betty Heming's children – Robert (1762-1819) in 1794; James (1765-96) in 1796; John (1775-1830+) in his will; Bett "Betty Brown's" son, Burwell (1783-1827+), and Mary's son, Joe "Joe Fosset" (1780-1827+) in his will. According to Sally Hemings' genealogy, her son, Beverley (1798-1822+) ran away in 1822 at age twenty-four; her daughter, Harriet (1802-22+) ran away in 1822 at age twenty, and was then freed by Jefferson; her sons Madison (1805-73+) and Eston (1808-54?) were freed after Betty Heming's sons, Robert and James, and Bett's son, Burwell, were emancipated, as proven by historic records.* The chairman of the board of Monticello's *The Thomas Jefferson Foundation, Inc.*, who is described as a "master historian" should be well-versed in these historic facts pertaining to Peter Carr's children by Sally Hemings.

Revisionism 4: "Sally Hemings was his wife's half sister, so the Hemings family itself, in the odd world of slavery…was a privileged slave family…"

Accuracy: There is no evidence whatsoever – either written, or eye-witness, that Sally Hemings was Jefferson's wife's half sister, apart from Madison Hemings' 1873 interview, truncated with disinformation, misinformation, false historic dates, events which never occurred historically, incorrect numbers and names of children, glaring falsehoods and fraudulent claims. The latter has been proven

---

*Source: Library of Congress, History and Genealogy Division.

to be a deliberate forgery. Furthermore, the Hemings family of servants were no more privileged than Ursula (1737-1800), Iris (1775-97+) and Squire (1793-97+), Jefferson's servant, Isaac's immediate family – namely, his mother, wife and son.

A June, 1774 page of Thomas Jefferson's wife, Martha Wayles Jefferson's Account Book, in which she records: "Paid Ursula…Gave Ursula two suits of clothes…Gave Ursula and Bet each a white skirt." Isaac's family and Jefferson's other servants were equally well taken care of, without preference.

Revisionism 5: "…And so, when Sally Hemings arrives in Paris, when Jefferson is the American minister there from 1785 to 1789, the relationship begins."

Accuracy: Firstly, Sally Hemings (1773-1835) arrived in Paris as Jefferson's daughter Mary's servant, in mid-July 1787. She accompanied eight-year-old Mary Jefferson to France at age fourteen.

Revisionism 6: Mr. Rubenstein's next question is revealing: "She was fourteen?" To which Meacham replied, "No. She was sixteen."

164

Accuracy: Sally Hemings (b.1773), historic records prove, arrived in Paris with Mary Jefferson in mid-July, 1787 at age fourteen – not sixteen, as asserted by Meacham. Hemings accompanied Mary Jefferson to the Convent of Panthemont, on the outskirts of Paris, where she lodged permanently as her maid; his eldest daughter Martha being already established at this Convent. Jefferson resided at a house in central Paris belonging to le Compte de l'Avongeac on the corner of la Grande Route des Champs Elysées et la Rue Neuve de Berry, with Col. Humphreys, Secretary of the American legation to France, and Mr. William Short, his private secretary. According to written evidence, Jefferson spent one day a week with his two daughters, during which time they spoke of nothing but "Eppington, Hors-du-Monde and Monticello." Madison Hemings' 1873 interview alleges that "Their stay (in Paris, Mary Jefferson's and his mother's)* was about eighteen months." However, Thomas Jefferson departed from France with his two daughters, Martha and Mary, and his staff on September 26, 1789, twenty-six months + after Mary and her servant arrived in Paris – *not* eighteen months. At Jefferson's departure from Paris, Martha and Mary Jefferson's, and her maid's ages were 17, 11 and 16, respectively.

Revisionism 7: "…Sally Hemings. She is in Paris, she has become pregnant by the man who owns her, who totally controls her fate, and he wants her to go back with him when he returns home to become the first secretary of state."

Accuracy: In this statement, Meacham is relying entirely upon Madison Hemings' fallacious 1873 interview – the one and only written source for his outlandish fraudulent claim. Secondly, Jefferson was not "returning home to become the first secretary of state." Jefferson wrote to Congress from Paris requesting a six-month leave of absence, to visit family and tend to personal matters at Monticello, after which he would resume his duties as Minister to France. Only after arriving in America, was he apprised that he had been appointed Secretary of State – the French Revolution having intervened.

Revisionism 8: "If she stays in France, all she has to do is go down to the Paris City Hall and declare that she is a slave being held in France, and she will be free…"

Accuracy: Slavery was abolished for the first time in 1794 by *la République Française*, five years after Jefferson's departure from France. Sally Hemings was therefore equally a slave in France, belonging to the newly-established American legation – as she was in Virginia. Is Mr. Meacham a master of French history, as well as being a "master historian" of American history? If so, he should be well versed in the French laws on slavery, its first abolition in 1794, its reinforcement under Napoleon in 1802, and the final, permanent abolition of this evil trade in France and her colonies in 1848.

Revisionism 9: "In what I find to be one of the most compelling moments, she negotiates with one of the most powerful men in the world, and she bends him to her will. She says, 'I will go back with you if any children we have are freed at the age of their majority'…But that relationship did last until the day Jefferson died forty years later."

*Author's text in parenthesis.

Accuracy: Here again, Meacham reiterates Madison Hemings' exploitative 1873 interview in which he fabricates an incredulous "such is the story that comes down to me," which has been classified a deliberate forgery. As Sally Hemings was equally a slave in France as in Virginia, she had no "bargaining power" to "bend Jefferson to her will." Again, historic records reveal that Sally Hemings' first child, Harriet was born in 1795 (d. 1797); followed by Beverley (1798-1822+), who ran away at age twenty-four; Harriet (1802-22+) who ran away in 1822 at age twenty, and was then freed by Jefferson; Madison (1805-1873+), freed in Jefferson's will after completing his apprenticeship with John Hemings, as well as Eston (1808-54?) freed at age twenty-one, after completing his apprenticeship with his uncle. There is absolutely no written, or eye-witness evidence supporting Meacham's statements, apart from Madison Hemings' "Such is the story that comes down to me" interview, and Annette Gordon-Reed's rewriting of Ellen Randolph Coolidge's October 24, 1858 letter, by removing ten words from Jefferson's third granddaughter's letter to her husband, Joseph, and attributing it to being – "just a mistake."

Revisionism 10: "…regarding the story of Hemings, beginning in September 1801. He had not been president for a year when the story – almost entirely accurate, with just two little mistakes – appeared in a Richmond newspaper, written by an alienated former ally of his…"

Accuracy: Meacham is, of course, referring to James T. Callender, the infuriated Scotsman, who fled England for sedition charges; who later served a nine-month conviction charge in the Richmond jail for sedition against John Adams, and who then launched his vengeful attack on Jefferson in the Richmond *Recorder* in 1802, following President Jefferson's refusal to appoint him postmaster of Richmond. Callender, reportedly a belligerent man, was found dead in three feet of water in the James River, after a drunken ordeal – hardly a credible source for a retaliatory "story" which he invented, after being refused a lucrative post by President Thomas Jefferson.

Meacham's book "Thomas Jefferson: The Art of Power – 'A Treaty in Paris' "

The 22nd chapter of Meacham's book, *Thomas Jefferson: The Art of Power* is entitled, **A Treaty in Paris**. It opens with a quotation from Madison Hemings' 1873 fallacious interview: "He desired to bring my mother back to Virginia with him, but she demurred. MADISON HEMINGS." [5]

Meacham's recitation and reliance upon Madison Hemings' forged interview for his vilification of Jefferson's noble character, is striking. He writes,

Revisionism 11: "…Sally Hemings was no lonely slave girl in Europe: Her big brother James was there with her, at the Hôtel de Langeac, and could have helped her win her freedom. According to their son Madison Hemings' later account, Sally, who had become 'Mr. Jefferson's concubine,' was pregnant when Jefferson was preparing to return to the United States. 'He desired to bring my mother back to Virginia with him but she demurred,' Madison Hemings said. To demur was to refuse, and Jefferson was unaccustomed to encountering resistance to his absolute will at all, much less from a slave. His whole life was about controlling as many of the world's variables as he could...Thomas Jefferson found himself in negotiations with a pregnant enslaved teenager who, in a reversal of fortune hardly likely to be repeated, had the means at hand to free herself. She, not he, was in control... For the first time in his life, perhaps, Jefferson was truly in a position of weakness at a moment that mattered to him. So he began making concessions to convince Sally Hemings to come home to Virginia. 'To induce her to do so he promised her extraordinary privileges, and made a solemn pledge that her children should be freed at the age of twenty-one years,' Madison Hemings said. Sally Hemings agreed. 'In consequence of his promise, on which she implicitly relied, she returned with him to Virginia,' said Madison Hemings. 'Soon after their arrival, she gave birth to a child, of whom Thomas Jefferson was the father. It lived but a short time. She gave birth to four others, and Jefferson was the father of all of them. Their names were Beverly, Harriet, Madison (myself), and Eston – three sons and one daughter.' Their father kept the promise he had made to Sally in Paris. 'We all became free agreeably to the treaty entered into by our parents before we were born,' Madison Hemings said. It was one of the most important pacts of Jefferson's life." [6]

Accuracy: Firstly, according to written historic facts, Sally Hemings resided permanently at l'Abbaye de Panthemont, on the outskirts of Paris, as a maid to Mary and Martha Jefferson. Jefferson did not live at an Hôtel, but at the house of le Compte de l'Avongeac in central Paris, on the corner of la Grande Route des Champs Elysées et la Rue Neuve de Berry, with Colonel Humphreys, Secretary of the American legation, and William Short, his private secretary. Jefferson spent one day a week with his two beloved daughters. As already factually established, Madison Hemings' "story as it comes down to me" is disproven in that Sally Hemings was equally a slave in France as in Virginia – no possible "bargaining leverage" being therefore available to her. Madison Hemings' account of a non-existent "child that lived but a short time," and his inaccurate count of his mother's children as four in lieu of five, from Harriet (1795-97), Sally Hemings' and Peter Carr's first child, is one of at least fifteen historic fallacies in Hemings' "interview." In addition, Sally Hemings' children were not all freed according to Hemings' alleged, non-existent "treaty" at the age of twenty-one – Beverley (1798-1822+) being twenty-four years old when he ran away.

The above, excerpted interview by Rubenstein – and review of *Thomas Jefferson: The Art of Power*, is a deliberate character assassination by Jon Meacham of Thomas Jefferson's pure, principled, virtuous and highly admired life and conduct, both at Monticello and in Paris, as borne out by eye-witness and written accounts. The latter evidence negates Madison Hemings' 1873 "oral tradition" – containing a litany of historic fiction – upon which Meacham's allegations are founded.

Unsurprisingly, John Meacham's book is advertised on its front and back cover as a #1 *New York Times* Bestseller; "This is probably the best single-volume biography of Jefferson ever written..." by Gordon S. Wood; "(Meacham) captures who Jefferson was, not just as a statesman but as a man...By the end of the book... the reader is likely to feel as if he is losing a dear friend" by *The Christian Science Monitor*; "Fascinating...a true triumph...In addition to being a brilliant biography, this book is a guide to the use of power...The result is a fascinating look at how Jefferson wielded his driving desire for power and control" by Walter Isaacson; named one of the best books of the year by *The Washington Post, Entertainment Weekly, The Seattle Times, St. Louis Post-Dispatch, BookPage* and *A New York Times* Notable Book.

Praise for *Thomas Jefferson: The Art of Power* begins on the first six pages of the book's opening, reprinted from: *The New York Times Book Review; The Washington Post; Chicago Tribune; The Seattle Times, The Associated Press; USA Today;* ANNETTE GORDON-REED, author of *The Hemingses of Monticello: An American Family* – "This is an extraordinary work;" *Entertainment Weekly; The Dallas Morning News; Bloomberg*: "Impeccably researched and footnoted...a model of clarity and explanation;" *Newsday; Fortune*: "Masterful and intimate;" *Garden & Gun; Booklist* (starred review); *Kirkus Reviews* and *Publishers Weekly*.

Revisionism 12: Of note, is that in David Rubenstein's sixth question to Jon Meacham on his book, *Thomas Jefferson: The Art of Power*, he affirms that, "He (Jefferson)* fathered six children with her (Sally Hemings)*, and he appears to have been an attentive father to those children..." [7]

Accuracy: The latter statement is diametrically opposed to Meacham's reliance upon Madison Hemings' 1873 error-strewn interview, in which is found Madison's statement, "He (Jefferson)* was not in the habit of showing partiality or fatherly affection to us children. We were the only children of his by a slave woman..." – his entire interview being "such is the story that comes down to me," of no known provenance.

The book "In the Hands of the People" – Edited by Jon Meacham

A "Project of the Thomas Jefferson Foundation at Monticello" published in 2020 by Random House, New York, *In the Hands of the People* is edited by John Meacham, with his Introduction. Its Afterword is written by Annette Gordon-Reed. Chapter 1 of the book, sub-titled, "The Ongoing Quest for Equality" discloses familiar accusations against Thomas Jefferson:

> "While Jefferson profited from slavery, America's tragic original sin, and failed to promote the rights of all the members of the American community, he nonetheless understood that a multi-ethnic nation needed to protect the rights of all of its citizens and actively engage them in its governance. The

*Author's text in parenthesis.

fundamental principle was adaptable for other people and other times. Human progress would expand its reach. African Americans, women, Native Americans, the LGBTQ communities, and others have, through their own great efforts, put living blood into the heart of the Jeffersonian principle. Jefferson's sight was often narrow – limited to white men – but his vision was broad and powerful, defining much of what is great about America…" [8]

Meacham's above-quoted, familiar accusations are as follows,

1. Thomas Jefferson profited from slavery.
2. Slavery is America's tragic original sin.
3. Jefferson failed to promote the rights of all the members of the American community.
4. The Jeffersonian principle (of self-government)* needed to have living blood put into its heart, that is, through other communities, including the LGBTQ community.
5. Jefferson's sight was often narrow – limited to white men…

The Declaration of Independence, the *U.S. Constitution* (based upon the 1776 Declaration) and the *U.S. Bill of Rights* have proved to the entire world, for the past two hundred and forty-four years, that America is a unique "Republic under God," her liberties stemming from these three Charters of Freedom, which far surpass the liberties granted to any other nation in the world.

The original U.S. Bill of Rights with its twelve articles, signed on March 4, 1789 in New York. At its ratification in 1791, *Article the third* became *Article the first*, containing the Freedom of Religion Clause. National Archives.

*Author's text in parenthesis.

As a "master historian" Jon Meacham should be proficient in the Jeffersonian principle of self-government through his well-known, published works, including his firm stand against slavery – the latter being first introduced in British America by the Crown of England. Jefferson's bold condemnation of the British Institution of slavery is stated in his 1774 *A Summary View of the Rights of British America*, published in Europe and America; his 1778 Anti-slavery bill, which his *Autobiography* again spells out; the 28th anti-Slavery Clause of his immortal *Declaration of Independence*, removed by Congress prior to its signing, but reaffirmed in Jefferson's *Autobiography*; and his *Notes on the State of Virginia*, published in France, England and America.

Slavery was first introduced to British America in 1619, subsequent to the capture and sale of innocent people by their West African Chieftains, who sold them to the British Slave Trade, transporting them thither on a Dutch man-of-war. The institution of slavery existed in the entire British Empire, including British America, enforced by monarchial rule, until King William IV abolished this evil trade throughout his colonies in 1833. The French Republic finally abolished slavery throughout France and her colonies in 1848. However, the despotic commerce existed in numerous countries worldwide.

The British Institution of Slavery – "America's original Sin"?

Only a narrow and illogical reasoning would accuse the American people of inheriting the "original sin" of slavery, leveling derogatory statements against Jefferson – and many founding fathers – for their English (Caucasian) origin by calling them "white men" with a "narrow sight" or view. The 56 signers of the 1776 *Declaration of Independence* were "white men," the 39 signers of the 1787 *U.S. Constitution* were "white men" and the signers of the 1789 *U.S. Bill of Rights* were also "white men" of European ancestry. In addition, the 41 signers of the 1620 Massachusetts Pilgrims' *Mayflower Compact* were "white men," and the signers of the 1639 *Fundamental Orders of Connecticut* were "white men." *The Fundamental Orders* was the first written known constitution in history that created a government – the foundation stone of democracy in America.

Additionally, the first 1607 permanent English settlement on American soil was founded in Jamestown, Virginia by "white men," whose Charter, dated April 10, 1606 proclaims, "We, greatly commending, and graciously accepting of their desires for the furtherance of so noble a work, which may, by the Providence of Almighty God, hereafter tend to the glory of His Divine Majesty, in propagating of Christian Religion to such people, as yet live in darkness and miserable ignorance of the true knowledge and worship of God…"

As historically proven, Jefferson's view far surpassed the "narrow" view of King George III, who enforced slavery in British America, as well as the even "narrower" view of King Louis XVI of France, who was tragically guillotined; or the French Republic's "narrow" view, whose motto "Liberté, Egalité et Fraternité" proved ineffective during the ensuing Napoleonic reign and wars. Europe in its entirety was peopled with "white men," many of whom emigrated to America, contributing to her innovations, inventions, achievements and expansion.

Jefferson's Louisiana Purchase and Lewis and Clark Expedition a "narrow" view?

In 1803, Jefferson's brilliant Louisiana Purchase from Napoleon – a "white man," for a mere fifteen million dollars, doubled the size of his country. His dispatch shortly thereafter in 1803, of Meriwether Lewis and William Clark, to explore and map these vast, newly-acquired lands in order to discover a feasible route to the west, and create an American presence there prior to Great Britain, or other European nations' claim to it – can hardly be termed a "narrow view." The successful outcome of the Lewis and Clark expedition enabled pioneers and missionaries to follow in their steps.

The Bible's view on Original Sin

The Bible clearly teaches that the only "original sin" is that passed down to every human being from Adam's willful disobedience to God's command – resulting in spiritual separation from Almighty God; the restoration of which broken fellowship with one's Creator is only possible through the merits of the Messiah – Jesus Christ's atonement on Calvary's Cross. No other "original sin" is inherently imputed upon a human being or a nation.

And again, the accusation that "Jefferson failed to promote the rights of all the members of the American community" is spurious – as he, compared to the British, French and other European leaders – did more to denounce, expose and attempt, with prohibitions, to abolish the slave trade – being consistently thwarted by the Crown of England. He nonetheless succeeded in terminating the importation of slaves into America in 1778, which is repeated in his *Autobiography*:

Jefferson's 1778 Bill ending the Importation of Slaves

From Jefferson's *Autobiography* we read,

> The first establishment in Virginia which became permanent was made in 1607. I have found no mention of Negroes in the colony until about 1650. The first brought here as slaves were by a Dutch ship; after which the English commenced the trade and continued ipso facto, their further importation for the present and the business of the war pressing constantly on the legislature, this subject was not acted on finally until '78 when I brought in a bill to prevent their further importation. This passed without opposition, and stopped the increase of the evil by importation, leaving to future efforts its final eradication.

Thomas Jefferson's anti-Slavery, 28th Clause in the Declaration of Independence

"Master historian" Jon Meacham should no doubt be well-acquainted with the Jeffersonian Principle enunciated in the 28th Clause of the *Declaration of Independence*, that is, the total emancipation of slavery in British America. In this clause, with its vehement denunciation of the King of England for thwarting Congress' repeated legislation to abolish the slave trade in British America, Jefferson called slavery an "execrable commerce" and "an assemblage of horrors." This clause was erased by Congress prior to its signing, in order to obtain the thirteen States' signatures required for its passage – two southernmost States otherwise dropping out of the union. Jefferson, however, reiterated the importance of his anti-Slavery clause by reproducing it in its entirety within his *Autobiography*:

The 28th Clause of Jefferson's Declaration of Independence

> He has waged cruel war against human nature itself, violating its most sacred rights of life and liberty in the persons of a distant people who never offended him, captivating & carrying them into slavery in another hemisphere, or to incur miserable death in their transportation thither. This piratical warfare, the opprobrium of <u>infidel</u> powers, is the warfare of the CHRISTIAN king of Great Britain. Determined to keep open a market where MEN should be bought & sold, he has prostituted his negative for suppressing every legislative attempt to prohibit or to restrain this execrable commerce. And that this assemblage of horrors might want no fact of distinguished die, he is now exciting those very people to rise in arms among us, and to purchase that liberty of which he has deprived them, by murdering the people upon whom he also obtruded them: thus paying off former crime committed against the LIBERTIES of one people, with crimes which he urges them to commit against the LIVES of another.

He continues to condemn the King of England for his "crime committed against the LIBERTIES" of those people, whose "most sacred rights of life and liberty" inherent in human nature itself, he has ruthlessly violated, stating that Congress' petitions for redress have only been met with further injury:

> In every stage of these oppressions we have petitioned for redress in the most humble terms: our repeated petitions have been answered only by repeated injuries. A prince whose character is thus marked by every act which may define a tyrant is unfit to be the ruler of a people who mean to be free. Future ages will scarce believe that the hardiness of one man adventured, within the short compass of twelve years only, to build a foundation so broad & undisguised for tyranny over a people fostered & fixed in principles of freedom.

From the foregoing, it is clear that all the citizens of British America were being oppressed and reduced to slavery under the tyrannical rule of King George III – including the slaves, which he refused to emancipate – this "execrable commerce" being highly lucrative to his Majesty.

Jefferson's Northwest Ordinance – Slavery is Banned

Described by David Rubenstein as one of "our greatest historians," Jon Meacham is no doubt cognizant of Thomas Jefferson's *Northwest Ordinance*, written on April 23, 1784, and ratified by Congress on July 13, 1787. Its 6th Article mirrors his 28th Clause of the *Declaration of Independence* – the anti-Slavery Clause, for in this vast territory west of the Alleghenies and northwest of the Ohio River, lands won from the British, Jefferson permanently banned slavery and involuntary servitude:

> **Article 6th**: There shall be neither slavery nor involuntary servitude in the said territory, otherwise than in the punishment of crimes whereof the party shall have been duly convicted: Provided, always, That any person escaping into the same, from whom labor or service is lawfully claimed in any one of the original States, such fugitive may be lawfully reclaimed and conveyed to the person claiming his or her labor or service as aforesaid.

The States from Massachusetts to Virginia had agreed to relinquish their claims to this wilderness territory.

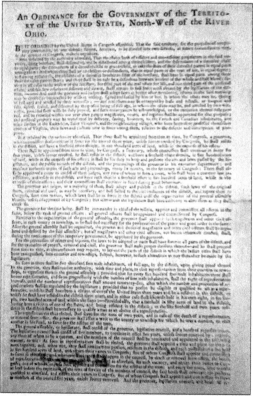

The Northwest Ordinance, 1787. Library of Congress, Rare Book Collection.

Jefferson's Northwest Ordinance refutes Meacham's statement in his book, *In the Hands of the People*, that America's third president "profited from slavery," and that he "failed to promote the rights of all the members of the American community." Of the Northwest Ordinance, Daniel Webster wrote,

> We are accustomed to praise the lawgivers of antiquity; we help to perpetuate the fame of Solon and Lycurgus; but I doubt whether one single law of any lawgiver, ancient or modern, has produced effects of more distinct, marked and lasting character than the Ordinance of 1787.
>
> – Daniel Webster.

The Northwest Ordinance – American Indians Protected

Jefferson's 3rd Article in his internationally-acclaimed *Northwest Ordinance*, disproves Meacham's claim that the Sage of Monticello's "sight was often narrow – limited to white men," as in it, he ensures the protection of the Indians' property, rights and liberty:

> **Article 3rd**: Religion, morality, and knowledge, being necessary to good government and the happiness of mankind, schools and the means of education shall forever be encouraged. **The utmost good faith shall always be observed towards the Indians**; their lands and property shall never be taken from them without their consent; and, in their property, rights, and liberty, they shall never be invaded or disturbed, unless in just and lawful wars authorized by Congress; but laws founded in justice and humanity, shall, from time to time, be made for preventing wrongs being done to them, and for preserving peace and friendship with them.

It is stunning that the chairman of Monticello's *Thomas Jefferson Foundation, Inc.*, would malign the author of America's liberties in his 2020 "Project of the Thomas Jefferson Foundation at Monticello," *In the Hands of the People*, published by Random House, when the Foundation's stated mission is historic "preservation and education" of Jefferson's home and legacy.

The Jeffersonian Principle against Sodomy

The Jeffersonian Principle against sodomy should be no stranger to Meacham, as it is enunciated in Section XIV of his well-known, published, *Bill for Proportioning Crimes and Punishments*,

> **Section XIV**: Whoever shall be guilty of rape, (*polygamy*), or sodomy with man or woman, shall be punished; if a man, by castration, if a woman, by boring through the cartilage of her nose a hole of one half inch in diameter at the least.

Thomas Jefferson's outline for his Bill for Proportioning Crimes and Punishments (from original, in Jefferson's handwriting). Library of Congress.

Far from displaying a "narrow sight" in his political creed of self-government, Jefferson, as well as his fellow-founding fathers, who themselves practiced and advocated virtue – condemned what Almighty God calls sin in the Bible – including sodomy, which He states is "an abomination in His sight."* Hence, this Jeffersonian Principle rightly and justly condemns what God condemns – the sin of LGBTQ, or sodomy. The author of *The Declaration of Independence* categorizes it as a punishable crime in America.

Annette Gordon-Reed and The Thomas Jefferson Memorial

Annette Gordon-Reed, in her Afterword to Meacham's book, *In the Hands of the People*, recounts that, in 2012, seventeen years subsequent to her initial visit to Monticello, and fifteen years after the publication of her first book, *Thomas*

---

*Leviticus 18:22; 20:13, Romans 1:26, 27, I Corinthians 6:9, 10, I Timothy 1:9-10. I Kings 14:24, 15:12; 22:46.

175

Jefferson and Sally Hemings – An American Controversy, she made her first visit into the Thomas Jefferson Memorial in Washington, D.C. She speaks of "Jefferson's famous words" reproduced upon its interior walls.[9] She then states that " 'The pen of the Revolution' wrote words that moved his generation and those that followed, in the United States and across the globe," [10] quoting part of the first – of his five original, excerpted writings upon these hallowed walls:

> "We hold these truths to be self-evident that all men are created equal, that they are endowed by their Creator with certain unalienable Rights, that among these are Life, Liberty and the pursuit of Happiness." [11]

Gordon-Reed then makes an astounding observation, imparting the following information to her readers:

> "I knew even before I arrived that other of Jefferson's words would be missing – the ones where he cast doubt on the capacity of forming a multiracial society in the country he helped to create. With those words, Jefferson was mostly a product of his time and place – a white Virginian of the eighteenth century. His prodigious imagination allowed him to see many things but did not allow him to take in the possibility that whites would be able to give up their prejudices and live in harmony with blacks as equal citizens in a republican society." [12]

How could a Pulitzer Prize-winning author and historian ignore Thomas Jefferson's excerpted anti-Slavery bill (also in his *Notes on the State of Virginia*, 1785) boldly condemning slavery, directly facing his *Declaration of Independence*, on the opposite inner wall of this memorial – both of which testify to Jefferson's republican creed? The four, large-paneled inscriptions, and a fifth, two-feet-tall inscription around the upper, inner dome were chosen by the Thomas Jefferson Memorial Commission "as being the most reflective of the principal founder of American political thought" prior to its dedication on April 13, 1943 – bicentennial of Jefferson's birth.

Jefferson's "Notes on the State of Virginia" denouncing Slavery, inscribed in the Jefferson Memorial

These words, engraved upon the inner wall of this national memorial honoring Thomas Jefferson, boldly denounce slavery. Jefferson asserts that God's justice and long-suffering cannot live forever – that the liberties of America are insecure without granting full emancipation to slaves, the equal inheritors of life and liberty from their Creator, as with every other human being. With the wisdom and foresight of a seer, he shudders at the thought of God's justice continuing to be violated – unless His gift of liberty is restored to all:

> God who gave us life gave us liberty. Can the liberties of a nation be secure when we have removed a conviction that these liberties are the gift of God? Indeed I tremble for my country when I reflect that God is just, that his justice cannot sleep forever. Commerce between master and slave

is despotism. Nothing is more certainly written in the book of fate than that these people are to be free. Establish the law for educating the common people. This it is the business of the state to effect and on a general plan.

If Gordon-Reed knew emphatically, prior to her first, 2012 visit to the Jefferson Memorial that "other of Jefferson's words would be missing," how is it that she refused to acknowledge in the Afterword of Meacham's book – *In the Hands of the People* – that she was "flat wrong"?

Jefferson's excerpted anti-Slavery bill (also in his *Notes on the State of Virginia*, 1785) – clearly exposed to Gordon-Reed's view on the inner wall of this memorial, and known to countless millions of visitors since its inauguration 1943, refute her statement that, "Jefferson was mostly a product of his time and place – a white Virginian of the eighteenth century" whose "prodigious imagination" did not permit him to understand that "whites would be able to give up their prejudices and live in harmony with blacks as equal citizens in a republican society."

The foregoing is simply another example of Annette Gordon-Reed's "just a mistake" philosophy in her portrayal of American history.

David McCullough's book – "The American Spirit, Who we Are and What we Stand For"

Another of David Rubenstein's master historian guests interviewed on Bloomberg Television, "The David Rubenstein Show," is David McCullough, a Pulitzer Prize-winner and Trustee Emeritus of Monticello's *The Thomas Jefferson Foundation, Inc.*, as well as a member of "Skull and Bones," secret society of Yale University, also called "The Brotherhood of Death."

On the front cover of McCullough's book, *The American Spirit – Who We Are and What We Stand For*, (Simon and Schuster, 2017) he is named "One of the great historical storytellers of his generation" by *The Wall Street Journal*.[13] In his chapter entitled "The Spirit of Jefferson – Independence Day Naturalization Ceremony at Monticello, Charlottesville, Virginia, 1994," after quoting the beginning lines of the *Declaration of Independence*, "We hold these truths to be self-evident, that all men are created equal, that they are endowed by their Creator with certain unalienable Rights, that among these are Life, Liberty and the pursuit of Happiness. – That to secure these rights, Governments are instituted among Men, deriving their just powers from the consent of the governed..."[14] he states,

> "Never, *never anywhere*, had there been a government instituted on the consent of the governed. Was Jefferson including women with the words "men" and "mankind"? Possibly he was, nobody knows. Was he thinking of black Americans when he declared all men are created equal? Ideally, yes, I think. Practically, no. He was an eighteenth-century Virginia planter, it must be remembered, as the slave quarters along Mulberry Row, just over there,

attest. He was an exceedingly gifted and very great man, but like others of that exceptional handful of politicians we call the Founding Fathers, he could also be inconsistent, contradictory, *human*." [15]

A prerequisite for a "master historian" of American history, is the mastery of the English language. *Webster's International Dictionary*, unabridged, describes the word, "man" n., plural, "men" as,

1. A human being; a person, whether male or female.
2. The human race; mankind: used without *the* or *a*.

The word, "mankind" is described as,

1. The human race; man taken collectively; all human beings. 'The proper study of mankind is man.' – Pope.

Any English Language major is fluent in the knowledge of collective nouns, which makes it all the more surprising that Mr. McCullough would raise this doubt of the *Declaration's* possible exclusion of women in the minds of "sixty-two" newly-naturalized citizens, from "twenty-four countries," during their naturalization ceremony at Monticello.

Building on this misconception conveyed to his audience – foreigners being accepted into the fold of English-speaking America – McCullough then casts aspersion at Thomas Jefferson and his *Declaration of Independence* by querying whether he included black Americans in his statement that "all men are created equal," emphasizing the slave quarters nearby. He concludes that, "…Practically, no. He was an eighteenth century Virginia planter…he could also be inconsistent, contradictory, *human*."

Once again, we see familiar Marxist accusations being leveled against the author of the *Declaration of Independence* – "he could also be inconsistent, contradictory, *human*" – "like the others…we call Founding Fathers." Mr. McCullough – described by the *Wall Street Journal* as "One of the great historical storytellers of his generation" should be a master of documents of American history, one of which is Jefferson's original, last draft of the *Declaration of Independence* – his 28th Clause condemning the Crown of England for thwarting the founding fathers' consistent efforts to eradicate slavery through legislation and prohibitions. This clause was so crucial to the mind and will of Jefferson, that he reproduced it in his *Autobiography*, exactly as he had presented it to Congress – thus negating McCullough's derogatory portrayal of Jefferson as "inconsistent and contradictory;" to which he added the word *"human,"* giving the impression that all human beings display the vices of inconsistent and contradictory behavior. The latter is at antipodes to the qualities of consistency, integrity, honesty, wisdom, truth, humility and virtue practiced by Thomas Jefferson, as witnessed to by his words and actions.

Jefferson's *Autobiography* – Slavery in America from 1650-1778

Jefferson's *Autobiography*, well known to historians, recounts the history of Slavery in America from 1650 to 1778, at which time the author of the *Declaration of Independence* terminated "the increase of this evil by importation," into the United States:

> The first establishment in Virginia which became permanent was made in 1607. I have found no mention of negroes in the colony until about 1650. The first brought here as slaves were by a Dutch ship; after which the English commenced the trade and continued it until the revolutionary war. That suspended, ipso facto, their further importation for the present and the busines of the war pressing constantly on the legislature, this subject was not acted on finally until '78 when I brought in a bill to prevent their further importation. This passed without opposition, and stopped the increase of the evil by importation, leaving to future efforts its final eradication.

We further read in *The American Spirit – Who We Are And What We Stand For*, under the sub-title, "History Lost and Found – National Trust for Historic Preservation Conference, Providence, Rhode Island, 2001," McCullough's statement: "Carpenter's Hall, much more importantly, was the gathering place for the First Continental Congress in the summer of 1774…John Adams was one of the fifty-six delegates who gathered in Carpenters Hall in 1774…" [16]

The original Resolutions of the First Continental Congress, housed in the Rare Book Collection of the Library of Congress, however, state that the delegates met from September 5, 1774 – October 26, 1774, in the Fall of 1774, not the preceding summer.

David McCullough's book – "John Adams"

In David McCullough's book, *John Adams* (Simon and Schuster, 2001) the author misrepresents historic fact in his account of Jefferson's eight-year-old daughter Polly's arrival in London, and her conveyance to Paris:

Revisionism 13: McCullough states,

> "…Jefferson was at last heard from. Rather than come himself to fetch the child, he was sending his valet, Petit. Having only just returned to Paris from his travels in the South, Jefferson explained, he had 'the arrearages of three or four months all crowded on me at once.' To the Adamses it must have seemed a lame excuse, knowing as they did how little there could be of a truly pressing nature to keep Jefferson in Paris and how competent William Short was to handle what business there was for a week or so, just as he had been doing for months…" [17]

The foregoing implies that Jefferson was less than eager to retrieve his daughter, that he lacked integrity as a father by sending his servant, Petit, to escort her to Paris, and that this "must have seemed a lame excuse" to the Adamses, "knowing as they did how little there could be of a truly pressing nature to keep Jefferson in Paris…"

Accuracy: The following factual evidence refutes McCullough's above-quoted account,

1. Jefferson's anxiety-filled letters from 1785-1787 to his sister-in-law, Mrs. Elizabeth Eppes and her husband, insisting that his daughter be sent to France, included his September 20th 1785 letter to Polly Jefferson, excerpted thus, "…I wish so much to see you, that I have desired your uncle and aunt to send you to me. I know, my dear Polly, how sorry you will be, and ought to be, to leave them and your cousins, but your sister and myself cannot live without you, and after a while, we will carry you back to Virginia…but above all things, by our care and love of you, we will teach you to love us more than you will do if you stay so far from us…"

2. His detailed instructions on the time and manner in which his beloved daughter should sail from America, stating in a September 22, 1785 letter to Mrs. Eppes, that, "No event of your life has put it into your power to conceive how I feel when I reflect that such a child, and so dear to me, is to cross the ocean, is to be exposed to all the sufferings and risks, great and small, to which a situation on board a ship exposes everyone. I drop my pen at the thought – but she must come…"

3. His letters to Polly and Mr. and Mrs. Eppes, expressing his yearning to enfold his daughter again in his arms, and his deep love and concern for her happiness when reunited with them in Paris.

4. His full knowledge and anticipation of her arrival after three years' pleadings and negotiations with her to join him in France.

5. His return to Paris from a voyage in mid-June, 1787 in order to welcome his daughter's arrival the ensuing July, having full knowledge that she was in the trusted care of Captain Ramsay – the latter having offered to escort Polly and her maid to Paris.

6. His gratitude to the Captain, but preference to dispatch a trusted servant, Petit, for her safe escort across the Channel to him.

7. His July 28, 1787 letter to his sister-in-law, Elizabeth Eppes, expressing their "great joy" and describing in detail his daughter's conveyance to him in Paris:

> "Polly's arrival has given us great joy. Her disposition to attach herself to those who are kind to her had occasioned successive distresses on parting with Captain Ramsay first, and afterwards with Mrs. Adams. She had a very fine passage, without a storm, and was perfectly taken

care of by Captain Ramsay. He offered to come to Paris with her, but this was unnecessary. I sent a trusty servant to London to attend her here. A parent may be permitted to speak of his own child when it involves an act of justice to another. The attentions which your goodness has induced you to pay her prove themselves by the fruits of them. Her reading, her writing, her manners in general, show what everlasting obligations we are all under to you. She will surely not be the least happy among us when the day shall come in which we may all be reunited. She is now established in the Convent, perfectly happy...She became a universal favorite with the young ladies and the mistresses. She writes you a long letter, giving you an account of her voyage and journey here..."

Regarding Polly's departure from London, McCullough informs readers in his book, *John Adams* that, "...as time would show, the love she (Abigail Adams)* felt for the child was to be her one enduring tie to Jefferson." [18]

There is no evidence, however, to prove that Abigail Adams' "one enduring tie" to Jefferson was to be his beautiful, gracious, well-mannered and lovable daughter, Polly. Abigail's sentiments for Jefferson, expressed in a letter to her niece from Paris, show her friendship and admiration for him as follows:

Abigail Adams: "He (Jefferson) is one of the Choice Ones of the Earth"

I shall really regret to leave Mr. Jefferson; he is one of the choice ones of the earth. On Thursday, I dine with him at his house. On Sunday he is to dine here. On Monday, we all dine with the Marquis (de Lafayette).*

Moreover, John Adams' voluminous correspondence with his friend, Thomas Jefferson until July 4, 1826 – the day they died – demonstrates the two families' enduring, mutual love and respect.

Revisionism 14: In his book, *John Adams*, McCullough again defames Jefferson by stating that,

"There were, as well, striking ironies. Jefferson, the Virginia aristocrat and slave master who lived in a style fit for a prince, as removed from his fellow citizens and their lives as it was possible to be, was hailed as the apostle of liberty, the "Man of the People..." [19]

Accuracy: Both Thomas Jefferson and George Washington** inherited English aristocracy and a refined education. Both lived in beautiful homesteads, surrounded by well-manicured gardens, overlooking spectacular views – the former, from Monticello, translated from Italian to mean "Little Hill," the latter, from Mount

---

* Author's text in parenthesis.
** George Washington descends from King John I of England, and nine of the 25 Baron sureties under oath to the Archbishop of Canterbury to obtain King John's signature on the Magna Charta, c. 1215.

Vernon, on an elevation overlooking the Potomac River – with a view of Maryland in the distance. Both inherited lands and plantations from their forebears, and both preferred being "gentleman farmers," at their beloved homes, surrounded by their families. Both forfeited this great blessing of family life by dedicating the choice years of their lives to the service of God and country – which entailed great sacrifices, laying down their lives, their fortunes and their sacred honor.

Jefferson, was "the pen," of the American Revolution – whether at Monticello or at Graff House in Philadelphia, where, at age thirty-three, he rented two little furnished rooms in which he wrote his immortal *Declaration of Independence*; or whether in New York, Philadelphia, or a rented house in Georgetown, as Secretary of State to Washington; or in Washington, D.C. as third U.S. president – he was separated from Monticello and his family for long periods of time serving his country.

Neither Jefferson nor Washington wished to remain in public life, nor did either claim power for himself. Jefferson was certainly not "…as removed from his fellow citizens and their lives as it was possible to be…" being a member of the House of Burgesses in Williamsburg; Governor of Virginia in Richmond; Minister to France in Paris; Secretary of State in New York, Philadelphia and Georgetown (then Maryland); Vice President of the United States in Philadelphia; and President of the United States in Washington, D.C. for two terms. His overseer of twenty years, Captain Edmund Bacon, states in *The Private Life of Thomas Jefferson*, that when Jefferson visited Monticello, it was the best-kept "tavern" in Charlottesville, as carriages of guests would descend upon him on week-ends, and that an ox would last only two days. Bacon recounts Jefferson's generous hospitality, as well as his refusal to turn away the poor, benevolently responding to their requests so that he had to continually remind "the Sage of Monticello" that his plantation could not sustain such lavish gifts to those in need.

Additionally, from Jefferson's pen at Monticello came his *Summary View of the Rights of British America*, his *Notes on the State of Virginia*, and many other renowned writings; his design of the Richmond Capitol building, his proposed design for the White House – chosen as one of the three semi-finalist designs – and submitted humbly under the pseudonym, "Mr. A-Z", second only to James Hoban's winning model; and his design for the world-acclaimed University of Virginia.

Captain Bacon also remarks that while at Monticello, Jefferson was indefatigably industrious with new inventions, such as a polygraph device and a dumbwaiter system operated by a pulley, as well as innovation improvements for his countrymen. He informs posterity that Jefferson "invented a plough that was considered a great improvement on any that had ever been used. He got a great many premiums and medals for it." Discovering in Washington that the U.S. Senate had no parliamentary manual for their proceedings, Jefferson authored *A Manual of Parliamentary*

Practice for the Use of the Senate of the United States, published in Georgetown in 1803. Documents of American history reveal a superlative statesman continually striving to improve the lives of his fellow-citizens.

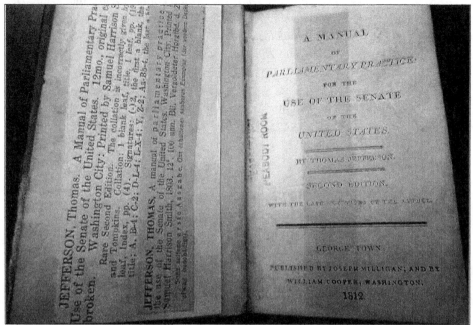

Thomas Jefferson's "A Manual of Parliamentary Practice for the Use of the Senate of the United States." First published in Georgetown in 1803.

Like Washington, he was not paid for many of his contributions to his countrymen – nor did he wish to be, being of a generous, refined education and upbringing. Jefferson's well-earned reputation as "the apostle of liberty" and the "Man of the People" cannot be described as a "striking irony," compared to the alleged "style" of life "fit for a prince" attributed to him by McCullough. Jefferson's life, whether at Monticello or in the public sphere, reflects an industrious, occupational, useful life, at antipodes to the self-indulgent, futile lives of monarchial princes – which "Common Sense" denounces. Moreover, Jefferson became an accomplished lawyer in Virginia in 1767 prior to his acceptance of national appointments.

George Washington was "the sword" of the Revolution, securing freedom for his country from Great Britain, being on the front lines of battle from 1775-1781; and again, sacrificing home and family to serve his countrymen two terms as America's first president. Washington was also a faithful member of Virginia's House of Burgesses and delegate to the First Continental Congress in Carpenters' Hall, Philadelphia, as well as President of the 1787 Constitutional Convention which framed the U.S. Constitution. At the young age of seventeen, George Washington obtained his Surveyor's License from the College of William and Mary in 1749.

David McCullough's book, *John Adams* is praised in the book's first two opening pages by the following list of 21st century media – *The Boston Herald, The New Yorker, The New Leader*, the President of *the American Museum of Natural History* (as quoted in *The New York Times*), *The Miami Herald, The Boston Globe, People* magazine, *The New Times Book Review, The Washington Post, The Charleston Gazette, Newsday, Los Angeles Times, The Houston Chronicle, San Diego Union-Tribune, American Way, The Plain Dealer* (Cleveland, OH), *The Times* (London), *U.S. News & World Report* and *The Chicago Sun-Times*.

"McCullough is one of our most gifted living writers," states *The Washington Post*.

Chapter XVII

The Council on Foreign Relations and Karl Marx – Origin and Goals – Members of the Council on Foreign Relations.

The Council on Foreign Relations and Karl Marx

The Council on Foreign Relations is a non-governmental council whose funding comes from private donors, and whose published pursuit is the study of global American economic, political and strategic problems. Incorporated in 1921, Edward Mandell House, its founder, was chief advisor to President Woodrow Wilson, who had spoken of him as "my alter ego." House proved to be a powerful influence during Wilson's presidency – 1913-1921. Edward House, however, was a Marxist whose design was the socialization of the United States.

His book, *Philip Dru: Administrator*,[1] published in 1912, reveals the author's goal to implement Karl Marx's plan of socialism for the conquest of America. He disclosed his conspiratorial Agenda in quest of controlling both Democrat and Republican Parties, with the aim of creating a Socialist World Government.

In his book, House advocated the implementation of a graduated income tax, as well as a central, state-controlled bank – both of which originate from Karl Marx' *Communist Manifesto*. The latter were signed into law in 1913, at the outset of the Wilson Administration, under House's influence. House's plan included the relinquishment of United States sovereignty to the League of Nations after WWI. He did, however, experience a major setback with the U.S. Senate's refusal to ratify it. Edward House saw this roadblock as "losing a battle, but not the war," founding with his followers, the Council on Foreign Relations, whose aim from its incorporation was to destroy the liberties and sovereignty of the United States, leading her into a global government.

House's frustrated "Plan A" became his "Plan B" – another "global organization" would supplant the League of Nations, following a future world war. Naturally, House and his colleagues would dominate this world government.

Origin and Goals

The Council on Foreign Relations, from its inception in 1921, was made up of powerful and influential individuals. Large contributions were received in the late 1920's from the Carnegie and Rockefeller Foundations. Beginning with Franklin Delano Roosevelt in 1940, the State Department was placed under the control of CFR members, and they have maintained that control through 2016. (Franklin Delano Roosevelt subsequently founded, with Winston Churchill and Josef Stalin, the United Nations on American soil after House's decease.)

In 1944, and in 1948, the Republican candidate for the presidency was Thomas Dewey, a member of the Council on Foreign Relations. Other CFR members were U.S. President Richard Nixon, a Republican, and Stevenson, Humphrey and McGovern, Democrats. Although the American citizen was led to believe he had the freedom to elect a president of his choice, the majority of candidates were CFR members. [2]

It is a fact that atheistic Marxism in the 20th century caused the extermination of about a hundred million people, enslaved approximately a billion, and has been the source of poverty, lack of freedom and hopelessness for the masses, excepting their despotic leaders who rule them with a rod of iron. The U.S. Administrative Branch of government has been dominated by Marxist infiltrators from 1940 through 2016, to include a total domination of the State Department. With decades of continuous control over the State Department, what goals have been accomplished by the CFR in their pursuit of America's entrance into a Global Socialist System?

And what devastation has been wrought in rewriting and removing America's original historic roots and identity – creating the anarchy, chaos and confusion now prevalent through counterfeit news, literature and media indoctrination?

Members of the Council on Foreign Relations

Following are but ten former Secretaries of State, their first year in office, and a foremost accomplishment of each in fulfilling the objectives of the CFR:

1. George P. Schultz 1982 – Diluted American protest over the U.S.S.R.'s shooting of KAL 007. [3]
2. Alexander M. Haig – 1981 – Facilitated the first sales of arms to China. [4]
3. Edmund S. Muskie – 1980 – Backed the ratification of SALT II. [5]
4. Cyrus R. Vance – 1977 – Handed over Nicaragua to the communists, as well as the Panama Canal. [6]
5. Henry A. Kissinger – 1973 – Handed over Southeast Asia to communists. [7]
6. William P. Rogers – 1969 – A traitor to Rhodesia. [8]
7. Dean Rusk – 1961 – Established no-win rules in Vietnam. [9]
8. Christian A. Herter – 1959 – Facilitated downfall of Cuba by Castro. [10]
9. John Foster Dulles – 1953 – A traitor to the Freedom Fighters in Hungary. [11]
10. Dean Acheson – 1949 – Handed over China to Mao Tse Tung. [12]

From *The Council on Foreign Relations 1986-1987* and *1990-1991 Annual Reports,* and from research published in *The Insiders* by John F. McManus, we learn the following about its membership:

At that time, the CFR membership consisted of 2,790 members. There were 712 business executives (including banking); 631 academic scholars and administrators; 382 U.S. government officials; 469 non-profit organization administrators; 303 journalists, correspondents and media executives; 249 lawyers; and 44 miscellaneous members. [13]

Business executives included: the chairmen of AT&T Company; American International Group Inc.; Salomon, Inc.; Levi Strauss & Company; Mobil Corporation; Exxon Corporation; Xerox Corporation and the Senior Partner of Goldman Sachs & Company.

Government officials included: Dick Cheney, Secretary of Defense; Nicholas F. Brady, Secretary of the Treasury; Lynn Martin, Secretary of Labor; Robert M. Gates, Director of the CIA; Brent Scowcroft, National Security Advisor; Colin L. Powell, Chairman, Joint Chiefs of Staff; James H. Billington, Librarian of Congress; S. Eagleburger, Deputy Secretary of State, and Sandra Day O'Connor, Justice of the U.S. Supreme Court.

Numerous U.S. Senators are listed, to include, William S. Cohen of Maine; Christopher J. Dodd of Connecticut; Daniel P. Moynihan of New York; J.D. Rockefeller, IV of West Virginia; William V. Roth, Jr. of Delaware and Joseph I. Lieberman of Connecticut. Of the many U.S. Representatives – members in the CFR, are Newt Gingrich of Georgia; Mel Levine of California; Les Aspin of Wisconsin and Richard A. Gephardt of Missouri.

Journalists, correspondents and media executives included, Katharine Graham, Chairman of *Newsweek & The Washington Post*; Roone Arledge, President of *ABC News and Sports;* Jason McManus, Editor-in-Chief of *Time*; Mortimer B. Zuckerman, Chairman of *U.S. News and World Report*; Max Frankel, Executive Editor of *The New York Times*; Norman Pearlstine, Executive Editor of *The Wall Street Journal*; William F. Buckley, Jr., President of *National Review*; Lewis W. Lapham, Editor of *Harper's*; William G. Hyland, Editor of *Foreign Affairs*; Lawrence A. Tisch, CEO of *CBS, Inc.*; and John F. Welch, Jr., Chairman of *General Electric Company,* (parent of *NBC*).

Print Journalists included: William F. Buckley, Jr.; Jeane K. Kirkpatrick, Robert L. Bartley and Hodding Carter, III.

Among the numerous Radio and Television Journalist members we read the names of David Brinkley; Tom Brokaw; Dan Rather; Barbara Walters; Jim Lehrer; Diane Sawyer; Irving R. Levine and Steve Bell.[14]

The current published list of CFR members include: David M. Rubenstein, Chairman; Jon Meacham, Chairman of Monticello, *The Thomas Jefferson Foundation, Inc.*; Janet Napolitano, President of the University of California, former U.S. Attorney (1993-1997), Attorney General of Arizona (1999-2003), Governor of Arizona (2003-2009) and President Barak Obama's first Homeland Security Secretary (2009-2013); Colin L. Powell, former U.S. Secretary of State (2001-2005); David Rockefeller, Chairman and CEO of Chase Manhattan Corp., Honorary Chairman of CFR; Eduardo J. Padrón, President, Miami Dade College, past board Chair of the Association of American Colleges and Universities, and of the American Council on Education, he serves on boards of Business – Higher Education Forum, the College Board Advocacy and Policy Center, and the International Association of University Presidents; Margaret Warner, Senior Correspondent, *PBS NewsHour*, previously reported for the *Wall Street Journal*; Fareed Zakaria, Host, *CNN's* Fareed Zakaria GPS, Editor-at-large of *Time Magazine* and a regular *Washington Post* columnist. From 2000-2010, he was the editor of *Newsweek International*, and managing editor of Foreign Affairs from 1992-2000; William M. McRaven, Chancellor, University of Texas Systems; James P. Gorman, Chairman and Chief Executive Officer, Morgan Stanley; Timothy Geithner, President, Warburg Pincus. He served as 75th U.S. Secretary of the Treasury; Leslie H. Gelb, former correspondent and columnist for the *New York Times*, President Emeritus of CFR; Madeleine K. Albright, Chair, Albright Stonebridge Group, LLC, and former U.S. Secretary of State. She currently serves on the U.S. Defense Department's Defense Policy Board; and Meghan L. Sullivan – Jeanne Kirkpatrick Professor of the Practise of International Affairs, Harvard Kennedy School.

The Council on Foreign Relations is headquartered in New York with an additional branch in Washington, D.C. The CFR'S published revenues for 2017 are $94,192,500. Its present membership is 4,900.

Chapter XVIII

Monticello designated a UNESCO "World Heritage Site" in 1987 – The United States and Israel quit UNESCO in 2019 – UNESCO'S "World Heritage Sites" – UNESCO'S "List of World Heritage in Danger" – The World Heritage Emblem, "Interdependence" – UNESCO'S Scheme to pervert Public Education – Attack upon Patriotism and its Parental Encouragement – Teachers Urged to Suppress American History – A Passage from Karl Marx's Communist Manifesto – 20th Century attacks, Jefferson the Atheist? – Thomas Jefferson, the anti-Evolutionist – Was he anti-Semitic?

Monticello – designated a UNESCO "World Heritage Site" in 1987

Monticello, and the University of Virginia in Charlottesville, were designated a "World Heritage Site" in 1987,* and as such, added to UNESCO'S (United Nations** Educational, Scientific and Cultural Organization) list of world historic sites under its provisions. It is therefore little wonder that the Trustees of Monticello, *The Thomas Jefferson Foundation, Inc.*, promote calumny to defame Thomas Jefferson, reaching multitudes of unwary visitors – particularly American students – with its slanderous report on the author of the *Declaration of Independence*.

The United States and Israel quit UNESCO IN 2019

A PBS news release from Paris dated January 1, 2019, entitled, "U.S. and Israel officially withdraw from UNESCO" reported that,

> The United States and Israel officially quit the *United Nation's Educational, Scientific and Cultural Agency* at the stroke of midnight, the culmination of a process triggered more than a year ago amid concerns that the organization fosters anti-Israel bias. The Admnistration filed its notice to withdraw in October, 2017, and Israeli Prime Minister Benjamin Netanyahu followed suit. The Paris-based organization has been denounced by critics as a crucible for anti-Israel bias: blasted for criticizing Israel's occupation of East Jerusalem, naming ancient Jewish sites as Palestinian heritage sites and granting full membership to Palestine in 2011.

Of note is the public statement made by former U.S. Ambassador to the United Nations that "the last straw" prior to withdrawal, was UNESCO's designation of *Hebron* in Israel, as a Palestinian "World Heritage Site." Ancient *Hebron* is the Jewish historic burial site of Abraham, Sarah, Isaac, Rebecca and Jacob, and therefore, a decidedly "Jewish Heritage Site."

---

* The Great Wall of China also became a World Heritage Site in 1987.
** The United Nations was founded after World War II by Sir Winston Churchill (United Kingdom), Franklin Delano Roosevelt (United States of America) and Josef Stalin (Union of Soviet Socialist Republics). The Charter was signed in San Francisco on the 26th June, 1945.

UNESCO'S "World Heritage Sites"

In 1999, UNESCO had 630 properties which the World Heritage Committee had inscribed on its "World Heritage List," twenty of which were United States "World Heritage Sites" – to include Independence Hall (1979), Monticello and the University of Virginia, Charlottesville (1987) and the statue of "Liberty Enlightening the World" (1984).

The World Heritage List was established under the terms of *The Convention Concerning the Protection of the World Cultural and Natural Heritage* adopted in November 1972 at the 17th General Conference of UNESCO. The World Heritage Committee is a 21-nation body elected from among all those that have ratified the Convention to carry out its program of recognition and mutual assistance. One of the main responsibilities of this Committee is to provide technical co-operation under the World Heritage Fund for the safeguarding of World Heritage properties to States Parties whose resources are insufficient. Through the World Heritage Fund, the committee can provide countries requesting assistance with studies, advice, training, and equipment in order to eliminate problems, restore damaged areas, and set up safeguards.[1]

UNESCO'S "List of World Heritage in Danger"

The committee also places properties on a "List of World Heritage in Danger." This action may be taken in view of such threats to the sites as natural disasters or civil strife.

The World Heritage Emblem – "Interdependence"

The World Heritage Site Emblem "symbolizes the interdependence of cultural and natural properties; the square is a form created by humankind and the circle represents nature, the two being intimately linked. The emblem is round like the world and at the same time it is a symbol of protection."[2]

Has UNESCO ever protected the original history of the United States, at her foremost national historic sites? To the contrary, she has vigorously pursued her program of rewriting and dismantling America's original heritage at these United Nations "World Heritage Sites," including Monticello.

UNESCO'S Scheme to Pervert Public Education

In the Congressional Record's Proceedings and Debates of the 82nd Congress, First Session, on Thursday, October 18, 1951, the following exposé was reported by the Honorable John T. Wood of Idaho. It commences thus,

> Mr. Speaker, I am herewith appending an article published by the American Flag Committee in Philadelphia, bearing the title, '**A Report to**

the American People on UNESCO. It is my sincere hope that every parent of every child in America may be able to read the inroads that this infamous plot has already made in the educational system of America and reading, may feel impelled to do something about it, both locally and nationally; and particularly at the voting booth:

UNESCO, the United Nations Educational, Scientific and Cultural Organization is a subversive association. It is consciously furthering a campaign calculated to pervert the teaching profession in this country, and to destroy the worth and integrity of America's first bulwark of freedom – our tax-supported public schools. UNESCO'S scheme to pervert public education appears in a series of nine volumes titled, "Toward World Understanding," which presume to instruct kindergarten and elementary grade teachers in the fine art of preparing our youngsters for the day when their first loyalty will be to a World Government, of which the United States will form but an administrative part. The booklets bear the following individual numbers and titles:

I. Some Suggestions on Teaching about the United Nations and its Specialized Agencies.
II. The Education and Training of Teachers.
III. A Selected Bibliography.
IV. The United Nations and World Citizenship.
V. In the Classroom with Children under 13 Years of Age.
VI. The Influence of Home and Community on Children under 13 Years of Age.
VII. Some Suggestions on the Teaching of Geography.
VIII. A Teacher's Guide to the Declaration of Human Rights.
IX. Some Suggestions on the Teaching of World History.

These booklets are cheaply priced for maximum distribution and are printed by *Columbia University Press*, New York. This seems appropriate, considering the role Columbia's Teaching College has long played in developing new methods for radicalizing and internationalizing public education in this country. The institution has become well known as a hotbed of British Fabianism, that peculiar type of creeping socialism which sired the present Labor Government which has reduced England to a fourth-rate power… **UNESCO'S booklets** read like the propaganda put out by United World Federalists, Inc., which has been denied tax exemption because of its specifically political nature. They begin by advancing the totally un-American doctrine that the prime function of public education in the United States must be that of capturing the minds of our children, at the earliest possible age, for the cause of political world government. The teacher is urged to devote every classroom minute to this end, and every subject taught must serve, or be revised in such a manner that it is made to serve, this same central objective.

The program is quite specific. The teacher is to begin by eliminating any and all words, phrases, descriptions, pictures, maps, classroom material or teaching methods of a sort causing his pupils to feel or express a particular love for, or loyalty to, the United States of America. Children exhibiting such prejudice as a result of prior home influences – UNESCO calls it the outgrowth of **the narrow family spirit** – are to be dealt an abundant measure of counter propaganda at the earliest possible age.

Booklet V. on page 9, advises the teacher that: "The kindergarten or infant school has a significant part to play in the child's education. Not only can it correct many of the errors of home training, but it can also prepare the child for membership, at about the age of seven, in a group of his own age and habits – the first of many such social identifications that he must achieve on his way to membership in the world society."

UNESCO'S Attack upon Patriotism and its Parental Encouragement

Following this same line of attack upon patriotism and its parental encouragement, the same booklet, on pages 58-60, goes on to further poison the minds of our teachers by adding:

As we have pointed out, it is frequently the family that infects the child with extreme nationalism. The school should therefore use the means described earlier to combat family attitudes that favor patriotism. Education for world-mindedness is not a problem that the school can solve within its own walls or with its own means. It is a political problem even more than an educational one, and the present position of teachers does not, in general permit them to intervene in the field of politics with the requisite authority. We thought with cautious optimism that educators could also try to influence public opinion. Certain members of our group thought that educators might now besiege the authorities with material demands in the manner of a trade union. In our opinion it is essential that, on the one hand, a *Children's Charter* should secure for all children such education as is summarized in this report, which alone can create the atmosphere in which development of world-mindedness is conceivable, and that, on the other hand, a *Teacher's Charter* should secure for all members of the teaching profession the liberty to provide such an education by the means they decide upon, as well as the right of access to commissions and councils responsible for the organization of public education.

Aside from encouraging the public school teachers to make war upon the ideals of patriotic national devotion which UNESCO sees as infecting our children in the home, precisely what kind of instruction would the authors of these UNESCO booklets introduce by influencing public opinion, besieging the authorities with material demands in the manner of a trade union, and by pressing for a *Children's Charter* and a *Teachers' Charter*, which refer to instruments prepared in treaty form, making UNESCO principles the supreme law of the United States? Let's see.

Teachers Urged to Suppress American History

First of all, teachers are urged to suppress American history and American geography, which might enhance pro-American sentiments which UNESCO wishes to sterilize. Here is how **Booklet V**, on page 11, treats the problem as it affects children aged 3-13 years:

"In our view, history and geography should be taught at this stage as universal history and geography. Of the two, only geography lends itself well to study during the years prescribed by the present survey. **The study of history**, on the other hand, raises problems of value which are better postponed until the pupil is freed from the nationalist prejudices, which at present surround the teaching of history."

Translated into less abstruse phraseology, the teacher is instructed to purge American geography from the elementary school classroom by divorcing it from its national element, and to completely ignore the teaching of history until the pupil enters high school since this subject cannot be similarly internationalized, and so is too risky to advance until the **youngsters' patriotic spirit has been thoroughly emaciated**. Parents who take a bit of time to investigate may find (as we found in eastern Pennsylvania) that a number of elementary schools have already dropped American history as a standard, required subject...

A Passage from Karl Marx's Communist Manifesto

UNESCO'S Teachers' Guides read like a passage from Karl Marx's Communist Manifesto. What better way to inculcate calumny against the founder of America's Republican creed of liberty, than to implement and promote the defamation of his character at his own home – Monticello, claimed by UNESCO in 1987 as a United Nations "World Heritage Site"?

20th Century Attacks – Jefferson the Atheist?

The calumnies against Jefferson do not stop here, however. Modern-day journalists continue to lambast the founder of republican political thought with false accusations of being an atheist – a product of the "Enlightenment" or "Reign of Terror" philosophy. For example, Steven Morris,* a self-pronounced atheist, in his Fall, 1995 article published by the *Pittsburgh Post Gazette*, entitled, "The Founding Fathers were not Christians," states that,

> **Thomas Jefferson**, third president and author of the *Declaration of Independence*, wrote, "The Christian priesthood, finding the doctrines of Christ levelled to every understanding and too plain to need explanation, saw, in the mysticisms of Plato, materials with which they might build up an artificial system which might, from its indistinctness, admit everlasting controversy, give employment for their order, and introduce it to profit, power and pre-eminence. The doctrines which flowed from the lips of Jesus himself are within the comprehension of a child; but thousands of volumes have not yet explained the Platonisms engrafted on them: and for this obvious reason that nonsense can never be explained." [3]

"The Christian priesthood" herein referred to by Jefferson in his July 5, 1814 letter to John Adams, is the Anglican clergy, which controlled the religious and civil liberties of Virginia under British rule, and which his 1786 *Act for Establishing Religious Freedom* disestablished. Plato (427-347 B.C.) was a Greek philosopher, a student of Socrates and teacher of Aristotle. Platonistic thought of the 13th century attempted to incorporate the body of Greek doctrine into Christian theology, and works in this direction have become the official attitude of the Roman Catholic Church.[4]

*Steven Morris, professor of physics at Los Angeles' Harbor College in Wilmington, California.

Additional correspondence by Thomas Jefferson to Jared Sparks on November 4, 1820, explains his view that "all subsequent innovations" were corruptions of Christianity. He asserts,

> I hold the precepts of Jesus, as delivered by himself, to be the most pure, benevolent, and sublime which have ever been preached to man. I adhere to the principles of the first age; and consider all subsequent innovations as corruptions of this religion, having no foundation in what came from Him... The religion of Jesus is founded in the unity of God, and this principle, chiefly, gave it triumph over the rabble of heathen gods then acknowledged. Thinking men of all nations rallied readily to the doctrine of one only God, and embraced it with the pure morals which Jesus inculcated. If the freedom of religion, guaranteed to us by law <u>in theory</u> can ever rise <u>in practice</u> under the overbearing inquisition of public opinion, truth will prevail over fanaticism, and the genuine doctrines of Jesus, so long perverted by his pseudo-priests, will again be restored to their original purity...

Again, in a letter to John Adams dated May 5, 1817, Jefferson applauds the fact that "this den of the priesthood is at length broken up and that a Protestant Popedom is no longer to disgrace the American history and character." He once more differentiates "sectarian dogmas" from "true religion, as taught by Jesus Christ:"

> ...I join you, therefore, in sincere congratulations that this den of the priesthood is at length broken up, and that a Protestant Popedom is no longer to disgrace the American history and character. If by *Religion*, we are to understand *sectarian dogmas*, in which no two of them agree, then your exclamation on that hypothesis is just, 'that this would be the best of all possible worlds, if there were no religion in it.' But if the moral precepts, innate in man, and made a part of his physical constitution, as necessary for a social being, if the sublime doctrines of philanthropism and deism* taught us by Jesus of Nazareth, in which all agree, constitute true religion, then, without it, this would be, as you again say, 'something not fit to be named, even indeed, a hell.'

Jefferson, the anti-Evolutionist

In another letter to John Adams, written on April 11, 1823, Jefferson asserts his belief in Almighty God's creation of the universe by "a Superintending Power," "an Intelligent and Powerful Agent," "an eternal pre-existence of a Creator:"

> I hold (without appeal to revelation)** that when we take a view of the universe, in its parts, general or particular, it is impossible for the human mind not to perceive and feel a conviction of design, consummate skill, and indefinite power in every atom of its composition. The movements of the heavenly bodies, so exactly held in their course by the balance of centrifugal and centripetal forces, the structure of our earth itself, with its distribution

---

* One God – as opposed to "the rabble of heathen gods."
** The Bible – The Word of God.

of lands, waters, and atmosphere; animal and vegetable bodies, examined in all their minutest particles; insects, mere atoms of life, yet as perfectly organized as man or mammoth; the mineral substances, their generation and uses; it is impossible, I say, for the human mind not to believe, that there is in all this, design, cause, and effect, up to an ultimate cause, a fabricator of all things from matter and motion, their preserver and regulator while permitted to exist in their present forms, and their regenerator into new and other forms.

We see, too, evident proofs of the necessity of a Superintending Power, to maintain the universe in its course and order. Stars, well known, have disappeared, new ones have come into view; comets, in their incalculable courses, may run foul of suns and planets, and require renovation under other laws; certain races of animals are become extinct; and were there no restoring power, all existences might extinguish successively, one by one, until all should be reduced to a shapeless chaos. So irresistible are these evidences of an Intelligent and Powerful Agent, that, of the infinite numbers of men who have existed through all time, they have believed, in the proportion of a million at least to a unit, in the hypothesis of an eternal pre-existence of a Creator, rather than in that of a self-existent universe. Surely this unanimous sentiment renders this more probable, than that of the few in the other hypothesis...

Worthy of note, is that the above-quoted testimony of Thomas Jefferson, as well as his *Declaration of Independence*, powerfully refute the inculcated atheistic Darwinian theory of evolution, forced into American public schools in the early 1900's. Its disastrous results are being demonstrated in society today.

Was he Anti-Semitic?

Another accusation voiced against Thomas Jefferson is that he was anti-Semitic. The question is easily put to rest by his gracious, respectful, admiring letter to Joseph Marx, dated July 8, 1820:

Monticello, July 8, 1820

Thomas Jefferson presents to Mr. Marx his compliments and thanks for the transactions of the Paris Sanhedrin, which he shall read with great interest, and with the regret he has ever felt at seeing, a sect the parent and basis of all those of Christendom, singled out by all of them for a persecution and oppression which prove they have profited nothing from the benevolent doctrines of Him whom they profess to make the model of their principles and practice.

Jefferson salutes Mr. Marx with sentiments of perfect esteem and respect.

Chapter XIX

Charles Thomson's "Synopsis of the Four Evangelists" – Jefferson's "wee-little book" – "The Philosophy of Jesus of Nazareth, an Abridgment of the New Testament for the Use of the Indians…" Jefferson to Charles Thomson, "I am a Real Christian" – Jefferson's "wee-little book," the work of 2-3 nights at Washington – Jefferson's "wee-little book" and the Smithsonian Institution – The History of Jefferson's "wee-little book" – 1904, Jefferson's "wee-little book" becomes "Thomas Jefferson's Bible" – 2011, Jefferson's "wee-little book" becomes "The Jefferson Bible, by Thomas Jefferson" – Smithsonian's "The History and Conservation of the Jefferson Bible" narrative continues – Three Charters of Freedom of the American Republic – Jefferson's Writing Desk – Inauguration of Smithsonian Books' 2011 "The Jefferson Bible," a Deliberate Fake.

Charles Thomson's "Synopsis of the Four Evangelists"

Charles Thomson (1729-1824) served as Secretary of the Continental Congress and the Congress of the Confederation from 1774-1789. A scholar of the Greek Bible, he published in 1789, the first American translation of the Septuagint (Greek Old and New Testaments.)

Jefferson to Charles Thomson – "I am a real Christian"

On January 9, 1816, Jefferson wrote to his life-long friend, praising him for the accuracy of his "Synopsis of the Four Evangelists;"* emphasizing its "usefulness, to those, who, not taking things on trust, recur for themselves to the fountain of pure morals." He announces to his Revolutionary-era friend that he, also, has made a wee-little book from the four Gospels, naming it "The Philosophy** of Jesus," and that it is "a paradigma"*** of His doctrines,**** by cutting the texts out of the book, and arranging them on the pages of a blank book, in a certain order of time and subject:"

> An acquaintance of fifty-two years, for I think ours dates from 1764, calls for an interchange of notice now and then, that we remain in existence, the monuments of another age, and examples of a friendship unaffected by the jarring elements by which we have been surrounded, or revolutions of government, of party and of opinion. I am reminded of this duty by the receipt, through our friend Dr. Patterson, of your *Synopsis of the Four Evangelists*. I had procured it as soon as I saw it advertised, and had become familiar with its use; but this copy is the more valued as it comes from your hand. This work bears the stamp of that accuracy which marks everything from you, and will be useful to those who, not taking things on trust, recur for themselves to the fountain of pure morals. I too, have made a **wee-little book** from the same materials, which I call the Philosophy of Jesus; it is a

---

* A Harmony of the Four Gospels, Matthew, Mark, Luke and John.

** Philosophy: Way of Life. Acts of the Apostles 22:4 and 24:22: "I persecuted this Way unto death" and "…having more perfect knowledge of that Way," respectively

*** paradigma: example, pattern, a model. From Latin and Greek, to show.

**** Doctrine: (Latin) *doctrina*; 1. teaching, instruction, from doctor: a teacher, instructor; from *docere*, to teach. 2. something taught, as the principles or creed of a Religion.

paradigma of his doctrines, made by cutting the texts out of the book, and arranging them on the pages of a blank book, in a certain order of time or subject. A more beautiful or precious morsel of ethics I have never seen: it is a document in proof that I am a real Christian, that is to say, a disciple of the doctrines of Jesus, very different from the Platonists, who call me infidel and themselves Christians and preachers of the gospel, while they draw all their characteristic dogmas* from what its Author never said nor saw. They have compounded from the heathen mysteries a system beyond the comprehension of man, of which the great Reformer of the vicious ethics and deism of the Jews, were He to return on earth, would not recognize one feature. If I had time I would add to my little book the Greek, Latin and French texts, in columns side by side...

Jefferson's "wee-little book"

In a prior letter to his former pastor, Charles Clay, dated January 29, 1815, Jefferson writes the following concerning his "wee-little book:"

> Probably you have heard me say I had taken the four Evangelists, had cut out from them every text they had recorded on the moral** precepts*** of Jesus, and arranged them in certain order, and although they appeared but as fragments, yet fragments of the most sublime edifice of morality which had ever been exhibited to man.

However, in this letter Jefferson disclaims any intention of publishing his little compilation saying, "I not only write nothing on religion, but rarely permit myself to speak on it."

"The Philosophy of Jesus of Nazareth – An Abridgment of the New Testament for the Use of the Indians..."

The entire **Title** given by Jefferson to his "wee-little book," is:

> The Philosophy of Jesus of Nazareth extracted from the account of His life and doctrines as given by Matthew, Mark, Luke and John, being an abridgement of the New Testament for the use of the Indians, unembarrassed with matters of fact or faith beyond the level of their comprehensions.

Its **Table of Contents**, hand-written by Jefferson, reads:

> A Table of the texts extracted from the Gospels, of the order in which they are arranged into sections, and the heads of each section.

---

* dogma: n. Greek: *dogma*, that which one thinks true, an opinion, decree, from *dokein*, to think, seem. a positive, arrogant assertion, dogmatic utterance. Dogmatic: an asserted a priori or without proof.
** moral: a. relating to, serving to teach or in accordance with, the principles of right and wrong. morality: n. a change of heart and moral character from being an enemy of God, to love of God and a holy life. Moral: n. the practical lesson inculcated by any story or incident, the significance or meaning (as in the parables of Jesus Christ.) A rule of action or conduct. *Webster's 1828 Dictionary.*
*** precept: n. to take beforehand, to admonish, a commandment or direction, a rule to be implemented.

I.	Luke 2. 1-7. 21. 22. 29-49. 51. 52 3. 29-38.	History of Jesus.
II.	Matthew 10. 5-31. 42.	Precepts for the Priesthood.
III.	Luke 22. 24-27. John 13. 4-17.	Preachers to be humble.
IV.	John 10. 1-16. Luke 11.52. 12.10-15.	False teachers.
V.	John 13. 34. 35.	Disciples should love one another.
VI.	Matthew 13. 24-30. 36-43	Parable of the Tares. man not to judge for God.
VII.	Matthew 20. 1-16.	Parable of the laborers.
VIII.	Mark 2. 15-17. Matthew 18. 10. 11. Luke 15. 9-32.	Physicians are for the sick. Parables of the lost sheep, the lost piece of silver, the prodigal son.
IX.	John 8. 1-11 Matthew 18. 15-17. Luke 19. 6-9.	The duty of mutual forgiveness & forbearance.
X.	Matthew 5. 1-10. 19-48. Matthew 6. 1-34. Matt. 7. 1-27.	The Sermon on the Mount.
XI.	Matthew 19.19-24. 29. 30. Matt. 22.25-40.	General moral precepts.
XII.	Matt. 12. 1-5. 11. 19. Luke 14. 1-6.	The Sabbath.
XIII.	Luke 11. 37-48. Matt. 15. 1-9.	Deeds and not ceremonies avail.
XIV.	Matt. 15. 10-20. Matt. 12. 33-37.	Words the fruit of the heart.
XV.	Matthew 13. 1-9. 18-23.	Parable of the sower.
XVI.	Luke 7. 36-47. Mark 12. 41-44.	The will for the deed.
XVII.	Matt. 11. 28-30.	General exhortation.
XVIII.	Luke 10. 25-37.	Parable of the Samaritan true benevolence.
XIX.	Matthew 23. 1-33. Luke 10. 9-14. Luke 14. 7-11. Matt. 18. 1-6.	Humility. pride, hypocrisy. Pharisaism.
XX.	Luke 16. 19-31. Matt. 22. 1-14. Matt. 12. 46-50. Matt. 8. 11.	Dives and Lazarus. The wedding supper. God no respecter of persons.

XXI.	Luke 13. 1-5.	Misfortune no proof of sin.
XXII.	Luke 14. 26-33.	Prudence and firmness to duty.
XXIII.	Luke 16. 1-13.	Parable of the unjust steward. worldly wisdom.
XXIV.	Luke 18. 1-8.	Parable of the unjust judge.
XXV.	Matt. 21. 33-41.	Parable of the unjust husbandman & their lord.
XXVI.	Luke 17. 7-10.	Mere justice no praise.
XXVII.	Luke 14. 12-14.	The merit of disinterested good.
XXVIII.	Matt. 21. 28-31.	Acts better than professions.
XXIX.	Matt. 22. 15-22.	Submission to magistrates.
XXX.	Matt. 19. 9-12.	The bond of marriage.
XXXI.	Matt. 25. 14-30.	The duty of improving our talents.
XXXII.	Luke. 12. 16-21.	Vain calculations of life.
XXXIII.	Matt. 25. 1-13. ⎫ Luke 12. 25-48. ⎭	Watch and be ready.
XXXIV.	John 12. 24-28.	The future life.
XXXV.	Matt. 22. 23-32.	The resurrection.
XXXVI.	Matt. 25. 31-46.	The last judgment.
XXXVII.	Matt. 13. 31-33. 44-52.	The Kingdom of Heaven.
XXXVIII.	John 4. 24.	God.
XXXIX.	John 18. 1. 2-9 Matt. 26. 49-50. John 18. 4. 5-8. Matt. 26. 55. John 18.12. Matt. 26.57. John. 18. 19-23. Matt. 26. 59-62. Luke 22. 67. 68. 70. Mark. 14. 60. 64. Luke. 23. 1-9. John 18. 36. Luke 23. 4-23. Matt. 27. 24. 25. Luke 23. 24. Matt. 27.26. John 19.16. Luke 23. 33. 34. John 19. 25-27. Matt. 27. 46. John 19. 28-30.	Crucifixion of Jesus.

> The Philosophy
>
> of Jesus of Nazareth
> extracted from the account of
> his life and doctrines as given by
> Mathew, Mark, Luke, & John.
>
> being an abridgement of
> the New Testament
> for the use of the Indians
> unembarrassed with matters of fact
> or faith beyond the level of their
> comprehensions.

Thomas Jefferson's handwritten *The Philosophy of Jesus of Nazareth extracted from the account of His life and doctrines as given by Matthew, Mark, Luke and John, being an abridgment of the New Testament for the use of the Indians, unembarrassed with matters of fact or faith beyond the level of their comprehensions.* Jefferson did not sign, nor did he put his name to this compilation of the teachings of Christ for the use of the Indians. Rare Book Collection, University of Virginia, Charlottesville, Virginia.

A Table of the texts extracted from the gospels, of the order in which they are arranged into sections, & the heads of each section.

§. I. Luke 2. 1–7. 21. 22. 39–49. 51. 52 } History of Jesus.
         3. 23–38.

II. Matt. 10. 5–31. 42. Precepts for the Priesthood.

III. Luke 22. 24–27. }
     John. 13. 4–17. } Preachers to be humble.

IV. John 10. 1–16 }
    Luke. 11. 52. } false teachers.
         12. 10–15 }

V. John. 13. 34. 35. disciples should love one another.

VI. Matt. 13. 24–30. 36–43. Parable of the tares. man not to judge for God.

VII. Matt 20. 1–16. Parable of the labourers.

VIII. Mark. 2. 15–17. } Physicians are for the sick.
      Matt. 18. 10. 11 } Parables of the lost sheep, the
      Luke 15. 3–32. } lost peice of silver, the prodigal son.

IX. John. 8. 1–11. }
    Matt 18. 15–17. } the duty of mutual forgiveness
    Luke. 17. 6–9 } & forbearance.

X. Matt. 5. 1–10. 19–48. }
         6. 1–34 } the Sermon in the mount.
         7. 1–27. }

Thomas Jefferson's handwritten *A Table of the texts extracted from the gospels of the order in which they are arranged into sections, and the heads of each secton.* Rare Book Collection, University of Virginia, Charlottesville, Virginia.

XI. Matth. 19. 13–24. 29. 30.
22. 35–40. } general moral precepts.

XII. 12. 1–5. 11. 12.
Luke 14. 1–6. } the sabath.

XIII. 11. 37–46.
matth. 15. 1–9. } deeds & not ceremonies avail.

XIV. 10–20.
12. 33–37. } words the fruit of the heart.

XV. 13. 1–9. 18–23. Parable of the sower.

XVI. Luke 7. 36–47.
mark 12. 41–44. } the will for the deed.

XVII. Matth. 11. 28–30 General exhortation.

XVIII Luke. 10. 25–37. Parable of the Samaritan true benevolence.

XIX matth. 23. 1–33.
Luke. 18. 9–14.
Matth. 14. 7–11.
18. 1–6. } humility. pride hypocrisy. Pharisaism.

XX. Luke 16. 19–31. Dives & Lazarus
matth. 22. 1–14. the wedding supper
12. 46–50.
8. 11. } God no respecter of persons.

XXI. Luke. 13. 1–5. misfortune no proof of sin.

XXII. 14. 26–33. Prudence & firmness to duty

XXIII. 16. 1–13. Parable of the unjust steward. wordly wisdom

A page of Thomas Jefferson's handwritten, *A Table of the Texts extracted from the gospels of the order in which they are arranged into sections, and the heads of each section*. Rare Book Collection, University of Virginia, Charlottesville, Virginia.

XXIV.	18. 1—8.	Parable of the unjust judge.
XXV.	Matt. 21. 33.—41.	Parable of the unjust husbandmen & their lord.
XXVI.	Luke. 17. 7—10.	mere justice no praise.
XXVII	14. 12—14.	the merit of disinterested good.
XXVIII	matt. 21. 28—31.	acts better than proffessions.
XXIX.	22. 15—22.	submission to magistrates.
XXX.	19. 3—12.	the bond of mariage.
XXXI.	25. 14—30.	the duty of improving our talents.
XXXII.	Luke. 12. 16—21.	vain calculations of life.
XXXIII	Matt. 25. 1—13. Luke. 12. 35—48.	watch and be ready.
XXXIIII	John. 12. 24—25.	a future life.
XXXV	matt. 22. 23—32.	the resurrection.
XXXVI.	25. 31—46.	the last judgement.
XXXVII.	13. 31—33. 44—52.	the Kingdom of heaven
XXXVIII	John. 4. 24.	God.

A page of Thomas Jefferson's handwritten, *A Table of the Texts extracted from the gospels of the order in which they are arranged into sections, and the heads of each section*. Rare Book Collection, University of Virginia, Charlottesville, Virginia.

In perusing Thomas Jefferson's hand-written "A Table of the texts extracted from the Gospels…" – the Scriptures he selected, and their corresponding descriptive categories – a true follower of Jesus Christ cannot but marvel at his belief and implementation of our Redeemer's solemn teachings. His categories prove his belief in eternal life; the resurrection; the last judgment; Christ's deity; His Kingship; the Judge of all men; eternal life for His true believers; and everlasting punishment for the wicked (cursed), cast into everlasting fire prepared for the devil and his angels (Matthew 25: 31-46); the Kingdom of Heaven; the Sabbath; humility and mercy, and Christ's admonition to watch and be ready. Jefferson's acknowledgment of sin, vain calculations of life, worldly wisdom, pharisaism, pride, hypocrisy, Heaven and hell (Dives and Lazarus) stand out. It should also be noted that at Calvary, Christ's full identity was written upon His cross: JESUS OF NAZARETH KING OF THE JEWS, in fulfillment of multiple Old Testament prophecies.

His inclusion of the miraculous, as in Matthew 25:31-46, proves his belief in the Last Judgment, when true disciples of Jesus Christ, King of kings, **inherit eternal life**; and the wicked are cast into everlasting punishment:

> When the Son of man shall come in His glory, and all the holy angels with Him, then shall He sit upon the throne of His glory: And before Him shall be gathered all nations: and He shall separate them one from another, as a shepherd divideth his sheep from the goats: And He shall set the sheep on His right hand, but the goats on the left. Then shall the King say unto them on his right hand, **Come, ye blessed of my Father, inherit the kingdom prepared for you from the foundation of the world**: For I was an hungered, and ye gave me meat: I was thirsty, and ye gave me drink: I was a stranger, and ye took me in: Naked, and ye clothed Me: I was sick, and ye visited Me: I was in prison, and ye came unto Me. Then shall the righteous answer Him, saying, Lord, when saw we thee an hungered, and fed thee? Or thirsty, and gave thee drink? When saw we thee a stranger, and took thee in? or naked, or in prison, and came unto thee? And the King shall answer and say unto them, Verily I say unto you, Inasmuch as ye have done it unto one of the least of these my brethren, ye have done it unto me. Then shall He say also unto them on the left hand, **Depart from Me, ye cursed, into everlasting fire, prepared for the devil and his angels**: For I was an hungered and ye gave Me no meat: I was thirsty, and ye gave me no drink: I was a stranger, and ye took me not in: naked, and ye clothed me not: sick, and in prison, and ye visited Me not. Then shall they also answer Him, saying, Lord, when saw we thee a hungered, or athirst, or a stranger, or naked, or sick, or in prison, and did not minister unto thee? Then shall He answer them, saying, Verily I say unto you, Inasmuch as ye did it not to one of the least of these, ye did it not to Me. **And these shall go away into everlasting punishment: but the righteous into life eternal**. Matt. 25:31-46.

And again, his selection of Matthew 22: 29-32 is evidence of his belief in the resurrection:

> And Jesus answered and said unto them, Ye do err, not knowing the Scriptures, nor the power of God. For in the resurrection they neither marry nor are given in marriage, but are as the angels of God in heaven. But as touching the resurrection of the dead, have ye not read that which was spoken unto you by God, saying, I am the God of Abraham, and the God of Isaac and the God of Jacob? God is not the God of the dead but of the living. Matt. 22: 29-32.

A striking Scripture verse chosen by Jefferson under his category for Almighty God is John 4: 24,

> God is a Spirit: and they that worship Him must worship Him in spirit and in truth.

Jefferson's acknowledgement that Christ's Kingdom was not of this world, but of the world hereafter, is amply proved by his selection of John 18: 36:

> Jesus answered, 'My kingdom is not of this world: if my kingdom were of this world, then would my servants fight, that I should not be delivered to the Jews: but now is my kingdom not from hence.'

"The Philosophy of Jesus of Nazareth..." contains many more supernatural Scriptural events.

Jefferson's "wee-little book" – "The Work of 2-3 Nights at Washington"

His "wee-little book" of a harmony of the teachings of Christ, compiled for the benefit of the Indians as a prelude to their understanding the entire Bible, cannot possibly be misconstrued to mean that the founder of America's political thought "wrote his own bible, removing the miraculous," – the latter being widely publicized by the enemies of republican liberty, who have wielded this political tool to denounce Jefferson as an "infidel, atheist, deist and/or anti-Christian."

Randolph G. Adams, in his book, *The Three Americanists*, expounds upon his compilation of the "Philosophy of Jesus...:"

> As a child of the 18th century, Jefferson's revolt against tyranny was colored by his knowledge that oppression was often the product of an autocratic church...Like John Eliot of New England, he was also concerned with the conversion of the Indians to Christianity. But when he proposed a bible for the use of the Indians, he insisted that it should not be embarrassed with passages containing matters of fact or faith beyond the level of the Red Man's comprehension. John Eliot must have been sorely puzzled while explaining some of the Old Testament to the Indians. In preparing his bible for the Indians, Mr. Jefferson adopted the simple device of clipping passages from copies of a printed Bible.

As Jefferson recalled years later, "It was the work of two or three nights only at Washington, after getting through the evening task of reading the letters and papers of the day." On March 4, 1804, the 46-page, "wee-little book" had been completed. Years later, Jefferson added a comparison of his English "Philosophy of Jesus of Nazareth..." with the corresponding Greek, Latin and French Scriptures, in four columns.

Jefferson's "wee-little book" and the Smithsonian Institution

The question arises: How did Thomas Jefferson's "wee-little book" get into the hands of the *Division of Political and Military History*, at the Smithsonian Institution's National Museum of American History?" Its conveyance there, where it is housed, is chronicled as follows:

The History of Jefferson's "wee-little book"

In 1895, Cyrus Adler, then Librarian of the Smithsonian Institution, persuaded Carolina Randolph, eighth daughter of Jefferson's eldest grandson, Thomas Jefferson Randolph, to sell the "wee-little book" with the corresponding Greek, Latin and French Scriptures in four columns, to the Smithsonian's National Museum for $400. Adler had been a Semitics student at Johns Hopkins University. In 1904, seventy-eight years after Jefferson's death, Adler persuaded the 57th Congress, first session, to order the printing of 9,000 copies of "The Life and Morals of Jesus of Nazareth, extracted textually from the Gospels in Greek, Latin, French and English," with its Table of Contents, "Table of the texts from the Evangelists employed in this Narrative and the order of their arrangement." This one-of-kind museum piece was neither signed, catalogued or printed by Jefferson. Neither did he put his name to it. The Congressional order was executed as follows:

Photograph of Cyrus Adler (1863-1940) while serving as Librarian of the Smithsonian Institution.

That there be printed and bound, by photolithographic process, with an introduction of not to exceed twenty-five pages, to be prepared by Dr. Cyrus Adler, Librarian of the Smithsonian Institution, for the use of Congress, 9,000 copies of Thomas Jefferson's Morals of Jesus of Nazareth, as the same appears in the National Museum; 3,000 copies for the use of the Senate and 6,000 copies for the use of the House.

1904 – Jefferson's "wee-little book" becomes "Thomas Jefferson's Bible"

Thus, in 1904, the "wee-little book's" new title page proclaimed – "by Thomas Jefferson," giving the false impression that Thomas Jefferson "wrote his own bible." Subsequent to the printing of this unique museum piece by the 58th U.S. Congress as "a Government Document," the Smithsonian lost no time in using it as a powerful political weapon to discredit the founder of America's liberties, by promoting it as "Thomas Jefferson's Bible."

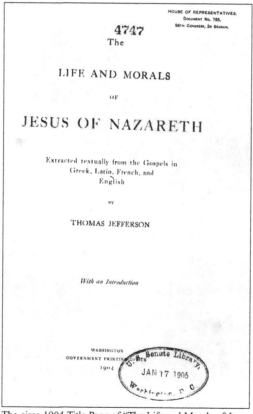

The circa 1904 Title Page of "The Life and Morals of Jesus of Nazareth extracted textually from the Gospels in Greek, Latin, French and English." "By Thomas Jefferson" and "With an Introduction" was added to Jefferson's original compilation which he neither signed nor put his name to. House of Representatives Document No. 765, 58th Congress, 2nd Session. Printed by the Washington Government Printing Office, 1904.

2011 – Jefferson's "wee little book" becomes "The Jefferson Bible, by Thomas Jefferson"

In 2011, the Smithsonian Institution republished Jefferson's one-of-a-kind artifact in their possession through Smithsonian Books, under the bold new revisionist title, "The Jefferson Bible, by Thomas Jefferson." However, the latter neither signed, nor put his name to it – nor did he title it a Bible. As a companion to this publication, Smithsonian Books published "The History and Conservation of the Jefferson Bible" by Harry R. Rubenstein (Curator of the *Division of Political and Military History,* National Museum of American History) and Barbara Cark Smith, © the Smithsonian Institution, printed in China through Oceanic Graphic Printing, Inc.

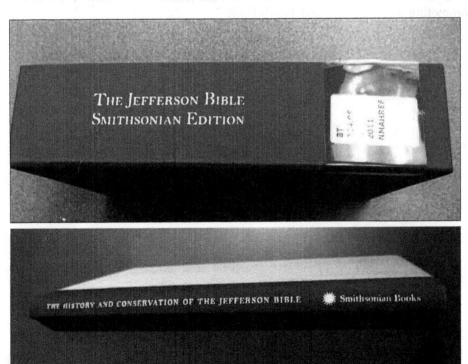

Above: The Smithsonian Institution's 2011 edition of "The Life and Morals of Jesus of Nazareth…" bearing their newly invented title: "The Jefferson Bible, by Thomas Jefferson," published by Smithsonian Books. Below: "The History and Conservation of the Jefferson Bible" by Smithsonian Books, a companion to the above publication, by Harry R. Rubenstein (Curator of the *Division of Political and Military History*, National Museum of American History), and Barbara Clark Smith.

Its Foreword, written by Brent D. Glass, Director of the National Museum of American History, contains statements contradicting the Christian philosophy of Thomas Jefferson, heretofore proven from factual evidence. They are as follows:

> "...no one can quarrel with the legacy that he valued most. Jefferson championed the ideals of the Age of Enlightenment..."

As previously discussed, the "Age of Enlightenment" is equated with the French Revolution's atheistic "Reign of Terror," – which is at antipodes to the Scriptural ideals embodied in Jefferson's greatest works undergirding the American Republic – *The Declaration of Independence* and his *Act for Establishing Religious Freedom*, as well as many others.

The Foreword continues,

> "...Jefferson's Bible – The Life and Morals of Jesus of Nazareth – offers further evidence of the personal philosophy that guided his public life. Any discussion about Jefferson's religious beliefs must reference this extraordinary text as a primary source..."

The above-referenced "wee-little book" is neither "Jefferson's Bible," nor could it possibly have guided his public life, being non-existent until 1804, at the completion of his "Philosophy of Jesus of Nazareth...An Abridgment of the Gospels for the use of the Indians...," four years prior to his exiting public life. This he did during two to three nights at the White House. Jefferson's custom of reading his large Old and New Testament Bible, which he called *his* Bible, on a continuing basis, refutes this statement.

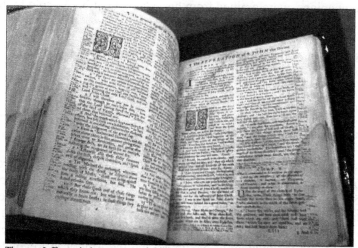

Thomas Jefferson's large personal Bible, containing the Old and New Testaments, opened between the General Epistle of Jude and Chapter 1 of the Book of Revelation. King James Authorized translation, Oxford: 1752. Rare Book Collection, University of Virginia, Charlottesville, Virginia.

Under the chapter heading, "History of the Jefferson Bible" by Harry R. Rubenstein and Barbara Clark Smith, we read,

> "...This then was Thomas Jefferson's Bible; it contained the one form of Christianity – however misshapen it appeared to others – that Jefferson believed."

Firstly, Jefferson did not entitle his compilation, nor did he call it, "a Bible." Secondly, his large Old and New Testament Bible, which Edmund Bacon, Monticello overseer for twenty years, witnessed him reading, "many and many a time" is preserved in the Rare Book vault of the University of Virginia, catalogued as "Thomas Jefferson's Bible" circa 1752. From *The Private Life of Thomas Jefferson*, we read Bacon's eye-witness account,

> Mr. Jefferson had a sofa or lounge upon which he could sit or recline, and a small table on rollers, upon which he could write, or lay his books. Sometimes he would draw this table up before the sofa, and sit and read or write; and other times he would recline on his sofa, with his table rolled up to the sofa, astride it. He had a large Bible, which nearly always lay at the head of his sofa. Many and many a time I have gone into his room and found him reading that Bible. You remember I told you about riding all night from Richmond, after selling that flour, and going into his room very early in the morning, and paying over to him the new United State Bank money. *That* was one of the times that I found him with the big Bible open before him on his little table, and he busy reading it. And I have seen him reading it in that way many a time. Some people, you know, say he was an atheist. Now if he was an atheist, what did he want with all those religious books, and **why did he spend so much of his time reading his Bible?**[1]

This is Thomas Jefferson's personal Bible, a King James Authorized translation of the Old and New Testaments published in 1752. Both his Bible and Prayer Book, constant companions, were omitted from his catalogue of books sold to the Library of Congress in 1815.

Smithsonian's "The History and Conservation of the Jefferson Bible" narrative continues

> "...it offers insight into the individual who created it, the thought of his times, and the American Revolution. It can be read as an historical document that illuminates the new nation..."

Jefferson's "wee-little book" as he called it, was initially completed in 1804 during two or three nights at the White House. The American Revolution spanned the years 1775-1783, concluding with the Treaty of Peace signed on September 3, 1783. This disqualifies his "wee-little book" from being credibly touted by the Smithsonian Institution as "an historic document that illuminates the new nation." Neither does it "offer insight into the thought of his times, and the American Revolution," as it was compiled twenty-three years subsequent to the final surrender of the British at Yorktown on October 19, 1781.

"Three Charters of Freedom" of the American Republic

The three great Charters of Freedom of the American Republic were signed as follows: *The Declaration of Independence* – July 4, 1776; the *U.S. Constitution* – September 17, 1787 and the *U.S. Bill of Rights* – March 4, 1789. These "historical documents that illuminate the new nation" did not originate from a compilation entitled, "The Philosophy of Jesus of Nazareth…being an Abridgement of the New Testament for the use of the Indians unembarrassed with matters of fact or faith beyond the level of their comprehensions," circa 1804.

Jefferson's Writing Desk

The Foreword of "The History and Conservation of the Jefferson Bible" informs the American public that their project is aimed at bringing,

> "the book to a wider audience through exhibitions, a website and this publication…The National Museum of American History was able to conserve and exhibit Jefferson's Bible through a public-private partnership – generous gifts… Through their work, Jefferson's Bible will take its place with the portable writing desk as twin reminders of the private and public life of one of America's greatest leaders, a complex and influential man who defined his own times and continues even today to shape our understanding of what it means to be an American."

Thomas Jefferson's writing desk is associated with the greatest documents of American history shaping the nation's political thought today – *The Declaration of Independence* (1776), the *Virginia Statute for Religious Freedom* (1786), *An Appeal to Arms* (1775), *Notes on the State of Virginia* (1785), *A Summary View of the Rights of British America* (1774), the first draft of the Virginia Constitution, his *Anti-Slavery Bill* (1778), his *Autobiography* (1743-1790) and numerous others – which cannot possibly be equated with what he himself titled "a wee-little book of the Philosophy of Jesus" and "a compilation which took me two to three nights at Washington," in 1804.

Least of all should it be sold by the federal government to Americans as "Jefferson's Bible" or "The Thomas Jefferson Bible," being a falsehood of the highest order – implying that Jeffersonian freedoms stem from a book first published in 1904 as a Government Document by the Washington Government Printing Office – at the behest of Smithsonian Librarian, Cyrus Adler. The fact that the liberty was taken by Adler to inscribe Jefferson's name thereon against his will, is proven by a letter dated April 25, 1816 to Mr. Fr. Adr. Vanderkemp, in response to a request that he use an "extract" in a publication of his own. Jefferson agreed, under the following terms: "**I ask only one condition, that no possibility shall be admitted of my name being even intimated with the publication.**"

Inauguration of Smithsonian Books' 2011 "The Jefferson Bible" – A Deliberate Fake

The grand inauguration of Smithsonian Books' 2011 publication entitled, "The Jefferson Bible – The Life and Morals of Jesus of Nazareth extracted textually from the Gospels, in Greek, Latin, French and English by Thomas Jefferson – Smithsonian Books, 2011," with his portrait thereon, took place on November 11, 2011.

An article in the October, 2011 issue of *The Smithsonian* by Wayne Clough, Secretary of the Smithsonian Institution, informs its global readership that,

> ...the conserved Jefferson Bible will be unveiled in an exhibition (November 11-May 28, 2012) at the National Museum of American History's Albert H. Small Documents Gallery. The exhibition will tell the story of the Jefferson Bible and explain how it offers insights into Jefferson's ever-enigmatic mind...The exhibition will be accompanied by an online version. Smithsonian Books will release the first full-color facsimile of the Jefferson Bible on November 1, and the Smithsonian Channel will air a documentary, *Jefferson's Secret Bible* in February, 2012...Now, nearly two centuries after he completed it, the Smithsonian Institution is sharing Jefferson's unique, handmade book with America and the world.

Hence, the Smithsonian Institution's 2011 publication of Jefferson's "wee-little book," with a counterfeit title and cover, inscribing his name thereon against his will, and advertised globally as being "Jefferson's Secret Bible" – which he wrote, **is a deliberate fake**.

Chapter XX

A Step Further, The Museum of the Bible – "Impact of the Bible in America" exhibit: "The Jefferson Bible," 2011 Smithsonian Edition – Thomas Jefferson and Revisionism – Smithsonian Books' 2011 "The Jefferson Bible," a 21st Century Fake Title and Cover – The Museum of the Bible's "Thanksgiving in America" – Thomas Jefferson's December 9th, 1779 "Day of Publick and Solemn Thanksgiving and Prayer to Almighty God" Proclamation – "The Missing Complement of 'Jefferson's Bible' " or his "Literary Commonplace Book"? – "The Literary Bible of Thomas Jefferson" – Inauguration of the Museum of the Bible - "The Shroud of Turin," Roman Catholic Relic – Counterfeit Papyri Fragments and Clay Objects – Ancient Gilgamesh Tablet forfeited – "All Dead Sea Scroll Fragments in the Museum of the Bible are Forgeries" – A one-of-a-kind, original "wee-little book"of known Provenance in the University of Virginia vault – The Jesuits, a Threat to this "wee-little book" – The English, 1791 and 1799 New Testament Bibles bought by Thomas Jefferson – Jefferson's reverence for the Bible.

A Step Further – The Museum of the Bible

An article by Cary Summers, entitled "The Real Museum of the Bible," appeared in the *Times of Israel's* May 3, 2016 edition. Summers, its President, responds to an interview on the museum's mission and focus, as follows:

> The Museum of the Bible is dedicated to the impact, history and narrative of the Bible. It's a non-sectarian institution. **It is not political** and it will not proselytize…our goal is straightforward: reacquaint the world with the book that helped make it, and let the visitor come to their own conclusions. The Museum of the Bible is a global education institution that invites all people to engage in the Bible. We don't exist to tell people what to believe about it.

"Impact of the Bible in America" Exhibit: "The Jefferson Bible," 2011 Smithsonian Edition

However, "Impact of the Bible in America" exhibit on the founding fathers of the American Republic is decidedly political. It prominently show-cases "The Jefferson Bible – 2011 Smithsonian edition," which constitutes a powerful political tool. The original, entitled "Morals of Jesus" is catalogued as an "artifact" in the *Division of Political and Military History* of the Smithsonian's National Museum of American History. It is not "a Bible" nor is it "Jefferson's Bible," nor "The Jefferson Bible," fallacious names given to it by the Smithsonian Institution.

This "wee-little book" as Jefferson called his compilation of *The Life and Morals of Jesus of Nazareth extracted textually from the Gospels in Greek, Latin, French and English,* in their exhibit, counterfeits his own personal Bible, circa 1752, King James Authorized translation, as heretofore established, which Edmund Bacon, his Monticello overseer for twenty years, witnessed him reading "many and many a time." The latter is housed in the Rare Book vault of the University of Virginia.

Marker at the entranceway to "Impact of the Bible in America" exhibit. The Museum of the Bible, Washington, District of Columbia.

"Impact of the Bible in America" exhibit's prominent display of Smithsonian Books' 2011 edition of its newly-entitled, "The Jefferson Bible, by Thomas Jefferson" – a fake title and cover. (Photograph taken through glass). The Museum of the Bible, Washington, District of Columbia.

"Impact of the Bible in America" exhibit's descriptive wording accompanying the Smithsonian Institution's 2011 edition states:

> Thomas Jefferson, while deeply committed to Enlightenment ideals and liberated reason, also believed in a Supreme Being who was the creator of the universe. Though he did not accept the Christianity that was taught by most of the churches of his day, he held Jesus in high regard and considered his teachings to be an important element in an ethical republic. In his later years, Jefferson compiled Jesus' teachings in the Gospels, while excluding miracles and most other supernatural elements. He called Jesus's moral system the "most perfect and sublime that has ever been taught by man."

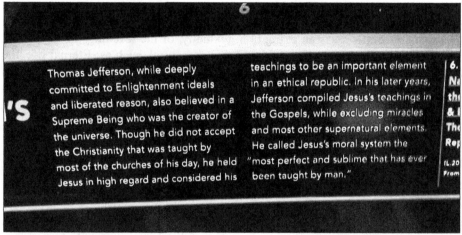

"Impact of the Bible in America" exhibit text on Thomas Jefferson. The Museum of the Bible, Washington, District of Columbia.

Thomas Jefferson and Revisionism

The exhibit's statement that Thomas Jefferson "called Jesus' moral system the 'most perfect and sublime that has ever been taught **by man**' " is rewritten to change the meaning of Jefferson's own words. Jefferson did not write, "...taught *by man*."

He wrote, in a letter dated June 17, 1804 to Henry Fry:

> I consider the doctrines of Jesus as delivered by Himself to contain the outlines of the sublimest system of morality that has ever been taught but I hold in the most profound detestation and execration the corruptions of it which have been invented by priestcraft and established by kingcraft constituting a conspiracy of church and state against the civil and religious liberties of mankind.

The curators of this exhibit's text have deliberately added the words, "**by man**", deceiving the public into believing that Jesus Christ, the Messiah, is a mere man – and that Thomas Jefferson wrote it. This is counterfeit history of the highest order.

Also, the curators' text that, "Thomas Jefferson did not accept the Christianity that was taught by most of the churches of his day" is inaccurate, implying that he disagreed with not only the Anglican Church (which he disestablished in 1786), but also the Presbyterian, Baptist, Episcopal, Methodist, Quaker, Huguenot, etc. dissident Protestant churches which he freed from control by the Civil Magistrate, enabling them to worship according to the tenets of the Bible.

As proven, Jefferson's 1804 English compilation titled, "The Philosophy of Jesus of Nazareth…" was an extraction, textually, of the teachings or sayings of Christ, which included the miraculous and supernatural, such as: Eternal life, the resurrection, Heaven, hell, Dives and Lazarus, the Last Judgement, the Kingdom of Heaven, the Wedding Supper, the Future life, and Matthew 25: 31-46: "When the Son of man shall come in His glory, and all His holy angels…"

Smithsonian Books' 2011 "The Jefferson Bible" – a 21st Century Fake Title and Cover

In conclusion, "The Jefferson Bible" or "Thomas Jefferson's Bible," published in 2011 by Smithsonian Books, with its counterfeit title and cover, is a 21st century fake, indoctrinating millions of visitors to the Museum of the Bible into believing the historical fallacy that Thomas Jefferson, author of the *Declaration of Independence*, "wrote his own bible, excluding miracles and most other supernatural elements."

As a fake, it needs to be immediately removed from the Museum of the Bible's "Impact of the Bible on America" exhibit and returned to its publisher, the Smithsonian Institution, prior to further deception being wrought upon an unwary American public.

The Museum of the Bible's "Thanksgiving in America"

The Museum of the Bible's articles sent to its global database recipients, include a November 26, 2019 article entitled, "Thanksgiving in America." The latter chronicles Thanksgiving Day in America from Abraham Lincoln's October 10th, 1863 Proclamation designating November 26, 1863, the last Thursday in November, as a National Day of Thanksgiving in perpetuity. The author(s) of the article conveniently omitted 240 years of America's history, the first Thanksgiving Day having been proclaimed in 1621 by Governor William Bradford of the Massachusetts Pilgrims. The article goes on to mention George Washington's 1789 Proclamation of a "Day of Public Thanksgiving and Prayer" but totally omits his February 19, 1795 "National Day of Thanksgiving and Prayer," decreed by Washington after the quelling of the "Whiskey Insurrection in Western Pennsylvania".

In keeping with the Museum of the Bible's revisionism of Thomas Jefferson's true historic identity, the article asserts that, "**Thomas Jefferson** believed public demonstrations of devotion to a higher power, like Thanksgiving, were unsuitable for a nation based in part on the separation of church and state." This misinformation, diffused globally under the label of a Bible Museum, is a powerful political method to indoctrinate millions into believing counterfeit history about the founder of America's republican creed.

Thomas Jefferson did, indeed, proclaim a "Day of Publick and Solemn Thanksgiving and Prayer to Almighty God."

Following is **Jefferson's December 9th, 1779 "Day of Publick and Solemn Thanksgiving and Prayer to Almighty God" Proclamation,** in which he extols publicly God the Father, God the Son and God the Holy Spirit:

On December 9th, 1779 **Thomas Jefferson,** Governor of Virginia, proclaimed,

> WHEREAS it becomes us humbly to approach the throne of Almighty God, with gratitude and praise, for the wonders which His goodness has wrought in conducting our forefathers to this western world; for His protection to them and to their posterity, amidst difficulties and dangers; for raising us their children from deep distress, to be numbered among the nations of the earth; and for arming the hands of just and mighty Princes in our deliverance; and especially for that He hath been pleased to grant us the enjoyment of health and so to order the revolving seasons, that the earth hath produced her increase in abundance, blessing the labours of the husbandman, and spreading plenty through the land; that He hath prospered our arms and those of our ally, been a shield to our troops in the hour of danger, pointed their swords to victory, and led them in triumph over the bulwarks of the foe; that He hath gone with those who went out into the wilderness against the savage tribes; that He hath stayed the hand of the spoiler, and turned back his mediated destruction, that He hath prospered our commerce, and given success to those who sought the enemy on the face of the deep; and above all, that He hath diffused the glorious light of the Gospel, whereby, through the merits of our gracious Redeemer, we may become the heirs of His eternal glory. Therefore,
>
> Resolved, that it be recommended to the several States to appoint THURSDAY the 9th of December next, to be **a day of publick and solemn THANKSGIVING to Almighty God for his mercies, and of PRAYER,** for the continuance of His favour and protection to these United States; to beseech Him that he would be graciously pleased to influence our publick Councils, and bless them with wisdom from on high, with unanimity, firmness and success; that He would go forth with our hosts and crown our arms with victory; that He would grant to His church the plentiful effusions of Divine grace, and pour out His Holy Spirit on all ministers of the Gospel; that He would bless and prosper the means of education, and spread the light of Christian knowledge through the remotest corners of the earth; that He would smile upon the labours of His people, and cause the earth to bring forth her fruits in abundance, that we may with gratitude and gladness enjoy them; that He would take into His holy protection our illustrious ally, give

him victory over his enemies, and render him finally great, as the father of his people and the protector of the rights of mankind, that He would graciously be pleased to turn the hearts of our enemies, and to dispense the blessings of peace to contending nations. That He would in mercy look down upon us, pardon all our sins, and receive us into His favour; and finally, that He would establish the independence of these United States upon the basis of religion and virtue, and support and protect them in the enjoyment of peace, liberty and safety. I do therefore by authority from the General Assembly issue this my proclamation, hereby appointing Thursday the 9th of December next, **a Day of publick and solemn Thanksgiving and Prayer to Almighty God,** earnestly recommending to all the good people of this commonwealth, to set apart the said day for those purposes, and to the several Ministers of religion to meet their respective societies thereon, to assist them in their prayers, edify them with their discourses, and generally to perform the sacred duties of their function, proper for the occasion. Given under my hand and the seal of the Commonwealth, at Williamsburg, this 11th day of November, in the year of our Lord, 1779, and in the fourth of the Commonwealth.

THOMAS JEFFERSON

Thomas Jefferson – a portrait of the founding father from life by Charles Willson Peale.

December 9th, 1779 Thanksgiving Day Proclamation by Thomas Jefferson, Governor of Virginia. Published in the *The Virginia Gazette*, November 30, 1779.

Of note, is that Jefferson wrote his Thanksgiving Day Proclamation *after* his 1777 authorship of *An Act for Establishing Religious Freedom*, which served as a model for the First Amendment's Establishment Clause in the *U.S Bill of Rights* – "Separation of Church from State Control."

The second paragraph of Jefferson's moving Proclamation of "a Day of Publick and Solemn Thanksgiving to Almighty God for His mercies, and of Prayer," discloses the reason for this timely decree: "for the continuance of His (God's) favour and protection of these United States; to beseech Him that He would graciously be pleased to influence our public Councils, and bless them with wisdom from on high, with unanimity, firmness and success; that He would go forth with our hosts and crown our arms with victory; that he would grant to His church the plentiful effusions of

Divine grace, and pour out His Holy Spirit on all ministers of the Gospel; that He would bless and prosper the means of education, and spread the light of Christian knowledge through the remotest corners of the earth; that He would smile upon the labours of His people, and cause the earth to bring forth her fruits in abundance, that we may with gratitude and gladness enjoy them…"

These public statements made by Thomas Jefferson refute the Museum of the Bible's November 26, 2019 "Thanksgiving in America" assertion that, "Thomas Jefferson believed public demonstrations of devotion to a higher power, like Thanksgiving, were unsuitable for a nation based in part on the separation of church and state."

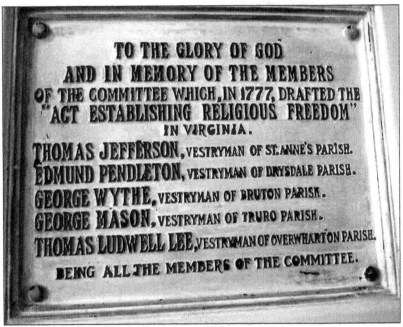

Historic plaque on the wall adjacent to Thomas Jefferson's Pew (no. 17), Bruton Parish Church, circa 1715, Williamsburg, Virginia: Memorializing Jefferson's 1777 Act Establishing Religious Freedom in Virginia.

The Missing Complement of 'Jefferson's Bible' – or – his "Literary Commonplace Book"?

The *Manuscript Division* of the Library of Congress houses a reference book entitled: "The Literary Bible of Thomas Jefferson," published in 1928 by the Johns Hopkins Press, and les Presses Universitaires de France, Paris, with an introduction by Gilbert Chinard, professor at Johns Hopkins University. Chinard writes,

This book is the missing complement of 'Jefferson's Bible.' It is quite as necessary for a true understanding of the personality of the man who wrote the *Declaration of Independence* and formulated the democratic creed of America.

Jefferson's "Literary Commonplace Book," newly-entitled "Jefferson's Literary Bible" published in 1928 by the Johns Hopkins Press. The Introduction advertises it as, "The missing complement of 'Jefferson's Bible.'" Manuscript Division, Library of Congress.

Jefferson's original hand-written "Literary Commonplace Book" of poetry and verses from Greek and Latin authors, which he neither signed nor put his name to. The cover bears no title or wording. Gift of his great-granddaughter. Manuscript Division, Library of Congress.

"The Literary Bible of Thomas Jefferson"

Upon further research, it was discovered that the original scrapbook belonging to Thomas Jefferson, comprising hand-written poetry and verses from Homer, Virgil, Horace, Cicero, Herodotus, the Odyssey, and other Greek and Latin authors, had neither title nor introduction. It is catalogued in the Library of Congress, Manuscript Division under: "Thomas Jefferson Papers – 'Literary Commonplace Book,' located in series 5 of the collection which consists of 'Commonplace Books, 1758-1772.'" The original plain brown leather cover has neither title nor wording, nor does it have a title page. Jefferson's great-granddaughter, who presented this scrapbook to the Library of Congress, wrote that,

Mrs. Randolph (Jefferson's daughter)* always kept this book of her father's among her treasures. Martha Jefferson Burke, née Trist. Alexandria, Virginia, January 29th, 1898."

From the foregoing, we understand that in 1895, Cyrus Adler, Smithsonian Librarian and former Semitics student at Johns Hopkins University, persuaded Thomas Jefferson's great-granddaughter, Carolina Randolph, to sell him Jefferson's "wee-little book" entitled, *The Life and Morals of Jesus of Nazareth extracted textually from the Gospels, in Greek, Latin, French and English*, for $400; after which, in 1904, Adler persuaded the 57th Congress, first Session, to publish it as a government document, placing Thomas Jefferson's name thereon. And that, in 1928, John Hopkins Press published Jefferson's scrapbook known as a "Literary Commonplace Book," giving it the new, invented title of "The Literary Bible of Thomas Jefferson," its introduction by Chinard asserting that "this is the missing complement of 'Jefferson's Bible' – it is quite as necessary for a true understanding of the personality of the man who wrote the *Declaration of Independence* and formulated the democratic creed of America"!

Accordingly, are Americans to believe the incredulous "story" that two scrapbook compilations belonging to Thomas Jefferson, published for the first time in 1904 and 1928, by the Washington Government Printing Office, and Johns Hopkins Press, respectively, fashioned the political thought and democratic creed of Thomas Jefferson, author of the *Declaration of Independence* and the *Act for Establishing Religious Freedom* – which documents secured America's civil and religious freedoms?

I submit that neither his "wee-little book" nor his "Literary Commonplace Book" played any part in the struggle to gain independence from the tyranny of monarchial rule – nor could either possibly have formulated the ideals enunciated in Jefferson's republican creed of self-government, as borne out by Congress' choice of Jeffersonian writings reflecting his political thought – boldly proclaimed upon the walls of The Thomas Jefferson Memorial in the nation's capital.

Inauguration of The Museum of the Bible

On November 17, 2017, the dedication ceremony of the Museum of the Bible received an official pontifical blessing from Pope Francis (a Jesuit). The ceremony's opening prayer was offered by Roman Catholic Cardinal Donald Wuerl (whose 2018 resignation followed in the wake of an abuse report.) The cost of the museum was $500 million, primarily from Hobby Lobby, founded by David Green. Steve Green, his son, is President of Hobby Lobby, as well as Founder and Chairman of the Board of the Museum of the Bible. This museum, officially described as a History Museum, reportedly houses 400,000 items in its collection.

*Author's text in parenthesis.

Roman Catholic theologian, Thomas L. McDonald, writing in the *National Catholic Register* on November 20, 2017, praised the abundance of material dedicated to the history of the Bible with respect to Roman Catholicism. Under the sub-title, *The Catholic Angle*, he writes:

> A crucial part of developing the museum was shedding sectarian biases, and part of that involved bringing Catholic scholars into the fold. In 2012, the museum brought its travelling Verbum Domini exhibit to the Vatican, which helped forge relationships with the Vatican museums and Vatican library. A similar exhibit was mounted in Philadelphia during the visit of Pope Francis, continuing the museum's process of courting Catholic leaders and press. The result is a permanent space on the first floor of the museum for rotating exhibits from the Vatican, including the giant illuminated Urbino Bible (15th century) and a number of reproduction frescos illustrating Church Councils. New items will be brought from Rome every six months. In addition, one of the special exhibits for the opening is a series of Stations of the Cross sculptures. **Catholicism permeates the art and exhibits**. A section of paintings and sculpture shows how artists depicted the Virgin Mary throughout history. **There's the prayer book of Emperor Charles V who condemned Luther as an outlaw** and various versions of the Vulgate and Douay-Rheims Bibles, among other Catholic versions. Pre-Reformation books and illuminated manuscripts, displays of Catholic architecture and art, the role of monks and nuns, and discussions of Catholic saints and scholars are all in the mix.

This author thoroughly agrees with McDonald's statement that "Catholicism permeates the art and exhibits." However, the museum's name – "Museum of the Bible," contradicts the Roman Catholic church's stance, which is not upon the Bible, but upon the Apocrypha (non-canonical books), recently dubbed "deuterocanonical" by the Catholic Church, as well as Popes' dogmas; the infallibility of the Pope in ecclesiastical matters; the Roman Catholic Catechism; prayers to "Mary, Queen of Heaven"*; Purgatory (a place where Catholics must go after death, to purge their sins prior to gaining access to heaven); the Rosary (repetitious prayers to "Mary, Queen of Heaven" while holding each bead); salvation by infant baptism and works; penance; sacerdotalism; confession of sins and absolution by a priest; transubstantiation; prayers to the Roman Catholic "saints;" the papal dogmas of the "Assumption of Mary into heaven;" and the "Immaculate Conception of Mary" that is, her invented sinless birth; Mary as Co-Redemptrice with Jesus Christ, the Messiah (which is blasphemy); Mass said for the dead; veneration of relics; the "Last Rites" administered by a priest, etc., all of which are not found in the Holy Bible – God's Word.

"The Shroud of Turin" – Roman Catholic Relic

On June 12, 2020, the Museum of the Bible announced to its global database readership: "Coming up on the Podcast: Explore the mystery of the Shroud of Turin. Join us for the first of five provocative discussions in which renowned

---

*Forbidden by Almighty God in the Old Testament Book of Jeremiah, chapters 7:18 and 44:19.

Shroud experts present the latest scientific evidence and in-depth information about this intriguing artifact that millions believe to be the burial cloth of Jesus of Nazareth."

This Roman Catholic relic is certainly *not* the burial cloth of Jesus Christ, Son of God, King of kings and Lord of lords.

Counterfeit Papyri Fragments and Clay Objects

On March 26, 2020, the Museum of the Bible's Chairman of the Board, Steve Green, published the following statement on past acquisitions:

> …Today I am announcing that we have identified approximately 5,000 papyri fragments and 6,500 clay objects with insufficient provenance that we are working to deliver to officials in Egypt and Iraq respectively…

Ancient Gilgamesh Tablet Forfeited

On May 18, 2020, an NBC article by Tim Stelloh stated:

> Authorities announce forfeiture of **Ancient Gilgamesh Tablet** from Hobby Lobby's Museum of the Bible – The Gilgamesh Dream Tablet was featured at the Washington, D.C. Museum. The Crafts Chain bought it in 2014 for 1.6 million. Civil Action filed to forfeit rare cuneiform tablet from Hobby Lobby. May 18, 2020. Cultural Property, Art and Antiquities Investigations. 'New York: Pursuant to ongoing Cultural Property, Arts and Antiquities investigations by ICE's Homeland Security Investigations (HSI), New York, a civil complaint was filed Monday, to forfeit a rare cuneiform tablet bearing a portion of the Epic of Gilgamesh, a Sumerian epic poem considered one of the world's oldest works of literature. Known as the Gilgamesh Dream Tablet, it originated in the area of modern-day Iraq and entered the United States contrary to federal law. The tablet was later sold by an international auction house (the "Auction House") to Hobby Lobby Stores, Inc. ("Hobby Lobby"), a prominent arts and crafts retailer based in Oklahoma City, Oklahoma for display at the Museum of the Bible ("the Museum"). Despite enquiries from the Museum and Hobby Lobby, the Auction House withheld information about the tablet's provenance. The tablet was seized from the museum by law enforcement agents in September, 2019.

"All Dead Sea Scroll Fragments in the Museum of the Bible are Forgeries"

In 2018, the Museum of the Bible announced that expert examination had led it to conclude the five of the sixteen fragments of the "Dead Sea Scrolls" in their collection were forgeries, and that the Museum had removed them from display. According to German researchers, those five showed "characteristics inconsistent with ancient origin."

In March, 2020, the Museum confirmed all sixteen "Dead Sea Scroll" fragments were forgeries. [1]

A one-of-a-kind original "wee-little book" of known Provenance in the University of Virginia vault

The University of Virginia, Rare Book Collection houses a one-of-a-kind, original "wee-little book" of known provenance. The opening of the book has a hand-written explanation of its contents:

> Given to me by my dear mother April 4th, 1876 M.J.T. Burke. Copied from the printed texts which great-grand-papa Jefferson cut from two copies of the New Testament, which he had bought for the purpose, these two copies my dear mother treasured and kept all her life. She gave them to me a short time before her death 1882, Alexandria, Virginia. My mother and Aunt Cornelia* and Aunt Mary* and their dear mother, Mrs. Randolph,** all wrote in this book. Aunt Mary helped my mother most in the copying. The original book of extracted texts was owned by Thomas Jefferson Randolph of "Edgehill." Albemarle County, Virginia. My mother, Martha Jefferson Trist Burke, gave me this book when my dear grandmother died, and I wish it to belong to the University of Virginia to keep it from ever falling into the hands of the Jesuits, who, I fear, have destroyed all of my grandmother's correspondence and valuable autographs. My grandfather Trist (Nicolas Philip Trist) considered the Jesuits the most dangerous element that possibly came into any country, and I, after thinking them of negligible influence, have by my personal experience, become convinced of the truth of my grandfather's views. Fanny Maury Burke.

The one-of-a-kind, "wee-little book" copied from Thomas Jefferson's compilation of "The Philosophy of Jesus of Nazareth..." by Martha Jefferson Randolph, his daughter, and granddaughters. Rare Book Collection, University of Virginia, Charlottesville, Virginia.

* Jefferson's granddaughters.
** Jefferson's daughter, Martha.

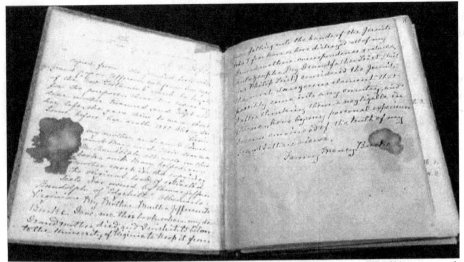

Jefferson's "wee-little book" copied by his daughter, Martha, and his granddaughters. Gift of his great-granddaughter to the University of Virginia, to "keep it from ever falling into the hands of the Jesuits, who, I fear, have destroyed all of my grandmother's correspondence and valuable autographs." Rare Book Collection, University of Virginia, Charlottesville, Virginia.

The Jesuits – A Threat to this "wee-little book"

Jefferson's great-granddaughter makes it clear that she is placing this "wee-little book" copied meticulously from the original, in the hands of the University of Virginia, in order to "keep it from ever falling into the hands of the Jesuits," whom, she affirms, have destroyed all of Jefferson's daughter, Martha Jefferson Randolph's "correspondence and valuable autographs."

"Edgehill," circa 1828, home of Thomas Jefferson Randolph, Jefferson's eldest grandson, and his family. Albermarle County, Virginia.

Painting of "Edgehill," the original wooden house, with its Ice House to the left, still standing – home of Thomas Mann Randolph, Jr. and his wife, Martha Jefferson Randolph. Built in 1799, it was moved to the brow of the hill on rollers to accommodate the brick mansion built by Thomas Jefferson Randolph. It became the notable "Edgehill School for Girls," run by Thomas Jefferson's great-granddaughters.

And again, his great-granddaughter pens this inscription:

The English, 1791 and 1799 New Testament Bibles bought by Jefferson

Thomas Jefferson Monticello. The selections from this book were cut out by Thomas Jefferson's own hand. Martha Jefferson T. Burke. Given to me by Cornelia Jefferson Randolph, Mr. Jefferson's granddaughter. This book, and a corresponding volume of the same was bought by Thomas Jefferson for the purpose of cutting out those verses which contain the sayings of Jesus of Nazareth. These verses were placed in a blank book and compared with the Greek and Latin translations of the same verses. These two books were given to me by my dear mother. Alexandria, Virginia, 1878. M.J.T. Burke. Given to the University of Virginia in her 86th year of age. By M.J.T. Burke, née Martha Jefferson Trist, Alexandria, Virginia, 1913. March 30th, 1913.

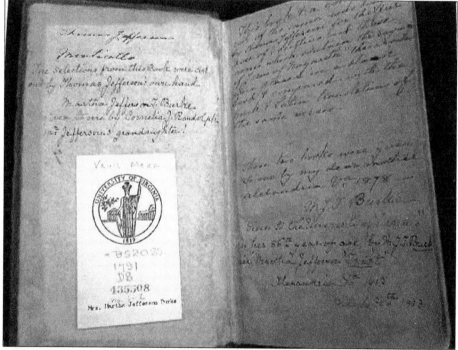

Inscription by Thomas Jefferson's great-granddaughter at opening of the 1791 New Testament Bible bought by Jefferson in order to "place verses which contain the sayings of Jesus of Nazareth in a blank book, and compared with the Greek and Latin translations of the same verses." Its accompanying volume is a 1799 edition. Rare Book Collection, University of Virginia, Charlottesville, Virginia.

The two New Testament Bibles referred to in the above inscription accompanied the hand-written "wee-little book," preserved for posterity in the University of Virginia Rare Book Collection vault. The 1799 New Testament Bible is catalogued as follows:

Jefferson, Thomas. Bible. New Testament. English 1799. Authorized. The New Testament of our Lord and Saviour Jesus Christ newly translated out of the original Greek: and with former translations diligently compared and revised. By his Majesty's Special Command. Appointed to be read in churches. Dublin: Printed by George Grierson, printer to the King's most Excellent Majesty, 1799. New Testament clipped by Thomas Jefferson in preparing 'The Philosophy of Jesus of Nazareth...Being an Abridgement of the New Testament for the use of the Indians.' Presented to the University of Virginia by Mrs. Martha Jefferson Burke.

Its counterpart Bible is catalogued identically, with a 1791 publication date.

Jefferson's Reverence for the Bible

The fact that Thomas Jefferson did not discard the two English New Testaments, circa 1791 and 1799 respectively, demonstrates his reverence for the Bible; as also shown by his daughter, granddaughters and great-granddaughter, all of whom treasured them. The latter finally delivered these precious volumes into the custody of the University of Virginia for safekeeping – protecting them from "ever falling into the hands of the Jesuits, the most dangerous element that ever came into any country."

As formerly demonstrated, Thomas Jefferson's Library of Congress Collection, under his hand-written category, "Religion" contains a hundred and ninety entries, the majority of which are Bibles in English, French, Greek, Latin and other languages.

CHAPTER XXI

The Museum of the Bible and Historic Revisionism, George Washington, John Adams and Benjamin Franklin – George Washington: "Impact of the Bible in America" exhibit – Washington's "Prayer for the Nation" – His "Sunday Evening Prayer" – George Washington's Addresses to the Churches – John Adams: "Impact of the Bible in America" exhibit – John Adams' May 9, 1798 "Day of Humiliation, Fasting and Prayer" Proclamation – John Adams' April 25, 1799 "Day of Humiliation, Fasting and Prayer" Proclamation – John Adams' 1780 Massachusetts Constitution – Benjamin Franklin: "Impact of the Bible in America" exhibit – Historic Revisionism: Benjamin Franklin – Accuracy: Franklin's Design Proposal for First U.S. Seal accepted by Congress – Biblical Symbolism of the First United States Seal – Benjamin Franklin and George Whitefield.

The Museum of the Bible and Historic Revisionism – George Washington, John Adams and Benjamin Franklin

In **"Impact of the Bible in America" exhibit, George Washington**, founder and First President of the United States is also targeted, by being unfavorably compared with Benjamin Rush, M.D., under the heading and text:

> *George Washington and Benjamin Rush M.D.* George Washington spoke often about religion and tolerance as essential for the new country's stability. But his personal beliefs about Christianity are not known for certain. His reticence contrasts with the outspoken Benjamin Rush. A Philadelphia doctor and founder, Rush frequently stated the importance of the Bible in sustaining the moral character of the American Republic.

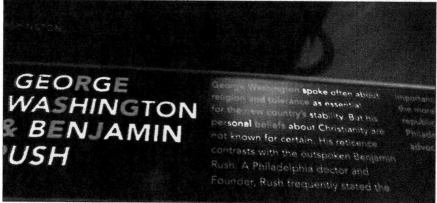

"Impact of the Bible in America' exhibit on "George Washington and Benjamin Rush." The Museum of the Bible, Washington, D.C.

229

and again,

> George Washington, Commander-in-Chief of the Continental Army, and America's first President, was strategically ambiguous in his stance on the Bible.

Why then, did the curators of this exhibit omit to display prominently George Washington's family Bible, as well as his Concordance to the Holy Scriptures, circa 1760 (housed in the Archives of Mount Vernon), his personal, three-volume hand-autographed Bible (housed in the Library of Congress, Rare Book Collection), and his original Bible presented to his parish church, *Pohick Episcopal Church*, inscribed by his adopted grandson "for the honor of Christianity" – the latter being housed in the Pohick Church vault?

Pohick Episcopal Church, (circa 1774), Parish Church of George Washington, George Mason and William Fairfax, vestrymen, who were on the Building Committee.

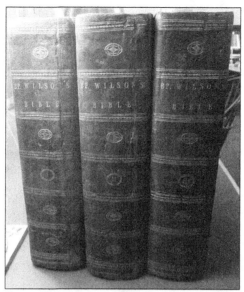

George Washington's three-volume, hand-autographed Bible. Library of Congress, Rare Book Collection.

Benjamin Rush, M.D., Signer of the *Declaration of Independence*, is certainly a great founding father, but George Washington far surpasses him as the father and first president of this nation.

The exhibit's statement that "George Washington's personal beliefs about Christianity are not known for certain" is historically disproven, revealing a lack of professional research. Following are some, of numerous, well-known public avowals of Christianity in print made by the illustrious Commander-in-Chief of the Continental Army and America's first President, General George Washington:

Washington's "Prayer for the Nation"

In Washington's circular letter to the governors of the States of the new nation, as Commander-in-Chief from his headquarters in Newburgh, New York, on June 8, 1783, he prays that,

> ...God would most graciously be pleased to dispose us all to do justice, to love mercy and to demean ourselves with that charity, humility and pacific temper of mind, which were the characteristics of the Divine Author of our blessed Religion, (Christianity)* and without an humble imitation of whose example in these things, we can never hope to be a happy nation...

---

*Author's text in parenthesis.

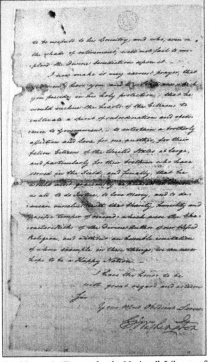

Washington's "Prayer for the Nation." Library of Congress, Rare Book Collection.

This prayer is now called "Washington's Prayer for the Nation."

Further proof of Washington's Christian beliefs are his hand-written, published prayers which he entitled "The Daily Sacrifice," constituting a morning and evening prayer for each day of the week. His *Sunday Evening Prayer* is hereunder reprinted:

Sunday Evening

O MOST GLORIOUS GOD, in Jesus Christ my merciful & loving father, I acknowledge and confess my guilt, in the weak and imperfect performance of the duties of this day. I have called on thee for pardon and forgiveness of sins, but so coldly & carelessly, that my prayers are become my sin and stand in need of pardon. I have heard thy holy word, but with such deadness of spirit that I have been an unprofitable and forgetful hearer, so that, O Lord, tho' I have done thy work, yet it hath been so negligently that I may rather expect a curse than a blessing from thee. But, O God, who art rich in mercy and plenteous in redemption, mark not, I beseech thee, what I have done amiss; remember I am but dust, and remit my transgressions, negligences & ignorances, and cover them all with the absolute obedience of thy dear Son, that those sacrifices which I have offered may be accepted by thee, in and for the sacrifice Jesus Christ offered upon the cross for me; for his sake, ease me of the burden of my sins, and give me grace that by the call of the Gospel I may rise from the slumber of sin unto newness of life. Let me live according to those holy rules which thou hast this day prescribed in thy holy word; make me to know what is acceptable in thy sight and therein to delight. Open the eyes of my understanding, and help me thoroughly to examine myself concerning my knowledge, faith and repentance. Increase my faith, and direct me to the true object, Jesus Christ the way, the truth and the life. Bless, O Lord, all the people of this land, from the highest to the lowest, particularly those whom thou hast appointed to rule over us in church & state. Continue thy goodness to me this night. These weak petitions I humbly implore thee to hear, accept and answer for the sake of thy dear Son Jesus Christ our Lord. Amen.

First pages of George Washington's hand-written Sunday Evening Prayer. Library of Congress, Rare Book Collection.

The foregoing prayer penned by George Washington, together with many others, is a clear testimony to the world of his belief in the saving grace of Jesus Christ, praying that God would remit his sins through the sacrifice Jesus Christ offered upon the cross for his salvation; that God would give him grace that by the call of the Gospel he may rise from the slumber of sin to the newness of life; enabling him to live according to His holy rules in His holy Word; imploring God to increase his faith and direct him to the true object, Jesus Christ, the way, the truth and the life – concluding by humbly asking God to hear, accept and answer his prayer for the sake of His dear Son, Jesus Christ our Lord.

Bronze Statue at the entranceway to Freedoms Foundation at Valley Forge, Pennsylvania – George Washington kneeling in prayer, as seen by Isaac Potts, the Quaker. His house (circa 1743) still stands in Valley Forge, Pennsylvania.

George Washington's Addresses to the Churches

On April 30, 1789, Washington was sworn into office as first President with his left hand upon the Bible, opened to Genesis, chapter 49-50. Genesis 49: 22-25c, upon which his hand lay, was his inauguration Scripture. He swore allegiance to the U.S. Constitution with his right hand upraised, the event taking place in Federal Hall, New York. As first President of the United States, Washington received letters of congratulations from numerous Protestant Christian churches. In response, he wrote his well-known, published "Addresses to the Churches," testifying to his outspoken stance on Christianity. Following are excerpts:

April 20th, 1789

To the Ministers, Church-wardens, and Vestry-men of the **German Lutheran Congregation**, in and near the City of Philadelphia, he requests their "intercession (for him) at the Throne of Grace. George Washington."

May 1789

To the General Assembly of the **Presbyterian Church in the United States**, Washington reiterates his "dependence upon Heaven, as the source of all public and private blessings," and adds that, "no man, who is profligate in his morals, or a bad member of the civil community, can possibly be a true Christian, or a credit to his own religious society." He concludes by requesting their "prayers to Almighty

God for His blessing on our common country, and the humble instrument, which He has been pleased to make use of in the administration of its government. George Washington."

May, 1789

To the Bishops of the **Methodist Episcopal Church in the United States**, he responds that he will "always strive to prove a faithful and impartial patron of genuine, vital religion," and assures them "in particular that I take in the kindest part the promise you make of presenting your prayers at the Throne of Grace for me, and that I likewise implore the Divine benediction of yourselves and your religious community. George Washington."

May, 1789

To the General Committee representing the **United Baptist Churches in Virginia**, he expresses the following: "If I could have entertained the slightest apprehension, that the Constitution framed in the convention, where I had the honor to preside, might possibly endanger the religious rights of any ecclesiastical society, certainly I would have never placed my signature to it…I beg you will be persuaded, that no one would be more zealous than myself to establish effectual barriers against the horrors of spiritual tyranny and every species of religious persecution." He concludes with, "be assured, gentlemen, that I entertain a proper sense of your fervent supplications to God for my temporal and eternal happiness. George Washington."

June, 1789

To the Ministers and Elders of the **German Reformed Congregations of the United States**, he writes, "I am happy in concurring with you in the sentiments of gratitude and piety towards Almighty God, which are expressed with such fervency of devotion in your address…May your devotions before the Throne of Grace be prevalent in calling down the blessings of Heaven upon yourselves and your country. George Washington."

July, 1789

To the Directors of the **Society of the United Brethren for Propagating the Gospel among the Heathen**, Washington pens the following: "You will also be pleased to accept my thanks for the treatise (An Account of the Manner in which the Protestant Church of the *Unitas Fratrum*, or United Brethren, preach the Gospel and carry on their mission among the Heathen)* you presented; and be assured of my patronage in your laudable undertakings…I pray Almighty God to have you always in His holy keeping. George Washington."

*Title of Treatise.

August 19th, 1789

To the **Bishops, clergy and Laity of the Protestant Episcopal Church*** in the **States of New York, New Jersey, Pennsylvania, Delaware, Maryland, Virginia and North Carolina, in General Convention assembled**: "Gentlemen, …On this occasion, it would ill become me to conceal the joy I have felt in perceiving the fraternal affection, which appears to increase every day among the friends of genuine religion. It affords edifying prospects, indeed, to see Christians of different denominations dwell together in more charity, and conduct themselves in respect to each other **with a more Christian-like spirit**, than ever they have done in any former age, or in any other nation…I request, most reverend and respected gentlemen, that you will accept my cordial thanks for your devout supplications to the Supreme Ruler of the universe in behalf of me. May you, and the people you represent, be the happy subjects of the Divine benedictions both here and hereafter. George Washington."

October, 1789

To the **Synod of the Reformed Dutch Church in North America:** "…You, gentlemen, act the part of pious Christians and good citizens by your prayers and exertions to preserve that harmony and good will towards men, which must be the basis of every political establishment, and I readily join with you, that 'while just government protects all in their religious rights, true religion affords to government its surest support.' George Washington."

October, 1789

To the **Religious Society called Quakers**, at their Yearly Meeting **for Pennsylvania, New Jersey, Delaware and the Western Part of Maryland and Virginia.** "Gentlemen, …We have reason to rejoice in the prospect that the present national government, which, by the favor of Divine Providence, was formed by the common counsels and peaceably established with the common counsels of the people, will prove a blessing to every denomination of them…The liberty enjoyed by the people of these States, of worshipping Almighty God agreeably to their consciences, is not only among the choicest of their blessings, but also of their *rights*…Your principles of conduct are well known to me; and it is doing the people called Quakers no more than justice to say, that (except their declining to share with others the burden of the common defence) there is no denomination among us, who are more exemplary or useful citizens… George Washington."

May, 1791

To the **Congregational Church and Society at Medway, formerly St. John's Parish**, in the State of Georgia. "Gentlemen,…You overrate my best exertions, when

*Washington's Protestant Church denomination.

you ascribe to them the blessings which our country so eminently enjoys. From the gallantry and fortitude of her citizens, under the auspices of Heaven, America has derived her independence…Continue, my fellow-citizens, to cultivate the peace and harmony, which now subsist between you and your Indian neighbours. The happy consequence is immediate. The reflection, which arises on justice and benevolence, will be lastingly grateful… George Washington."

January, 1793

To the members of the **New Church in Baltimore**. "Gentlemen…to the manifest interposition of an Overruling Providence, and to the patriotic exertions of United America, are to be ascribed those events, which have given us a respectable rank among the nations of the earth…We have abundant reason to rejoice, that, in this land, the light of Truth and reason has triumphed over the power of bigotry and superstition, and that every person may here worship God according to the dictates of his own heart…Your prayers for my present and future felicity are received with gratitude; and I sincerely wish, gentlemen, that you may in your social and individual capacities taste those blessings, which a gracious God bestows upon the righteous. George Washington."

The foregoing furnishes ample proof of George Washington's personal Christian beliefs, as well as his well-known, public stance for Biblical Christianity – refuting "Impact of the Bible in America" exhibit's statement that "his personal beliefs about Christianity are not known for certain," and that "his reticence contrasts with the outspoken Benjamin Rush."

John Adams and "Impact of the Bible on America" exhibit

"Impact of the Bible in America" exhibit next victimizes John Adams' Christian stance during his political life, by stating that, "John Adams, America's first vice president and second president, followed the strategic ambiguity of George Washington when it came to taking a stance on personal beliefs during his political career. Adams did, however, share his love for the Bible in letters with political colleagues like Thomas Jefferson."

Once again, the Museum of the Bible curators demonstrate historic revisionism by omitting Adams' two famous "Proclamations of a National Day of Humiliation, Fasting and Prayer" as President of the United States, on May 9th, 1798; and April 25th, 1799, respectively. Both are public testimonies of his personal belief in God the Father, God the Son our Mediator and Redeemer, and God the Holy Spirit, as hereunder excerpted:

John Adams' May 9th, 1798 "Day of Humiliation, Fasting and Prayer" Proclamation

> …That all Religious Congregations do, with the deepest humility, acknowledge before **God** the manifold sins and transgressions with which we are justly

chargeable as individuals and as a nation; beseeching Him, at the same time, of His infinite grace, through **the Redeemer of the world**, freely to remit all our offences, and to incline us, by **His Holy Spirit**, to that sincere repentance and reformation which may afford us reason to hope for His inestimable favour and Heavenly benediction…That the principles of genuine piety and sound morality may influence the minds and govern the lives of every description of our citizens; and that the blessings of peace, freedom and pure religion, may be speedily extended to all nations of the earth… John Adams.

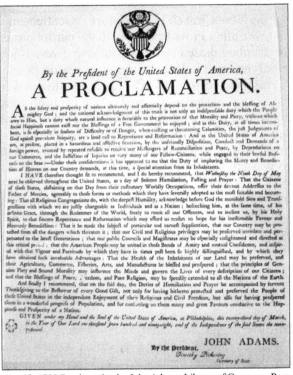

May 9th, 1798 Proclamation by John Adams. Library of Congress, Rare Book Collection.

John Adams' April 25th, 1799 "Day of Humiliation, Fasting and Prayer" Proclamation

…That they call to mind our numerous offences against the **most High God**, confess them before Him with the sincerest penitence, implore His pardoning mercy, through **the great Mediator and Redeemer**, for our past transgressions, and that, through the grace of **His Holy Spirit**, we may be disposed and enabled to yield a more suitable obedience to His righteous requisitions in time to come…And I do, also, recommend that with these acts of humiliation, penitence and prayer, fervent thanksgiving to the Author of all good be united, for the countless favors which He is still continuing to the people of the United States, and which render their condition as a nation eminently happy, when compared with the lot of others. John Adams.

April 25th, 1799 Proclamation by John Adams. Library of Congress, Rare Book Collection.

John Adams' 1780 Massachusetts Constitution

Moreover, John Adams drafted the famed 1780 *Massachusetts Constitution*, wherein he affirmed his stance for "the public worship of God, and for the support and maintenance of public Protestant teachers of piety, Religion and morality, in all cases where such provision shall not be made voluntarily:"

> As the happiness of the people, and the good order and preservation of civil government, essentially depend upon piety, religion and morality, and as these cannot be generally diffused through a community, but by the institution of public worship of GOD, and of public instructions in piety, religion and morality: Therefore, to promote their happiness, and to secure the good order and preservation of their government, the people of this Commonwealth have a right to invest their legislature with power to authorize and require, and the legislature shall, from time to time, authorize and require, the several towns, parishes, precincts, and other bodies politic, or religious societies, to make suitable provision, at their own expense for the institution of the public worship of GOD, and for the support and maintenance of public Protestant teachers of piety, religion and morality, in all cases where such provision shall not be made voluntarily.

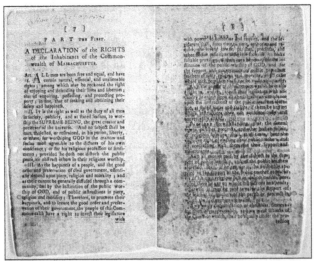

The Massachusetts Constitution (1780). Library of Congress, Rare Book Collection.

The above historic evidence refutes "Impact of the Bible on America" exhibit's statement to millions of its viewers that "John Adams followed the strategic ambiguity of George Washington when it came to taking a stance on personal beliefs during his political career." It proves, to the contrary, that John Adams did not hesitate to make known, and to proclaim publicly, his personal belief in the truth of the Christian Religion during his political career.

Benjamin Franklin: "Impact of the Bible in America" exhibit

The exhibit's next victim, under the heading, *Benjamin Franklin and Samuel Seabury*, is Benjamin Franklin, who is unfavorably compared to Samuel Seabury, a Connecticut clergyman, and loyalist to King George III, "whose argument" the curators write, "was straightforward and blunt: 'Fear God, Honour the King.' (I Peter 2:17 KJV.)" The weapon used in this exhibit against Franklin, Signer of the *Declaration of Independence* and the *U.S. Constitution,* is the Word of God itself, taking sides with the King of England. However, no mention whatever is made of the "Divine Right of Kings" which Benjamin Franklin and the founders of the American Republic vanquished through copious Scriptures denouncing tyranny, such as God's miraculous deliverance of the children of Israel from the bondage of slavery in Egypt.

The exhibit text states:

> **Benjamin Franklin** was the oldest of the founders, and a devoted patriot. As a member of the Continental Congress, he spoke passionately for American Independence from Great Britain, often using moral aphorisms and sometimes citing the Bible to make his points. **Samuel Seabury**, a Connecticut clergymen, was loyal to Britain. In the years leading up to the Revolutionary War, Seabury and his fellow loyalists opposed American Independence. Their argument was

straightforward and blunt: ' Fear God, Honour the King' (I Peter 2: 17 KJV). Seabury was a notable loyalist to the Crown of England. During the war, he served as a chaplain among the British forces where he gave emboldened sermons based on submission to authority found in the New Testament.

Historic Revisionism: Benjamin Franklin

"Impact of the Bible in America" exhibit on *Benjamin Franklin and Samuel Seabury* continues to contradict historic records with the following information:

> Benjamin Franklin, Thomas Jefferson and John Adams comprised the first committee assembled to design America's national seal. Franklin proposed the dramatic biblical scene from the Exodus of Moses and the Israelites' successful escape from Pharaoh and his warriors. The image was encircled with the timely phrase, 'Rebellion to Tyrants is Obedience to God.' **Franklin's design was rejected**. 1. Proposal for the U.S. Seal (facsimile) Benjamin Franklin, Philadelphia, Pennsylvania, 1776. Museum of the Bible Facsimile 000149.

Above: "Impact of the Bible in America" exhibit on "Benjamin Franklin and Samuel Seabury." The Museum of the Bible, Washington, D.C. Below: "Impact of the Bible in America" exhibit: "Franklin's 'Proposal for the Great Seal of the United States.' August, 1776."

Accuracy: Franklin's Design Proposal for the First U.S. Seal Accepted by Congress

The facsimile displayed in this exhibit is taken from Benjamin Franklin's original hand-written proposal for the first United States Seal, housed in the Manuscript Division of the Library of Congress, together with the design of the seal itself, which was, indeed, **accepted by Congress** – as published in my book, *The Truth about the Founding fathers of the American Republic* © 2013. They are hereunder reprinted:

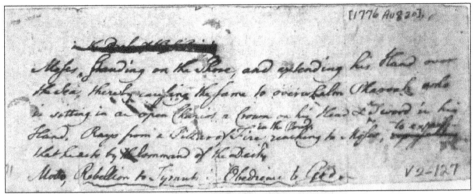

Benjamin Franklin's hand-written proposal and motto. Manuscript Division, Library of Congress.

Reverse

[Drawing by Benson J. Lossing from the description]

Design of First Seal of the United States. Thomas Jefferson Papers. Manuscript Division, Library of Congress.

Biblical Symbolism of the First United States Seal

Benjamin Franklin's and Thomas Jefferson's descriptive designs concurred, and John Adams was in agreement. The committee unanimously selected the miraculous deliverance of the children of Israel from Pharaoh's tyranny, Almighty God parting the Red Sea for their flight, and drowning Pharaoh and his chariots in pursuit. Benjamin Franklin, Thomas Jefferson and John Adams equated Pharaoh with monarchial rule, placing King George III's crown upon his head; the pillar of fire and the pillar of cloud above, guiding the Israelites to freedom. Hence, they drew a comparison between the deliverance of Israel, and Almighty God's miraculous intervention, freeing the American colonists from enslavement to an alien power. Their chosen motto: "Rebellion to Tyrants is Obedience to God," reflects the founders' triumph over the centuries-long ecclesiastical weapon of "Divine Right of Kings," wielded by monarchs to subdue empires.

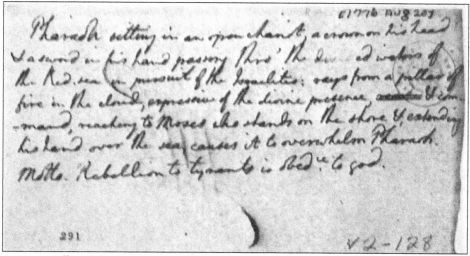

Jefferson's hand-written proposal and motto. Manuscript Division, Library of Congress.

Benjamin Franklin and George Whitefield

Additionally, this exhibit omits any mention of Benjamin Franklin having encouraged and promoted George Whitefield, famed Evangelist of the Great Awakening in America. Not only did Franklin attend Whitefield's sermons at Christ Church, Philadelphia, but he also printed, published and sold them in two volumes, testifying to his stand for Biblical Christianity.

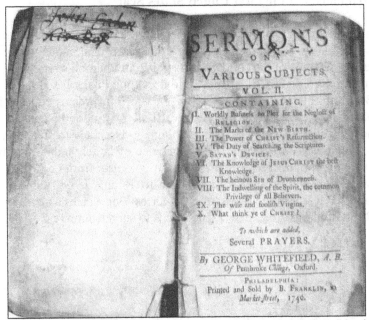

Title page of George Whitefield's "Sermons on Various Subjects." Vol. II. 1740. Printed and sold by Benjamin Franklin. Library of Congress, Rare Book Collection.

Benjamin Franklin – a portrait of the founding father from life by Charles Willson Peale.

Chapter XXII

The Thomas Jefferson Memorial

The dedication of the Jefferson Memorial took place on April 13, 1943, the two-hundredth anniversary of Thomas Jefferson's birth. The memorial commemorates Thomas Jefferson, a foremost founding father of the United States, who championed the values of democracy, religious freedom and education. The memorial has become a symbol of these values around the world.

Jefferson Memorial Chamber Inscriptions

Jefferson's articulation of the philosophy of self-government, notably in the *Declaration of Independence* (1776), established his popular reputation as the principal founder of American political thought.

On the walls of the Thomas Jefferson Memorial are excerpts of Jefferson's views on democracy and his advocacy of a system of government that would allow citizens to govern themselves. These five inscriptions were chosen by the Thomas Jefferson Memorial Commission as being the most reflective of Jefferson's thought:

Around the inner dome, in two-feet-tall lettering, we read,

I HAVE SWORN UPON THE ALTAR OF GOD ETERNAL HOSTILITY AGAINST EVERY FORM OF TYRANNY OVER THE MIND OF MAN.

Taken from a letter to Dr. Benjamin Rush, September 23, 1800.

The following four, beautifully-inscribed panels adorn the walls:

We hold these truths to be self-evident: that all men are created equal, that they are endowed by their Creator with certain inalienable rights, that among these are life, liberty, and the pursuit of happiness, that to secure these rights governments are instituted among men. We…solemnly publish and declare, that these colonies are and of right ought to be free and independent states…And for the support of this declaration, with a firm reliance on the protection of Divine Providence, we mutually pledge to each other our lives, our fortunes and our sacred honour.
Taken from the Declaration of Independence, 1776.

Almighty God hath created the mind free. All attempts to influence it by temporal punishments or burthens…are a departure from the plan of the Holy Author of our religion…No man shall be compelled to frequent or support any religious worship or ministry or shall otherwise suffer on account of his religious opinions or belief, but all men shall be free to profess and by argument to maintain, their opinions in matters of religion. I know but one code of morality for men whether acting singly or collectively.

Taken from A Bill for Establishing Religious Freedom, 1777 (Passed by the Virginia Assembly in 1786.) The last sentence is taken from a letter to James Madison, August 28, 1789.

God who gave us life gave us liberty. Can the liberties of a nation be secure when we have removed a conviction that these liberties are the gift of God? Indeed I tremble for my country when I reflect that God is just, that his justice cannot sleep forever. Commence between master and slave is despotism. Nothing is more certainly written in the book of fate than that these people are to be free. Establish the law for educating the common people. This it is the business of the state to effect and on a general plan.

Taken from *Notes on the State of Virginia*, 1785. The last two sentences are taken from a letter to George Washington, January 4, 1786.

I am not an advocate for frequent changes in laws and constitutions, but laws and institutions must go hand in hand with the progress of the human mind. As that becomes more developed, more enlightened, as new discoveries are made, new truths discovered and manners and opinions change, with the change of circumstances, institutions must advance also to keep pace with the times. We might as well require a man to wear still the coat which fitted him when a boy as civilized society to remain ever under the regimen of their barbarous ancestors.

Taken from a letter to Samuel Kercheval, July 12, 1816.

The handsome bronze, 19-feet tall statue of Thomas Jefferson, executed by celebrated American sculptor, Rudulph Evans of New York, stands majestically in the center of this memorial's imposing interior. He is donned with a fur-collared great coat, gift of his Revolutionary friend, Thaddeus Koscuiszko – freedom fighter from Poland. Jefferson's face beams with intelligence and benevolence. He holds in his left hand his greatest accomplishment – *The Declaration of Independence*.

Statue of Thomas Jefferson by Rudulph Evans. Jefferson holds the *Declaration of Independence* in his left hand. The first, of four panelled inscriptions upon the miner walls is the *Declaration of Independence*, excerpted. Jefferson Memorial, Washington, District of Columbia.

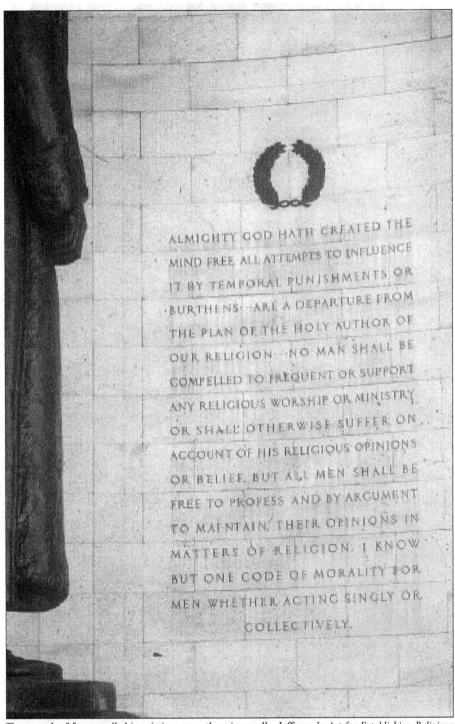

The second, of four panelled inscriptions upon the miner walls. Jefferson's *Act for Establishing Religious Freedom*, excerpted. Jefferson Memorial, Washington, District of Columbia.

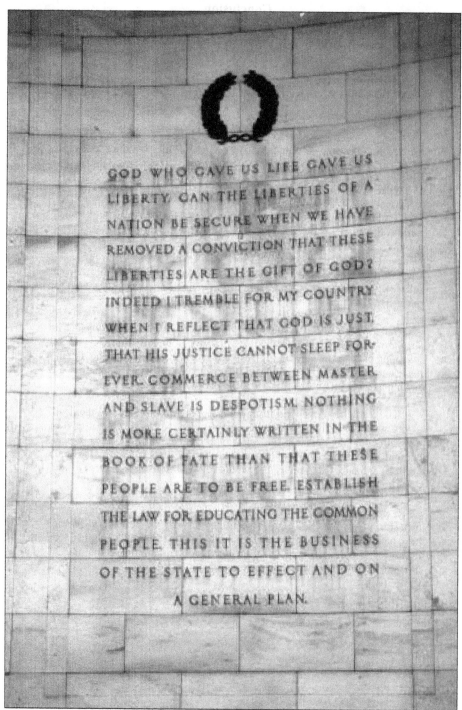

The third, of four panelled inscriptions upon the inner walls. Jefferson's *Notes on the State of Virginia* 1785, excerpted. Jefferson Memorial, Washington, District of Columbia.

Conclusion

A fitting conclusion to this book on "the Sage of Monticello," author of the immortal *Declaration of Independence*, the *Act for Establishing Religious Freedom* and the father of the University of Virginia, is the testimony of Captain Edmund Bacon at his departure from Monticello, after faithfully serving twenty years as Jefferson's overseer.

For he was a constant eye-witness observer of his life, conduct, principles, morals and virtues. From *The Private Life of Thomas Jefferson*, we read Captain Bacon's moving account of his departure:

> …I know that he thought a great deal of me. I had proofs enough of that, besides the letter I showed you. I know that if one man ever tried to serve another faithfully, I did him – and he was satisfied. One day he was at the blacksmith-shop and _____ found some fault with me, and said my salary was too large. The blacksmith, who heard the conversation, told me of it, and said Mr. Jefferson replied, 'Not one man in a thousand would do as well for me as Mr. Bacon has done.'
>
> When we parted, it was a trying time to me. I don't know whether he shed any tears or not, but I know that I shed a good many. He was sitting in his room, on his sofa, where I had seen him so often, and keeping hold of my hand some time, he said, 'Now let us hear from each other occasionally;' and as long as he lived I heard from him once or twice a year.
>
> The last letter I ever had from him was when I wrote him of the death of my wife, soon after I got to this country. He expressed a great deal of sympathy for me; said he did not wonder that I felt completely broken up, and was disposed to move back, that he had passed through the same himself; and only time and silence would relieve me. That is the letter I told you I so much regretted I had lost.
>
> I am now (1862) in my seventy-seventh year. I have seen a great many men in my day, but I have never seen the equal of Mr. Jefferson. He may have had the faults that he has been charged with, but if he had, I could never find it out. I don't believe that, from his arrival to maturity to the present time, the country has ever had another such a man.[1]

And let it be so.

FOOTNOTES

Chapter I

[1] Jefferson, Thomas. *Autobiography*. Original Manuscript in Rare Manuscript Collection, Library of Congress, Washington, D.C.

[2] Official documentation. The College of William and Mary, Williamsburg, Virginia.

[3] Jefferson, Thomas. *Autobiography*. Original Manuscript in Rare Manuscript Collection, Library of Congress, Washington, D.C.

[4] Ibid.

[5] Ibid.

[6] Randolph, Sarah N. *The Domestic Life of Thomas Jefferson*. Compiled from family letters and reminiscences, by his great-granddaughter. New York: Harper and Bros., Publishers, 1871, pp. 10, 11.

Chapter II

[1] Rives, Barclay. *A History of Grace Church, Walker's Parish*, Cismont, Virginia. The Church: 2010, p. 16.

[2] *American Peoples Encyclopedia*. Vol. 15. Chicago: Spencer Press, Inc., 1954, pp. 15895-15897.

Chapter III

[1] Jefferson, Thomas. *Autobiography*. Original Manuscript in Rare Manuscript Collection, Library of Congress, Washington, D.C.

[2] 'Americanus,' Pennsylvania, July, 1800. Library of Congress, Rare Book Collection, Washington, D.C.

Chapter IV

[1] Jefferson, Thomas. The Writings of Thomas Jefferson, Vol. II, 1776-1781. Manuscripts, October, 1776. *Notes on Religion*. New York: G.P. Putnam's Sons, 1892, pp. 92-102. Library of Congress, Rare Book Collection, Washington, D.C.

[2] Ibid.

Chapter V

[1] *American Peoples Encyclopedia*. Vol. 19. Chicago: Spencer Press, Inc., 1954, pp. 19736, 19737.

[2] Ibid., Vol. 16, p. 16827.

[3] Ibid., pp. 16966, 16968.

[4] Ibid., Vol. 8, pp. 8003, 8004.

[5] Ibid., Vol. 11, p. 11488. *Webster's International Dictionary of the English Language, Unabridged.*

[6] Ibid., Vol. 12, pp. 12633, 12634.

[7] Millard, Catherine, D. Min. *Sir Isaac Newton's Proof of Creationism*. Virginia: CHM, 2015.

[8] Ibid., p. 99.

Chapter VI

[1] Pierson, Hamilton W., D.D. *Jefferson at Monticello. The Private Life of Thomas Jefferson*. From entirely new materials, with numerous facsimiles. New York: Charles Scribner, 1862, pp. 108-110.

[2] Catalogue of the Library of Thomas Jefferson, Vol. II. Rare Book Collection, Library of Congress, Washington, D.C.

[3] Thomas Jefferson to Messrs. Nehemiah Dodge, Ephraim Robbins and Stephen S. Nelson, a committee of the Danbury Baptist Association in the State of Connecticut, January 1, 1802, Washington, D.C.

[4] Smith, Samuel Harrison (Mrs.) Margaret Baynard. *The First Forty Years of Washington Society*. Portrayed by the family letters of Mrs. Samuel Harrison Smith. New York: C. Scribner's Sons, 1906. Rare Book Collection, Library of Congress, Washington, D.C.

[5] Christ Church – Washington Parish. *A Brief History*, p. 30. Library of Congress Collection.

[6] The Presbyterian Congregation in George Town – 1780-1970. Published by the Session of the Presbyterian Congregation in George Town. Washington, D.C.: 1971, pp. 23, 24.

[7]Jackson, Richard P. A Native of Georgetown and Member of the Washington Bar. *The Chronicles of Georgetown, D.C. from 1751-1878*. Washington, D.C.: R.O. Polkinhorn, Printer, 1878, pp. 145, 146.

[8]Ibid., p. 145.

[9]The Presbyterian Congregation in George Town – 1780-1970. Published by the Session of the Presbyterian Congregation in George Town. Washington, D.C.: 1971, p. 31.

[10]The Sunday Star, Washington, D.C. *Church Observes 150th Birthday*. November 9, 1930.

[11]Butler, Clement Moore, Rector. *An Historical Account of St. John's Episcopal Church, Georgetown*. October 17, 1843.

[12]Ibid.

[13]Pierson, Hamilton W., D.D. *Jefferson at Monticello. The Private Life of Thomas Jefferson*. New York: Charles Scribner, 1862, pp. 74, 75.

[14]Gould, W.D. The Religious Opinions of Thomas Jefferson. Mississippi Valley Historical Review, 1933-34, Vol. XX, p. 204.

Chapter VII

[1]Jefferson, Thomas. *A Summary View of the Rights of British America*. Manuscript Division, Library of Congress, Washington, D.C.

[2]Jefferson, Thomas. The Writings of Thomas Jefferson. Vol. I – 1760-1775. Jefferson manuscripts, July 6th, 1775. *Second Draft of 'Declaration on Taking up Arms.'* New York: G.P. Putnam's Sons, 1892, pp. 162-176.

Chapter VIII

[1]Paine, Thomas. *Common Sense*. January 8th, 1776. Rare Book Collection, Library of Congress, Washington, D.C.

[2]Jefferson, Thomas. *The Declaration of Independence*. The National Archives, Washington, D.C.

[3]Jefferson, Thomas. *Autobiography*. Original Manuscript in Rare Manuscript Collection, Library of Congress, Washington, D.C.

Chapter IX

[1]Pierson, Hamilton W., D.D. *Jefferson at Monticello. The Private Life of Thomas Jefferson.* New York: Charles Scribner, 1862, pp. 97-103.

[2]Jefferson at Monticello. *Memoirs of a Monticello Slave, as dictated to Charles Campbell by Isaac* (1847). Charlottesville: University of Virginia Press, 1951, pp. 22, 23. Library of Congress Collection, Washington, D.C.

[3]Pierson, Hamilton, W., D.D. *Jefferson at Monticello. The Private Life of Thomas Jefferson.* New York: Charles Scribner, 1862, pp. 71-73.

[4]Ibid., pp. 75-77.

[5]Ibid., pp. 77, 78.

[6]Ibid., pp. 78, 79.

[7]Jefferson, Thomas. *Autobiography.* Original Manuscript in Rare Manuscript Collection, Library of Congress, Washington, D.C.

[8]Ibid.

Chapter X

[1]Randolph, Sarah N. *The Domestic Life of Thomas Jefferson.* Compiled from family letters and reminiscences, by his great-granddaughter. New York: Harper and Bros., Publishers, 1871, pp. 26, 27.

[2]Ibid., pp. 27, 28.

Chapter XI

[1]Martha Jefferson's account of her father, Thomas Jefferson's permanent residence in Paris as Minister to France. From, *The Domestic Life of Thomas Jefferson*, p. 73.

[2]Official documentation. Monticello, 1986.

[3]Ibid.

[4]Jefferson, Thomas. *Autobiography.* Original Manuscript in Rare Manuscript Collection, Library of Congress, Washington, D.C.

⁵Randolph, Sarah N. *The Domestic Life of Thomas Jefferson*. Compiled from family letters and reminiscences, by his great-granddaughter. New York: Harper and Bros., Publishers, 1871, pp. 40, 41.

⁶Ibid. p. 41.

Chapter XII

¹Randolph, Sarah N. *The Domestic Life of Thomas Jefferson*. Compiled from family letters and reminiscences, by his great-granddaughter. New York: Harper and Bros., Publishers, p. 102.

²Ibid., p. 73.

³Ibid., p. 76.

⁴Ibid., p. 104.

⁵Ibid.

⁶Ibid.

Chapter XIII

¹Randolph, Sarah N. *The Domestic Life of Thomas Jefferson*. Compiled from family letters and reminiscences, by his great-granddaughter. New York: Harper and Bros., Publishers, pp. 150, 151, 152.

²Ibid.

³Ibid.

⁴Ibid., p. 153.

⁵Virginia State Library and Archives, Richmond, Virginia.

Chapter XIV

¹*American Peoples Encyclopedia*. Vol. 16, Chicago: The Spencer Press, Inc., 1954, pp. 16319-16320.

²Skousen, W. Cleon. *The Naked Communist*. "The Forty-five Current Communist Goals." Salt Lake City: The W. Cleon Skousen Library and Izzard Ink Publishing Company, 1958, p. 297.

³Gordon-Reed, Annette. *The Hemingses of Monticello – An American Family*. New York: W.W. Norton and Company, Inc., 2008, p. 182.

⁴Ibid., pp. 326, 327.

⁵Ibid., p. 670.

⁶Skousen, W. Cleon, *The Naked Communist*. "The Forty-five Current Communist Goals." Goal #20. Salt Lake City: The W.W. Cleon Skousen Library and Izzard Ink Publishing Company, 1958, p.297.

Chapter XV

¹Skousen, W. Cleon. *The Naked Communist*. "The Forty-five Current Communist Goals." Goal #30. Salt Lake City: The W. Cleon Skousen Library and Izzard Ink Publishing Company, 1958, p. 297.

Chapter XVI

¹Rubenstein, David M. *The American Story: Conversations with Master Historians*. New York: Simon and Schuster, 2019. Front Interior Book Jacket.

²Ibid., pp. 53, 54.

³Ibid., p. 54.

⁴Ibid. pp. 55, 56.

⁵Meacham, Jon. *Thomas Jefferson: The Art of Power*. New York: Random House, 2012, p. 216.

⁶Ibid., pp. 217, 218, 219.

⁷Rubenstein, David M. *The American Story: Conversations with Master Historians*. New York: Simon and Schuster, 2019, p. 54.

⁸*In the Hands of the People*. Edited and with an Introduction by Jon Meacham. Afterword by Annette Gordon-Reed. New York: Random House, pp. 3, 4.

⁹Ibid., p. 91.

¹⁰Ibid., p. 92.

¹¹Ibid.

[12] Ibid.

[13] McCullough, David. *The American Spirit – Who We Are and What We Stand For.* New York: Simon and Schuster, 2017. Front Cover inscription.

[14] Ibid., p. 28.

[15] Ibid.

[16] Ibid, p. 85.

[17] McCullough, David. *John Adams.* New York: Simon and Schuster, 2001, p. 373.

[18] Ibid.

[19] Ibid., pp. 544, 545.

Chapter XVII

[1] House, Edward Mandell. *Philip Dru: Administrator.* New York: New York, 1912.

[2] McManus, John F. *The Insiders.* Appleton, WI: The John Birch Society, 1983, pp. 6-8.

[3] State Department Briefing #327, September 1, 1983.

[4] State Department Briefing #208, June 25, 1981.

[5] State Department Briefing #290, October 16, 1980.

[6] Gwertzman, Bernard. *Cyrus Vance Plays it Cool.* New York Times Magazine, March 18, 1979.

[7] Allen, Gary. *Kissinger.* Seal Beach: CA, '76 Press, 1976.

[8] Department of State, GIST #8 (rev. 2), September, 1972.

[9] "Who Runs This Whole U.S. Show in the World." *U.S. News and World Report,* June 5, 1967.

[10] Laza, Mario. *Dagger in the Heart.* N.Y.: Twin Circle Publishing Company, 1968.

[11] Stang, Alan. *The Actor.* Appleton, WI: Western Islands, 1968.

[12]Welch, Robert. *May God Forgive Us*. Chicago, IL: Henry Regnery Company, 1952.

[13]CFR Annual Report, July 1, 1986. June 30, 1987. N.Y.: CFR, 1987, p. 86, and 1990-91 Annual Report.

[14]Partial Membership List is taken from "Membership Roster, June 30, 1987," Council on Foreign Relations Annual Report, pp. 132-148.

Chapter XVIII

[1]Official documentation. UNESCO World Heritage Centre, 7, Place de Fontenoy, 75352 Paris, 07 France; and Office of International Affairs, National Park Service, United States Department of Interior, Washington, D.C. 20240.

[2]Ibid.

[3]Thomas Jefferson to John Adams, July 5, 1814.

[4]*American Peoples Encyclopedia*. Vol. 15, pp. 15895-15896.

Chapter XIX

[1]Pierson, Hamilton W., D.D. *Jefferson at Monticello. The Private Life of Thomas Jefferson*. From entirely new materials, with numerous facsimiles. New York: Charles Scribner, 1862, p. 119.

Chapter XX

[1]B.B.C. News – U.S. and Canada. *U.S. Museum Dead Sea Scroll Collection found to be Fakes*. March 16, 2020.

Conclusion

[1]Pierson, Hamilton W., D.D. *Jefferson at Monticello. The Private Life of Thomas Jefferson*. New York: Charles Scribner, 1862, pp. 128, 129.

Appendix VI

[1]Hammond, Peter. *Frontline Fellowship*. Cape Town, South Africa. (Used by permission.)

APPENDIX I

Aleksandr Solzhenitsyn (1918-2008) – Nobel Laureate, writer and historian, was the 1970 winner of the Nobel Prize for Literature. He was a Russian novelist, historian, philosopher, writer and political prisoner. Born in 1918 in Kislovodsk, Russia, he died in 2008 in Moscow. Solzhenitsyn was an outspoken critic of the Soviet Union and Communism, and helped to raise global awareness of its Gulag labor camp system. Author of the *Gulag Archipelago* and *One Day in the Life of Ivan Denisovitch*, he studied Mathematics at Rostov University, simultaneously taking correspondence courses from the Moscow Institute of Philosophy, Literature and History. During World War II, he served as the Commander of a sound-ranging battery in the Soviet Army, was involved in major action at the front and was thrice decorated for personal heroism. In 1945 he was arrested for criticizing Stalin in private correspondence and sentenced to an eight-year term in a Labor Camp, to be followed by permanent internal exile. The experience of the camps provided him with raw material for *One Day in the Life of Ivan Denisovitch*, which he was permitted to publish in 1962. It would remain his only major work to appear in his motherland until 1990. Solzhenitsyn's exile was cut short by Khruschev's reforms, allowing him to return from Kazakhstan to central Russia in 1956. He taught Mathematics, astronomy and physics at a high school while continuing to write.

In the early 1960's he was allowed to publish, in addition to *One Day in the Life of Ivan Denisovitch*, only four stories, and by 1969 he was expelled from the Writers' Union. The publication in the West of the initial version of *August, 1914* (the first part of *The Red Wheel*) and of *Gulag Archipelago* soon brought retaliation from the Soviet authorities. In February, 1974, Solzhenitsyn was arrested, stripped of his Soviet citizenship, and flown against his will to Frankfurt, West Germany. After a sojourn in Zurich, Solzhenitsyn moved to Vermont in 1976 with his wife and sons. Over the next eighteen years, spent mostly in the quiet of rural seclusion, Solzhenitsyn would complete his epic historical cycle, *The Red Wheel*, as well as several shorter works. In his essay and speeches throughout the free world, he decried the weak will displayed by Western governments in the face of continuing manifestations of Communist aggression. He also warned against the dangers of encroaching materialism for the East and West alike.

In May, 1994, Solzhenitsyn returned to his native Russia via the Pacific port of Vladivostok and travelled extensively, meeting with thousands of people throughout the country. He continued to write prodigiously, publishing *Between Two Millstones*, a memoir of his years in the West; *Russia in Collapse*, which rounded out the quadrilogy of historical essays begun with *Letter to the Soviet Leaders*, *Rebuilding Russia*, and *the Russian Question*; eight, two-part stories, exploring a new genre;

twelve essays of literary criticism on 20th century writers; and, in 2001-03, a work on the mutual history of Russian and Jewish peoples in Russia, *200 Years Together: 1795-1995*. In 1997, the Russian Academy of Sciences elected Solzhenitsyn as a member, and in 2007, awarded him the Russian State Prize. Meanwhile, 2006 saw the beginning of the publication of a major new 30-volume of collected works. Aleksandr Solzhenitsyn died in Moscow in 2008 at age 89. Solzhenitsyn's other works, include the novels, *The First Circle* and *Cancer Ward*; his literary memoirs, *The Oak and the Calf*, and their addendum, *The Invisible Allies*; collections of plays and early works, and numerous speeches and essays, including his Nobel Lecture and his Harvard Address – "A world Split Apart." (Source: A Biography from *The Aleksandr Solzhenitsyn Center*.)

APPENDIX II

Thomas Jefferson's Last Will and Testament

I, THOMAS JEFFERSON, of Monticello, in Albemarle, being of sound mind, and in my ordinary state of health, make my last will and testament, in manner and form as follows:

I give to my grandson, Francis Eppes, son of my dear deceased daughter, Mary Eppes, in fee simple, all that part of my lands at Poplar Forest, lying west of the following lines, to wit: beginning at Radford's upper corner, near the double branches of Bear Creek and the public road, and running thence in a straight line to the fork of my private road, near the barn; thence along that private road, (as it was changed in 1817), to its crossing of the main branch of North Tomahawk Creek; and from that crossing in a direct line over the main ridge which divides the North and South Tomahawk, to the South Tomahawk, at the confluence of two branches where the old road to the Waterlick crossed it, and from that confluence up the northernmost branch, (which separates McDaniel's and Perry's fields), to its source; and thence by the shortest line to my western boundary. And having, in a former correspondence with my deceased son-in-law, John W. Eppes, contemplated laying off for him, with remainder to my grandson, Francis, a certain portion in the southern part of my lands in Bedford and Campbell, which I afterwards found to be generally more indifferent than I had supposed, and therefore determined to change its location for the better; now, to remove all doubt, if any could arise on a purpose merely voluntary and unexecuted, I hereby declare that what I have herein given to my said grandson Francis, is instead of, and not additional, to what I had formerly contemplated. I subject all my other property to the payment of my debts in the first place.

Considering the insolvent state of the affairs of my friend and son-in-law, Thomas Mann Randolph, and that what will remain of my property will be the only resource against the want in which his family would otherwise be left, it must be his wish, as it is my duty, to guard that resource against all liability for his debts, engagements, or purposes whatsoever, and to preclude the rights, powers, and authorities over it, which might result to him by operation of law, and which might, independently of his will, bring it within the power of his creditors, I do hereby devise and bequeath all the residue of my property, real and personal, in possession or in action, whether held in my own right, or in that of my dear deceased wife, according to the powers vested in me by deed of settlement for that purpose, to my grandson, Thomas J. Randolph, and my friends, Nicholas P. Trist and Alexander Garret, and their heirs, during the life of my said son-in-law, Thomas M, Randolph, to be held and administered by them, in trust, for the sole and separate use and behoof of my dear daughter, Martha Randolph, and her heirs; and, aware of the nice and difficult distinction of the law in these cases, I will further explain by saying, that I understand and intend the effect of these limitations to be, that the legal estate and actual occupation shall be vested in my said trustees, and held by them in base fee, determinable on the death of my said son-in-law, and the remainder during the same time be vested in my said daughter and her heirs, and of course disposable by her last will, and that at the death of my said son-in-law, the particular estate of the trustees shall be determined, and the remainder, in legal estate, possession, and use, become vested in my said daughter and her heirs, in absolute property forever.

In consequence of the variety and indescribableness of the articles of property within the house of Monticello, and the difficulty of inventorying and appraising them separately and specifically, and its inutility, I dispense with having them inventoried and appraised; and it is my will that my executors be not held to give any security for the administration of my estate. I appoint my grandson, Thomas Jefferson Randolph, my sole executor, during his life, and after his death, I constitute executors, my friends, Nichols P. Trist and Alexander Garret, joining to them my daughter, Martha Randolph, after the death of my said son-in-law, Thomas M. Randolph. Lastly, I revoke all former wills by me heretofore made; and in witness that this is my will, I have written the whole, with my own hand, on two pages, and have subscribed my name to each of them, this sixteenth day of March, one thousand eight hundred and twenty-six.

TH. JEFFERSON

I, Thomas Jefferson, of Monticello, in Albemarle, make and add the following codicil to my will, controlling the same so far as its provisions go:

I recommend to my daughter, Martha Randolph, the maintenance and care of my well-beloved sister, Anne Scott, and trust confidently that from affection to her, as well as for my sake, she will never let her want a comfort. I have made no specific provision for the comfortable maintenance of my son-in-law, Thomas M. Randolph, because of the difficulty and uncertainty of devising terms which shall vest any beneficial interest in him, which the law will not transfer to the benefit of his creditors, to the destitution of my daughter and her family, and disablement of her to supply him; whereas, property placed under the exclusive control of my daughter and her independent will, as if she were a *femme sole*, considering the relation in which she stands both to him and his children, will be a certain resource against want for all.

I give to my friend, James Madison, of Montpellier, my gold-mounted walking-staff of animal horn, as a token of the cordial and affectionate friendship which for nearly now an half century has united us in the same principles and pursuits of what we have deemed for the greatest good of our country.

I give to the University of Virginia my library, except such particular books only, and of the same edition, as it may already possess, when this legacy shall take effect; the rest of my said library, remaining after those given to the University shall have been taken out, I give to my two grandsons-in-law, Nicholas P. Trist and Joseph Coolidge. To my grandson, Thomas Jefferson Randolph, I give my silver watch in preference of the golden one, because of its superior excellence, my papers of business going of course to him, as my executor, all others of a literary or other character I give to him as of his own property.

I give a gold watch to each of my grandchildren, who shall not have already received one from me, to be purchased and delivered by my executor to my grandsons at the age of twenty-one, and granddaughters at that of sixteen.

I give to my good, affectionate, and faithful servant, Burwell, his freedom, and the sum of three hundred dollars, to buy necessaries to commence his trade of painter and glazier, or to use otherwise, as he pleases.

I give also to my good servants, John Hemings and Joe Fossett, their freedom, at the end of one year after my death; and to each of them respectively, all the tools of their respective shops or callings; and it is my will that a comfortable log-house be built for each of the three servants so emancipated, on some part of my lands convenient to them with respect to the residence of their wives, and to Charlottesville, and the University, where they will be mostly employed, and reasonably convenient also to the interests of the proprietor of the lands, of which houses I give the use of one, with a curtilage of an acre to each, during his life, or personal occupation thereof.

I give also to John Hemings the service of his two apprentices, Madison and Eston Hemings, until their respective ages of twenty-one years, at which period, respectively, I give them their freedom; and I humbly and earnestly request of the Legislature of Virginia a confirmation of the bequest of freedom to these servants, with permission to remain in this State, where their families and connections are, as an additional instance of the favor of which I have received so many other manifestations in the course of my life, and for which I now give them my last, solemn, and dutiful thanks.

In testimony that this is a codicil to my will of yesterday's date, and that it is to modify so far the provisions of that will, I have written it all with my own hand in two pages, to each of which I subscribe my name, this seventeenth day of March, one thousand eight hundred and twenty-six.

TH: JEFFERSON.

APPENDIX III

The History of the United States of America – Mount Rushmore Historic Plaque

Almighty God, from this pulpit of stone the American people render thanksgiving and praise for the new era of civilization brought forth upon this continent. Centuries of tyrannical oppression sent to these shores God-fearing men to seek in freedom the guidance of the benevolent hand in the progress toward wisdom, goodness toward men, and piety toward God.

1776 – Consequently, on July 4, 1776, our forefathers promulgated a principle never before successfully asserted, that life, liberty, equality and pursuit of happiness were the birthrights of all mankind. In this *Declaration of Independence*, formulated by **Jefferson**, beat a heart for all humanity. It declared this country free from British rule and announced the inalienable sovereignty of the people. Freedom's soldiers victoriously consecrated this land with their life's blood to be free forevermore.

1787 – Then, in 1787, for the first time a government was formed that derived its just powers from the consent of the governed. General Washington and representatives from the thirteen states formed this sacred constitution, which embodies our faith in God and in mankind by giving equal participation in government to all citizens, distributing the powers of governing threefold, securing freedom of speech and of the press, establishing the right to worship the Infinite according to conscience, and assuring this nation's general welfare against an embattled world. This chart of national guidance has for 145 years weathered the ravages of time. Its supreme trial came under pressure of Civil War, 1861-65. The deadly doctrines of secession and slavery were then purged away in blood. The seal of the union's finality set by President Lincoln, was accomplished like all our triumphs of law and humanity, through the wisdom and the power of an honest, Christian heart. Farsighted American statesmanship acquired by treaties, vast wilderness territories where progressive, adventurous Americans spread civilization and Christianity.

1850 Texas willingly ceded the disputed Rio Grande region, thus ending the dramatic acquisition of the west.

1867 – Alaska was purchased from Russia.

1904 – The Panama Canal Zone was purchased as authorized by President Theodore Roosevelt, whereupon our people built a navigable highway to conveniently enable the world's people to share the fruits of the earth and of human industry. Now, these areas are welded into a nation possessing unity, liberty, power, integrity and faith in God with responsible development of character and the steady performance of humanitarian duty.

Holding no fear of the economic and political, chaotic clouds hovering over the earth, the consecrated Americans dedicate this nation before God, to exalt righteousness and to maintain mankind's constituted liberties so long as the earth shall endure.

William Andrew Burkett
Author

This 560-word "History of the United States of America, 1776-1904," was chosen in 1935 by a nationwide competition conducted by the *Mount Rushmore National Memorial Inscription Committee*, the President of the United States, Chairman. This plaque was presented by the National Historical Foundation, July 4, 1971, and prominently installed on the terrace facing Gutzon Borglum's historically-accurate sculpture of George Washington, **Thomas Jefferson**, Abraham Lincoln and Theodore Roosevelt, carved in stone in the black hills of South Dakota.

Mount Rushmore, in the black hills of South Dakota. Sculpture of George Washington, Thomas Jefferson, Abraham Lincoln and Theodore Roosevelt by Gutzon Borglum.

APPENDIX IV

COMMUNIST "BLUEPRINT FOR WORLD CONQUEST"

On a dark night in May, 1919, two lorries rumbled across a bridge and on into the town of Dusseldorf. Among the dozen rowdy, singing "Tommies" apparently headed for a gay evening were two representatives of the Allied Military Intelligence. These men had traced a wave of indiscipline, mutiny, and murder among the troops to the local headquarters of a Revolutionary organization established in the town.

Pretending to be drunk, they brushed by the sentries and arrested the ringleaders – a group of thirteen men and women seated at a long table.

In the course of the raid the Allied Officers emptied the contents of the safe. One of the documents found in it contained a specific outline of "Rules for Bringing about a Revolution." It is reprinted here to show the strategy of materialistic Revolution, and how personal attitudes and habits of living affect the affairs of a nation.

COMMUNIST "BLUEPRINT FOR WORLD CONQUEST"
Communist Rules for Revolution
(Captured in Dusseldorf May, 1919 by the Allied Forces*)

Corrupt the young, get them away from religion. Get them interested in sex. Make them superficial, destroy their ruggedness.

Get control of all means of publicity and thereby:

Get people's minds off their government by focusing their attention on athletics, sexy books and plays and other trivialities.

Divide the people into hostile groups by constantly harping on controversial matters of no importance.

Destroy the people's faith in their natural leaders by holding the latter up to contempt, ridicule and obloquy.

Always preach true democracy, but seize power as fast and as ruthlessly as possible.

By encouraging government extravagance, destroy its credit, produce fear of inflation with rising prices and general discontent.

Foment unnecessary strikes in vital industries, encourage civil disorders and foster a lenient and soft attitude on the part of government toward such disorders.

By specious argument cause the breakdown of the old moral virtues; honesty, sobriety, continence, faith in the pledged word, ruggedness.

Cause the registration of all firearms on some pretext, with a view to confiscating them and leaving the population helpless.

*NOTE: The above "Rules for Revolution" were secured by the State.

INVESTIGATION OF UN-AMERICAN PROPAGANDA ACTIVITIES IN THE UNITED STATES

HEARINGS
BEFORE A
SPECIAL COMMITTEE ON UN-AMERICAN ACTIVITIES HOUSE OF REPRESENTATIVES
SEVENTY-SIXTH CONGRESS
FIRST SESSION
ON
H. Res. 282

TO INVESTIGATE (1) THE EXTENT, CHARACTER, AND OBJECTS OF UN-AMERICAN PROPAGANDA ACTIVITIES IN THE UNITED STATES, (2) THE DIFFUSION WITHIN THE UNITED STATES OF SUBVERSIVE AND UN-AMERICAN PROPAGANDA THAT IS INSTIGATED FROM FOREIGN COUNTRIES OR OF A DOMESTIC ORIGIN AND ATTACKS THE PRINCIPLE OF THE FORM OF GOVERNMENT AS GUARANTEED BY OUR CONSTITUTION, AND (3) ALL OTHER QUESTIONS IN RELATION THERETO THAT WOULD AID CONGRESS IN ANY NECESSARY REMEDIAL LEGISLATION

VOLUME 9
SEPTEMBER 28, 29, 30, AND OCTOBER 5, 6, 7, 9, 11, 13, AND 14, 1939
AT WASHINGTON, D. C.

Printed for the use of the Special Committee on Un-American Activities

UNITED STATES
GOVERNMENT PRINTING OFFICE
WASHINGTON : 1939

94931

Title Page of Kenneth Goff's Hearings before a Special Committee on Un-American Activities, House of Representatives, 1939.

APPENDIX V

Investigation of Un-American Propaganda Activities in the United States. Hearings before a Special Committee on Un-American Activities – House of Representatives, Seventy-sixth Congress, First Session of H. Res. 282.

In light of the "collapse" of the Berlin wall and the "dissolution" of the Soviet Empire, let us heed the words of Soviet leader Mikhail Gorbachev in a speech to the Politburo, November 1987, as reported by Sir William Stephenson, head of the Combined Allied Intelligence Operations during World War II (i.e., the man called "Intrepid"):

> Gentlemen, comrades, do not be concerned about all you hear about glastnost and perestroika and democracy in the coming years. These are primarily for outward consumption. There will be no significant internal change within the Soviet Union, other than for cosmetic purposes. Our purpose is to disarm the Americans and to let them fall asleep. We want to accomplish three things: One, we want the Americans to withdraw conventional forces from Europe. Two, we want them to withdraw nuclear forces from Europe. Three, we want the Americans to stop proceeding with Strategic Defense Initiative.

For three years until 1939, Kenneth Goff of Milwaukee, Wisconsin, had been a dues-paying member of the Communist party and had been thoroughly trained in Communist warfare, both psychological and physical, in order to destroy Christianity, American society and government. After accepting Jesus Christ as his Lord and Savior, he defected from the party and published the Russian textbook **Psycopolitics** used in Lenin University by the communists to train young American students to penetrate this nation from within. Excerpts from that textbook are included in the conclusion to my book, *The Rewriting of America's History*. As is usually the case with communist defectors, Goff was assassinated. Further documentation by Goff which I have acquired, is *Confessions of Stalin's Agent*, published by him in 1948. A photocopy of the only existing copy in the C.I.A. files was obtained for me by a C.I.A. agent, himself a Christian. It is hereunder reprinted, unveiling the insidious hidden agenda of the enemies of America to undo this nation, by removing her greatest strength and anchor – Christianity.

When I came upon *Confessions of Stalin's Agent* by Goff, my eyes were opened to the fact that I was experiencing just one facet of this dilemma. Other key areas have also been targeted, such as: churches, youth groups, schools, government, organizations and movies. Following is Goff's book, reprinted in its entirety:

Confessions of Stalin's Agent

This is My Story
by
Kenneth Goff

Chapter I

My Introduction to Stalin's Missionaries

I was born and raised in a conservative southern Wisconsin community. While working on a weekly newspaper in 1935, I received a letter through the **FERA** (Federal Employment Relief Administration) informing me that I could attend without cost, a "Worker's School" at the University of Wisconsin. I accepted the offer, went to Wisconsin and enrolled. It was a typical New Deal project, completely Communist controlled.

We were daily taught in the classrooms how to organize a worker's society. The alleged advantages of a Socialist or Communist system were constantly discussed. In the evening, students would gather around the piano and sing revolutionary songs, such as the "The Internationale."

One night, a student invited a group of us to attend a closed Communist lecture. The meeting was held in the basement of the home of a Party member. The speaker was a young man from New York by the name of Cohen. He gave a report on the Seventh World Congress of the Communist Party.

He called us Liberals, and said we were like armies without generals, or plans to carry out our campaign. He said our hit-and-miss policy would lead the working classes to destruction. Only by developing trained leadership could we attain the goal of a new world order, or international communism!

Cohen declared that the Communist Party was the vanguard of the masses and its membership comprised the generals for the coming revolution.

During the course of the meeting, he made some remarks against the LaFollette brothers which caused me to protest. This angered the speaker. I was literally thrown out by two husky fellows. Within a year the speaker and I had become close friends. We had many laughs over the experience.

My parents were old-fashioned Christians. Sunday mornings always found the entire family in Church. It was a little white frame building. Here we barefooted boys would gather with other youngsters around an old coal stove, in one corner, and be taught from the pages of God's Word. After Sunday school, we joined our parents for morning worship. This was usually followed by a picnic dinner on the lawn of the Church.

There would be all-day services some Sundays, lasting until late in the evening. Then we would start home in the family automobile, under moonlit skies, with my father leading the group in singing such songs as, "Come Thou Fount of Every

SPECIAL COMMITTEE ON UN-AMERICAN ACTIVITIES
WASHINGTON, D. C.

MARTIN DIES, Texas, *Chairman*

JOHN J. DEMPSEY, New Mexico
JOE STARNES, Alabama
JERRY VOORHIS, California
JOSEPH E. CASEY, Massachusetts

NOAH M. MASON, Illinois
J. PARNELL THOMAS, New Jersey

ROBERT E. STRIPLING, *Secretary*
RHEA WHITLEY, *Counsel*
J. B. MATTHEWS, *Director of Research*

II

5582   UN-AMERICAN PROPAGANDA ACTIVITIES

(At the conclusion of the executive session, the committee proceeded, at 10:45 a. m., in open session, as follows:)

TESTIMONY OF OLIVER KENNETH GOFF

The CHAIRMAN. Will you raise your right hand. You solemnly swear to tell the truth, the whole truth, and nothing but the truth, so help you God?
Mr. GOFF. I do.
Mr. WHITLEY. What is your full name, Mr. Goff?
Mr. GOFF. Oliver Kenneth Goff.
Mr. WHITLEY. What is your address?
Mr. GOFF. Rural Route 3, Delavan, Wis.
Mr. WHITLEY. How old are you, Mr. Goff?
Mr. GOFF. Twenty-five.
Mr. WHITLEY. Where were you born?
Mr. GOFF. In Darien, Wis.
Mr. WHITLEY. What is your occupation?
Mr. GOFF. Salesman.
The CHAIRMAN. What does he sell?
Mr. GOFF. For the McNess Products Co. at Freeport.
Mr. WHITLEY. Mr. Goff, are you a member of the Young Communist League?
Mr. GOFF. Yes.
Mr. WHITLEY. When did you join the Young Communist League?
Mr. GOFF. In May 1936.
Mr. WHITLEY. May 1936?
Mr. GOFF. That is the second day of May.
Mr. WHITLEY. Where did you join?
Mr. GOFF. In Milwaukee, Wis.
Mr. WHITLEY. And under what name did you join the Young Communist League?
Mr. GOFF. John Keats.
Mr. WHITLEY. John Keats?
Mr. GOFF. Yes.
Mr. WHITLEY. Was it suggested to you at the time you joined that you join under an assumed name?
Mr. GOFF. I was asked by Gene Dennis and Fred Keller to take this name for the records.
Mr. WHITLEY. Is that a general practice of the Young Communist League?
Mr. GOFF. Yes; that is carried out both in the Young Communist League and the Communist Party.
Mr. WHITLEY. Are you a member of the Communist Party, Mr. Goff?
Mr. GOFF. Yes, sir.
Mr. WHITLEY. When did you join the Communist Party?
Mr. GOFF. The same day I joined the league, I joined the party.
Mr. WHITLEY. In other words, you were recruited into the Young Communist League and into the Communist Party itself both on the same day?
Mr. GOFF. That is true.
Mr. WHITLEY. And under what name did you join the Communist Party?

Testimony of Kenneth Goff before the Special Committee on Un-American Activities, House of Representatives, Washington, D.C., October 9, 1939, Page 1.

Blessing," "Shall We Gather at the River?" "In the Sweet Bye and Bye"...and scores of other grand old hymns of the Faith.

These were the "unbearable" conditions from which the Communist Party was sent into Wisconsin to "save" us.

Then the day came when the headquarters of the denomination decided to sell our little old dilapidated Church building. This brought about a change in our lives. We had to attend Church in town.

Services were conducted differently there. The Pastor proclaimed a new faith. He called it the Social Gospel. This was the first time I ever heard the validity of the Scriptures questioned. We were told that many of the Bible stories were mere allegories. The meetings were quite formal.

Each Sunday morning, the Preacher would march in while the choir sang, "Praise God from Whom all Blessings Flow." Then he would make the announcements. After that, we listened to a canned sermon devoid of spiritual power, anointing and fervency.

One day, I asked him about some of the things he was teaching. Without the least hesitation, he disclaimed belief in such rock-ribbed truths as the inspiration of God's Word, Christ's virgin birth, the blood atonement and other doctrines of the Faith. He said we must build a better world based upon the "brotherhood of man."

My faith was further attacked in public and high school by evolutionary hypothesis. As youngsters, we were told that God had nothing to do with creation... and that the human family evolved from a one-celled animal called the amoeba.

I had no idea then, that I was being conditioned in heart and mind to receive the atheism of Communism in years to come. Without this background of doubt, it is to be questioned if I would have succumbed to Communism as taught in the New Deal school at Madison.

When I finished my course in the **FERA**, I received several invitations to attend Communist rallies. At one such meeting I was introduced to Gene Dennis, district organizer of the party, stationed in Milwaukee. He is now its National Secretary. Dennis invited me to his office at 113 East Wells Street. While there, on May 2, 1936, I joined the Communist Party.

I signed a membership card which pledged my allegiance to the Communist International for the revolutionary overthrow of our government...and in its place, the establishment of a Soviet America. I then assumed another name so that if my membership book was ever found, it could not be traced to me.

I chose the alias John Keats and received the number 18-B-2. The latter was to be used if the Party went underground.

I was told that I would not have to give up my religious beliefs. All they asked was that I read the material on religion as prescribed by Moscow. An official of the Party later explained with brutal candor, that if I clung to any form of religion, I would die along with all Ministers and Priests of the United States after the revolution.

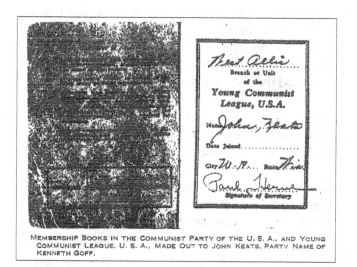

MEMBERSHIP BOOKS IN THE COMMUNIST PARTY OF THE U. S. A., AND YOUNG COMMUNIST LEAGUE, U. S. A., MADE OUT TO JOHN KEATS, PARTY NAME OF KENNETH GOFF.

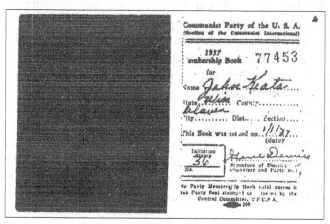

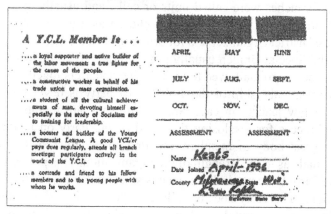

Membership Books in the Communist Party of the U.S.A. and Young Communist League, U.S.A of Kenneth Goff, alias John Keats – (Un-American Activities Committee).

Dennis said: "Dialectic materialism and religion don't mix. Anyone with religious tendencies would be a menace to the Communist State." He gave me a number of anti-religious books to read in the hope that I would quickly renounce my faith. I asked him about the thousands of **Modernist Ministers** who have defended and furthered the Communist cause. He replied:

> These liberal chameleons are of great value at present, but once our goal is reached, they will either have to change their belief, or pay the price with their heads along with the rest.

Communism was presented to me as "Twentieth Century Americanism." Browder and Foster were built up as the Washington and Lincoln of our day. Large posters were displayed at all mass meetings showing the American flag alongside the Soviet flag, with pictures of Browder, Foster, Washington and Lincoln in the background.

During the Spanish civil war of 1936, the two battalions of American Communists were named after Washington and Lincoln. It was a common thing to see in our meeting places, large posters of Lenin and Washington, side by side, draped with the Red flag displaying the hammer and sickle.

I was told that I could deny being a member of the Communist party but never to make any statement damaging to the reputation of the Soviet Union. It was presented to us as the fatherland of all workers. We were NOT told, however, that the laboring classes of Russia live in chains of slavery with the last vestige of human liberty abolished. I was assigned to the Special Branch of the Party made up of individuals who of necessity had to hide their affiliations. In some cases, even other members could not know that these particular people belonged to the Party. This was required because a slip of the tongue could handicap our work with outside groups.

The Party branches were called units or cells, and usually met once a week to plan their programs. One member was chosen as a go-between in reporting activities to the District Organizer and for bringing back his instructions. Individual members of the Special Branch usually reported directly to the district office for orders. They were seldom allowed to visit the headquarters together.

The general membership of the Communist party is never disclosed to the public. Only a few leaders in each State admit they are members. These men become mouthpieces for disclosing the stand of the Party on matters of public concern. The great body of members remains under cover so that no accurate check can be made as to the strength of the organization. This policy has led many to believe the Party to be weak. Reference is sometimes made to the small vote in general elections. The Party does not allow its power to be shown through votes cast for the Presidential candidates. It only uses elections as channels for carrying on propaganda to further the destruction of our Republic - the system which gives them the right to vote.

The New York Times

"All the News That's Fit to Print."

VOL. LXXXIX...No. 29,844.   NEW YORK, TUESDAY, OCTOBER 10, 1939.

ROOSEVELT NAMES USED BY RED CHIEFS, SAYS DIES WITNESS

Communist Leaders Bragged of having Tea With First Lady, He Testifies

PRESIDENT'S NOTE CITED

Praise of National Youth Congress Was Quoted as Aiding 'United Front'

By The United Press.

WASHINGTON, Oct. 9 – Kenneth Goff of Delavan, Wis., who said he had been a leader in the Young Communist League, told the Dies committee today that Communists used the names of President and Mrs. Roosevelt to advance their activities.

Mr. Goff said that he personally had made use of Mr. Roosevelt's letter of greeting to an American Youth Congress meeting in Washington in order to answer charges among church groups that the Washington meeting was communistic.

He said he displayed to them Mr. Roosevelt's letter, which was the first thing in a book distributed at the meeting. The last greeting in the same book came from the central committee of the United States Communist party.

Mr. Goff said that William Hinckley and other youth congress leaders who had tea with Mrs. Roosevelt at Hyde Park were all Communists. These Communists, he said, "bragged" that they had ea with Mrs. Roosevelt.

"Did this give them added prestige among Communists and in their work in the front organizations?" asked Chairman Dies.

"Sure," Mr. Goff replied, "I was looking forward to the day when I could have tea with her too."

Dies Assails "Prominent Officials"

Other developments at today's hearings included:

1. Mr. Dies charged that "Prominent government officials" are giving aid and support to the Communist party in the United States by continuing to appear before gatherings sponsored by "Communist Front" organizations. He mentioned particularly a "national conference of civil liberties" to be held in New York Oct. 13 and 14.
2. Mr. Goff resigned from the Communist party and an affiliated youth organization by submitting a communication to party officials which was read during the session.
3. Mr. Goff said he first was asked to join the party while attending a Summer "workers school" held at a University of Wisconsin fraternity house. He said the school was financed by Federal funds. Later he joined the party and was elected a national committee member of the Young Communists League.
4. The committee investigated theft of documents by someone who broke into its offices over the week-end.

Regarding the tea given by Mrs. Roosevelt for the members of the Youth Congress, Mr. Dies asked how it helped the Communist members of the congress. Mr. Goff replied that Mr. Hinckley, whom he described as a representative of Christ Episcopal Church of Missouri, and the others at Mrs. Roosevelt's tea were able to cite this fact in allaying fear among prospective Communist party members.

"They were able to say 'Don't be afraid to join the party. Look at the people we associate with.'"

Official Cooperation Asserted

Discussing the Washington meeting of the Youth Congress to lobby for the proposed "American Youth Act," Mr. Goff identified Young Communist League reports which said the meeting resulted in "closer ties with the Administration." The report mentioned free auditorium and the cooperation of Aubrey Williams, NYA Administrator; Robert Fechner, CCC director; Senator La Follette and Mr. Roosevelt. Each of these persons was listed by his last name. Mr. Goff supplied the first names and official positions.

When J.B. Matthews, chief committee investigator, read the name "Roosevelt" Mr. Goff interjected: "That's Franklin D."

AT DIES HEARING
Kenneth Goff

The committee members grinned. Mr. Goff identified a Y.C.L. report dated July 23, 1938, in which a program was outlined for Communists to work in the Young Democratic clubs.

This plan was adopted, he said, after Communists decided that it was not necessary to build a national Farmer-Labor party in America "as long as the Leftist groups were supporting the New Deal."

The Communists, he said, did not want "known Communists" to join the Young Democratic clubs and only put in persons whose Communist affiliation was not known.

Roosevelt Letter Is Quoted

The Roosevelt letter which Mr. Goff said was used by Communists to aid their "united front" activities was dated June 21, 1937, and said in part:

"The problems and the opportunities which we face as a nation are numerous, varied and challenging. This is no time for complacency or indifference; it is a time when vigorous and intelligent participation in the solution of our common problems is needed from every citizen in our democracy. The American Youth Congress has become an important instrument in achieving this end and, as such, has the good-will and the best wishes of all who are concerned with the future of American democracy."

When Mr. Goff mentioned organizations into which Communists had "infiltrated," such as the American Youth Congress and the National Negro Congress, Chairman Dies called attention to a "so-called national conference of civil liberties" to be held in New York Oct. 13 and 14, and said he understood that "prominent government officials" would speak at that meeting.

Mr. Dies said that the New York civil liberties meeting would be sponsored, among other organizations, by the American League for Peace and Democracy, the National Negro Congress and the International Labor Defense, which, he said, the committee had found to be Communist "fronts."

Mr. Goff said that he had been a member of the Communist party since 1936 under the name of "John Keats," and had worked for the party in such groups as the Young Townsend Old-Age Pension Movement in Wisconsin, where he held the post of State secretary.

He testified that Communists were infiltrating into religious groups. He declared that two national board members of the Young Women's Christian Association were members of the Young Communist League and had attended the national training school of the Communist party in New York. The board members who are Y.C.L. members are Rose Troiano and Rose Terlin, both of New York, he said.

Mr. Goff said he attended the eighth national convention of the Y.C.L. and at that meeting met Joseph Curran, president of the national Maritime Union (C.I.O.). He exhibited a card autographed by Mr. Curran at that meeting.

He testified that Joseph Cadden, national chairman of the American Youth Congress and executive secretary of the American Student Union, also attended the meeting.

Officers of the Young Communist League, the witness went on, urged "progressive students" to join the Reserve Officers Training Corps, and, from within, fight against "reactionary" R.O.T.C. officers and against compulsory military training.

Mr. Goff testified he lost his leg when struck by an automobile and knocked under a rapid transit train after addressing a meeting in Sheboygan, Wis. The Communist party, he said, hired lawyers and persuaded him to settle for $5,000 "because the party needed money."

The "party lawyers," he said, took one-third of the $5,000 settlement, and the party persuaded him to make loans or contributions so that his own share was reduced "until about all I got out of it was about $1,000."

There are more Communists in America today than there were in Russia, before the revolution...and in Spain before their civil war. Since the so-called "dissolution" of the **Comintern**, Party membership has increased by leaps and bounds.

Following my induction into the Communist Party, I was sent to the **Debs Labor School** in Milwaukee. This was one of the many Communist training centers operating in all parts of the United States. Such schools are usually located in thickly-populated industrial sections. The largest one is in New York State.

Prior to 1935, students were sent to Moscow for their training courses, which lasted from six months to two years. After that date, schools were established in the United States with half of the expenses of maintaining them contributed by the Communist International, and the balance by the local Party.

These centers of instruction were organized by the late Abraham Markoff, national head of the Communist school system in the United States. He of course acted upon direct orders from Moscow. Every such school is a well of ideological poison from which young citizens drink atheistic and revolutionary ideas. Earl Browder says in his book "Communism in the United States," page 310:

> The workers school is that institution where we are providing our leaders with weapons, ideological weapons of Marxism and Leninism, to be used in the mass struggle.

George Dimitroff, President of the World Comintern, said:

> The masses must be stirred to struggle, and Communist schools must be used to help them grasp the mighty, fertile all-powerful Bolshevik theory, the teachings of **Marx, Engels, Lenin** and **Stalin**.

We received instructions every day on how to organize and promote the revolution...how to bore from within existing organizations, and lead them toward the Left.

Gene Dennis told us one evening not to report to school the following day, but to wander around the downtown area of Milwaukee until we received further instructions. I went down to the main business section the next morning and did some window shopping.

About 10 o'clock, while gazing in a window, a newsboy tapped me on the elbow and asked me if I wanted to buy a "Milwaukee Sentinel." I said no, that I had already read it. He continued to insist that I purchase one, and I ordered him away. He then handed me a copy and said, "Read comrade." I took the paper and across the top was written in pencil, "Go to Bues Hall."

I immediately went there and found many of the comrades had already arrived. More were coming in every minute. When assembled, we were told that if the Party ever went underground, it would be necessary to meet this way. We were instructed how to dismantle and assemble mimeograph machines, to print handbills if the party was forced to operate secretly.

Then Gene Dennis gave us the blueprint of how to seize a city when the revolution breaks. At that hour, two large riots are supposed to take place in every city of any size. Leaders of these mobs are to be carefully chosen and trained in advance. The disturbances are to be of such extent as to require sending large forces of police to those areas. While the authorities are trying to quell these riots, picked bands of Communists are to seize the radio stations and telephone exchanges. With the aid of their comrades who are employed inside, all communication systems are to be instantly crippled.

Flying squads of Communists are to seize control of the water supply and shut it off; also the electrical power and gas. This means that no elevators or street cars are to be running. Homes would be without water, fuel, or light. It would be impossible to communicate with friends or loved ones, even in another part of the city.

Goon squads of professional murderers are to round up the people in business districts. Men are to be held as hostages in some of the larger buildings. Women are to be turned over to the sex-crazed mobs to be ravished and raped.

These are exactly the **methods used in Russia, Spain and other places** where the Communist Party has been allowed to organize and come to fruition. They firmly expect to do the same thing in the United States.

Bridges, subways and street car stations are to be blown up. Downtown areas are to be isolated from the rest of the city. Sharpshooters and snipers are to be detailed in taxicabs and vehicles, which are to be taken over, to wipe out the police, soldiers, uniformed persons and known vigilantes. Smoke bombs properly located in subways, buildings and large stores are to add to the terror of the people.

This is the day – the big day toward which every Communist in America is looking...and for which he is preparing. His entire training focuses at that point.

When night comes, the city is to be in pitch darkness. Murderous bands of communists will roam the streets, plundering shops and starting fires in old buildings. This will increase the panic and facilitate the surrender of women, children and old people, who will be held as hostages to hasten the surrender of unarmed men.

Then as the morning sun casts her first rays on the community, one will be able to see blood flowing in the streets. This is no idle dream. The Communist Party is working methodically and with deadly precision toward this objective. It is now happening in Bulgaria, Romania, Hungary, etc. It can happen here. Unless we destroy the Communist menace in America the day is at hand when we shall suffer the same fate as our Christian brethren in Europe.

Let it be borne in mind that what I shall now say about revolutionary tactics, as planned and plotted by the great conspiracy, comes from inside Party circles.

We were instructed regarding alternate plans for gaining control of the United States. These were in the nature of interim objectives, which if realized would only be regarded as stepping stones toward the ultimate goal of Bloodshed and Mob Violence. The following schemes were outlined as temporary targets and measures of expedience:

(1) To completely saturate the public mind with Communist propaganda so there would be such confusion that the democratic system could not possibly operate.
(2) To set up innumerable front organizations for smearing and ruining before the public, every man or woman of prominence who dared raise a finger against us.
(3) To promote pacifist groups and have them cry out against war in order to keep America disarmed while Russia prepared for world conquest.
(4) To create unemployment in the United States by "dumping" products produced by slave labor, on the markets of the world.
(5) To create a general strike through Communist controlled labor unions thereby paralyzing the Nation and creating waves of mob violence.

These are a few of the broad objectives kept before Party members.

It is hoped by the Communists that once Russia is able to convert the potential industrial capacity of Europe's satellite nations to a productive status, she will, because of lower living a wage standards, produce goods to **permanently undersell the United States** in Central and South America. Unemployment will thereby increase because of the loss of foreign trade.

To further their aim of gaining political control of our Country, the conspirators are setting up numerous political organizations as fronts. These enterprises have produced results highly gratifying to leaders of the Party in Moscow. They have as their over-all purpose the final overthrow of the United States Government. Such groups encompass every phase of American life...and all of them have several things in common – including the condemnation of the foreign policy of the United States and approval of the foreign policy of the Soviet Union.

When William Z. Foster made his speech in May, 1928, accepting the Presidential nomination as candidate of the Communist Party, he said:

> Our Party creates no illusions amongst the workers that they can vote their way to emancipation. The working class must shatter the capitalist state. It must build a new state, a new government, a workers and farmers government - the Soviet government in the United States. **When a communist heads the government of the United States** - and that day will come just as surely as the sun rises, that government will not be a capitalist government but a soviet government and behind this government will stand the communist army to enforce the dictatorship of the proletariat.

This is a bold statement, but one hundred percent true as far as Moscow's designs and Communist Party objectives are concerned. We were told that when he Party came into power, a United States of Soviet America would be established... that this Nation would be divided into Soviets, with a Commissar over each one. When such statements were made in our meetings, it was a habit for all of us to rise with clenched fists and sing lustily:

> We march down the streets with our banner unfurled; fighting for bread and the Communist World. The bosses all quake at the challenge we hurl. Advance to the U.S.S.A.

One comrade would then step forward and ask what was to be done with the religious people of the country. We would then quote what comrade Lounstcharski had declared, namely:

> We hate Christians. Even the best of them must be regarded as our worst enemies. All religions are poison. A fight to the death must be declared upon all religions.

Fred Bassett Blair, a local Community Party organizer, told us that we would turn the Churches into workers' clubs; and that these clubs would be healthier for workers than a dead religion.

Chapter II

I Become a Number Instead of a Name

After finishing my course in the **FERA New Deal** "Worker's School" at the University of Wisconsin, I was one of the group regarded as being properly "conditioned" for membership in the Communist Party.

A few years later when testifying before the Dies Committee, I described my experience with the FERA as follows:

> In 1935 I received a letter granting me the right to attend a worker's school to be held in Madison, Wisconsin. The money was contributed by the United States Government. We were to attend for six weeks, and all expenses would be paid. During this time we were given material that was rather of the leftish view. The director of the school, Lucille Cohen, was a left-wing Socialist from New York. At this school about 80 percent of the young people were either Communists or leftists or fellow travelers.

Before my course was completed a man came out from New York to look us over. His name was also Cohen. He assured us that we were Liberals in the truest sense of the word.

As I write these words, I have open before me a book dealing with Marxism, which Eugene Dennis autographed on the fly leaf: "To a real friend and comrade - with best wishes, Gene." Perhaps he now feels that I have fallen from grace! **The Lord Jesus Christ has since saved me from my sins**, and I pray that Dennis will come into a like experience, some time before he is called to cross the great divide. He has been much in the headlines of late due to an investigation into his affairs by the Committee on Un-American Activities. Representative Karl E. Mundt, a member of the Committee, had this to say in a speech before Congress, April 22, 1947:

> Mr. Speaker, Mr. Eugene Dennis is the general secretary of the Communist Part of America, which makes him either the No. 1 or No. 2 official Communist in the country, depending upon whether W.Z. Foster, the chairman of the party is considered by party followers to have more authority than the general secretary. In either event, that man is before you on an incident of contempt of Congress.

Referring to the fact that Dennis' real name is Waldron – Francis Waldron, Mr. Mundt continued: "We did not know until later just why Mr. Eugene Dennis refused to identify himself by his proper name, but it has since developed that he is a fugitive from justice in California under one of his aliases; that he has been a draft dodger in the United States under one of his numerous names; that he obtained a passport fraudulently under one of his aliases; and, consequently, he was unprepared to reveal his correct name before the committee at that time."

As the foregoing debate progressed in Congress, Mr. Mundt and other Representatives, vigorously denounced Attorney General Tom Clark for allegedly failing to prosecute Communists who are known to be law violators.

"I am sure we all wonder this afternoon what it is that a Communist has, that an ordinary American citizen has not." said Mr. Mundt, "how is it, for example, that Mr. Eugene Dennis can violate the draft law as he has and be a draft evader with complete immunity, and nobody in the Department of Justice prosecutes him for his law violation." At this point, Representative Dondero of Michigan made the following shocking contribution to the discussion:

> I think the speaker might also add to the list that in wartime, Communists were able to steal a truckload of files of the most secret nature out of the State Department and Naval Intelligence, and were arrested by the FBI, but then were dismissed with nominal fine.

Mr. Mundt continued:

> Yes. The list can be extended as long as a bamboo fishing pole of law violations which have occurred in the last 6 or 8 years in America by Communists, without anybody in the Attorney General's office taking any step whatsoever to punish them. In fact, it was only after repeated speeches in the well of the House this year that we succeeded in getting the Attorney General to move in on the contempt proceedings which the House of Representatives voted by overwhelming majorities nearly a year ago.

Thereupon Representative Smith of Ohio suggested Mr. Clark's impeachment on the charge of coddling Communists. As the debate continued, Representative Marcantonio of New York was the only one who spoke in defense of my former comrade. Finally the House voted that Mr. Clark and the Department of Justice would be required to hold Dennis and bring him to trial.

The party did not send me to a regular Communist school. I was chosen one of a select group to attend what they called a "special class" – at national headquarters, 35, Twelfth Street, New York City.

Only uninformed and gullible people think of the Communist party like Republicans and Democrats. **The Communist organization** can be more correctly thought of as **an underground revolutionary army**. It is a cult or secret order into which members are initiated. New members, going into a regular school, are ordered first to report at Party headquarters. They are then blind-folded. From New York they are driven a good distance from the city into a rural district. They must remain in camp until their training is finished. It takes some longer than others to be inoculated with the virus.

Students cannot write letters telling what they are doing. Both incoming and outgoing mail is censored. Letters written by members at camp are carefully scrutinized, then taken to New York for mailing. All mail from friends or relatives must be sent to the Party office for censorship prior to delivery.

While in the school, one is denied all contact with the outside world, except through heads of the organization. Their expenses are paid and personal matters arranged. Both sexes attend these schools. There are no moral restraints. My classes at Party headquarters were addressed by such top ranking leaders as Earl Browder, William Foster, Bob Minor, Clarence Hathaway, Ella Reeve Bloor, Joe Curren, Elizabeth Gurley Flynn, Ray Hansborough and others.

These schools were organized by Abraham Markoff on instructions from Moscow. They are wells of ideological arsenic from which new recruits in the Party consume great draughts of un-American, atheistic and revolutionary poison.

I still have notes on some of the lectures attended during the early days of my training for leadership in the Party.

Here are a few words from Early Browder, explaining the purpose of the secret Communist school system:

> The worker's school is that institution where we are providing our leaders with weapons - ideological weapons of Marxism and Leninism, to be used in the mass struggle.

He then quoted Georgi Dimitroff, president of the **World Comintern**, as saying: "The masses must be stirred to struggle, and the Communist schools must be used to help them grasp the mighty, fertile, all-powerful Bolshevik theory – the teachings of **Marx, Engels, Lenin** and **Stalin**."

Browder told my class that young members should fix their dreams on the hour when they would become commissars in a Soviet America. He told us to think of the day when filthy democracy would be at an end in the United States, decide what industries we would take over, and prepare ourselves accordingly.

He said we should never look for victory through the ballot – that Communist triumph could come only by bloodshed and revolution. We were told to drive steadily toward the day and hour when blood would flow in gutters and make it possible for us to take over. I distinctly recall hearing him announce that the "last vestige" of the bourgeois state would be destroyed – and that even small children who had been exposed to bourgeois teaching would have to be put to death.

Foster was even more violent in his lectures. He spoke with candor about plans for a "blood bath" in the United States, to precede the dictatorship of the proletariat. Foster of course was pushed into the background and Browder brought forward during the years of close collaboration between Roosevelt and Stalin.

When it became apparent that the Country was about to make a right turn, thereby ending the White House-Kremlin honeymoon, the Comintern ordered old "blood and thunder Foster" to again assume Party leadership. I have notes on a lecture by Foster instructing us how to fight the R.O.T.C. We were told to join the organization, learn its secrets, worm our members into positions of authority and be ready to use it in the revolution. He gave us instructions on street fighting, explained how to build barricades, and stated bluntly that some students would probably have to kill their parents and others members of the family in the interest of setting up a "Soviet State."

Among the most depraved leaders to teach our classes was the notorious Ella Reeve Bloor. I can best introduce her by quoting from the House Report 209 on the Eightieth Session of Congress, pages 14 and 15:

> The Communist Party of America held its first convention from September 1 to 7, 1919, at the headquarters of the Russian Federation of the Socialist Party in Chicago. The call for the meeting, was published in the (Russian) 'Nory Mir,' on July 7, 1919, and in the 'Revolutionary Age' of August 23, 1919, both

being left wing Socialist organs. It called upon all those who favored an 'international alliance of the Socialist movement of the United States only with the Communist groups of other countries' to answer 'the clarion call of the Third International'... Earl Browder and Ella Reeve Bloor who is now a National Board member, were charter members of the Communist Labor Party.

Comrade Ella warned the girls of our classes that they had been called to an important task in building a "worker's society." She spoke in glowing terms about becoming "whores of the revolution." No racial boundaries or color lines must be permitted, she said. White girls would be expected at all times to submit themselves to Negroes, Chinese and others.

"Your body belongs to the Party," she would shout. Girls were instructed to "become prostitutes for the advancement of Communism." They were ordered to resort to whatever means necessary for the purpose of enticing men into the Party and committing acts of violence against **"this damned democracy."**

Every organism has a sewer. The Communist Party is the sewer of the American politic body. Our teachers directed their hardest blows against **"Fundamentalist Christianity."** But I never heard one of them say, at any time, a single word against Modernism. In fact, they assumed a benevolent attitude toward Modernist preachers. Eugene Dennis put it this way:

> These liberal chameleons are of great value at present, but once our goal is reached, they will either have to change their belief, or pay the price with their heads along with the rest.

A favorite phrase in the classes that I attended was a quotation from Zinovieff who said: "We shall grapple with the Lord God in due season. We shall vanquish Him from the highest heaven and wherever He seeks refuge, we shall subdue Him forever." Yaroslavesky's statement, "Remember that the struggle against religion is a struggle for socialism," was prominently displayed in the literature they gave us to study. He is president of the **"Society of Militant Atheists."**

The same was true of Lounatcharski's remark: "We hate Christians. Even the best of them must be regarded as our worst enemies. All religions are poison. A fight to the death must be declared upon all religions."

We were given the most detailed instructions on how to fight the Church. Only to the degree that Christianity was weakened, could the movement toward revolution become strong and powerful. The followers of Christ were therefore to be regarded as our worst enemies. We were given methods for indoctrinating the thinking of both believers and unbelievers with anti-religious theories.

Our textbooks against religion included "The Origin of the Family" by Frederick Engels and "The Foundations of Christianity" by Karl Kautsky. Both of these, as well as other titles used, are one hundred percent atheistic. Talmudic teachings were hammered into our minds – including the charge that Jesus was born to Mary through an illicit affair with a Roman officer; that Jesus was a Maccabean, who wanted to abolish Roman rule over Judea; that He was a member of the working class and a revolutionist, and that He practiced free love. We were taught that the Romans killed Him for attempting to seize control of the government; that the writers of the four gospels falsified and shaded their writings to accommodate the conditions of their time.

Paul, we were told, was an agent of Roman capitalism sent out to organize the scattered followers of Christ into an ecclesiastical order for the interests of the state and that the Church of Jesus Christ offers opium to the people. **Dialectic materialism** was presented as the foundation of Communist belief. There is no such thing as soul, according to this teaching. Everything is material. The only heaven or hell is what one gets here on earth. We were told that no appetite should go unsatisfied, whether it be of sexual promiscuity, theft, murder, or other base desires. One should never restrain himself at any point.

Evenings found the students in dimly lit rooms at national headquarters, engaging in the basest practices that the human mind can imagine. Negro boys made love to white girls and vice versa. Anti-religious songs were sung to prove that God could not destroy the revelers. Strange enough, students thus indulging themselves, had an inward feeling that they were insulting God – despite the fact of denying His existence.

I recall a particularly revolting picture hanging on the wall, picturing Christ's intestines protruding from His stomach, while workers gnawed at His arms, legs and entrails; and they were also shown drinking blood from His veins. Beneath this large cartoon were the words, "Take eat, this is my body broken for you."

During these orgies, comrades would sing both in Russian and English, such songs as the **Communist hymn of hate** called the "**Internationale**," the second stanza of which is as follows:

> We want no condescending saviour,
> To rule us from a judgment hall;
> We workers ask not for their favors,
> Let us consult for all.
> To make the thief disgorge his booty.
> To free the spirit from the cell,
> We must ourselves decide our duty,
> We must decide and do it well.
> 'Tis the final conflict
> Let each stand in his place;
> The International Soviet,
> Shall be the human race.

Another favorite song used on such occasions went like this:

> Blow the bloody bugles,
> Beat the bloody drums, boys.
> Blow the bloody Bourgeois,
> To bloody kingdom come.
> Build the big bonfire,
> As high as the big church spire;
> And blow the bloody bastards,
> Higher one by one.

We would also sing the following blasphemous parody on the Gospel Message of the Lord Jesus Christ:

1. Long-haired preachers come out every night,
   Try to tell you what's wrong and what's right;
   But when asked about something to eat,
   They will answer with voices so sweet:
   Refrain:
   You will eat by and by, in that glorious land above the sky,
   Work and pray, live on hay,
   You'll get pie in the sky when you die.
2. Oh, the salvation army they pray,
   They sing and they clap and they play.
   When they get all your money on the drum,
   They will tell you that you're a bum.
3. If you fight hard for children and wife,
   Try to get something good in this life,
   You're a sinner and bad man, they tell;
   When you die you will sure go to hell.
4. Workingmen of all countries, unite!
   Side by side we for freedom will fight.
   When the world and its wealth we have gained
   To the grafters we'll sing this refrain:
   Last Refrain:
   You will eat bye and bye, when you've learned to cook and to fry,
   Chop some wood, 'Twill do you good, and you'll eat in the sweet bye and bye.

I had grown up in a **Christian family**, around a praying fireside. No matter how much I was exposed to Communism, even as it exists inside the Party, these righteous home influences could not be discarded. My conscience continued unbearably active. God was all the time speaking to my heart.

I was assigned by national headquarters to duty in District 18 of the Party, which comprises the State of Wisconsin. It became my special duty to bore into Church groups and youth organizations. While engaged in these activities I met a girl comrade, who was working under the alias of Doris Berger. She was a clever and hardened Bolshevik.

During the Boston Store strike in Milwaukee, she had been arrested. This experience toughened her for more useful work in the Party. She was exactly the type of fearless, fighting red that any Communist would want for a wife. We were married. She is the present Mrs. Goff.

We were socially-minded and toiled for the Party. Both of us were sincere in entering its ranks. We wanted something better, and desired a solution for the perplexing economic problems of the United States. But neither of us was quite satisfied in his heart.

Apologists for Communists try to make out that great freedom exists within the Party. But when one becomes a member, he soon finds that his life is no longer his own. He cannot travel from one State to another without the permission of the District Organizer. Neither can he marry or raise a family without approval. Women are forced to have abortions when party leaders decide that the work of the organization is such that the parents should not have children. Every comrade, male and female, is required to take all problems to the District Organizer.

One evening, after Mrs. Goff and I were married, found us together in the kitchen of the place where the Party gave us permission to live. Looking back, I have no way of explaining what caused me to start singing a hymn learned at home in my boyhood, "**Rescue the Perishing**."

It was the farthermost thing from my mind to chant such a melody, because I was then taking my Communism very seriously. My back was turned to Mrs. Goff as I sang the words:

> Down in the human heart,
> Crushed by the tempter;
> Feelings lie buried
> That grace can restore.
> Touched by a loving heart,
> Wakened by kindness,
> Chords that are broken
> Will vibrate once more.

I heard my hardened Bolshevik wife sobbing. The entire episode made me mad. Communists are not supposed to cry. I asked what was ailing her anyway! The tears continued to flow. She said that she knew in her heart that Jesus Christ was different than the Communists explained; that He was truly God on earth; that heaven was real and that Christ could make her life clean, and true Christians were the only truly happy people in the world.

I flew into a rage and told her to forget that nonsense. I promised that I would never again by guilty of singing such bunk in her presence. She refused to listen to me and was miraculously converted a short time later. It was in the dead of winter and the preacher had to cut a hole in the ice to baptize her. I tried to make myself believe she had "gone crazy over religion." But I knew better! Childhood memories came vividly before me. She continued to pray for me...and before long those prayers were answered. And that is the real reason why I left the Communist Party.

Chapter III

My Part in the Conspiracy
I Begin to Know the Big Shots

The Communist Party is not a party. It is a **revolutionary army within our borders**, masked as a political organization. It is a conspiracy, promoted by a foreign country, for the overthrow of our Government. We hear it said that to outlaw the movement might drive it underground. This line of reasoning is defective for the reason that, by its very nature, the Party already operates as an Underground Organization. One does not join the Communist Party in the way that one becomes a Republican or a Democrat. The new member has to be "recruited" – the same term used in joining a military organization.

As one who worked three years on the inside, I am in a position to know that the organization relies upon deception for promoting its schemes. Its chief weapon is the lie method. Truth is alien to its program. Jesus denounced the anti-Christ progenitors of the modern Communist movement as follows:

> Ye are of your father the devil, and the lusts of your father ye will do. He was a murderer from the beginning, and abode not in the truth, because there is no truth in him. When he speaketh a lie, he speaketh of his own; for he is a liar, and the father of it.

A person becomes a Republican or Democrat by merely casting a ballot for the candidate of his choice. But when one is recruited into the red Party, he is compelled to take a rigid course of training in revolutionary technique. He is immediately assigned to one of a group of Communist schools set up for this purpose. When his training is finished, the leaders decide where he can best serve the interests of the Party. Thereupon he is given an assignment. He is told what organizations to bore into, with the aim of eventually taking them over. These may include churches, clubs, civic societies, fraternal groups, political bodies and others. It is a known fact that Communists even occupy some pulpits.

After completing my courses at the Debs Labor School of Milwaukee, and "special classes" in New York national headquarters, I was made a member-at-large. This was a highly confidential and important post. The Congressional Record of April 16, 1947 contains a factual statement regarding this phase of the Communist program on page A-1812:

> Members-at-Large: Those active in strategic positions where a Communist label would be disadvantageous are affiliated as Members-at-Large so that they do not have to meet with any unit or branch of the Party and can, therefore, work in front organizations and church groups and not be known as members of the organization. Among such Members-at-Large have been Kenneth Goff, alias John Keats, former member of the National Committee of the Young Communist League, and Edward Strong, a member of a special branch, and head of the Southern Negro Youth Congress, which the Young Communist League surreptitiously controlled.

Church people need to be alerted to tactics for boring Communists into their denominations. The Committee on Un-American Activities of the House of Representatives has something to say on this subject, in its report to the first session of the Eightieth Congress:

> **Penetrating Religious Groups**: Those who deal with Communist youth organizations are frequently deceived by the number of religious organizations apparently represented. Religious groups are notoriously naive and easy prey for the young Communist power politicians. Every young Communist is instructed as a first step to join a mass organization such as YMCA, YWCA, or a church, a trade union or a student group. With religious groups, the Communist strategy is to speak in terms of Christian principles but actually to exploit them to establish contact and use them for Communist propaganda often with considerable success. Out of a total of 52 members of the National Council of the American Youth Congress, 22 have been identified as Communists. This list is given here for the purpose of indicating the technique employed whereby they appear not as Communists, but as the representatives of religious and other respectable groups.

The following list of names and organizations were then published in the Committee's report to Congress:

William Hinckley, Christ Episcopal Church, Mo.
Irma Garner, South Side Settlement House.
Howard W. Lederer, Ninety-second Street,
    YWCA, New York City
Elizabeth Scott, St. James Presbyterian Church,
    New York City
Rose Terlin, student secretary, student division,
    YWCA.
Rose Trojano, national industrial council, YWCA.
Hazel Lehman, Youth Forum and Commonwealth
    Federation, Washington
Robert Clemmons, Epworth League, Cleveland,
    Ohio
William Dorsey, City-wide Young People's Forum, Baltimore
Bert J. Duzykowski, Central Committee of Polish
    Youth, Milwaukee
Kenneth Goff, Wisconsin Townsend Clubs
Florence V. MacDonald, Wisconsin Young People's Conference
Harold Peterson, Minnesota Junior Farmer-Labor
    Association, Minneapolis

It is Communist strategy to prostitute the names of prominent persons, as well as to bore into reputable groups. In pursuance of this policy, numerous front organizations have been created, bearing names of persons serving in advisory capacities, printed on imposing letterheads.

Some people have been innocent dupes, roped in by designing propagandists. Others are well known in Party circles to be friends and supporters of the red cause.

Take **Eleanor Roosevelt** for instance. As a member of the Communist Party and an official in the Young Communist League, I never regarded the former first lady as being other than a secret friend and supporter of our program. As recently as April 23, 1947, she was vociferously praised in a speech by Helen Gahagan Douglas, the Congresswoman from Hollywood, wife of the Jew, Melvyn Hesselberg, known as Melvyn Douglas, as follows: "I say that Eleanor Roosevelt, and those like her who have walked down through history with light around their heads, are the true disciples of Jesus Christ and the true practicing Christians." We will agree that this is eloquent language, but I have often heard Mrs. Roosevelt praised in terms equally flattering within the secret circles of the Communist Party.

I gave some three hundred pages of testimony before the Dies Committee explaining the inner workings of the Party and its tie to the Third International, but none of my disclosures were more important than the sections that related to Mrs. Roosevelt's fraternization with the Young Communist League and the American

Youth Congress. This matter was covered in part by my testimony of October 9, 1939, which ran as follows...reprinted from the Government records:

"The Chairman. The Committee will come to order. You may proceed, Mr. Matthews.
Mr. Matthews. Mr. Chairman, we have a number of documents that have to do with the American Youth Congress of which the witness has already testified he was a member of the National Committee.

I should like to have you identify a list of the National Council of the American Youth Congress in order to have them incorporated in the record.
Mr. Goff, is that the list (handing list to witness),

Mr. Goff.	Yes; that is the National Council.
Mr. Matthews.	On this council the National Chairman is listed as William Hinckley, representing Christ Episcopal Church, Missouri.
The Chairman.	He is a member of the Communist Party?
Mr. Matthews.	He is a member of the Communist Party. The Executive Secretary is listed as Joseph Cadden, representing the National Student Federation of America. He is identified as a Communist.
The Chairman.	Is it not a fact that Hinckley managed in some way to get an invitation to Hyde Park and was entertained there?
Mr. Goff.	Yes; he had tea at Eleanor Roosevelt's house one day.
The Chairman.	Were others invited to that tea?
Mr. Goff.	Yes.
The Chairman.	When was it that this tea was given?
Mr. Matthews.	That was last summer?
Mr. Goff.	It was at the time of the pilgrimage, or preparation for the **World Youth Congress**.
The Chairman.	Did they not brag about it afterwards?
Mr. Goff.	They bragged about having tea at Eleanor Roosevelt's house.
The Chairman.	It gave them added prestige in their work, in that front organization; the fact that they had had tea with the President's wife helped them considerably?
Mr. Goff.	Yes."

For Mrs. Roosevelt to entertain officials of our organization in her home, was tantamount to endorsing our principles. At least it was so regarded by the Communist Party and a large section of the public. I know we found it easier to line up new members, among young people, after we were invited to the Roosevelt home at Hyde Park, and to have tea in the White House.

While giving my testimony before the Dies Committee, I placed in the record an address by O. Kuusinen, delivered at the Seventh World Communist Congress in Moscow, which stated in part:

> We want to attack our class enemies in the rear, when they start the war against the Soviet Union. But how can we do so if the majority of the toiling youth follow not us, but the Catholic priests or the liberal chameleons? We often repeat the slogan of transforming the imperialist war into a civil war against the bourgeoisie. In itself, the slogan is a good one, but it becomes an empty and dangerous phrase if we do nothing serious in advance to create a united youth front. In these organizations, our American young comrades have discovered a large number of functionaries and cadres who are prepared to fight side by side with the Communists against reaction, and in the course of not quite a year, the Young Communist League in the United States has succeeded in creating 175 fractions in these mass organizations. Comrades, these are only a few - not all - of the positive experiences gained by the Young Communist League of the United States, in course of the work recently carried on by our American young comrades.

This shows the kind of an outfit that Mrs. Roosevelt entertained at Hyde Park. The so-called "**Friends of Democracy**," headed by L.M. Birkhead's record of cooperation with the Party in Kansas City was explained to us. He was presented as a useful "friend," whose objectives were regarded as identical with those of the Party.

As I write these words, a grand jury investigation of Birkhead, his associates and the Friends of Democracy, is just getting under way in New York City. Perhaps I cannot do better in this regard, than quote from a Chicago Tribune editorial of May 15th which says:

> Magistrate Peter M. Horn of New York has done well to order a grand jury investigation of the aggregation of high-binders parading as Friends of Democracy. The inquiry is long overdue. It has been ordered now because the organization's National Director, the Rev. Leon M. Birkhead, has been caught in one of the libels he perpetrates incessantly in pursuit of his vendettas. Birkhead's racket has been operating for eleven years.
>
> His principal associated poison penman is a bearded writer of 'whodunits' named Rex Stout, who was a member of the original executive board of the Communist New Masses, and a character with a penchant for aliases, Avedis Derounian, more commonly known as John Roy Carlson. Derounian was the author of a book

called 'Under Cover,' a wilderness of lies and libels. On the losing end of one of several libel actions, Derounian heard himself characterized by federal Judge Barnes in Chicago, as a congenital liar who would do anything for a dollar. All in all, the combination has a fat graft. The grand jury should be interested not only in discovering the dimensions of the take, but in exploiting the motives of the smear campaigns, and the identity of those who evidently think they stand to benefit sufficiently to pay for them.

Having engaged in this educational work, the grand jury can then proceed with its other mission of returning the indictments which will send Birkhead, Stout, and Derounian to the penitentiary for the many criminal libels they have employed in their dirty business.

Death did not rid the White House of the Roosevelt family too soon, for the good of our Country. Many things served to sicken me with the Party while I was yet a member. The greatest incentive to a change in attitude was the conversion of my wife. I had been advocating world revolution...and now a complete revolution was taking place in my soul.

I was day and night conscious of Mrs. Goff's prayers.

I followed orders one night and delivered a street corner speech against Fascism and Nazism. I shouted: "Down with Fascism. Kill Hitler, Kill Mussolini." While I was yet speaking, a comrade stepped up, tapped me on the shoulder and said. "Don't say that anymore, Keats. Russia and Germany have signed a pact. The Party line is changed. Go to headquarters and get the latest dope."

I felt like a fool. One minute **I was supposed to hate Hitler**. The next minute **I was supposed to love him**...all because a handful of men in the Kremlin said so! The record says:

"In other words, you found that the things you were supposed to do were things that were dictated to you from some other source, and that it was a case where you were in conflict with your own conscience completely?

Yes, sir.

Were you also impressed with the fact, as time went on, that those changes in the Party line were matters that not only did not always allow your own conscientious views, but were also dictated from outside your own country?

Yes, sir.

Did that have an influence with you?

Yes, sir; it bothered me because, in the first place, I never found the party giving both sides. There was a question of a lot of things in regard to the Soviet Union, and I wanted to hear both sides of the story. They would not let me go there and look around for myself. I asked them, when I wanted to go there, if I could go around the find out things in Russia, but they said, 'You will have to take the charted course like everybody else.' Although I had inwardly renounced the Party several weeks in advance, I waited to announce my resignation while testifying before the Dies Committee. I wanted to make my stand count for as much as possible.

My task completed, I left Washington and began my journey home. Every time the train stopped in a large city, newsboys came through the coaches and I would see my story on the front page. It is impossible to describe my feelings. The Communist Party was the consuming factor of my life. I had resigned, gone over to the enemy, and publicly exposed the innermost secrets of the conspiracy. I was warned in advance that if I ever made such a move, it would mean my death. Today, I bear marks in my body which prove that my former comrades tried to make good their threat.

Chapter IV

I Provoke Revolt among Negroes and Aliens

I see from Press reports that Eugene Dennis, my former mentor in the Communist Party...the man who recruited me into the organization in 1936, and gave me the alias John Keats, has been sentenced to prison.

By an interesting paradox, six of the twelve Washington jurors who found Dennis guilty, were Negroes. This must have been a hard blow, because the Communist Party – of which he is General Secretary, has for years concentrated their propaganda upon the Negro population of the United States. We were told in Party circles that the Negro was to be robbed of his religion...organized into shock troops to do the dirty work, and bear the brunt of the street fighting, when the revolution came...and to be encouraged toward acts of violence, particularly rape, as the Nation became more and more sovietized by propaganda. Sheer duplicity prompts the Party to choose a Negro to run for Vice President, from time to time, on the Communist ticket. I know what the leaders really think of the black race!

Considerable progress has been made in generating **hatred for Christianity and democratic government** among Negroes. Langston Hughes, the Negro poet, is an example. His song "Goodbye Christ," symbolizes a trend, and illustrates what Communism is accomplishing, to an alarming degree, among the members of this race. The words go as follows:

> Listen, Christ,
> You did all right in your day, I reckon –
> But that day's gone now.
> They ghosted you up a swell story, too.
> Called it the Bible -
> But it's dead now.
> The popes and the preachers've
> Made too much money from it.

They've sold you to too many
Kings, generals, robbers, and killers –
Even to the Tsar and the Cossacks,
Even to the Rockefeller's Church,
Even to the Saturday Evening Post.
You ain't no good no more.
They've pawned you
Till you've done wore out.
Goodbye.
Christ Jesus Lord God Jehovah,
Beat it on away from here now.
Make way for a new guy with no religion at all –
A real guy named
Marx Communist Lenin Peasant Stalin Worker ME –
I said, ME!
Go ahead on now,
You're getting in the way of things, Lord,
And please take Saint Ghandi with you when you go,
And Saint Aimee McPherson,
And big black Saint Becton
Of the Consecrated Dime.
And step on the gas, Christ!
Move!
Don't be so slow about movin'!
The world is mine from now on –
And nobody's gonna sell ME
To a king, or a general,
Or a millionaire.
Goodbye Christ, good morning Revolution!

Negroes who have been exposed to the Moscow virus are all familiar with the name Eugene Dennis. The fact that members of their race served on the jury that convicted him, will have a wholesome effect. Speaking of Dennis...let me say that information regarding his close connections with the Kremlin, came to me while I was active in the Party. I learned that he and Stalin were warm personal friends. In fact Dennis discussed with me some of the secret exchanges, that passed between himself and the dictator. This will be made clear as I proceed.

The winter of 1936 and '37 was a momentous period for the **International Communist Party**. It was engaged in **civil war**, within the borders of **Spain**. Party members throughout the world were instructed to cooperate in recruiting an International Army. A place was made on every agenda, of Party meetings in the United States, for the discussion of Spain. Official Washington approved the procedure. The Germans gained the everlasting animosity of President Roosevelt when they sent armed forces to help on the side of France.

Every comrade had to take a physical examination, by a Party doctor, to determine whether he was fit for military service overseas. This confirms that fact that the Communist Party is NOT a party. It is rather, an underground, revolutionary army, representing a foreign power. Dennis instructed me and other members of the Milwaukee branch, that in the event of being sent to Spain we were to learn every method of street fighting, to qualify as officers when the revolution would break in our American cities.

Thousands of **American comrades** were assigned to duty **in Spain**, with the two International Divisions - the Abraham Lincoln Brigade and the George Washington Brigade. During this period, a change took place in the Party leadership of Wisconsin. Joe Stalin personally ordered Dennis to Spain, with instructions to send his reports directly to the Kremlin. This instantly elevated our Wisconsin leader to a place of supreme importance in the thinking of all American comrades. Practically all party members, sent from the United States to participate in the Spanish civil war had to be smuggled out of the Country. They encountered no opposition from **New Deal departments at Washington**. Wisconsin comrades were equipped with **fake passports** obtained under aliases. My father-in-law's apartment became the clearing house for this illegal practice.

These were picked up daily by Dorothy Hartman, alias Doris Berger, whom I later married - and whose conversion was ultimately responsible for my acceptance of Christ and complete repudiation of Communism. Dorothy would deliver the passports to Party headquarters at Milwaukee, where they were assigned to those ordered to Spain. The enlistees were then sent to New York, where they embarked for France. There the Blum government gave them arms, after which they were smuggled through the Pyrenees Mountains under cover of darkness. Many never came back.

Those who returned were made heroes at specially planned home comings. Elaborate parties were given them at New York. Here the most brazen experiences in sexual promiscuity, ever produced by human degeneracy were publicly related. Under the influence of liquor, these returning soldiers of the revolution poured out to gleeful listeners, their unspeakable, barbaric adventures in Spain. They told of raids on convents, where every nun would be repeatedly raped by alternating Communist beasts until dead. Then their bodies would be piled high, like cordwood, in public places. After being swathed in oil, the torch was applied, and the stench of burning flesh became a sweet odor to the nostrils of these half-crazed Communists. Returning comrades told of their vandalistic destruction of church property.

Protestants, though fewer in number, suffered in proportion. I shall never be able to erase these horrible atrocity stories from my memory. Would to God that I could. Such meetings were held behind carefully guarded, closed doors. Only Party members were treated to these sadistic demonstrations, called "home comings." When Dennis left for Spain, his position was filled by an old time revolutionist from Russia, who went under the name of Ned Sparks. This man remained in Wisconsin until the close of World War II...after which he was assigned to the Los Angeles area. Southern California is regarded by Moscow is being one of the most important parts of the country, because the Hollywood branch is there.

Lenin understood the propaganda value of films and this fact prompted him to say: "Of all the arts, the movies is for us." Hollywood is a vital nerve center for the Communist program of the Untied States. The greatest single contribution for carrying on the revolutionary struggle originates at that point. Communism and the motion picture industry grew to adulthood together in this part of the world. Time and again, I have sat in secret meetings where red strategy was being mapped, and observed exactly where and how Hollywood fitted into the projects under consideration. Lenin gave specific orders that the American tentacle of the International Communist Party was to **utilize the movies as a revolutionary weapon**. These instructions have never been forgotten. The "right people" have always been kept at the heart and core of the industry.

Party membership is, of course, a secret. I was, for instance, a "Member-at-Large" – which meant that I was not obliged to discuss my connections with the movement to anyone except immediate superior officers. Moreover, the system of assuming fictitious names, makes it difficult to ferret out Party affiliations. But we were told that nearly a third of all actors and actresses, had connections in one way or another, with the red underground. I feel the necessity of digressing at this point, to invite the reader's attention to a section of a report filed with Congress by the Committee on Un-American Activities, June 6, 1947.

The document was prepared by the sub-committee of the Committee, charged with **investigating Communism in the motion picture industry**. After explaining, that testimony was taken at Hollywood and other places...and after discussing some of the things that came to light, this group of Congressmen list seven conclusions as follows:

"(1) That scores of **screen-writers who are Communists** have infiltrated into the various studios and it has been through this medium that most of the Communist propaganda has been injected into the movies. These writers belong to the Screen Writers Guild, which has a membership of some 1,300 and which, according to the testimony of competent witnesses, is under the complete domination of the Communist Party. These writers receive anywhere from $500 to $5,000 per week.
(2) That some of the most flagrant Communist propaganda films were produced as a result of White House pressure, during the Roosevelt regime.
(3) That Communist screen writers, directors and producers have employed subtle techniques in pictures, in glorifying the Communist system and degrading our own system of Government and institutions. (The subcommittee was furnished with a complete list of all the pictures which have been produced in Hollywood in the past 8 years which contain Communist propaganda). The Committee was fortunate in having before it a prominent and experienced screen-writer and critic

who analyzed these pictures from the standpoint of Communist propaganda and degradation of American institutions.

(4) That the **National Labor Relations Board** has given great aid to the Communists in their efforts to infiltrate and control the motion picture industry.

(5) That up until recently, there has been no concerted effort on the part of studio heads to remove the Communists from the industry, but that in fact they have been reflected in the propaganda which they have been successful in injecting in numerous pictures which have been produced in the last 8 years.

(6) At the present time there is a rebellion within the industry on the part of a number of top actors, directors, and producers who are refusing to play, direct, or produce pictures that contain Communist lies, or which were written by a well-known Communist, or in which well-known Communist actors have been given a role.

(7) That the Communists have succeeded in preventing certain good American pictures, which ought to glorify America and the American system, from being produced."

After our marriage, Mrs. Goff and I moved to her parents' apartment house on the east side of Milwaukee...

Chapter V

The Call of Christ

I resigned from the Communist Party on October 9, 1939 - the day I first appeared before the **Committee on Un-American Activities** at Washington. Representative Martin Dies was the Chairman at that time.

After finishing my training in revolutionary methods at the Communist school of Milwaukee and Party headquarters in New York City, officials appointed me a "Member-at-Large." This meant that I had to be ready to accept assignments any time to work in whatever group the leaders might decide.

Because I came from a Christian family, it was my special duty to **bore into Churches, perverting as many believers** and religious bodies as possible. I served the Communist Party with fanatical zeal for several years. No member can call his soul his own! Every detail of his life is rigidly regulated. This applies to both mind and body. My whole being was consumed with Party interests. The day a man or woman becomes a Communist, that day the victim steps into a strait jacket. Wives are not even allowed to give birth to children, without the consent of the district organizers. For this reason abortion is a common practice.

My wife's acceptance of Christ was making a deeper impression upon me in 1939, than I realized at the time. Her prayers were beginning to tell! Finally, I joined her in the Faith...first inwardly, and later by public profession. I had long since become disillusioned by the Party program. There no longer remained any question in my mind, as to the true objectives of the organization. Far from wanting to better conditions for working men, I had learned from the inside that the real purpose was to bind them with chains, thereby making slaves and serfs of the laboring classes.

I knew that the **lowest standard of American laborers were better than the highest standards of the Soviet Union**. I finally came face to face with the fact, that the ultimate objective of the Communist movement was the **establishment of a World State**. When the full force of this realization descended upon me, I felt as though the bottom had dropped out of everything. I saw that I had played the fool. It was under these circumstances that I read one morning, about Mr. Dies coming to Chicago. I immediately collected a quantity of material together, including a large amount of documentary evidence regarding the inside operations of the Party, that I knew would interest Government investigators.

Early the next day, I knocked at the door of Mr. Dies' suite in the Palmer House...only to be politely informed by a subordinate, that he was too busy to see me. I confess to a degree of nervousness, because I knew the danger of carrying around a briefcase full of Communist documents on the streets of Chicago. Had I been caught, Party comrades would have murdered me. I decided to remain in the hotel, rather than risk returning to the street. Every Communist is a spy, spying on another spy. The average red will lick the boots of the officer above him. Advancement frequently comes by squealing on somebody.

I got what I wanted, an interview with Mr. Dies. He saw that I was sincere. He also attached great importance to the information that I possessed. My break with the Party came as a blow to the organization...because (1) of what I knew about its illegal operations, and (2) the fact that my resignation was so widely publicized. In addition to my Party affiliation, I was a member of the **National Committee of the Young Communist League** - a position of importance in the Communist movement, because of the League's close connection with the Kremlin in Moscow.

The following excerpt from my testimony before Congress leads up to a vital matter.

MR. WHITLEY. Mr. Goff, will you explain to the committee the relationship between the Young Communist League, in the United States, and the Young Communist International?

MR. GOFF: Have you a copy of the Communist International constitution?

MR. WHITLEY: The program?

MR. GOFF: The program of the Communist International.

MR. WHITLEY: This is the program of the Communist International, Mr. Chairman. Mr. Goff, is this the program which has been adopted and is used by the Communist Party of the United States?

MR. GOFF: This is right.

MR. WHITLEY.	You are positive of that?
MR. GOFF:	I am sure of that.
MR. WHITLEY:	Mr. Chairman, this is the program which Mr. Browder in his testimony stated, I believe, was not the official program of the Communist Party of the United States.
MR. GOFF:	This is the official program, and under section 35 it reads: "The International League of Communist Youth, Communist International, is a section of the Communist International with full rights and is subordinate to the Executive Committee of the Communist International."
MR. GOFF:	That is right.

The foregoing information is important, at this particular time, because an organization known as the **American Youth for Democracy**, is operating on school and college campuses, in all parts of the United States.

The AYD protests loudly that it is not Communist. This is in keeping with the Party line. Their protestations are false...for the reason that the **Young Communist League** held a special convention in New York City, October 15, 1943 and voted to change its name to American Youth for Democracy.

The organization must be eventually broken up and abolished, in the interests of rescuing the Republic from the tentacles of the Moscow octopus. The conditions under which I submitted my resignation are suggested in the transcript of the testimony, given before the Committee on Un-American Activities...October 9, 1939. The record says:

MR. WHITLEY.	Mr. Goff, do you plan to resign from the Young Communist League and the Communist Party?
MR. GOFF.	I do.
MR. WHITLEY.	Following your testimony here?
MR. GOFF.	I have my resignation here (indicating document).
MR. WHITLEY.	You have your resignation prepared?
MR. GOFF.	Yes.
THE CHAIRMAN.	I think it would do well to have him give his reasons for testifying.
MR. WHITLEY.	That is incorporated in this resignation.
THE CHAIRMAN.	Very well.
MR. WHITLEY.	I will read this resignation of Mr. Goff's.

To the **Young Communist League** and the Communist Party:

Three years ago, like many other young Americans, I entered your party and movement, believing that your aims were for the bettering of America, both economically and socially, and that you were the true defenders of democracy. After three years' work in your movement, I have come to the conclusion that joining your party was the greatest mistake of my life. You have proven to me by your teachings and actions that your aims are not for the bettering of America, but are for furthering your own selfish ambitions and those of your fatherland in the Union of Soviet Socialist Republics. Had your aims been true and for the best interest of our Nation, you would not have to call upon your father and high priest, Joseph Stalin, for every move you make, but would have found your leadership here in the United States of America.

Many of your members have come from foreign shores to our land to escape oppression, but like termites, do not become members of our household, but gnaw at the pillars of our democracy with hopes that it will crumble, that you might profit by its fall. You shout to high heaven your praise for the Bill of Rights and all it stands for, yet in your own party, you pry into every member's private life, and see to it, with all your power, that he cannot live a life of his own.

Yes, your speakers rave for hours about the mad dogs of Fascism and how your fatherland, the **Union of Soviet Socialist Republics** and its leader, Josef Stalin, are the greatest bulwark against Fascism and defender of democracy, and while these words are yet wet upon your lips, the Red Army of the fatherland, and your beloved peace leader, Joseph Stalin, join hands in accord with **Adolf Hitler**, one of the biggest Fascist leaders, and one of the greatest enemies of democracy in our times, and together they destroy Poland and bring little Latvia, Estonia and Lithuania to their knees. Yes, all this your fatherland does, in the name of peace and democracy. But do you who have the protection of a democracy, tell your fatherland, the Union of Soviet Socialist Republics, that you do not approve of the action taken by the Red Army in the conquest of Poland? No! And by these and many other actions you prove, that you and your organization, are no more than puppets dancing on the strings pulled by Joseph Stalin and the Comintern.

Because of your un-American ways and your lie of your so-called defense of democracy, I hereby submit my resignation from the Young Communist League and the Communist Party, to take effect immediately. I shall take my stand with those who are fighting for **real Americanism and democracy**. I know that this is a long and bitter fight, and I am enlisted for the duration of the war.

Yours truly,
(signed) KENNETH GOFF

This done, I left Washington for the home of my parents in Wisconsin. My wife approved the stand I had taken. Her interest in the Communist Fascism ended when she accepted Christ. I felt blue, discouraged and despondent. Like the man who gambles, I had bet everything I possessed – so to say, on one throw of the dice...and I had lost! My interests had been for years, wrapped up in the Communist Party. I did not know which way to turn. **The Nation was being propagandized in favor of Communism, from the White House down!**

Mrs. Roosevelt was entertaining officials of the Young Communist League in the White House. I knew from inside sources, that Party members were being given posts in the Army, Navy, and State Department and other branches of the national government. The Committee on Un-American Activities was the object of bitter attacks. Its hands were being weakened by constant attacks on the floor of Congress by Representatives Sabath, Celler, Marcantonio, and others.

Walter Winchell, Drew Pearson and others of their ilk, had not yet found out... so that their blasts at the Committee, and propaganda in favor of Russia, were proving hurtful. I was not even able to arouse Pastors and Churches, whom I contacted, to the danger. I was fighting a terrific inner battle during those months. My spirits dropped and a heavy depression settled over me. I found myself so weak that it was necessary to remain in bed. I did not care to live. Then, one day a light suddenly dawned in my soul.

Mrs. Goff quietly laid a Bible on my bed. It was within easy reach. In her absence I picked it up and the pages opened of themselves, to the fourteenth chapter of **John's Gospel**. I read those beautiful promises of eternal life. I read the story of Christ's victory over death, the story of redemption, the promise of the Holy Spirit's presence, and the influence of the Gospel message upon the Apostles. Right then and there, in bed – without a preacher, without an altar call, through the Word of God alone, **I accepted Jesus Christ as my personal Saviour**. I have no words to describe the joy that flooded my soul.

My whole attitude toward life instantly changed. In a little while I was up, writing, lecturing, preaching and teaching. From earliest boyhood, I had dreamed of some day becoming a Minister of the Gospel. My detour into Communism interrupted the plan. But like Jonah of old, the hand of Providence was upon my life. God permitted me to go by the way of the whale's belly of Communism, but I finally reached Nineveh. Today, I am happiest when standing behind the sacred desk, declaring the unsearchable riches of Christ. I am driven forward, with the knowledge that He is with me. For years, I have been smeared and opposed by the Communists and their front organizations. But nothing that they have done, has in any way destroyed the inward peace and assurance I enjoy, because He is with me.

I was speaking a few weeks ago, when suddenly the lights in the auditorium were turned off. Three hundred communists began smashing their way into the building. They had planned to take my life. But the police arrived in the nick of time and escorted me to safety. In St. Louis recently, I was struck down by local Communist leaders. When Gene Tunney and I went to the Lake Geneva Youth

Conference, to oppose a Communist rally, I was beaten in one of the committee rooms. This is only to mention a few of the many perplexing experiences that Mrs. Goff and I have encountered, since renouncing the Party!

But we are not discouraged, because we worship a God who "works in mysterious ways His wonders to perform," and we have even seen Him get glory through our suffering – and, after all, nothing else matters.

Chapter VI

The Trojan Horse
Every Communist rides the Trojan Horse.

As a former member of the Communist Party, I know that the **Kremlin** expects to eventually gain control of the world, by infiltrating and taking over important organizations in every country. In fact Georgi Dimitroff, head of the Comintern in 1935, issued exactly those orders. He used the term "Trojan Horse" and manifested unlimited audacity, in explaining what was expected of Party members everywhere. The instructions were given publicly at the Communist World Congress at Moscow. The legend of the **Trojan Horse** takes us back to ancient Greece. There was supposed to have been a powerful city called Troy, surrounded by high walls. The Trojans repeatedly attacked but were unable to pierce the defenses. After a long time of fighting, they feigned defeat and withdrew a considerable distance. The people of Troy thought the war was over. Before the Trojans left they made a huge, mechanical horse out of wood. The hollows of the beast were secretly filled with soldiers. Citizens of Troy pulled the monster into the city. During the night, the enemy soldiers climbed out, opened the gates from the inside and admitted the Trojan armies. Troy was taken. Enemies used deception and subterfuge. They finally destroyed the city from the inside.

There is nothing mysterious about the way Communists operate. They have an international program which is applied with minimum variation in each Country, Christianity and democratic government are their natural foes – behind whose lines they strive constantly to work.

If Walter Winchell and others of his race are now sincere in their opposition to Communism, it means a complete reversal of a historic attitude. I hope they are sincere...but my fingers are crossed for the present. Marshall Field has hit a compromise by saying, through his newspapers, that he does not endorse Communism "for the United States."

This infers that the system is satisfactory for Russia and other countries. He knows the international Communist Party is so cohesively organized, each segment being dependent upon the whole, that its successful operation in one place brings a curse upon other places. Victor A. Kravchenko, a native of Russia who has turned against Communism and lives in mortal fear of assassination for having written the book, "I Chose Freedom," regards Marshall Field as the arch propagandist of

America on the side of Communist Fascism. This is indicated by the following testimony recorded before the **Committee on Un-American Activities on July 22, 1947**:

MR. NIXON. How would you control or curb the Communist Party and the Communist influence in the United States?

MR. KRAVCHENKO. We must fundamentally **change the entire system of propaganda in America**. I have already said a great deal on this subject at this hearing. If you wish to go into the question in serious details, I fear that the scope of this hearing will not permit it.

MR. NIXON. Do you feel that it would be at all helpful, to take legal action to outlaw the Communist Party, as such, in the United States?

MR. KRAVCHENKO. I consider the fellow-travelers in America to be a more dangerous force than the official Communist Party, and I will tell you why. For instance, say I am an American citizen. I buy the Daily Worker. I know that it is the Daily Worker.

I know that it is the official organ of the Communist Party of the United States. But say I buy the Chicago Sun or PM (edited by Marshall Field). They are not Communist Party official papers, but they give me, to a great extent, the same ideas. That is more serious. If we have in the left hand Marshall Field, and in the right hand about 30 percent official members of the official Communist Party in the United States, my opinion is Marshall Field is more dangerous and will cause more trouble than the same 30 percent of Communists, of whom we know what they are doing and the nature of their aims. I was speaking with Marshall Field for several hours, and if you think that I could succeed in persuading him on anything, you are mistaken.

But should it develop that any considerable number of Jewish leaders in countries outside of Russia, have formulated a revised policy contrary to the wishes of the Kremlin, I predict an attack upon Palestine from the North, surpassing in fury anything known in the last war.

The Comintern will not – it dare not, tolerate **double-crossing**. Those who learn its secrets and turn against the leaders, are usually "liquidated." I can speak from experience in this regard, having felt the wrath of the Party after accepting Christ and renouncing the organization. The Communists are murderers at heart. Daily they plot and plan a way to destroy and ruin those who stand in the way of their bid for power. The members soon become as accustomed to talking about killing fellow-human beings, as calmly as the average farmer would talk about killing a chicken for Sunday dinner. One occasion I was assigned by Eugene Dennis to go to Cleveland, Ohio in 1936, to attend a Convention. I was instructed by the Party, to do everything in my power to defeat any motion proposed by Gerald L.K. Smith at the Convention; and do everything possible to destroy his influence, because of his vigorous "anti-Communist Crusade." When we failed to outwit and defeat Smith at the Convention, the Party members present, were called to a special meeting in the Ohio Headquarters of the Communist Party. Presiding over this meeting was Earl Browder. He and other Party Leaders, proposed that we work out plans for the assassination of Gerald L.K. Smith at an opportue time, when it would not bring the Party into bad repute.

I know the **Communist Party** to be a Trojan Horse. I know how orders came through from Moscow, to train and equip members for the purpose of boring into reputable organizations.

I know how Party members gloat in their secret councils, when they succeed in taking over the leadership of some organization previously **marked for demoralization**. Stalin expects to apply this method to our entire national Government. Here are his words:

> It is necessary that the American Communist Party should be capable of meeting the moment of crisis, fully equipped to take direction of future class wars in the United States. You must prepare for that, comrades, with all your strength and by every possible means.

During those treacherous years that the New Deal was in power, the Kremlin succeeded in establishing a powerful beachhead in the United States. Our enemies were aided and abetted from the White House. I know their methods, because I was on the inside at the time. How has the Communist Party been able to develop the kind of leadership necessary for gaining control of reputable organizations? The answer is simple. It is done by calling a never-ceasing stream of recruits to Moscow from all the countries of the world. These people are trained in revolutionary warfare and sent back home, to be leaders in the "class struggle." The name of their principal educational center is the **"International Lenin School**." They now maintain schools in all parts of the United States, patterned after their parent center in Moscow.

Large numbers of American Communists have been trained there. They are now back in our midst, working the Trojan Horse plan, undermining our Churches, free institutions and system of Government. The organization chosen for infiltration may be a labor union, club, civic body, political party, school, teacher's group, newspaper, magazine, youth movement, patriotic society – or some other organization. I have even known Church leadership being thus demoralized. I have seen Epworth Leagues and youth groups of all other denominations transformed into youth centers of radicalism. I have observed whole groups of Pastors changed into becoming Communists at heart, under the impact of the Trojan Horse technique.

Earl Browder claims there are eight thousand professed Ministers in the United States, secretly allied with the Communist Party, for the purpose of destroying the Church from within. I have found Communist propaganda, wearing the badge of **Christian Fundamentalism**. And of course, every Modernist Preacher is allergic. These are not pleasant things to contemplate, but our Country is faced with a factual situation. The time has come for the American people to become sensitized to Communist technique.

I like **J. Edgar Hoover's** statement that,

> The Communist Trojan Horse has now become the Trojan Snake in American Life.

Instead of sending me to Moscow to be taught revolutionary tactics in the "Lenin School," I was ordered to New York for highly technical training as a "Member-at-Large." I was sincere in joining the Party. I was led to suppose that it actually had the welfare of the poor at heart. I began to be disillusioned as I got deeper into the affairs of the organization. The leaders above me failed to destroy my conscience. The whole conspiracy spread before me like an open book, when I learned what went on at Secret Caucuses held by Jewish Members. Negroes and other races were not allowed to meet secretly and formulate plans for local Party groups to follow. I made the mistake of making a public protest against the procedure at an open meeting. From that hour I became a marked man...

Jack Kling, a national leader in the **Young Communist League** spent the night with me in Milwaukee. Unfortunately my Bible was in sight. I had turned again to reading the Scriptures, as my faith in the Party began to wane. Kling got mad. He demanded an answer then and there, why I read that kind of "**Capitalist propaganda**." My reply was that Party literature said Christ was killed for leading an uprising against the Roman Government, and I wanted more information on the subject. This, of course, did not satisfy him. He immediately reported me to my superior officers. I was hauled before the County Organizer the next day. **He forbade me to engage in any more Bible reading**, on threat of disciplinary action. The whole performance was such as to convince me that I had lost favor with the Party. Such a thought is sufficient to strike terror into the heart of any Communist.

For several weeks I had been organizing a Youth Rally in West Allis - a suburb of Milwaukee, to be held that evening. At 7 o'clock, about an hour before being due at West Allis, I was ordered to the Party office. There I was instructed to leave immediately for Sheboygan, to address a worker's meeting. Another comrade, Paul Herve, was assigned to my place in West Allis. This all seemed strange. I had no choice but to obey. No Communist can call his soul his own.

I spoke to a small group of workers at Sheboygan. At the close of the meeting, I hurried to the place where the interurban railroad stopped to pick up passengers for Milwaukee. My train was scheduled to leave at 11 o'clock. I waited in the safety zone on the street. I did not notice the automobile, loaded with enemies, that was parked a short distance away. I stood there alone, waiting for the interurban. An innocent young man, with no knowledge of what was about to occur, was also in the car. He told me later that Schultz, the driver, and others of the group, were watching every move I made.

As the interurban approached, Schultz timed himself perfectly and drove directly toward me, at a terrific rate of speed. In a split second, I realized that I was being caught between a speeding automobile and a rapidly approaching train. I was hit with a sickening thud and hurled under the wheels of the latter. Everything went black! Then a few minutes later, I found myself under the train, in a pool of blood, my leg severed from the rest of my body. Schultz stopped the automobile, jumped out, ran back and began kicking me in the face, cursing with every movement of his body. Trainmen grabbed him and called the police. This is part of the price I paid for daring to criticize Communist Party policy while belonging to the organization.

I was confined to a hospital bed six weeks, a hundred miles away from home and friends. During this time, my comrades were doing a sinister job! Before I left the operating room, they had arranged for Sam Berg, a Party lawyer, to take charge of my affairs. First, they ordered that no charges be preferred against the driver. Second, they took my insurance. Five thousand dollars was collected. They allowed me $900.00 for the hospital bill and kept the rest. There was nothing I could do. Members are at the mercy of their leaders.

In closing...let me say that the **God**, Who "works in mysterious ways His wonders to perform," finally **delivered me from Satanic Communism**...and for this I shall be eternally grateful. Mrs. Goff and I have come through many trying experiences but in our hearts we enjoy peace and soul rest which "the world cannot give and the world cannot take away." We are now trying daily, to make our lives count for Him, who died for us. We solicit the prayers of all believers in Jesus Christ.

Chapter VII

The Reorganized Comintern
A War Against Christian Civilization

Only during the war against **the Nazis** did sorely pressed Russia pretend to abandon the Communist International. This was thought necessary to get the full degree of aid from the United States and Britain. Stalin believed this aid essential to defeat the invading Germans, even though he never let the Russian people know the aid was necessary, the amount of aid obtained, and continually taught the Russians that they alone were winning the war. Even today the people are taught that the war was won by state socialism and not be a joint endeavor with a capitalistic government.

The recent conference attended by Communists from nine nations marked one change in fundamental Communist policy. It merely shows the abandoning of a fruitless pretense. Whatever the technical changes in the operation of the Communist International, worldwide communism has never ceased to function since the formation of the "First International" in the year 1864. To understand fully this world conspiracy of Communist Boshevism, we must study its origin and its final motives.

On the first day of May in the year 1776 in Munich, Germany, an organization called the "**Illuminati**" was launched by a group of atheists and free thinkers. The founder and leader of this organization was **Adam Weishaupt**. Weishaupt was a cunning human-devil, whose dream in life was to place the whole **world under one government** headed by his God-hating "Illuminati." To accomplish this, Weishaupt set forth the following program:

1. Abolition of all government. 2. Abolition of inheritance. 3. Abolition of private property. 4. Abolition of patriotism. 5. Abolition of family. 6. Abolition of religion.

These six principles by which they had proposed to destroy all orderly society have remained a part of the **Communist program** until this day. During the years that followed, Weishaupt built a strong underground movement in Germany which penetrated through its Trojan Horse policies, the economic, religious and political groups of that nation. Later, the citizens of Germany became aware of the fact that a diabolical plot was being carried out by the "Illuminati" to destroy their nation. They immediately passed laws to outlaw the traitorous organization and arrested many of its leaders.

Adam Weishaupt and some of his followers escaped and found a refuge in France. Here, again, they went to work on their plans for a world revolution. They formed a new organization called the "**Jacobins**" and made Weishaupt its Grand Patriarch. These clubs spread like wildfire throughout France and played an important part in the **bloody French revolution**. The teachings of Weishaupt and his followers caused widespread strike and an increasing class struggle throughout the continent of Europe. New Revolutionary movements sprung up in many different countries. Each of these new movements had their own program. Without unity there seemed to be no hope for a "working class" victory.

During this period a new leader was developing. His name was **Karl Marx**. Marx, the Jew, had come from a well-to-do family. Marx first joined a circle called the "Left Hebelians" which sought to draw atheistic and revolutionary conclusions from Hegel's philosophy. While Marx was a member of this group, he published many magazines and papers. Together with a friend of his, **Frederik Engles**, Marx worked out the theory and tactics of revolutionary **Proletarian Socialism**, otherwise known as **Communism**.

Both men were banished from Germany and France as dangerous revolutionists. In 1847, they joined a secret propaganda society in Brussels bearing the name

"Bund Der Komunisten" (Communist League). It was while a member of this league that in 1848 Marx wrote the infamous **"Communist Manifesto"** that has been the bible of the Communist Revolutionist ever since. This manifesto called for the workers of the world to unite and destroy all existing government by bloody revolution. Following the issuance of the Manifesto, a revolution broke out in Belgium causing Marx to be banished from that country. He later went to London, England, where, on September 28, 1864, the "First International" was formed. This united front of the Revolutionist was called the "International Workingmen's Association." This first International remained in force until it was weakened by the Bakunists split which caused it finally to dissolve on July 15, 1876.

The "Second International" was formed of right wing socialist groups in 1889 and lasted until 1914. It was weaker than the first because it did not receive the full support of the extreme left-wing who were called Communists. In 1905 the leftists attempted a revolution in Russia and failed. The year 1917 found the Czarist government in Russia very weak. This time under the skilled **Marxist leadership of Lenin, Stalin** and **Trotsky**, the Communists were able in the month of October to carry through a successful revolution and seize the reins of the state.

Hardly had the **Czarist government** been overthrown when the free revolutionary leaders came to bitter disagreement on the policy to follow. Trotsky wanted to take the revolutionary army and conquer Europe at once. Lenin and Stalin felt that they should first build a strong Socialist state in Russia, then through infiltration they could penetrate all other nations.

Once the other nations were weakened, they could lie in wait for an imperialist war at which time they could easily cause dissention and take control. This plan worked well. Following the October revolution, Communist parties began to spring up all over the globe. This called for an International organization and so the "Third International" was formed in 1920.

This "Third International," commonly called the Comintern, was a congress with representatives from every nation in the world. The congress was ruled over by a president, Georgi Dimitroff of Bulgaria, and its secretary, Josef Stalin of Russia. Josef Stalin being the secretary, became the highest officer in the Comintern as is common in Communist party organization. The Comintern, a union of Communist parties of the various nations, is in reality the **World Communist Party**.

As the leader and organizer of the world revolutionary movement of the proletariat and the protagonist of the principles and aims of Communism, the Communist International strives to win over the majority of the working class. It fights for the establishment of a world dictatorship of the proletariat. This world dictatorship would then continue to establish a **world union of Socialist Soviet Republics** for the achievement of Socialism, the first stage of any Communist society.

Soon after the formation of the Third International, Lenin was shot by a young woman. He lingered in ill health for some time before he died. Lenin believed at the time of his death that the government of the Soviet Union would continue under the leadership of the revolutionary leader, Leon Trotsky. However, Stalin had already determined that this should not be. During Trotsky's absence from the capital, Stalin seized power and began spreading wild rumors aimed at breaking down the faith of the Russian people in Trotsky. This sly plot succeeded and Trotsky was forced to flee the country to save his life. Once outside Stalin's domain, Trotsky organized the Fourth International. This Fourth International (Trotskyites) exists to this day and carries on an undercover fight against the Third International, commonly called the Stalinists.

Warning! Some of the most bitter foes of Stalinism in America are the followers of Leon Trotsky. Their opposition to Stalin, however, and to Soviet Russia represents merely a factional quarrel among the disciples of the Jew, Karl Marx. In fact, Trotskyites, as they are called, are as bloodthirsty, and in some instances more bloodthirsty, if possible, than the authorized representatives of Moscow. Once Stalin became the supreme leader of the Third International and the Communist Party of Russia, he began to organize for the conquest of the world. He called several **World Congresses of the Comintern** where the economic and political problems of each nation were discussed. It was then agreed that they would go underground in the majority of nations and quietly strengthen their forces. This master plan was carried out with success until 1935. In that year they called the Seventh World Congress in Moscow. The delegates at this congress felt that the hour had come for them to come out in the open and launch a United Front campaign. It was believed that this policy would give more strength to the Party and possibly gain control of some countries.

Spain was chosen as the first country with which they would experiment. The "Experiment" was the direct cause of the bloody Spanish Revolution. During the revolution the Communists tried to unite the Trotskyites, Anarchists and the Socialists under one banner. This maneuver failed and the Reds were defeated in the revolution.

By this time, **Hitler** was on the rise and many nations who had been leaning toward Communism were now lining up in the Nazi camp. Stalin called for an all out campaign against Fascism at home and abroad. A blood purge took place in the Soviet Union and anyone who was suspected of not being a 100 percent pro-Stalin was liquidated. In other countries where trials were held, the guilty members were expelled from the party. When Stalin saw that Hitler was beating him to the punch, he craftily cooked up the Soviet-Nazi Pact. This gained him time, and gave him parts of Poland, Latvia, Lithuania, Estonia, and Finland without much fight.

With the Soviet-Nazi Pact in force, Stalin could wait until Hitler's troops were scattered all over Europe, then strike. Adolf Hitler evidently got wise to Stalin's game and struck first. Meanwhile, word had gotten to Stalin that his ally might turn on him, and use Trotsky as his puppet in his Russian campaign. Stalin ordered the immediate assassination of Trotsky who was living in exile in Mexico. Leon Trotsky was beaten to death by his own secretary after the order was issued by the **Comintern**. This, I am sure, was the contributing factor to Hitler's defeat in the

Russian campaign. Had Trotsky lived, the picture might have been quite different.

In the United States during this time the Communists had been raising the slogans, "Keep America Out of War," and "The Yanks Are Not Coming." With the invasion of Russia by Hitler, these slogans changed overnight. They began to call for America to "Save the World from Fascism" and "Let the Democracies of the World Unite."

With our entrance into the war in 1941, the whole picture changed. **Our shipments of Lend Lease to Russia** began to slow the advance of Hitler's armies. The average American said, "Let's give them just enough to keep them fighting until both are exhausted." Stalin sensed this feeling and pulled his prize trick out of the bag. In May, 1943, he held a small conference of a few of the International Communist leaders and announced that the Comintern had been dissolved. This was hailed by many Allied leaders as the "dawn of a new day" and as "heralding greater cooperation between Russia and the Western world."

Those of us who had been members of the Party knew this to be a lie, and a clever trick on the part of Stalin. We knew that the Constitution of the Third International stated that it could not be dissolved without a majority vote of the World Congress of the Comintern. No World Congress had been held at that time. This fact has been borne out by recent actions of the Communists. Documents seized from Russian agents during the Atomic Bomb trials in Canada established irrefutably that the Kremlin-directed international spy ring functioned throughout the war. Igor Sergeivitch Gouzenko, the code clerk in the Russian embassy in Canada, after fleeing the Reds sent to apprehend him, informed the Royal Commission that "the announcement of the dissolution of the Comintern was probably the greatest farce of the Communists in recent years.

He told the startled Canadians, to whom he fled with coded documents from Moscow directing spying activities in Canada and the United States, that actually the Comintern exists and continues the work. The Soviet leaders have never relinquished the idea of "establishing a communist dictatorship throughout the world."

Gouzenko furnished documentary proof to bear out his assertions. He added that "it is clear that the Communist Party in democratic countries had changed long ago from a political party into an agency net of the Soviet government."

Well, now do the doubters finally understand that the Bolshevist world revolution for the establishment of a World Soviet is really under way, and has been for the past thirty years? If not, let them study the Communist conference which was held in Moscow on October 5, 1947. At this conference, Communist leaders of nine countries participated openly. The rest of the countries were represented, but not openly for fear of repercussion.

Earlier this year, secret delegates of the Communist Party of America obtained passports to Europe. They were present at this conference. The delegates who operated in the open were from Russia, France, Italy, Czechoslovakia, Poland, Romania, Bulgaria, Yugoslavia, and Hungary. These agents are setting up an information and propaganda bureau in Belgrade under Marshall Tito's watchful eye. Thus, we find the Comintern working from two Communist capitals, Belgrade and Moscow, but working jointly for the same purpose. "To banish God from the skies and capitalism from the earth," and to establish a **World Soviet State**.

The picture is growing clearer each day. We see the world gradually being divided into **two camps, U.S.A. and U.S.S.R**. Soon these two camps will clash. When, only time can tell.

Chapter VIII

Hollywood's Corruption
The Fulfillment of Stalin's Dream

One of the greatest breeders of juvenile delinquency in America is the movies. More crime, adultery, drinking and filth is poured into the minds of American youth from Hollywood than any other source.

This scheme fits well into the plans of the Communist Party, to demoralize American youth; for it is hoped by the Communists that there will be a breakdown of our economic and moral structure, which will make it easy for them to step in and take over our Republic and establish in its place the **United States of Soviet America**. During the last fifteen years, the Communist Party has been busy getting a firm foothold in Hollywood, and today, we find them well established with more than one third of all the actors and actresses holding membership in the Communist Party. Many of those who haven't joined as yet are aiding in their program by following the line of the fellow-traveler.

During the past few years, there has been close ties between this **Sodom and Gomorrah of America** and the **White House**. Because of the Roosevelt approval of these sex-perverts and morons, many of our young people have begun to idolize them as gods. At the present time these social degenerates are setting the mode of dress, talk, and even political thinking. Fifty years ago, it would have defeated a candidate to have some burlesque star endorse him; today it's the popular thing.

Have our people grown so weak that they must turn to these half-baked nitwits in Hollywood for our political thought; or have we become suckers to the Communist intrigue of using Hollywood as a means of destroying our way of life. The parents of America pay the movie industry millions of dollars every week, to train their youngsters how to become sex perverts and atheists. Young people attending the movies, see enacted before their very eyes base sex crimes and bloody murders. These scenes are so real, they leave an imprint upon the child's memory which cannot be removed, and many times when it is recalled at a weaker moment, it may cause the child to commit the same crime.

In a city in northern Illinois, a dog ran howling down the street and fell dead in front of the Apollo Theater. Upon examination, a pen-knife was found stuck into the back of his neck. An investigation by the local police brought out the fact that

22 dogs had been killed in that community over a period of two months. Some had been shot, then wrapped in stolen blankets and buried. Others had been put into gunny sacks and thrown in the river while still alive. These fiendish crimes had been committed by youngsters, none of them over 15 years of age. Their only excuse was that they wanted to re-enact crime scenes they had seen at the local movies. Girls have testified that after seeing an extremely passionate movie, they have gone out of the theatre to find a man with whom they could have illicit relations, and if they happened to have a young man with them, they would go out with him for the same purpose.

Youths have testified that they take girls to the movies for the express purpose of arousing them, that they might influence them to commit adultery. What else can we expect from these young people when they are given money by their parents to attend movies where they can see displayed on the screen before them a seduced woman lying in bed where the act of seduction took place; a house party where scantily-clothed women are seen drinking liquor, and sucking on cigarettes; a married woman has a baby by a friend whom she loves better than her husband; a Communist revolutionist glorified as a hero; congressmen ridiculed as crackpots; Gospel preachers made to look like flea-brained nincompoops; and gangsters living in luxury surrounded by young prostitutes. These scenes help promote juvenile delinquency, and are a menace to the welfare of our nation.

Earl Barnes, a noted educator says, "Any person brought up on the psychology of the movie-world is unfit for life. The lower minds go to the movies and the longer they go, the lower they will be."

Dr. Edward A. Ross, famous sociologist, lays this to the movie industry.

> Never has there been a generation so much in revolt against their elders as this. In my judgment, this psychic revolt springs from the motion films. We have a generation of youth, sex-excited, self-assertive, self-confident and parent-critical.

Theodore Dreiser, famous American novelist and by no means a church man, had this to say about movies, "I have seen movies that would curl your hair, in spite of the motion picture censorship we are supposed to have."

If the Communist Party was to open a training school in your town and would issue invitations for your children to attend free of charge I would venture to say very few American parents would allow their children to go anywhere near the place. Yet these same parents would pay good money night after night for their children to attend movies and be slyly indoctrinated with the same damnable atheistic Communist teachings.

Several years ago G. Allison Phelps, the prominent Los Angeles journalist, prepared a list of movie bigwigs, who are responsible for the type of pictures shown across America. Phelps calls this list the 'all alien team.' Let's look at the line-up, and see who some of the men are, who make up this modern **Tower of Babel**.

THE HOLLYWOOD

ALL-American (ALL ALIEN?) Eleven
of
INDISPENSABLES

Head Coach
Nick Schenck
Born: Russia - Salary $275,673

Bob Rubin
First Assistant Coach
Born: Syracuse
Salary: $218,423

Darryl Zanuck
Third Assistant Coach
Born: Wahoo
Salary: $265,000

Second Assistant Coach
Born: Hoboken
Salary: $249,482

Fourth Assistant Coach
Born: Hungary
Salary: $170,000

THE TEAM

Name	Born	Salary
Harry M. Warner	Russia	$156,000
Joseph M. Schenck	Russia	106,000
Anatole Litvak	Rumania	117,857
Sam Katz	Russia	247,000
Harry Cohen		185,000
Sam Goldwyn	Poland	156,000
Al Lichtman	Hungary	229,392
Joe Pasternack	Hungary	119,875
Alexander Korda	Hungary	
Gregory Ratoff	Russia	104,333
Louis B. Mayer	Russia	688,369

SUBSTITUTES

Dave Bernstein, Jerry Mayer, Mendel Silverberg, Harry Rapf, Eddie Loeb, Sol Lessor, Sam Briskin, Lee Marcus, Frank Orsatt, Nat Goldstone, Lew Schreiber, J.J. Cohen, Arthur Loew, Jack Cummings, Melvyn Douglas, Louis K. Sidney, Herman Mankiewiez, L. Weingarten, Sam Sischoff, Hunt Stromberg, Bill Goetz, Pandro Berman, Mervyn LeRoy, Murry Silverstone, Sal Wurtsel, S.P. Skouras, Fred Pelton, Joe Maniewiez, Lep Friedman, Bernie Hyman and Henry Ginsberg.

Just name one remark by anyone from this group of men that ever exalted

Christ or helped the church. John Rankin (Dem.-Miss.,) member of the House Committee on Un-American Activities, says:

One of the most dangerous plots ever instigated for the overthrow of this Government, had its headquarters in Hollywood.

The Communist Party is re-organizing for a tough, bitter fight. The orders for this change came from Joe Stalin and were transmitted to the American Party by comrade Duclos of France. This move was made to prepare the American Communist for revolutionary action in case there is a falling out between Stalin and Truman. Plans are being put into effect by the Communists to paralyze American industry, by a general strike if we should disagree with Stalin's program to communize Europe and Asia.

The Communists have moved their strategic base of operation from New York City to Hollywood. Already many party leaders are being shifted to key industrial cities in preparation for the revolt. Ned Sparks, former secretary of the Communist Party in Wisconsin has been transferred to Los Angeles. Sparks was chosen for this post because of his past revolutionary experience. **He fought in the Russian Revolution under Lenin** and knows well how to butcher Christians.

When we see such an outstanding Communist as this, being assigned to the Hollywood district, then we can begin to realize the important position of the movie industry in the coming Communist Revolution. It is no strange phenomena that when leading Communists come to America, one of the first places they visit is Hollywood; for it was from this city, that the largest sums were contributed to aid the Communist forces during the Spanish Civil War.

Recently, a Russian Journalist, Konstantin Simonov, toured Hollywood, and paid homage to Bette Davis, Charlie Chaplin and the **Hollywood Writer's Association**. He reported that he found most actors and actresses displayed a great interest in the Soviet Union and Soviet Culture. He also stated that Bette Davis and Charlie Chaplin had deep contempt for the Anti-Communist press and its attitude toward the Soviet Union. This is not at all strange.

On November 16, 1944, a group of **Communist stars of screen** sent a wire of greeting to the U.S.S.R. Amity Rally. Among the signers was Charlie Chaplin, the Communist parasite, who has made millions of dollars in America and shamed the name of American womanhood; yet never to my knowledge has he become an American citizen. He tells us how to vote and how to run our foreign affairs, (as can be seen in the following telegram signed by nineteen of the Hollywood Communist gang.)

"In time to come the recognition of the Soviet Union by the United States will be remembered as the beginning of an era which brought savagery, ignorance and hunger to an end. It will be remembered as the first step taken toward new horizons of a world where security and culture are meant for the happiness of all people everywhere. On this occasion, Hollywood wishes to add its voice to the voices of all Americans hailing the mutual bond which exists and which will continue to grow between our great country and our Allies. In this friendship lies not only the hope but the future of the world."

Signed - Larry Adler, James Cagney, Eddie Cantor, Charles Chaplin, Dorothy Commingor, George Colouris, Olivia De Havilland, John Carfield, Ira Gershwin, Rita Hayworth, Katharine Hepburn, Gene Kelley, Alexander Knox, Groucho Marx, Harpo Marx, Edward G. Robinson, Sylvia Sidney, Gail Sondergaard, and Orson Welles.

One of the outstanding young Communists in Hollywood is **Frankie Sinatra**, the young man, who expects every young maiden to swoon at the sound of his rasping voice. Yet behind that voice, is the voice of Bloody Joe, enticing our youth into his deadly Marxian philosophy. Sinatra co-operates closely with the **American Youth for Democracy** and the C.I.O. - P.A.C. Early this year he was one of eight who was awarded medals from the A.Y.D. (the Young Communist League) for 'major contributions to democracy and to the war effort. He has been active in appearances in racial troubled zones.

Other awards, were to Peggy Ryan, entertainer; Bill Mauldin, left-wing cartoonist; Slim Aaron of 'Yank' magazine; Lt. Edvina Todd, navy nurse; Edward Carter, Negro service man; and Harry Tanuye, Japanese-American. Frank Sinatra, commonly called 'The Voice,' is one of the star performers at A.Y.D. rallies, where young people are recruited into the Communist Party. His bold promotion of 'bobby-soxism,' has added to the great wave of juvenile delinquency in America.

In San Francisco on March 23, 1946, fifty-six adolescent Sinatra fans were taken into custody by police as they stood shivering in a waiting line in front of the Golden Gate Theater at 4:30 a.m. in the morning, six hours before 'the voice,' was scheduled to appear. The police hauled 53 indignant bobby-soxers and three boys to the juvenile home on technical charges of violating the curfew law, which prohibits anyone under eighteen from being on the streets between 11:00 p.m., and 6:00 a.m. Most of the children were from Oakland.

One father said, "The police were well justified in picking up the girls. I think Sinatra should be run out of town."

This young Stalinite has been touring the country swooning bobby-soxers with his baritone voice, while he tells their parents how to vote. He appeared before 16,000 left-wingers in Madison Square Garden last year, at the opening of a nationwide campaign, the Communist Party and the **New Deal's 'Russian Firsters,'** to capture the veteran's votes. Frank Sinatra, defiant in bow-tie, demanded freedom for the Chinese; a campaign against the Spanish Government; and public recognition of the political possibilities of radio crooners. While Sinatra and others demanded the overthrowing of Franco; Red Fascists passed out handbills in the crowd, which read, "Veterans - join the Communist Party...our Party stands for the ownership and control of the nation's economy by the workers and farmers."

Through this one performance alone, any intelligent person should be able to see how 'Communist Frankie,' with his purring voice, is swooning the youth of

America into the arms of atheistic Communism.

I can think of no better way to close this chapter on Hollywood than with this clear call to action by G. Allison Phelps, who said, "It will take more than MICE CHRISTIANS, to drive from Christian America, the filth columnist of Hollywood. Christians who will not only preach about, but who also will sternly uphold the principles of our Saviour, will have to rise in this land, and use their influence to combat the atheistic ideologist of the modern Augean stable, known in Hollywood as the 'Tower of Babel.'

The author of this book was formerly a leader in the Communist Party. He was assigned by Stalin's agents in the United States to work among young people and help bring about a bloody Communist revolution.

> He fought the church.
> He fought the American way of life.
> He plotted the death of officials and Christian leaders.
> He used a number instead of a name.
> He worked with Communist plotters from New York and Hollywood.
> While a Communist he was invited by Eleanor Roosevelt to be a guest at the White House.

This book tells the inside story of a man who, in repentance, **left Josef Stalin to serve Jesus Christ.**

In conclusion, let us heed Soviet Premier Nikita S. Khrushchev's "blueprint" for the transition to full communist society. Delivered in his major speech at the 21st Communist Party Congress - the 1st week in February, 1959, it was reported in the *New York Times*' February 10, 1959 edition, as follows:

> Premier Khrushchev's blueprint is the most detailed treatment of a key subject on which leading communist writers from Marx to Stalin tended to be very general...Premier Khrushchev's pronouncement depicts the pattern of transition from socialism to communism in the following manner: There can be no quick jump from capitalism to communism. The transition from socialism to communism will be a gradual one and 'there will be no particular moment' when socialism will end and communism will begin...

APPENDIX VI

What is the modus operandi of Marxists? Marxists aim to demoralize their targeted victims through psychological warfare (**Psychopolitics**, alias, the Russian textbooks of the 1930's, described as "The Art and Science of Manipulating Masses of Minds of People without their Knowing it.") Using guilt manipulation, vilifying the victims and victimizing the villains, their politics of guilt and pity seek to undermine Christianity and nationalism.

1. **Playing the Victim Card While Demonizing Opponents**

    Marxists employ double standards to enable them to always play the victim while demonizing the opponents of Marxism. Along with demonizing opponents, Marxists seek to promote hero worship of their idols of the New World Order.

2. **Intimidation.** Through politically correct censorship and intimidation, cyber-bullying and cry-bullying, they seek to mobilize hysterical, spiteful, vindictive opposition to silence all dissent. Anyone daring to express a different opinion will find themselves a target of malicious slurs and smear tactics.

3. **Poisoning the Well and Weaponizing Words**

    They seek to weaponize words and poison the well, calling free speech: "Hate speech!" Marxists seek to silence opposition by accusing anyone who dares to introduce facts and reason into the discussion: *"Racist!" "Nazi!" "Islamaphobe!" "Homophobic bigot!"* and other toxic labels designed to intimidate opponents into silence and retreat.

4. **The Gramsci Strategy**

    The Frankfurt School of Cultural Marxism utilized the Gramsci Strategy, also called the Termite Strategy, of eating the heart out of every pillar of Western civilization until the entire edifice rots and collapses. Their goal is the secularization of society – to side-line Christianity and deal with all issues without reference to the Bible. "Shouldest thou help the ungodly, and love them that hate the Lord? Therefore is wrath upon thee from before the Lord." II Chronicles 19:2.

5. **Marxists identify Primary Culture, Transforming Institutions for Infiltration and Subversion**

    a. Education
    b. Entertainment
    c. News Media
    d. Religious institutions
    e. Political institutions

6. **Marxist Revolutionaries identify their Stages of Operation for Ideological Subversion:**

a. Demoralization
   b. Destabilization
   c. Crisis
   d. Normalization
   e. Second Phase of the Revolution

7. **Subversion and Slander**

   Everything is designed to undermine the strength of the targeted enemy through subversion and slander. Straw man arguments are frequently used to weaken the resistance of targeted individuals or groups.

8. **Smokescreens and Distractions**

   Distraction is essential to provide a smoke screen behind which Marxist subversives can destroy everything that could be a strength in the congregation, community or country targeted. The issue focused on is seldom the real concern. Their motivation is normally the furthering of the revolution by discrediting all resistance.

9. **Character Assassination**

   As Socrates famously declared, "When the debate is lost, slander becomes the tool of the loser.

10. **"Confuse, Divide and Conquer"**

    If a people can be confused, then they can be divided, which makes it easier to defeat them. Hence Marxists aim at: **Disinformation, Division** and **Defeat** for the country targeted. "While they promise them liberty, they themselves are servants of corruption…" II Peter 2:19.

11. **"Corrupt and Conquer"**

    Degenerate entertainment, defiled art and **decadent culture** are the strategy of cultural Marxists to rot the soul of a nation.

12. **Treason from Within**

    As Cicero warned: "A nation can survive its fools and even the ambitious, but it cannot survive treason from within. An enemy at the gates is less formidable, for he is known and carries his banners openly, but the traitor moves amongst those within the gates freely, his sly whispers, rustling through all the alleys, heard in the very halls of government itself. For the traitor appears not a traitor; he speaks in accents familiar to his victims, he wears their face and their arguments, he appeals to the baseness that lies deep in the hearts of all men, he rots the soul of a nation, he works secretly and unknown in the night, to undermine the pillars of the city, he infects the body politic, so that it can no longer resist. A murderer is less to be feared." [1]

APPENDIX VII

The American Civil Liberties Union

In researching the history of the ACLU in the International Law Library of the Library of Congress, I discovered the following: In 1917, this organization was founded under the name, National Civil Liberties Bureau. In 1920, its name was changed to The American Civil Liberties Union. Excerpts from the Associate Director's book on its history are hereunder quoted:

> ...The ACLU backed or led numerous court tests which resulted in the Supreme Court checking the marauding of investigating committees and voiding loyalty oaths...In 1925, the ACLU attacked Tennessee's anti-evolution law in the famous Scopes Trial. While Scopes was convicted and fined $100.00, the Bryan-Darrow courtroom confrontation was instrumental in ending a serious governmental threat to freedom of thought and academic liberty...(Author's note: The Scopes Trial was valiantly won by William Jennings Bryan, distinguished Senator, lawyer, Christian statesman, and Nebraska's greatest hero in the U.S. Capitol's Hall of Fame)...The House un-American Activities Committee initiated new forays into colleges and professions which underscored the ACLU's call for the Committee's abolition...Historians have correctly characterized the 1950's as the period in which civil liberties faced its most severe threat because of the inexorable pressure of the US-USSR confrontation. And the dark night of McCarthyism called up the ACLU's most vigorous and vigilant efforts...Whether it was the Wisconsin Senator's vicious assault on the ACLU itself, on State Department and army personnel; the unrelenting hearings of the House Un-American Activities Committee; the scare-induced firings of teachers for refusing to inform on past associates, the witch hunts of the government's security investigations, paralleled by State and local probes, loyalty oaths and investigations of private industry...the ACLU was challenged again and again...Even though unceasing effort was required to make the yeast of freedom rise over the Cold War oven, other areas were not neglected. The wall between church and state was cemented in decisions ending Bible-reading and prayers in schools. For the first time, movies were legally recognized as enjoying the protection of the First Amendment... *

The devastating results of the ACLU's anti-American agenda are all around us today.

---

*see Thomas Jefferson's 1786 *Statute for Religious Freedom* – "Separation of Church from State Control," forerunner to the First Amendment's Establishment Clause of the U. S. Constitution.

ABOUT THE AUTHOR

Catherine Millard is the president of *Christian Heritage Tours, Inc.*® and *Christian Heritage Ministries*®. She received her B.A. from George Mason University in American Studies, her M.A. from Capital Bible Seminary in Old and New Testaments, and her doctorate in Christian Education from Luther Rice College and Seminary (*summa cum laude*). She also studied Hebrew at the Hebrew University of Jerusalem.

She has spent thirty years as a scholar and researcher at the Library of Congress, utilizing the original documents, writings, papers, addresses and proclamations of the founding fathers – many of which have been removed from public view. She is the author of twenty historical books, including *The Truth about the Founding Fathers of the American Republic*, *Great American Statesmen and Heroes*, *The Dismantling of America's History*, and the awarding-winning, *The Rewriting of America's History*.

Recipient of the George Washington Honor Medal sponsored by the Freedoms Foundation at Valley Forge, and the Faith and Freedom, Religious Heritage of America Award, she was elected to "Who's Who Among Students in American Colleges and Universities" for outstanding academic achievement.

Dr. Millard has lectured and taught extensively in colleges, universities and schools throughout the United States and abroad.

You may contact her through the following address:

Christian Heritage Ministries®
P.O. Box 797
Springfield, Virginia 22150
United States of America

Telephone: 703-455-0333
www.christianheritagetours.org
www.christianheritgemins.org

Additional copies of this book are available through the above address.